# The Landscape Photographer's Guide to Photoshop

# The Landscape Photographer's Guide to Photoshop

## A Visualization-Driven Workflow

**Guy Tal**

rockynook

The Landscape Photographer's Guide to Photoshop
A Visualization-Driven Workflow

Guy Tal
guytal.com

Editor: Joan Dixon
Project manager: Lisa Brazieal
Marketing coordinator: Mercedes Murray
Layout and type: Hespenheide Design
Cover design: Aren Straiger

ISBN: 978-1-68198-218-2
1st Edition (1st printing, November 2017)


Rocky Nook, Inc.
1010 B Street, Suite 350
San Rafael, CA 94901
USA

www.rockynook.com

Distributed in the U.S. by Ingram Publisher Services
Distributed in the UK and Europe by Publishers Group UK

Library of Congress Control Number: 2016952034



This book is printed on acid-free paper.
Printed in China

*If a view of geography does not imply something more enduring than a specific piece of terrain, then the picture will hold us only briefly; we will probably prefer the place itself, which we can smell and feel and hear as well as see—though we are also likely to come away from the actual scene hoping somewhere to find it in art. This is because geography by itself is difficult to value accurately—what we hope for from the artist is help in discovering the significance of a place.*

—ROBERT ADAMS

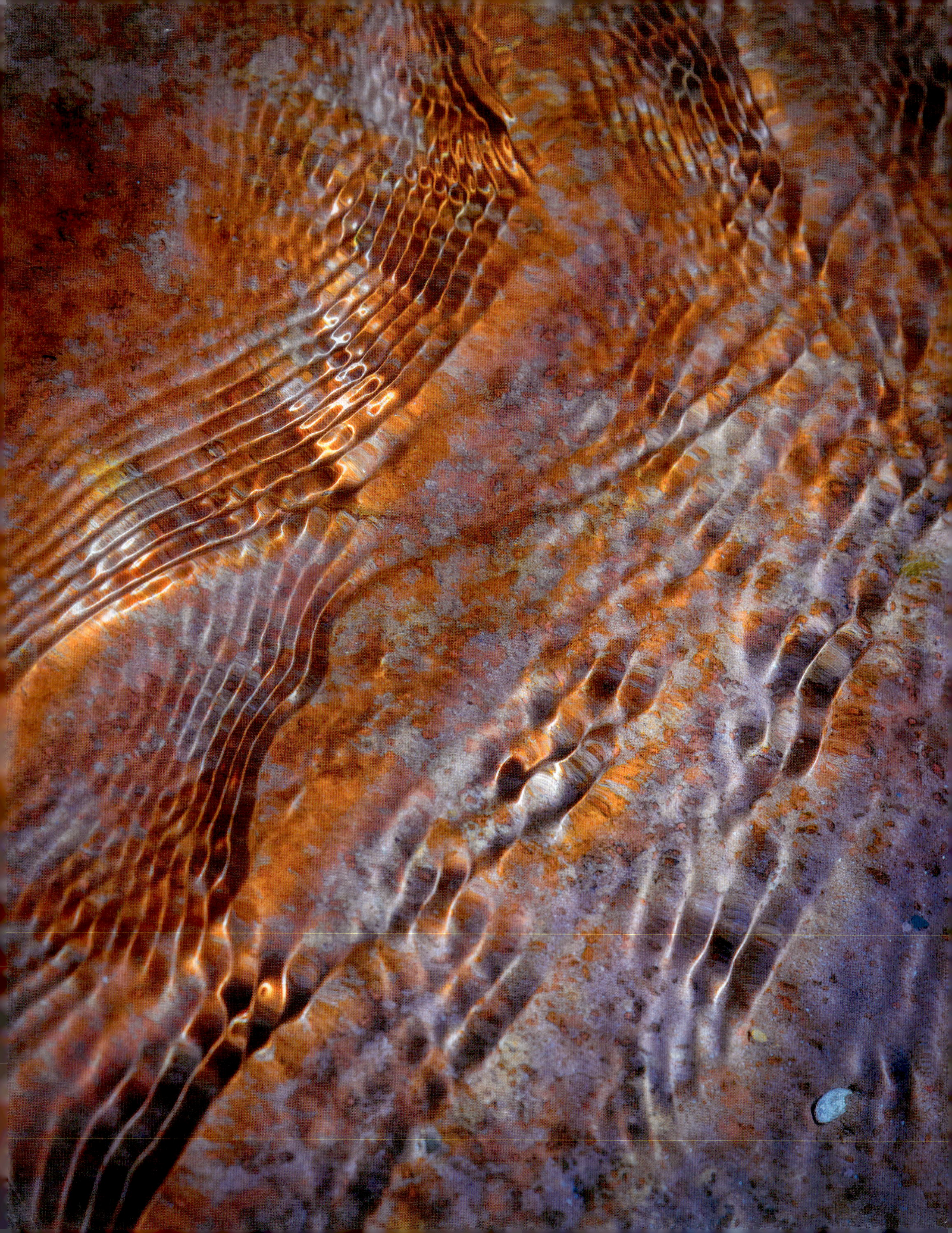

# About the Author

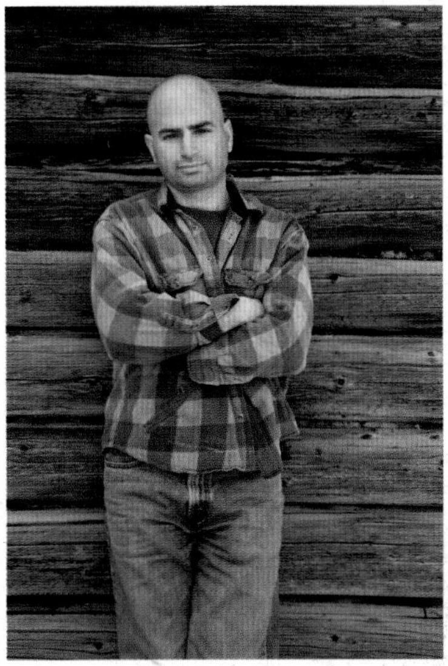

Guy Tal spent the first 26 years of his life in Israel where he was born, served a mandatory military service, and studied and taught at the Tel Aviv University. As a youth, he loved to explore the natural areas around his home by the Mediterranean Sea, as well as the Negev Desert and the Golan Heights. It was during one of these outings that Guy first picked up a camera to document the things that fascinated him about the natural landscape and its wild inhabitants. This prompted a passion for and deep interest in photography that continues to grow and intensify to this day—three decades later.

At odds with the political turmoil and rampant urbanization of his homeland, Guy immigrated to California where he embarked on a career in information technology. He also began an enduring love affair with the wild places of the American West. Guy found that he was unfulfilled by the urban, career-driven life, and decided to move closer to his beloved deserts and mountains of the Colorado Plateau. He ultimately settled in a tiny, remote town at the foot of Utah's Aquarius Plateau, on the edge of Utah's famous canyon country—a place that inspires him deeply and where he practices most of his work.

A lifelong learner and explorer, Guy's interest in art, science, and philosophy converged with his intense love of wild places, which he expresses through his photography and writing. He is a public speaker, educator, and frequent contributor to several photographic publications. Guy's first book, *More Than A Rock*, was published by Rocky Nook in 2015.

# Table of Contents

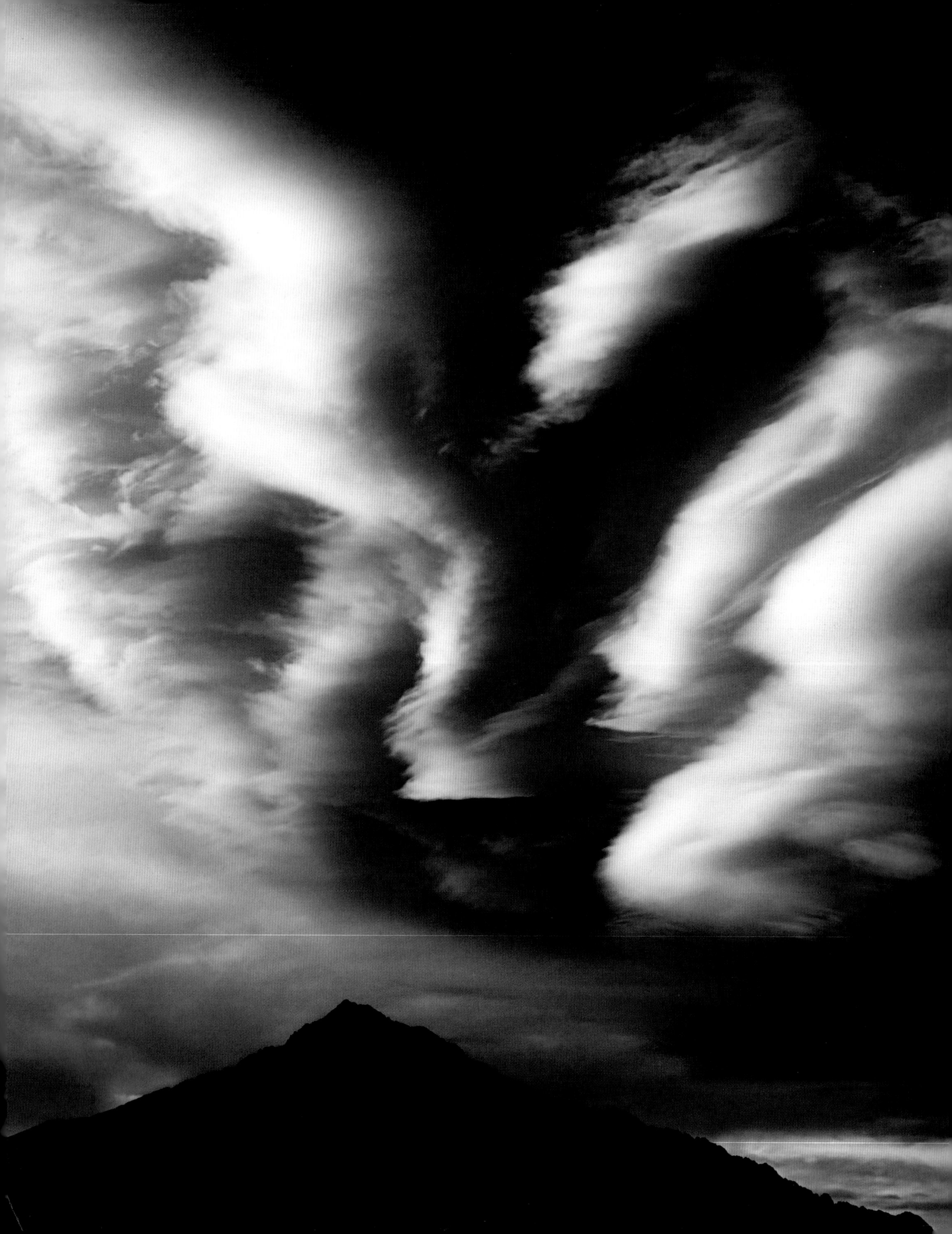

# Foreword

The mind of Guy Tal is equal parts artist, philosopher, and scientist. Many artists are content with using tools that simply work. Guy carefully dissects his tools and thought processes not just so he understands how something works, but rather to determine if better or more efficient alternatives may exist.

Not just another book of regurgitated Photoshop techniques, *The Landscape Photographer's Guide to Photoshop* is guided by Guy's own expressive photographs and thoughtful workflow. Explicitly intentional and visualization driven, these workflows and techniques stand apart from presets and popular processing recipes.

Guy's professional experience runs the gamut of camera formats from film to digital, and dates back to the earliest versions of Photoshop (now more than 25 years old). There are many programs and apps today that offer unquestionably greater ease of use than Photoshop, and most often with considerably faster execution. But should you treat your art like fast food?

You owe it to your photographs to dig deeply into this book. You'll learn how a few of Photoshop's most basic tools will fill most of your creative needs, complete with reversible and nondestructive adjustments. No other software offers the visionary artist more control and precision.

From pixels to prints, this is a soup to nuts book for the expressive landscape photographer. Whether you are new to photography or are a long-time photographer and Photoshop power user, *The Landscape Photographer's Guide to Photoshop* offers something for everyone. It is perhaps the only book of its kind and may be the only one you will ever need.

—Michael E. Gordon
Long Beach, California
www.michael-gordon.com

# Introduction

> *Mastery of craft is directly proportional to the sheer number of hours you throw into the effort, but vision unfolds in concert with your total life experience—in other words, slowly, and only across extended periods of time.*
>
> —TED ORLAND

This book is intended for landscape photographers who wish to pursue their work as expressive art and who want to use the tools provided in Adobe Photoshop to accomplish their goals. It is not meant to be an exhaustive review of the features of Photoshop—rather, it is an introduction to the visualization-driven workflow I employ in my own work and that I teach in my workshops.

I believe making expressive images—images that convey not only appearances but also the photographer's thoughts and feelings—requires a holistic approach that starts with a stroke of inspiration and carries forth that inspiration, using it to guide the forming of a visualized outcome in the photographer's mind, and then applying precise control of color, tone, and contrast toward realizing that visualization in the final image, whether electronic or printed.

Expressive photography relies on a combination of technical and cognitive skills. In expressive images, we seek to employ visual qualities—color, value, contrast, lines, textures and shapes—to elicit predictable emotional responses from the viewer. To do so successfully, the photographer must know something about visual perception and must understand photography—not just as a set of technologies for recording and processing images, but also as a form of language and as a medium for creating art.

Visualization, which I describe in detail in the book, is the ability to see in the "mind's eye" a finished image—a desired end result—before and during its making. With a visualized image, the photographer has a target to aim for and a reference point to use in selecting the tools needed to realize it. Visualization is not an easy skill to master, but with time and effort proficiency can be achieved. To visualize is to recognize not just what there is, but also what can be—how visual ingredients, creative ideas, expressive intent, and technical skills can be brought together to produce images that are not just aesthetically pleasing, unique, and original but that also reflect the photographer's thoughts, feelings, and personality.

Throughout many years of practicing photography, teaching workshops, and working with students of all skill levels, I have developed and refined the workflow presented here. Though photographic technology and digital processing tools have evolved at a staggering pace, the tools and techniques I describe in this book are those that have consistently proven to be the most effective and intuitive, and which are conducive to the goal of making expressive landscape photographs.

I believe there is no one-size-fits-all recipe when it comes to processing expressive images. Each image is unique, both in its visual characteristics and in what it is intended to express.

—Guy Tal
Torrey, Utah
November 2017

# Part I:
# Theory

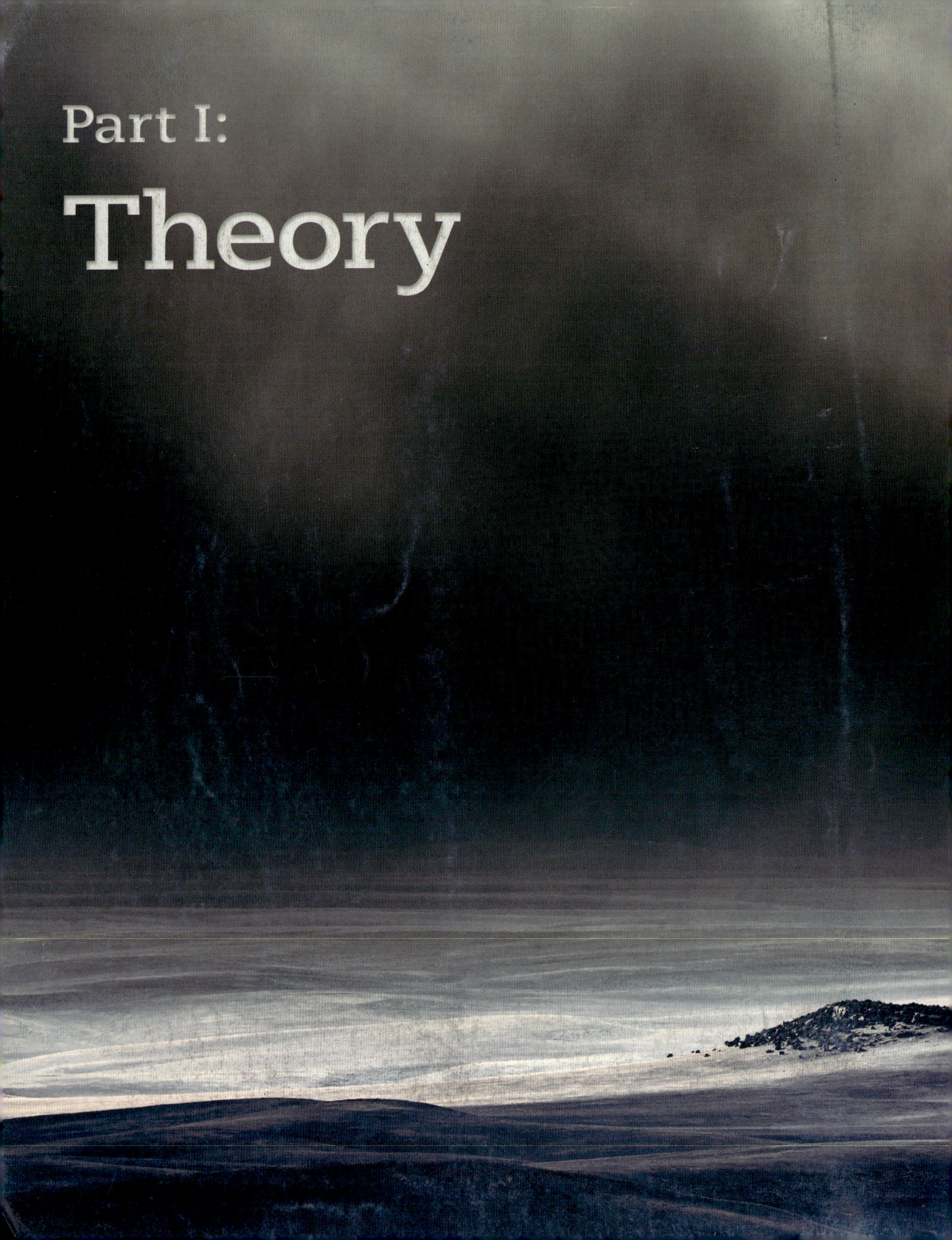

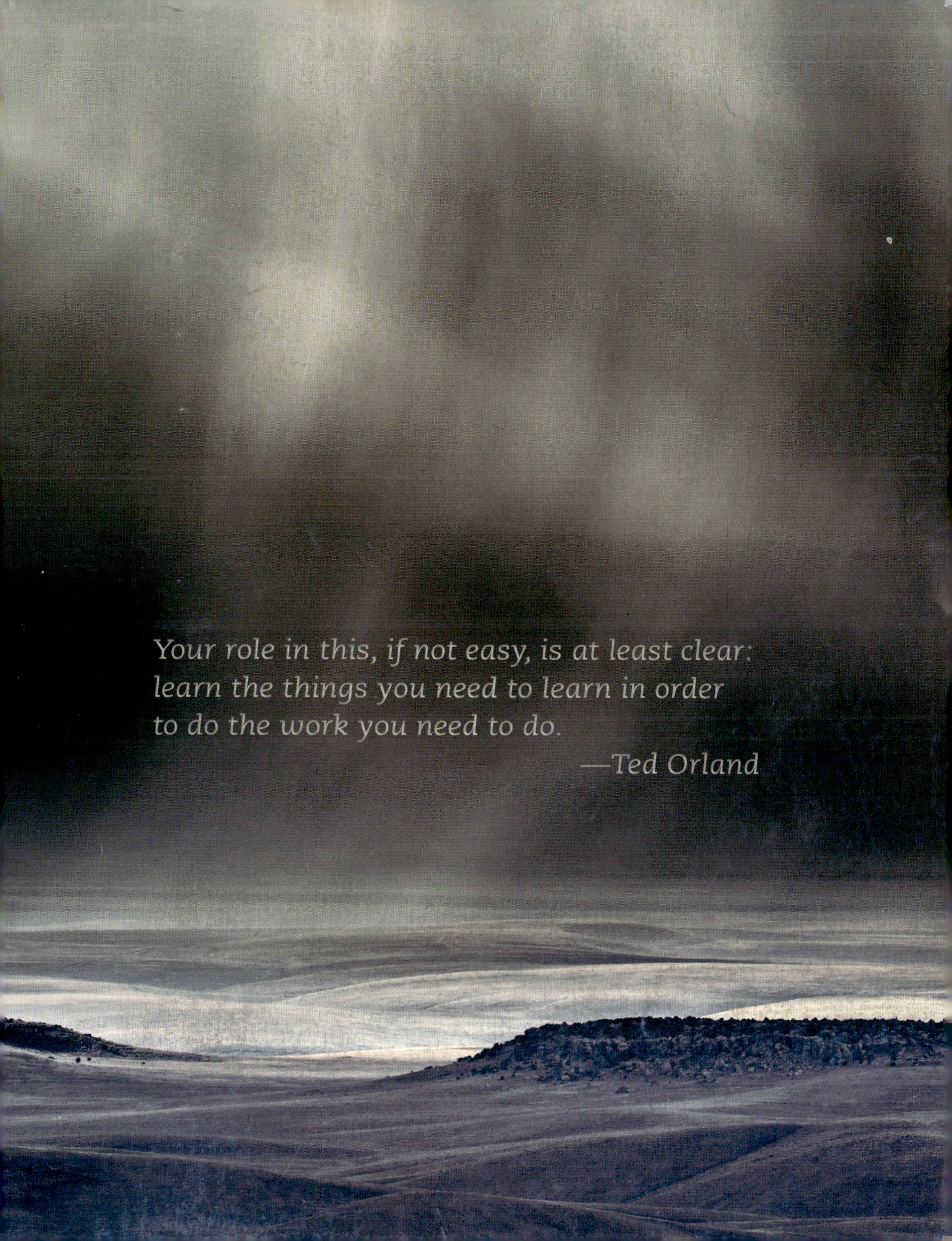

*Your role in this, if not easy, is at least clear:
learn the things you need to learn in order
to do the work you need to do.*

*—Ted Orland*

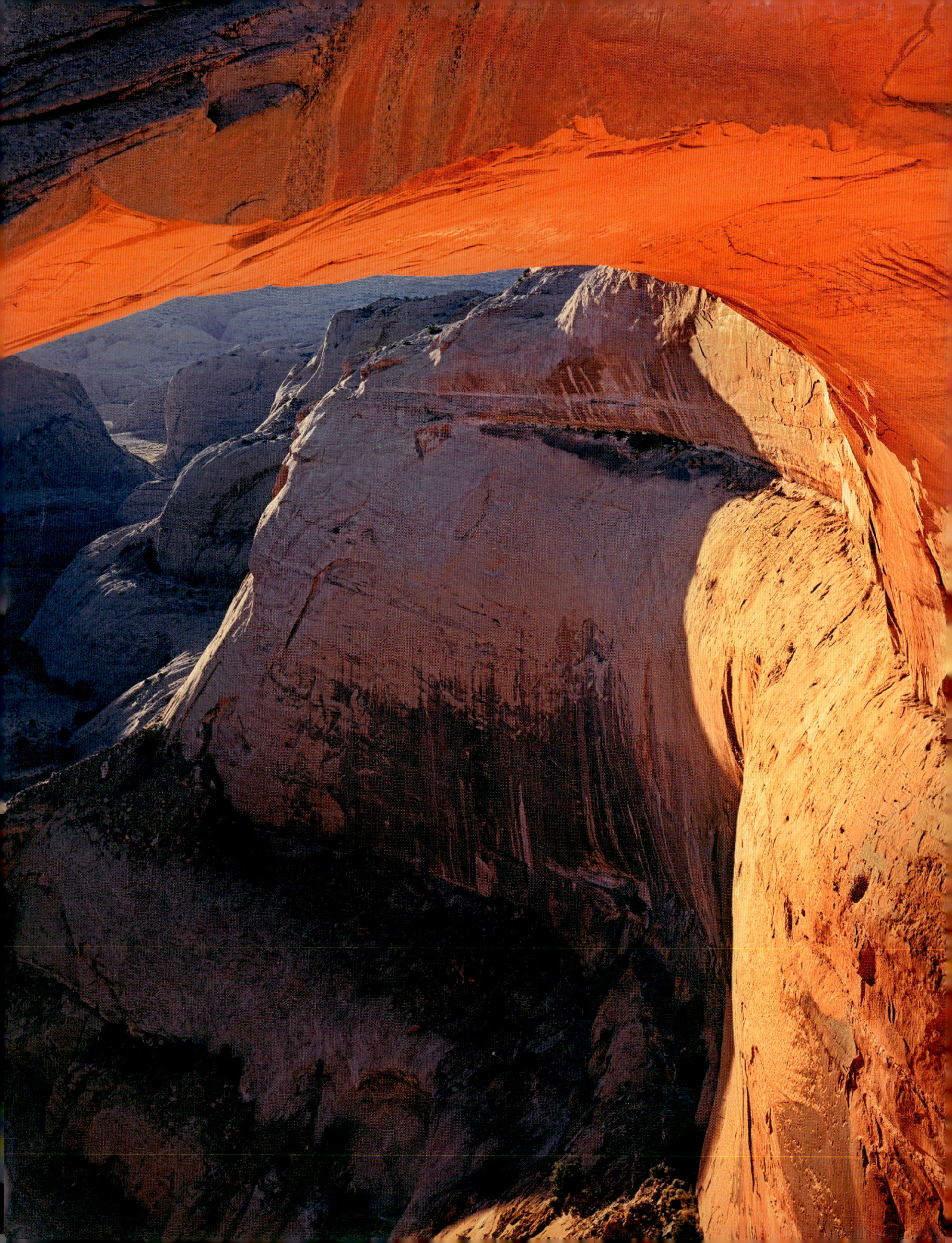

# Photography and Art

1

*It cannot be too plainly stated that it is quite unimportant whether photography produces "art" or not. Its own basic laws, not the opinions of art critics, will provide the only valid measure of its future worth.*

—LASZLO MOHOLY-NAGY

Most of us have an intuitive notion of what art is, although to venture a formal definition for art is likely to arouse contention. Consider that when we define what qualifies as art, we also implicitly declare what does *not* qualify as art. With something so broad and subjective as to include, among many other things, paintings and autographed urinals; ancient glyphs and computerized holograms; great cathedrals and Shakespearean plays; woven rugs and calligraphy; pottery and interpretive dance; music and cinema; business management and strategies for war—and at least some genres of photography—where should the line be drawn?

The word art derives from the Latin *artem*, referring specifically to things created by human skill and craftsmanship, as distinct from things occurring randomly and naturally. Other words of the same origin include *artifact* and *artificial*. This is an important distinction and one that is not intuitive to most—art, independent of any other qualification, is something deliberately created by human beings.

## Art Defined

The *Encyclopedia Britannica* offers this definition for visual art: "a visual object or experience consciously created through an expression of skill or imagination." The inclusion of "object or experience" implies that just about anything we are capable of perceiving with our senses may qualify as a work of art. Still, the more revealing part of the definition is in the words "consciously created," affirming that art is a product of a deliberate act by a conscious being. The definition suggests that naturally or randomly occurring phenomena, as well as creations made by unconscious machines, no matter how aesthetically pleasing or inspiring they may be, do not meet the criteria to be considered as art. This can be a point of concern to landscape photographers who rely to a great degree on found aesthetics; and to various degrees on automated tools, in the production of our work. The definition implies that to be considered art, photographs must venture beyond mere representation of things (literally re-presenting them). Art should also possess a consciously created element originating in the photographer's mind.

Indeed, many who propose that photography is unsuitable to be a means for making art base their objection on the assumption that photography is, and can only be, a mechanical and representational medium, leaving little or no room for expressing the subjective imagination, intent, and sensibilities of an artist. I believe that such characterization is both wrong and unfortunate, and is largely a product of misinformation, as well as a degree of prejudice that may be better understood when considering the history of western art.

Photography struggled for recognition as an artistic medium almost since its inception, which happened to coincide with the decline of Romanticism—a movement in art that emphasized emotion and individuality, sublime beauty and natural aesthetics—some of the very things we celebrate in landscape photography.

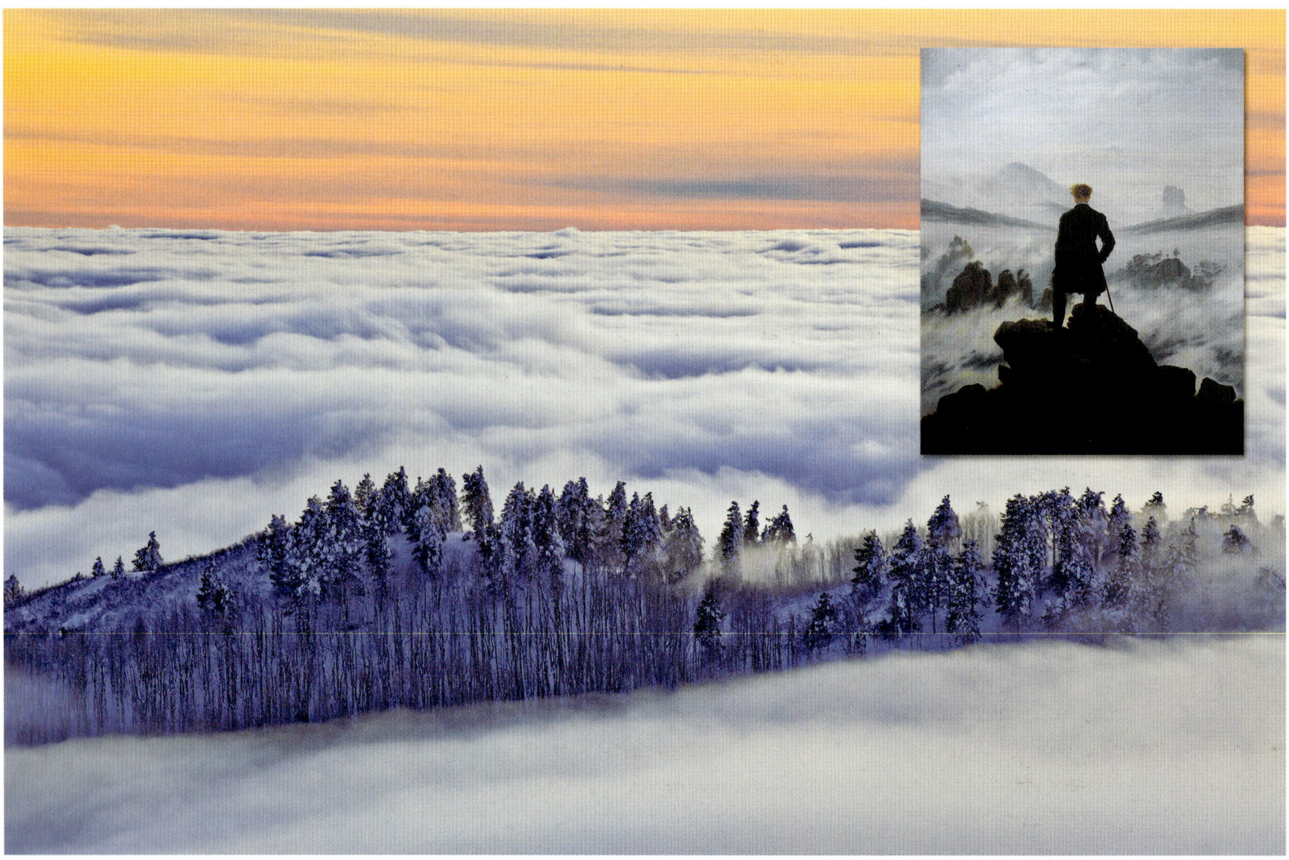

**Figure 1.1:** It is fair to say that much contemporary landscape photography is rooted in Romanticism, emphasizing the purity and beauty of the natural world and the artist's reverence for it. As landscape photographers, however, our motivation often transcends mere aesthetic appeal and derives also from the experience of being present in wild, natural settings. When I made this image, titled *Kingdom of Ravens*, I was standing on the steep edge of one of Utah's high plateaus. I distinctly recall feeling like I was the person in Caspar David Friedrich's painting, *Wanderer Above the Sea of Fog* (inset).

Current attitudes toward topics such as the role of beauty in art, why photography is considered by some not to be a proper medium for art, and notions of meaning and purpose in art are often not intuitive to photographers (indeed, to most people).

## Western Art Before Photography

Following is an overview of Western art before the invention of photography. This history is important to know for the following reasons: 1) The evolution of photography as art follows patterns seen in painting. 2) It sheds light on the debate of photography as an art form.

### Classical Art

What we commonly refer to as western art is rooted in the classical period of Ancient Greece, occurring around 500 BCE.

The advent of democracy liberated artists in both the literal and the creative sense. With the exception of prehistoric art, for the first time real people and real events, rather than gods and other mythological subjects, began to appear as subjects of art.

By Hellenistic times, artists had achieved such mastery of their crafts that mere realistic renditions no longer were considered sufficient, and art took on an overly idealized look. Sculptures of this era celebrate the human figure in such glorified perfection as to be wholly unrealistic.

Rome overtook the Greek Empire, although Roman art preserved many of the sensibilities of Greek art. In fact, the Romans made many copies of famous Greek sculptures, which would otherwise not be known to us today as the originals were since lost. Like their Greek predecessors, Roman artists continued to also celebrate gods and heroes, but their style was more documentary and less idealized. More important to readers of this book is the introduction of natural elements—landscapes and animals—into the visual narrative of Roman art. In time, Roman painters also evolved visual techniques for rendering of perspective, proper use of color, texture and shading, etc., that were not available to Greek artists.

A study of landscape photographs over the last few decades reveals a similar trend. In the past, the mere act of capturing a well-composed and well-exposed image and printing it with proper tonality or color was considered a worthy accomplishment. Improvements in photographic technology increasingly allowed for greater control and more precise renditions to be made, leading to present time, when many landscape photographs venture beyond the capacities of human vision.

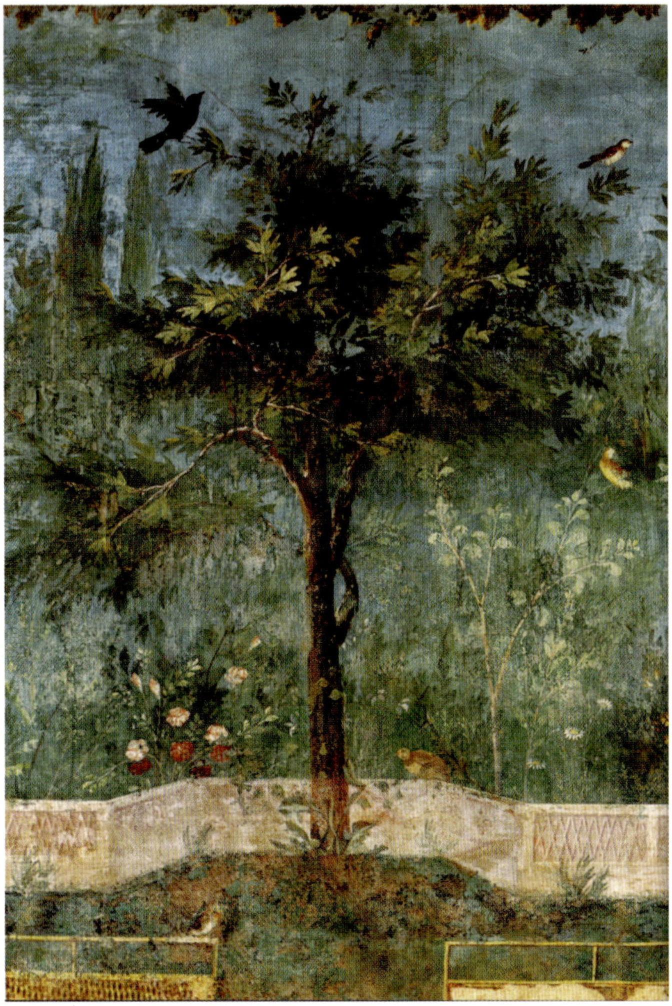

FIGURE 1.2: Detail from a fresco found at the Villa di Livia in Rome, thought to have been owned by the wife of Roman emperor Augustus. The fresco shows an abundance of natural subjects—trees, flowers, birds—although this early example of Roman art still appears mostly two-dimensional and does not feature techniques for rendering perspective, light, and shadow, which were developed in later times.

## The Middle Ages

The period following the fall of the Roman Empire is known as the Middle Ages, or the Medieval period. Some literature also refers to this period as the Dark Ages, signifying an era that, for many in Europe, was marked by poverty, war, disease, persecution, and religious fundamentalism. Despite being diverse in style, nearly all art during this period—spanning about a thousand years—revolved around religious motifs. Churches became powerful and wealthy, and they commissioned artists to glorify their beliefs, mostly to be enjoyed by wealthy patrons. Most of those in the working class were too poor to afford art, let alone have the resources to engage in it.

## The Renaissance

The Renaissance, starting in fourteenth century Florence and fueled by the riches of the Medici family, marks the end of the Middle Ages, and a spectacular flourishing of the arts and sciences. In terms of style, Renaissance art is, to a large degree, a revival of the classical art of Rome and Ancient Greece, expressed in exquisite realism and a perfection of skill. Still, there was much more to Renaissance art than just mimicry of classical art. Although religious depictions still dominated much of the art produced during the Renaissance, we also see a renewed interest in portraying natural subjects. The realism of the classical era was further enhanced during the Renaissance with greater emphasis on use of perspective, light, and shadow. Renaissance art celebrated beauty; enhanced and glorified and studied it. Artists such as Michelangelo and Leonardo da Vinci created works of spectacular skill, scale, and complexity.

The Renaissance was an era of significantly greater freedom, compared with medieval times, and creative individuals could express their talents in a manner not usually seen in the Middle Ages. Yet, despite its enlightened and humanistic legacy, Renaissance art still was mostly created under the patronage of a rich, powerful, and religious elite. In that sense, some consider the Renaissance's true importance as being a transitional period between the strict and dogmatic art of the Middle Ages and the artistic freedom of the Modern era, in which artists finally rebel against all that confined their expressive powers before that, both aesthetically and politically.

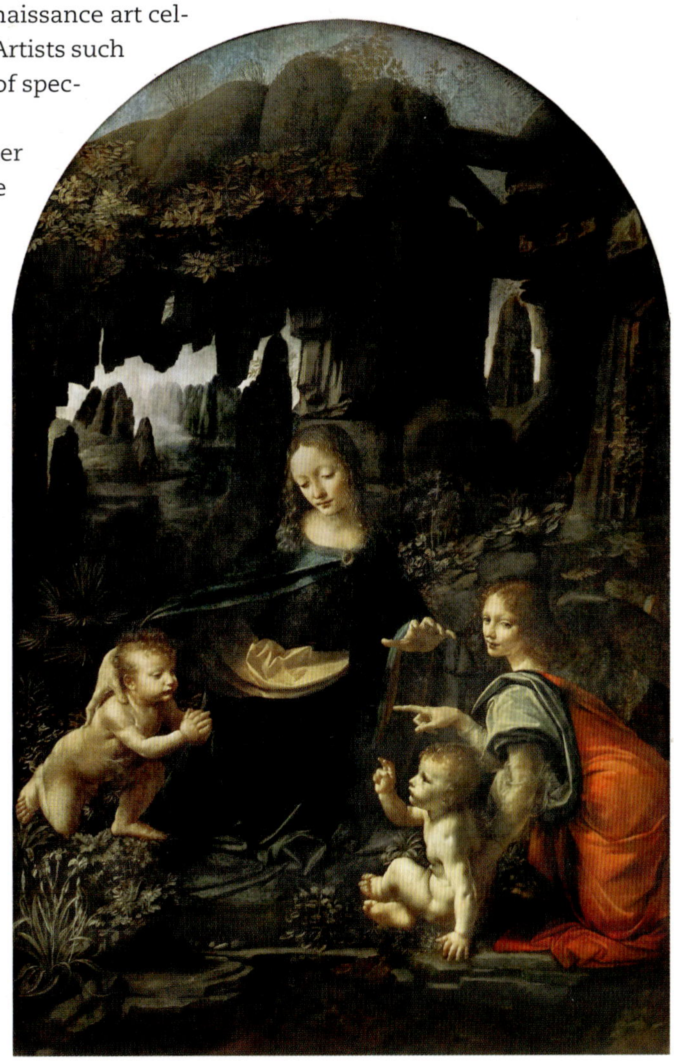

FIGURE 1.3: Leonardo da Vinci's *Virgin of the Rocks*, like many of his other paintings, includes a backdrop of dramatic natural scenery, rendered to simulate the interplay of light and shadow, atmosphere, and a sense of depth, using techniques developed during the Renaissance.

## Baroque and Rococo Periods

After the Renaissance, came the Baroque and Rococo periods, marked by lavish aggrandizing of all things beautiful, emotional, and dramatic. Art became adorned to the extreme in graceful flowing lines, bold colors, gilded accents, and intense renditions of light. Emotional scenes, still mostly of a religious nature, were rendered with exaggerated flair and grandeur, and architecture assumed exquisite ornamental details on a monumental scale. Artists like Gian Lorenzo Bernini took the Renaissance legacy of

Michelangelo and Rafael, and made it even more extravagant and luxurious. Art was designed to be accessible to the masses and to be appealing to anyone irrespective of their level of education or social status, usually with the simple intent of celebrating biblical themes and the teachings of the Roman Catholic Church. Illustrations were direct, simple, and appealing primarily to the senses rather than to the intellect.

Baroque art had little to do with matters of daily life, politics, or social justice. Instead, it showcased the skill of the artist in rendering easily relatable scenes with bombastic gusto. Similarly, many works of contemporary landscape photographers seek to overwhelm viewers in obvious and easily digestible creations using overly saturated colors and majestic scenery, but often lacking a more complex, nuanced, and personal narrative.

### Neoclassicism and Romanticism

The Enlightenment of the eighteenth century gave rise to two interesting and related developments. The new science of archaeology led to renewed interest in the classical arts, resulting in Neoclassicism—an evolutionary, rather than revolutionary, rehashing of the past. More important, a parallel movement—Romanticism—gained in prominence. In Romantic art we see the beginnings of art wresting itself free from the bidding of political powers, whether religious or aristocratic. Gone were the days of socially benign renditions of biblical scenes sanctioned by the Roman Catholic Church.

Following on the heels of the Enlightenment, artists of the Romantic period sought to express subjective values and sensibilities, often in defiance of the social elite. Romantic art celebrated the sublime in natural scenes but also did not sidestep such negative emotions as fear and apprehension that were previously not considered proper subjects for art (perhaps with the exception of the suffering of Christ).

Juxtaposed against the backdrop of rampant urbanization and industrialization, artists of the Romantic era may have been the forbearers of environmental art, highlighting the purity and beauty of natural subjects and seeking to elevate the human spirit from the grim realities of the industrial age through emotionally powerful imagery. Great emphasis was placed on originality, both in terms of expressing the sensibilities of an individual artist, and in defiant departures from former trends in art that did not allow for free expression or social commentary.

Landscape painting, not formerly considered of high status, gained prominence in the Romantic era. Painters rendered a variety of subjects, often in very large paintings, most depicting dramatic natural scenery as a backdrop or even as their main subject. Although there is no strict commonality in subject matter, a defining characteristic of Romanticism is the expression of the artist's inner world and personal narrative, as opposed to prescribed (biblical) stories.

It is fair to say that much landscape photography today celebrates similar values, sensibilities, and subject matter as art of the Romantic era. However, the art world has long shifted its focus to other—at times antithetical—movements. This is part of the challenge landscape photographers face when attempting to introduce our work in venues that align themselves with more recent trends in art.

## Realism

The exaggerated emotions and sublime renditions of the Romantic era fell out of favor after the French Revolution when artists, true to the social turmoil of their day, decided to do away with all embellishment and, instead,

FIGURE 1.4: This rendition of *The Oxbow* by Romantic painter Thomas Cole (c. 1836) shows many elements revered by landscape photographers today: dramatic light and weather, a sweeping long view, and a progression from foreground to background.

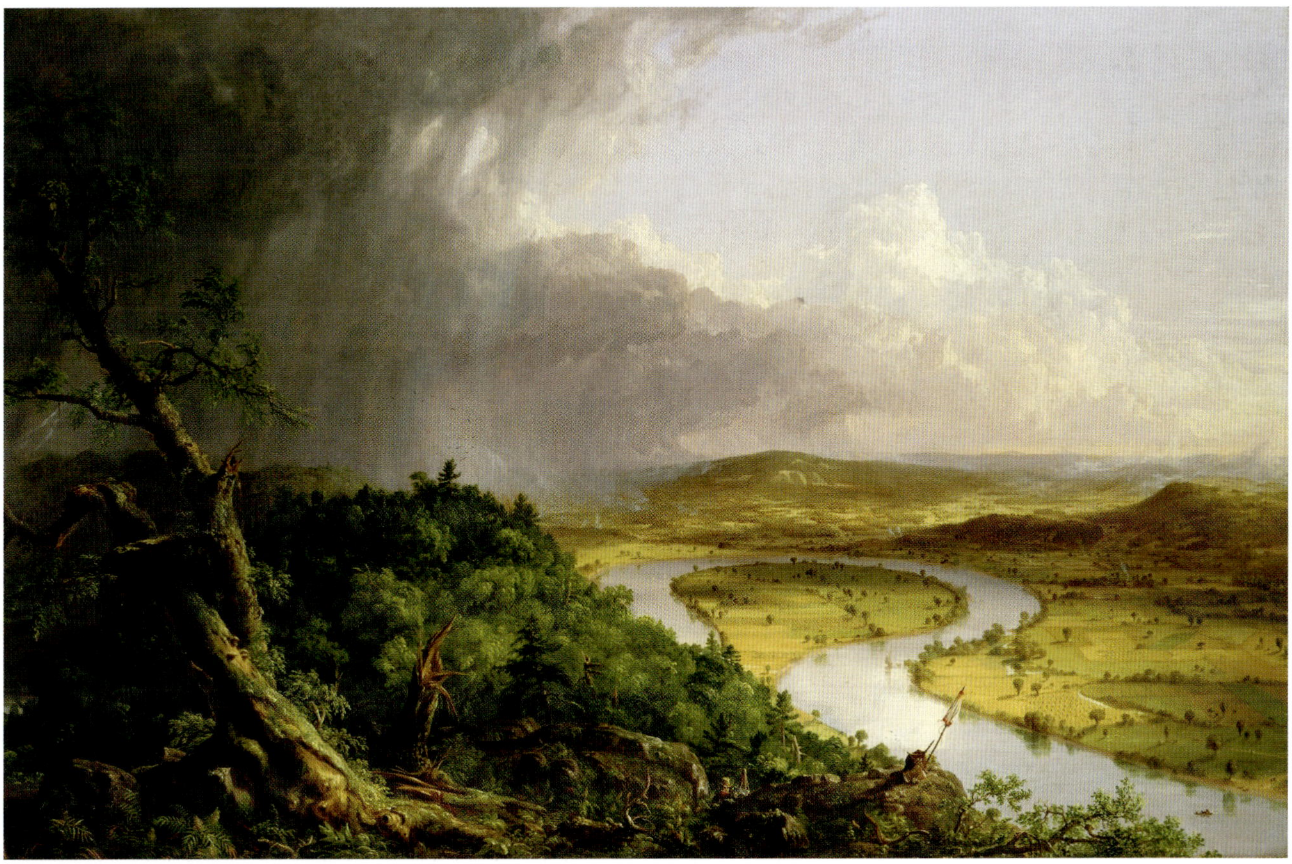

strive to remain truthful to realistic appearances. The resulting art movement is, therefore, known as Realism.

Other than realistic style, Realism also marked a shift in preference of subject matter. Ordinary working class people and simple scenes, once considered unworthy as subjects of art, now received the attention of artists. Similarly, social commentary, including unpleasant subject matter, also became fair game for artists wishing to make social and political statements within their work.

It is at this point, around the middle of the nineteenth century, that we first see the clash of traditional arts with the newly invented medium of photography. It might seem that photography would be the perfect complement for Realism, considering its ability to produce accurate and truthful representations; but, as human nature would have it, photography was greeted with great skepticism by artists of the day. Moreover, as photographs became rapidly popular, Realism already was in the process of giving way to the novel concepts of modern art, marked by an ongoing trend toward abstraction, rather than realistic renditions.

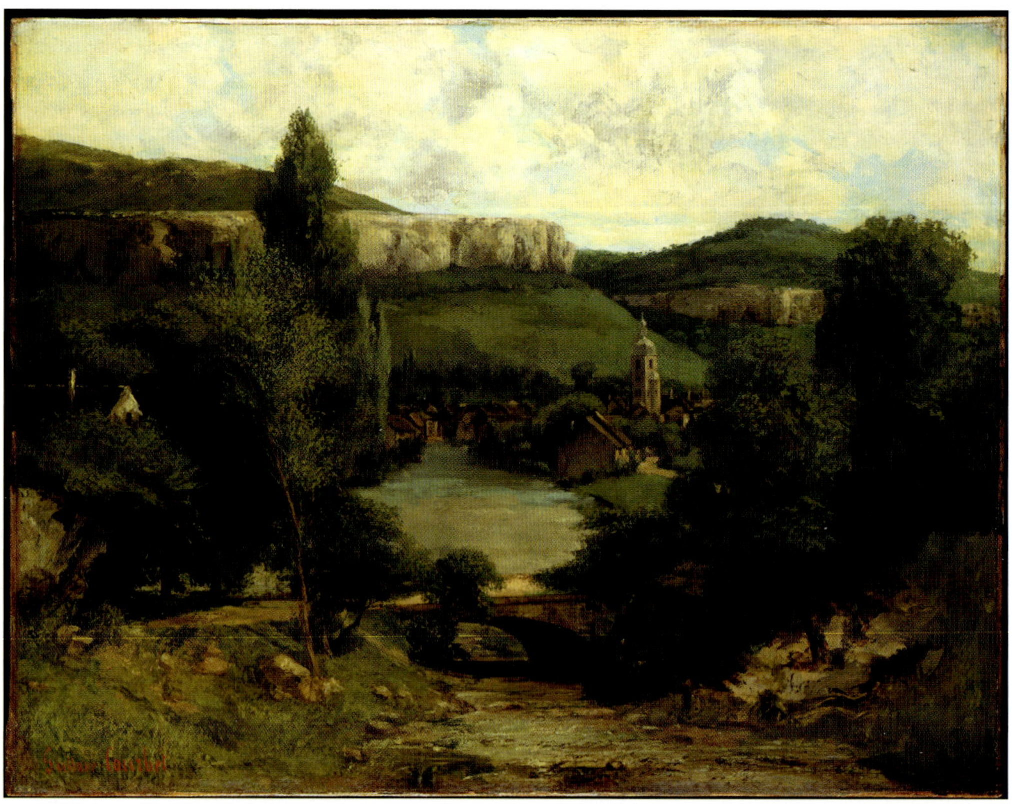

**FIGURE 1.5:** Realist artists strived to render scenes in a manner that is true to natural light and detail, rather than exaggerate them for dramatic effect. Note the lack of flourish and drama, and the use of natural and realistic colors and light in this painting by Gustave Courbet titled *View of the Ornans*, c. 1858.

## Photography as Art

Nicéphore Niépce invented photography in the early nineteenth century, although it did not become widely popular until after Niépce's death, when his former partner, Louis Daguerre, introduced the daguerreotype process. Allowing for relatively short exposure times, the daguerreotype process offered a means of making inexpensive (relative to commissioned paintings) portraits, which became wildly popular. Although widespread in Europe, daguerreotypes became especially prevalent in the United States, where several million of them were produced each year around the middle of the nineteenth century. Still, despite its popularity, very few regarded photography as a medium for the creation of art.

Since its early days, photography was the subject of resistance and ridicule from painters. Impressionist painter Pierre-Auguste Renoir suggested mockingly that, "Photography freed painting from a lot of tiresome chores, starting with family portraits."

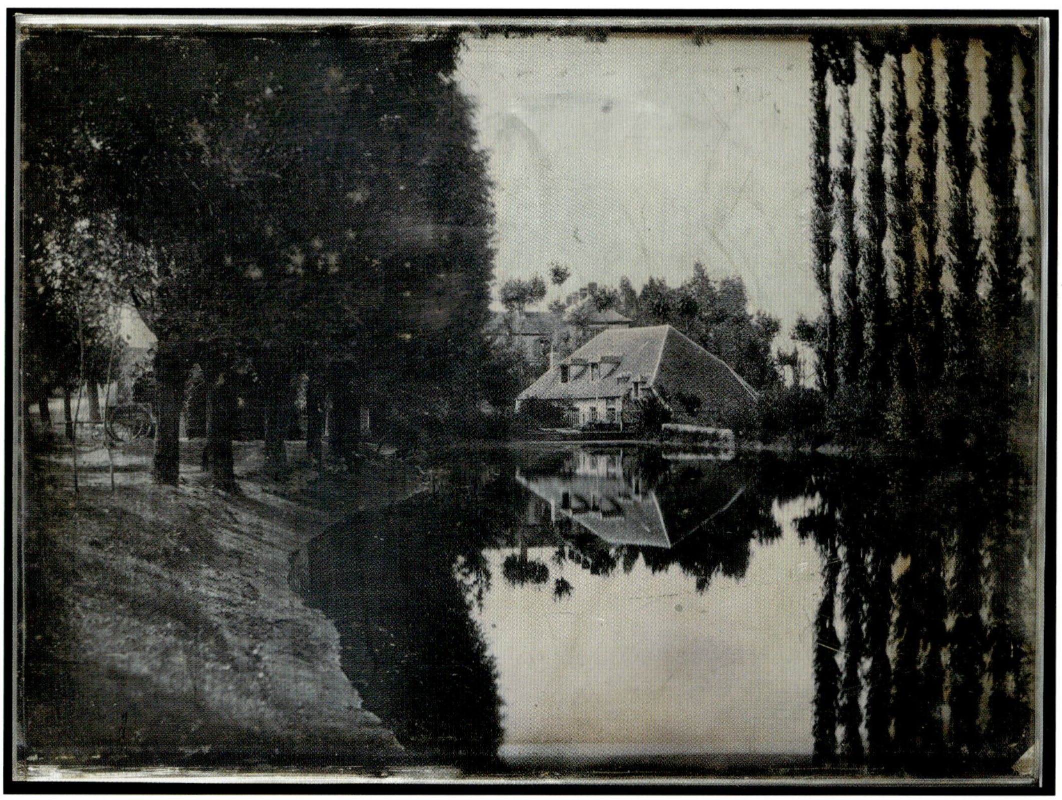

**FIGURE: 1.6:** The daguerreotype process was most notably used for portraits, however some photographers also used it to make landscape images, such as this scene photographed in 1844 by Marie-Charles-Isidore Choiselat.

The distinction of being photography's harshest critic likely is reserved for poet and art critic Charles Baudelaire. In 1859, when daguerreotypes were at the height of their popularity, Baudelaire penned a scathing essay in which he wrote:

> *As the photographic industry was the refuge of every would-be painter, every painter too ill-endowed or too lazy to complete his studies, this universal infatuation bore not only the mark of a blindness, an imbecility, but had also the air of a vengeance. I do not believe, or at least I do not wish to believe, in the absolute success of such a brutish conspiracy, in which, as in all others, one finds both fools and knaves… If photography is allowed to supplement art in some of its functions, it will soon have supplanted or corrupted it altogether, thanks to the stupidity of the multitude, which is its natural ally. It is time, then, for it to return to its true duty, which is to be the servant of the sciences and arts.*

To put the essay in context, it was written at a time when many artists preoccupied themselves with the celebration of idealized natural beauty. Baudelaire feared that photography, having the power to render natural scenes more accurately than other media, and requiring less skill, might become the downfall of the fine arts. Baudelaire continues:

> *In matters of painting and sculpture, the present-day Credo of the sophisticated…is this: "I believe in Nature, and I believe only in Nature (there are good reasons for that). I believe that Art is, and cannot be other than, the exact reproduction of Nature… Thus an industry that could give us a result identical to Nature would be the absolute of Art." A revengeful God has given ear to the prayers of this multitude. Daguerre was his Messiah. And now the faithful says to himself: "Since photography gives us every guarantee of exactitude that we could desire (they really believe that, the mad fools!), then photography and Art are the same thing.*

Baudelaire may have been the first (although by far not the only) critic to dismiss photography on the assumption that it can be nothing more than a mimetic, representational medium.

Since the Romantic era, art came to be associated with subjective and original expressions of an artist's unique and creative mind. Baudelaire correctly makes the same point reflected in present-day definitions of art as being something "consciously created." Creation means bringing something new into existence—something that did not exist before the artist created it—as opposed to re-presenting something already in existence. As suggested by Ansel Adams, "Most creative photographs are departures from reality and it seems to take a higher order of craft to make this departure than to simulate reality."

**The "Inward Significance" is What Really Matters**

There are some who adamantly defend the idea that all photographs must abide by the strict rules of photojournalism, but such a claim only validates the fact that art, by its very nature, is subjective and ambiguous. It is my belief that photography—like any other medium for communicating information, concepts, stories, and emotions—can serve many expressive purposes and that its validity is determined by context, rather than by some technical quality. To require that all photographs should be factual and literal is as silly as to require that all writing should be factual and literal. Just as readers can derive different meanings from factual and fictional accounts, viewers of photographs can make a similar distinction between representational and creative images. While the aim of photojournalism is to communicate facts, in the words of Aristotle, "The aim of art is to represent not the outward appearance of things, but their inward significance."

## Pictorialism

By the end of the nineteenth century, photography was already well established and widely practiced. Although primarily used for portraits, it also developed a devout following as a means of making visual art, meaning that photographic images were also produced for their aesthetic and decorative value and not only as formal representations of the likenesses of people and other subjects. These early artistic photographs generally featured posed subjects and often were heavily manipulated to resemble paintings. This style of photography earned the name Pictorialism.

Pictorialist photographers often employed various techniques to achieve soft focus and to create ethereal and moody effects; and their prints were further enhanced using specialized brushes, chemistry, or even pigments to achieve the desired painterly appearance.

Beyond tools and fashions, Pictorialism marked an important trend in photography, venturing beyond the inherent representational nature of the medium and into the realm of creative expression, where images are created rather than just captured by the photographer.

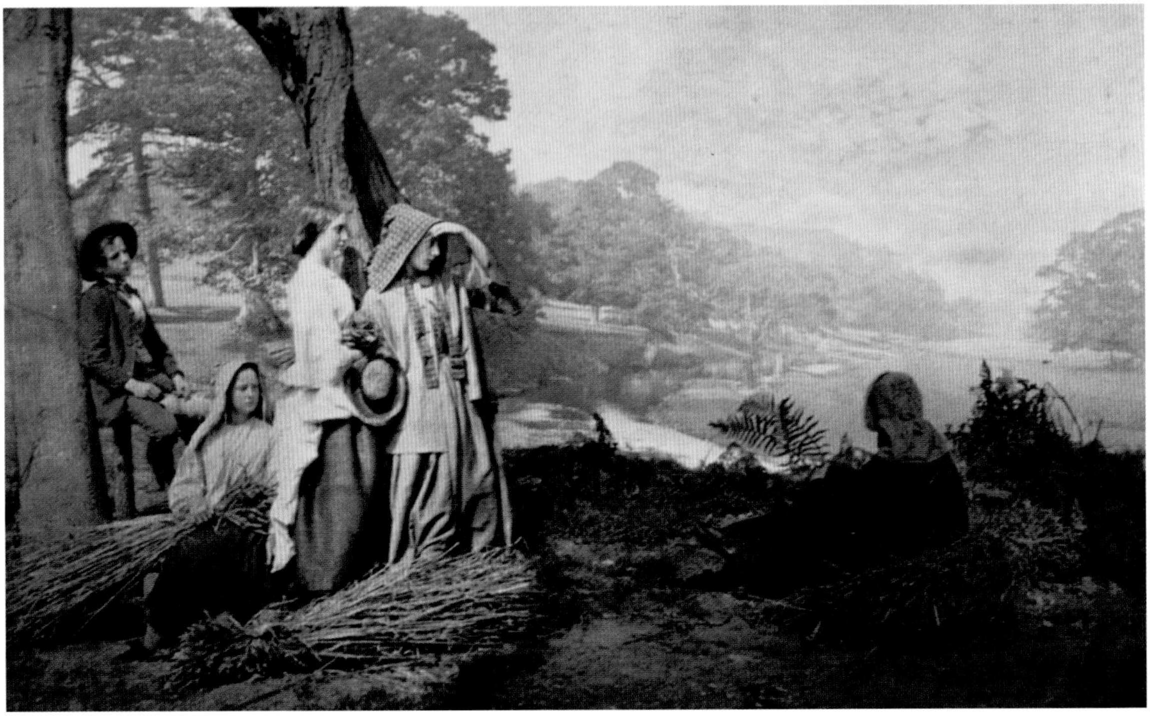

FIGURE 1.7: A photograph in the Pictorialist style by Henry Peach Robinson.

## Straight Photography

Pictorialism thrived well into the early twentieth century but ultimately fell out of favor, to a large degree due to efforts of photographers like Alfred Stieglitz and Paul Strand, and later also Ansel Adams, Edward Weston, and a group of western photographers who came together to form Group f/64 (named after what is commonly the smallest aperture on a view camera lens, which renders the greatest depth of field possible—an affront to the stylized blurring effects used in Pictorialism). These photographers promoted what came to be known as "straight" photography, which sought to emphasize the innate qualities of the photographic medium and which differentiates photographs from paintings—primarily the ability to render fine and accurate details.

It is commonly believed that straight photography precludes techniques for manipulating the photographs after capture. This is patently untrue. Practically all early masters of straight photography manipulated their images in various ways. Their goal was not to make the photographs more "truthful," but rather to limit their tools strictly to those unique to the photographic medium rather than those employed in painting or in pictorialist photography. Photographer Sadakichi Hartmann—a highly regarded photographer and critic in his day—penned an article about straight photography in which he wrote:

> *"And what do I call straight photography," they may ask, "Can you define it?" Well, that's easy enough. Rely on your camera, on your eye, on your good taste and your knowledge of composition, consider every fluctuation of color, light, and shade, study lines and values and space division, patiently wait until the scene or object of your pictured vision reveals itself in its supremest moment of beauty. In short, compose the picture which you intend to take so well that the negative will be absolutely perfect and in need of no or but slight manipulation. I do not object to retouching, dodging, or accentuation, as long as they do not interfere with the natural qualities of photographic technique. Brush marks and lines, on the other hand, are not natural to photography, and I object and always will object to the use of the brush, to finger daubs, to scrawling, scratching, and scribbling on the plate, and to the gum and glycerine process, if they are used for nothing else but producing blurred effects.*

## Color Photography

Since its inception, and for nearly a hundred years until the mid-1930s, practically all photography was monochromatic. For about half that period, photographs were primarily captured on sensitized glass plates; then, starting in 1889, on flexible film. For most of the history of photography, photographers developed their own images and could apply a variety of corrections, retouches, and other adjustments to their images using various chemical processes. Each plate, sheet, or roll of film could be developed separately, and the development process could be adjusted to accomplish specific effects or appearances. Prints were made using techniques that allowed for selective lightening and darkening (i.e., dodging and burning), and other manipulations.

Kodachrome color film, introduced in 1935, marked two photographic milestones. For starters, it was the first color film to become popular and widely available. But, just as important, it was also the first film to rely on a standardized development process (in fact, the process was so complex that the film had to be sent back to Kodak for development, and could not be processed by the photographer). The result was that, while black-and-white photographers had a broad range of creative options to choose from when processing and printing their work, photographers using color film had no such choices.

As more manufacturers began to offer color films—both positive and negative—some processes, such as C-22 (later superseded by C-41) and E-6, were created. These processes were simple enough that photographers could, potentially, implement them in their own darkrooms, but they offered no latitude for creative variations from the standard formulas.

Standard processes, other than offering the convenience of outsourcing film development to professional laboratories, also had the unfortunate effect of restricting color photographers' creative options.

In time, and for many, exposed film became the photographer's final product. Once film was exposed, development and printing were handled in a standard manner, usually by third parties, allowing little control other than push/pull processing (increasing or decreasing development time). A tremendous field of creative possibilities formerly available to those who mastered chemical processes and darkroom techniques was no longer available for the great majority of photographers.

In addition, color photographers were at a further disadvantage when it came to precise control of color, contrast, and tonality. These were, for the most part, dictated by the film's chemistry, leaving the photographer with only a handful of emulsions to pick from. For a long time, no good tools were available to control and fine-tune color and contrast in color photographs.

## Digital Photography

The advent of digital imaging signaled a greater revolution than just a change in photographic technology. Digital tools put all the fine controls (and much more) once reserved to those versed in processing and printing black-and-white images in their own darkrooms into the hands of anyone with a computer. Digital technology liberated photographers to decide for themselves things once dictated by fixed properties of chemical emulsions and standardized processes. Digital tools today allow precise control over color and contrast that far exceeds what was previously available to photographers relying on standard emulsions and chemical processes.

Just as important, whereas most films were created to maintain relatively close fidelity to color and contrast as seen (under given lighting conditions), digital photographers today have a tremendous degree of freedom to depart from such appearances.

A point can be made that pushing creative options to extremes is a slippery slope toward loss of meaning and reliance on visual gimmickry, rather than creative expression. Ultimately, the degree to which such options are applied is entirely within the photographer's discretion. I contend that it is better to have them than to be constrained by a dearth of options or by the arbitrary decisions of others.

The era of film, regrettably, also gave rise to an unfortunate form of militarism in photography. When a piece of film could act as "proof" of a photograph being realistic, many came to rely on such perceived "truthfulness" as an inherent characteristic of the photographic medium, and on strict realism as a measure of worth for a photograph. However, such truthfulness was always a matter of degree and never unequivocal. When considered objectively, realism is not always a necessity or a virtue in a photograph. There are many contexts in which realism in a photograph, just as in writing and other media, is an entirely unnecessary imposition.

Truthfulness, honesty, morality, and other terms sometimes used to judge photographs are, in fact, not qualities of photographs—digital or traditional—they are qualities of people. Both truth and deception in photography are ultimately about how people use the medium and present their creations.

While some prejudice, rooted in ignorance about the many ways in which photography may be used, is still very much prevalent with the creative options now available to digital photographers, photography has gained a rich array of tools and controls, making it more suitable than ever for the creation of expressive art

FIGURE 1.8: The rich array of tools available in Photoshop rivals and exceeds those available in the traditional darkroom, and especially for processing of color photographs, allowing the photographer precise control over color and contrast formerly unavailable to film photographers constrained by standard emulsions and processes.

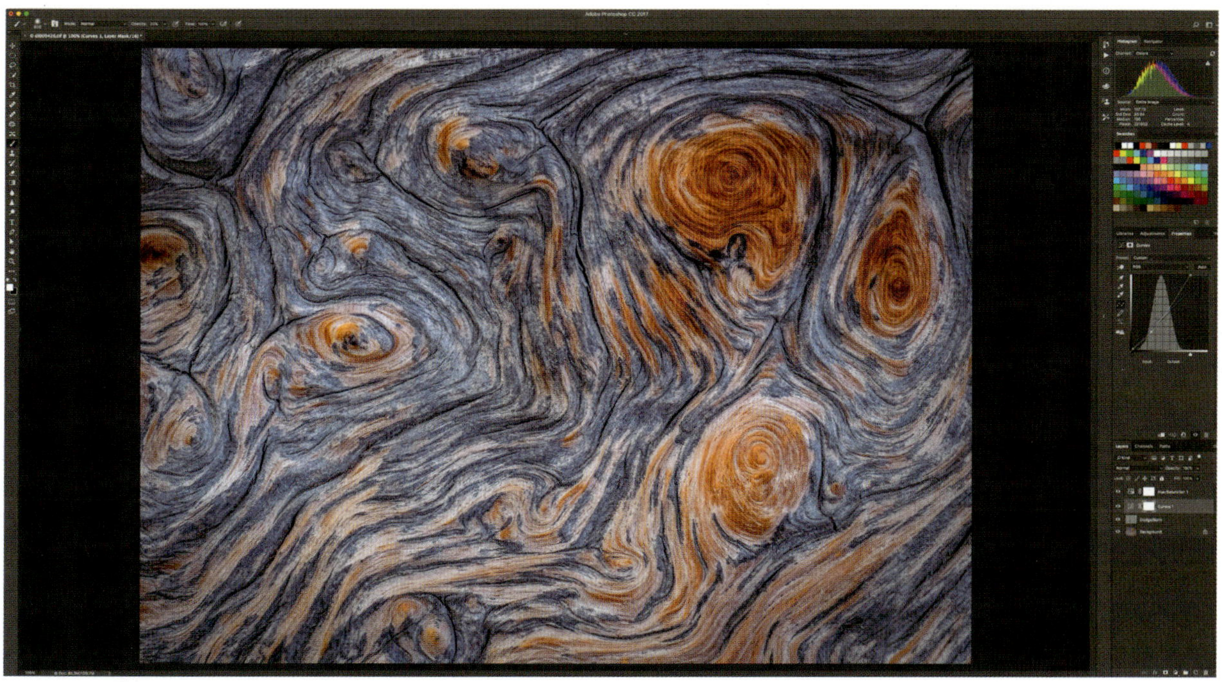

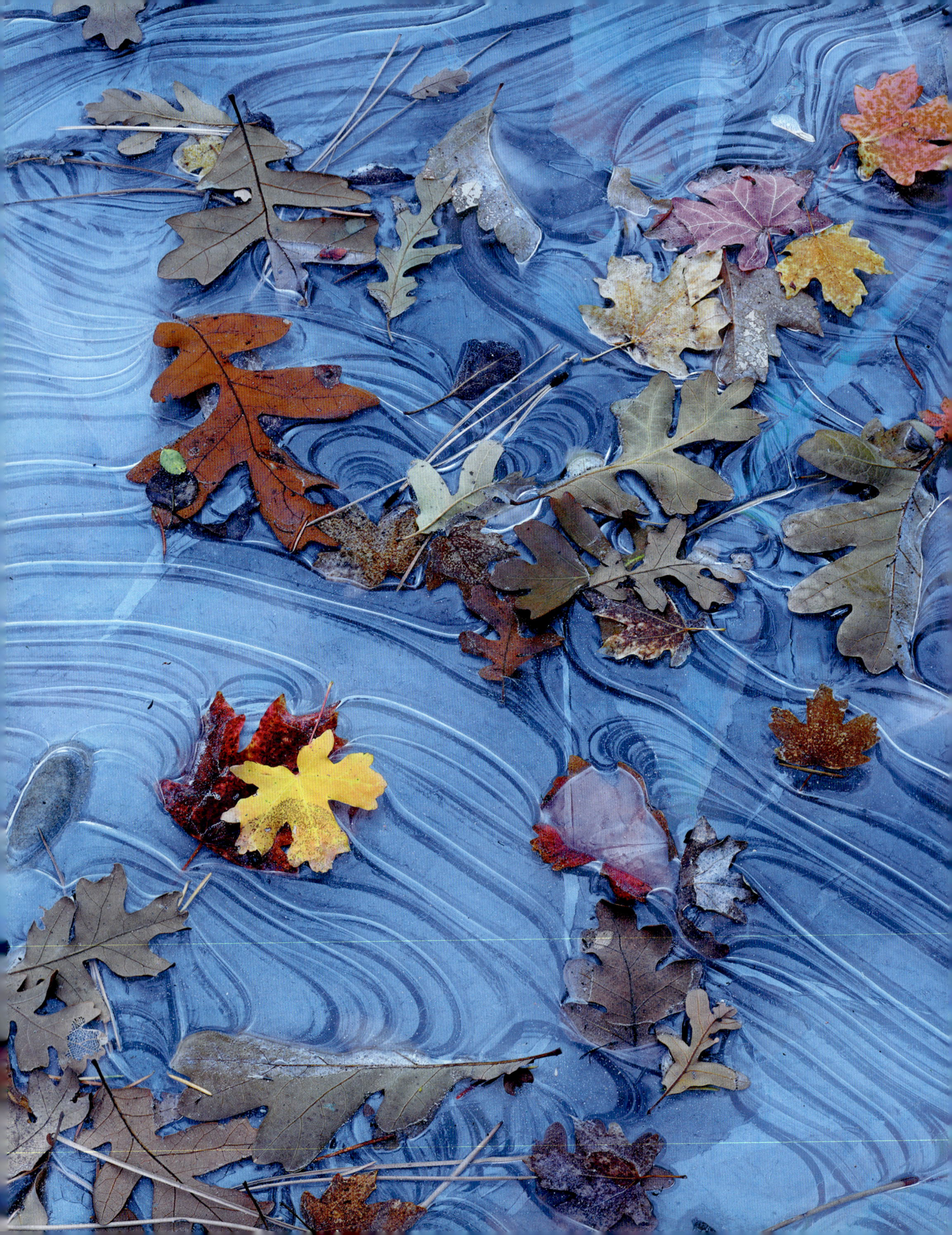

# Visualization

2

*The subject and the picture were not the same thing, although they would afterwards seem so. It was the photographer's problem to see not simply the reality before him but the still invisible picture, and to make his choices in terms of the latter.*

—JOHN SZARKOWSKI

Visualization was an important and revolutionary concept to photographer Ansel Adams, who opens his seminal trilogy of books—*The Camera*, *The Negative*, and *The Print*—with a chapter on visualization. In this chapter, Adams offers this definition:

*The term visualization refers to the entire emotional-mental process of creating a photograph, and as such it is one of the most important concepts in photography. It includes the ability to anticipate a finished image before making the exposure, so that the procedures employed will contribute to achieving the desired result.*

—ANSEL ADAMS

Expanding on Adams's definition, visualization can be thought of as the ability to imagine—to see in the so-called "mind's eye"—a finished image before, and during, its making. To visualize is to imagine ways in which *objective* appearances can be composed and then transformed by the application of photographic tools to accomplish a desired, *subjective* outcome.

**FIGURE 2.1:** When I first saw this section of a dead tree trunk, it immediately reminded me of the swirly sky patterns in Vincent van Gogh's famous painting, *Starry Night* (inset). I visualized the image rendered in blue and gold, similar to those in van Gogh's painting. I could not accomplish these colors in midday light, so I waited for afternoon when the tree was in shade, and returned to make the image in the blue-tinted light found in open shade, and without the harsh shadows that would otherwise be present under direct sunlight. My clear visualization of what I wanted dictated not only the lighting conditions (and time of day) required to realize my desired outcome, but also my later choices of RAW conversion settings (particularly white balance), and subsequent processing. This illustrates Ansel Adams's reference to visualization as "the entire emotional-mental process of creating a photograph."

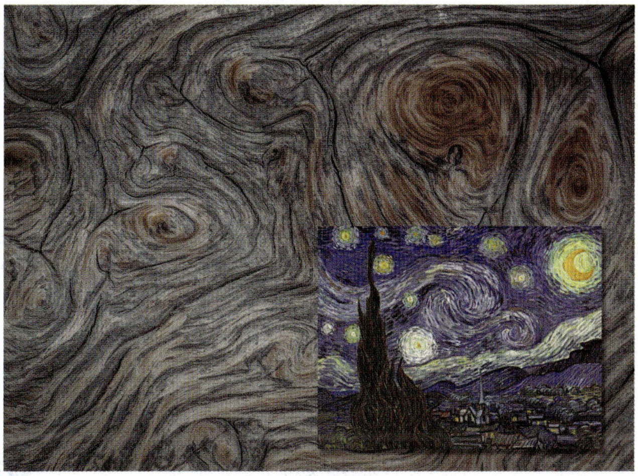

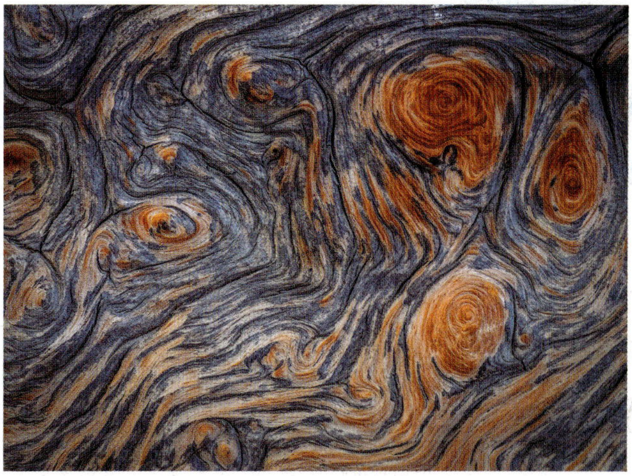

It is the nature of the photographic process that some tasks are done in the field, where we experience whatever inspiration prompts us to capture an image, and other tasks are done in the studio (or darkroom, or anywhere we process our captured images), separated from the initial experience.

When spending time processing an image, it is easy to become bogged down in technical minutiae or other distractions as we work. Having a visualized image in mind gives us a reference point—both visual and emotional—for what we felt and what we wish for our viewers to feel, as well as a means of ensuring that we stay true to our expressive goal—the appearances, thoughts, and emotions we wish our image to communicate. Our goal in applying processing tools and techniques can therefore be described as the process of shaping the image captured by the camera into the visualized image in our mind.

Photography is sometimes described as "the art of seeing," although such characterization, while useful in some genres of representational photography, is somewhat misleading when it comes to photographs meant to serve an expressive, rather than illustrative, purpose. As I explain in the previous chapter, art is a deliberate—conscious—creation originating in the artist's mind and brought into being by the artist's skill. As such, expressive photography—aimed at portraying not just objective appearances but also (sometimes, only) subjective thoughts and feelings—can better be described as *the art of visualization*. The better you become at visualizing what you can *make* from the visual elements available to you, rather than simply to *capture* them, the greater your expressive vocabulary will be.

Although *seeing* is sometimes used metaphorically to refer to visualization, visualization transcends mere seeing (if they were the same thing, we would not need separate terms for them). Seeing is a passive act, requiring no conscious effort—we open our eyes and we see. Visualization, on the other hand, is a conscious and deliberate act requiring investment of cognitive effort and relying on acquired skill.

The goal of seeing is to make us aware, as quickly and as effectively as possible, of the things in our surroundings that the unconscious brain evolved to consider most important—things that may indicate threat or reward. The goal of visualization, on the other hand, is not just to become aware of things as they are, but to do something with them—to create something out of them; to deliberately compose and arrange them in specific ways; to emphasize some aspects over others; to utilize emotional associations inherent in such visual elements as colors, lines, shapes, textures, and juxtapositions; to transcend what a random person—indeed, any person other than you—would see by default.

Considering visualization as *seeing in the mind's eye*, as opposed to seeing using the actual, physical eye (more accurately, the physical visual system,

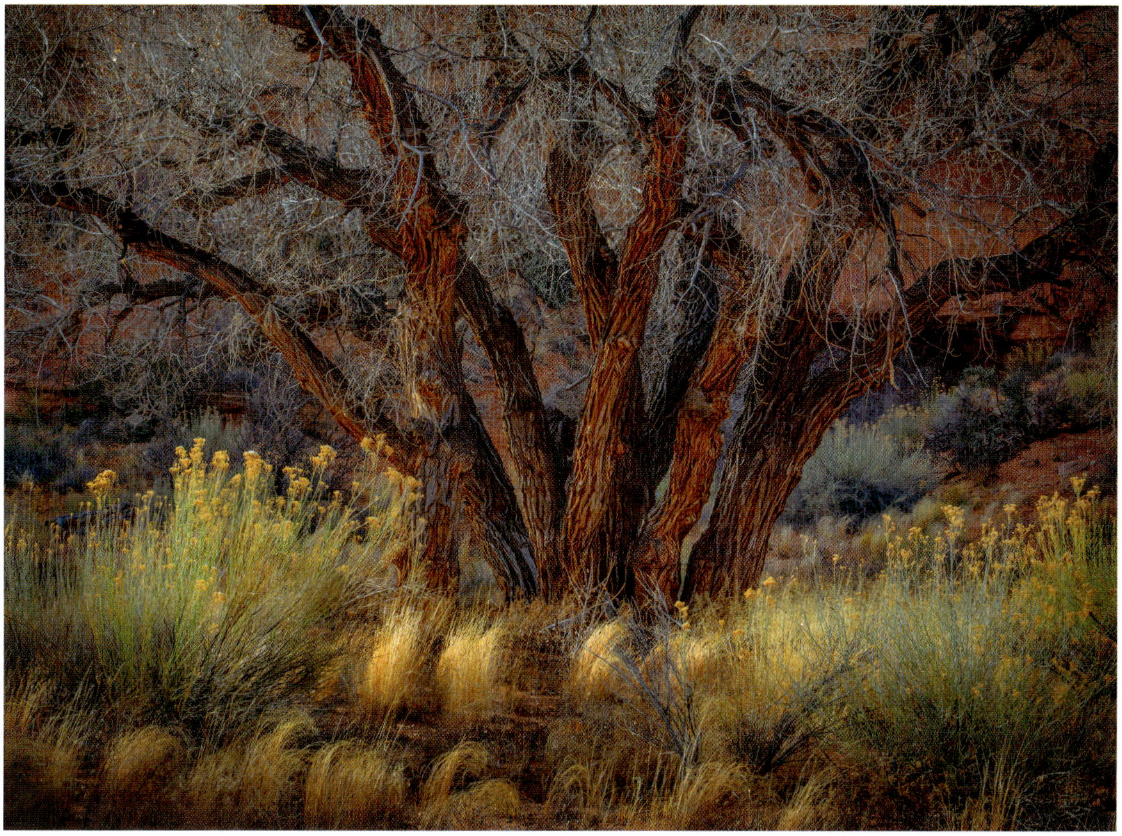

which is mostly in the brain) is important to grasp—it means that the visualized image is, by definition, not the same as what we might passively perceive in the normal course of seeing. Rather, visualization is bringing into being a novel creation, utilizing physical elements but also transforming them and overlaying them with subjective meaning. As Ansel Adams described, "When I'm ready to make a photograph, I think I quite obviously see in my mind's eye **something that is not literally there** in the true meaning of the word. I'm interested in something which is built up from within, rather than just extracted from without" (emphasis added).

Remarkably, the same processes in one's brain that form the perception of seeing based on signals originating from stimulation by reflected light can also form images without such stimulation (this is what

FIGURE 2.2: Over the years, I camped by this cottonwood tree dozens of times. I have seen it in all seasons and all hours of the day, on many occasions. I first visualized this image several months before conditions aligned to allow me to capture it in the right season and light conducive to realizing my visualization. In other seasons, the tree would be covered in foliage, obscuring its intricate arrangement of trunks and branches; and the position of the sun would not produce the highlights in the grasses and the subtle glow on the red sandstone. These are the elements I wanted to emphasize in both my composition and processing, as they communicate a sense of welcoming warmth and a balance between the stalwart old tree and the delicate desert brush surrounding it. Such remote and natural campsites are, in a literal sense, my home on many days. My goal is to express to you—the viewer, who may not share my love for, and familiarity with, this place—what the place means to me: the comforting sense of familiarity and shelter.

happens when we hallucinate, or visualize). Visualization can therefore also be thought of as the ability to conceive an image in the mind without information coming from the eyes; or to enhance the information coming in from the eyes, and to transcend our default perception of seeing.

**Redundant Prefixes**

There is a strange tendency among photographers to attach redundant prefixes to some terms. Accordingly, many use such terms as *previsualization*, *postprocessing*, and *postproduction*. If visualization means, in the words of Ansel Adams, "the ability to anticipate a finished image," and since anticipation already implies prescience, then "previsualization" literally means anything that comes before that anticipation, and may as well refer to brushing your teeth in the morning. Similarly, if processing means editing your captured image to accomplish your visualized outcome, then "postprocessing" literally means anything that comes after that—perhaps a celebratory glass of wine?

It is believed that photographer Minor White, after learning about visualization and the principles of the Zone System from Ansel Adams, divided visualization into two phases: previsualization, which is visualizing the final print before making an exposure; and postvisualization, which involves recalling the visualized intent while making the print in the darkroom. The term postvisualization has since fallen out of favor, and previsualization made it into the photographic vernacular as a synonymous, albeit redundant, term to visualization.

## Visualization and Composition

A visual composition is an arrangement of visual elements within a frame. Although beyond the scope of this book, composition is still worth mentioning as it is the first consideration when visualizing an image. Photoshop offers powerful tools that can be used to create and enhance a wide range of visual effects. However, if the composition is lacking there may ultimately be little we can do in processing to make an image successful.

All images begin with a concept in the photographer's mind—an idea of what the image is about—something that prompted the photographer to stop and consider making a photograph, or a desired effect that the photographer wishes to evoke in the viewer. The concept may be as simple as an interesting subject or the beauty of a witnessed scene or phenomenon; or it can be something more nuanced and subjective, such as a specific emotion or feeling, which may or may not be directly inspired by the scene photographed.

Composition is the photographer's primary means of distilling and arranging visual elements so the image expresses the desired concept. In composing an image, the photographer can isolate, juxtapose, place emphasis, distort, eliminate distractions, change the viewer's perception of the size of some elements relative to others, etc., all of which are powerful means for visual expression, and which cannot be applied in processing.

If we compare the process of making an image to that of baking a cake, composition can be thought of as the selection of the right ingredients in the right proportions. Processing can then be considered as the equivalent of baking the ingredients into an actual cake and then frosting and decorating it to make it as appealing to the eye as to the palate. However, if some ingredients are missing, used in the wrong proportions, or are of inferior quality, the cake is not likely to be very appetizing regardless of the skills of the baker or the quality of their cookware.

Our goal in processing is not to create an image from scratch, but rather to use the captured composition as a starting point toward a visualized outcome. To that starting point we then apply the tools at our disposal, with the goal of transforming the captured data into the desired visualized image. But if we start with a weak or ambiguous composition, it is doubtful that any amount of processing will make an image successful in expressing its original concept. So, be very deliberate in composing and capturing the best possible data that you can while in the field. While Photoshop may help overcome some of the limitations of camera and subject, these limitations (and the tools you will use to address them) should be considered (visualized) in advance. Don't assume that an image composed and captured without such consideration can later be "fixed" in Photoshop.

### Knowing When to Move On

Landscape photographers, dependent to a large degree on natural arrangements of visual elements to compose with, should acknowledge that not all visualized images can ultimately be composed as we would like. Sometimes, it is good to know when to give up and to seek other opportunities. Ansel Adams describes such an experience in his book *Examples: The Making of 40 Photographs*:

> *I had been photographing in the Chama Valley, north of Santa Fe. I made a few passable negatives that day and had several exasperating trials with subjects that would not bend to visualization. The most discouraging effort was a rather handsome cottonwood stump near the Chama River. I saw my desired image quite clearly, but due to unmanageable intrusions and mergers of forms in the subject my efforts finally foundered, and I decided it was time to return to Santa Fe.*
>
> —ANSEL ADAMS

Later that day, after giving up on the cottonwood tree that "would not bend to visualization," Adams made his most famous image, *Moonrise, Hernandez, New Mexico.*

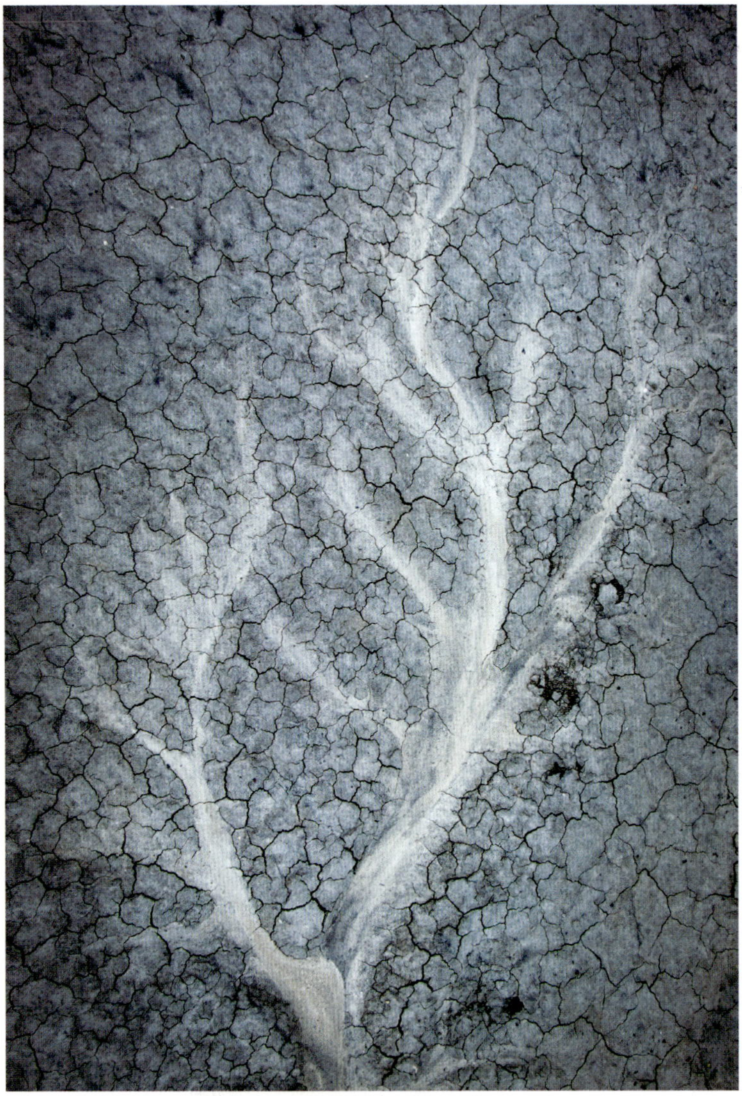

FIGURE 2.3: Even simple subjects lacking in bold colors or impressive scenery, when carefully composed can elicit profound emotional responses and communicate such feelings as grace, calmness, and tenderness that may not be possible when the photographer focuses all their attention on maximizing visual impact. The more you nurture the ability to visualize a variety of image styles that have known emotional effects rather than always reaching for the "eye candy," the greater your range of visual expression will be.

## Self-Expression and Equivalence

Self-expression in art refers to the expression of an artist's subjective thoughts, feelings, and personality in their work.

It might seem that the medium of photography, designed to fix literal appearances—impressions of actual light reflecting off real objects—is more suitable for representational imagery, rather than for making expressive works (which transcend objective appearances). Indeed, when compared with painting, writing, or other media, which allow an artist to conjure whatever subjects and compositions best fit his or her expressive goals, it is undoubtedly more difficult to express a subjective narrative using the medium of photography. However, it is certainly possible. In fact, it is exactly because photographs are, to a substantial degree, derived from reality that they also invoke certain perceptions in viewers that are not afforded to other media and that allow a creative photographer to evoke powerful emotions.

The manual skill and the mechanics of making photographic images are decidedly easier than those required in other media, especially in our digital age when cameras and computers can automate much of the image-making process, and can effortlessly produce interesting visual effects with just a few clicks. Technological advancements, combined with simple and easy-to-learn formulas, allow photographers to produce striking images of such things as the night sky, to expand dynamic range beyond what was possible even just a few years ago, and to perform a variety of other visually compelling effects. Indeed, it is quite possible for budding photographers to produce images of very high technical quality and popular appeal after just a short learning period, where other media may require much more prolonged study and practice to master.

> *For artists diving into a new technology, it is a triple short-cut to mastery: you get a free ride on the novelty of the medium; there are no previous masters to surpass; and after a few weeks, you are the master. Try that with the violin.*
>
> —STEWART BRAND

But, while photographic technology may in many ways be easy to learn and master, visual self-expression is not. Beyond just mastery of tools and techniques, *expressive* photography requires investment of emotion and cognitive effort, a degree of maturity and depth, and an understanding of visual perception—specifically, how visual cues can be employed to elicit known responses from viewers.

When considered in terms of a language, visual expression can be considered to have a vocabulary and grammar. Such skills indeed can never be mastered to a point where you know everything about visual expression, just like you can never know everything about written expression. Creative writers are not likely to ever run out of ideas and stories, and novel ways to express them in written or verbal language, and they are not dependent on always using the same settings, characters, or plotlines in all their stories. And the same is true for creative photographers.

As photographic artists—and unlike painters who start with a blank canvas—we must know not only what we wish to express, but also how to do so within the hard constraints imposed by qualities of light and subjects that are often beyond our ability to control or predict, and using the processes and tools unique to photography. Just as important, we must be cognizant of the perceptions, expectations, and yes, also prejudices that our audience inherently associates with the medium of photography. However, do not allow such hurdles to deter you because, despite such difficulties, expressive photographic images are not only possible but can be every bit as powerful and moving as images created using any other medium. Also, as suggested by various studies, having to accomplish a goal within limitations is an essential condition for creative thinking.

**Dogma vs. Expression**

Discussions of transcending reality in photography often arouse strong feelings among those who place greater value on the purity of the photographic process than on the goals a given photographer might have in employing it. Many believe that photographs should maintain dogmatic allegiance to the distinguishing characteristics of the medium: its ability to record accurate and detailed impressions of objective appearances. In the minds of some, any deviation from these inherent qualities, even when strict adherence to such qualities serves no practical or creative purpose whatsoever, should not be tolerated. I find such attitudes to be shortsighted and irrational. As an expressive artist, I am far more concerned with what I wish to express than with the mechanics of my medium; and my allegiance to my tools only goes as far as the degree to which they serve my expressive purposes.

How, then, do we transcend objective appearances to weave personal and subjective expressions into a photograph? One of the first to contemplate this question was photographer and art connoisseur, Alfred Stieglitz. Among his most revolutionary works was a portfolio of cloud images that he titled *Equivalents*. Here is his explanation of the title:

> *My cloud photographs are the equivalents of my most profound life experiences, my basic philosophy of life. In looking at my photographs of clouds, people seem freer to think about the relationships in the pictures than about the subject matter for its own sake.*
>
> —ALFRED STIEGLITZ

Photographer Minor White, who considered Stieglitz a mentor and was greatly influenced by Stieglitz's thoughts on Equivalence, wrote about the topic extensively in Aperture Magazine, which he helped found. Here is how White describes it in one of his essays:

> *When the photographer shows us what he considers to be an Equivalent, he is showing us an expression of a feeling, but this*

*feeling is not the feeling he had for the object that he photographed. What really happened is that he recognized an object or series of forms that, when photographed, would yield an image with specific suggestive powers that can direct the viewer into a specific and known feeling, state, or place within himself.*

—MINOR WHITE

Stieglitz and White are making two important points that are crucial to expressive photography: first, that photographs may be used to evoke meanings and feelings, rather than just capture appearances; and second, that photographs can be deliberately designed so they can arouse "specific and known feelings" in the viewer, which may be entirely unrelated to the things photographed.

Equivalence, then, is the effect we seek in expressive photography: the ability to compose visual elements in such a way that their combined effect communicates more than just what something looked like, but also inspire emotions of the photographer's deliberate choosing.

FIGURE 2.4: In my workshops, I often present this image and ask participants to call out words that come to their minds. I often hear the words *peace, calm, drama,* and *beauty*. These are emotional equivalents to the visual experience. To date I have never heard anyone say *trees, hills, sky, clouds,* or *cows*. The image serves not as an illustration of literal things, but as a metaphor for emotions. The identity of the things that come together to accomplish the total impression—known as the *gestalt*—of the image are of little or no importance to its expressive effect.

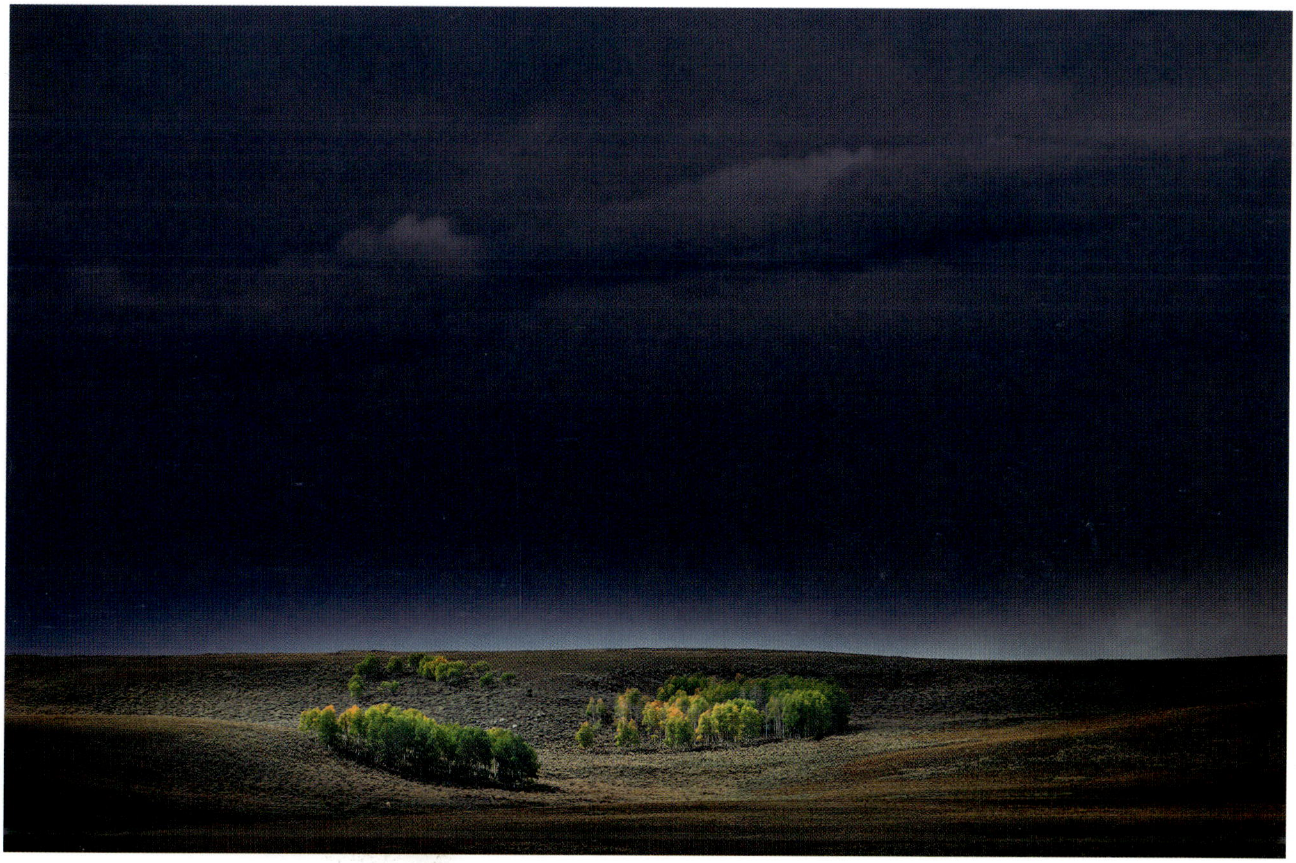

## Awareness and Knowledge

To be aware is to know that something exists. In the context of image processing, being aware of what is possible using the tools provided in Photoshop allows us to visualize their effect while on location.

As you gain experience using the tools available in Photoshop, you also will become a more effective visualizer. For example, once you become proficient in converting color images to black-and-white, you will also become better at visualizing possible black-and-white images that you may not have been aware of before. And, when you become proficient in the use of selective dodging (lightening) and burning (darkening) techniques, or adjusting color and contrast to accomplish a specific mood, you will also be able to visualize what moods can be accomplished using elements in a scene that may not be obvious to someone who does not know these options are available to them.

When not deliberately visualizing images, we are prone to accepting our default visual perceptions, rather than to consider alternatives. Indeed, if we were to consciously question everything we see, we'd never get anything done. However, when it comes to creating expressive work, to instinctively follow familiar patterns may be a great limitation, because it means that we are only aware of what (or some of what) there is, rather than what could be.

For most photographers, the creative process is entirely reactive: something presents itself that is interesting or aesthetically pleasing (per our default way of seeing); it is recorded with a camera; perhaps it is enhanced a little using simple adjustment of contrast and color saturation, or effects created by automated tools; and the image is then considered "finished." This type of formulaic approach is known as *convergent thinking*, and is useful when performing repetitive and familiar tasks that do not require creativity. Creative work, where novel ideas may produce useful and previously unknown results, requires a different approach known as *divergent thinking*, which involves considering multiple possibilities—and venturing beyond the most obvious one(s)—before selecting the most effective approach, which was not known in advance.

To be most effective and to lead to divergent thinking, visualization should occur only *after* something grabs the photographer's attention. Visualizing possible ways of composing the available elements and the possibilities available in processing, and then selecting the most effective outcome (or outcomes) is the first step in turning the photographer's intuitive emotional response into a tangible image. Conversely, to visualize an outcome in advance, before spontaneously encountering a moving experience, is known as *preconception* and has the disadvantage of suppressing creativity. When

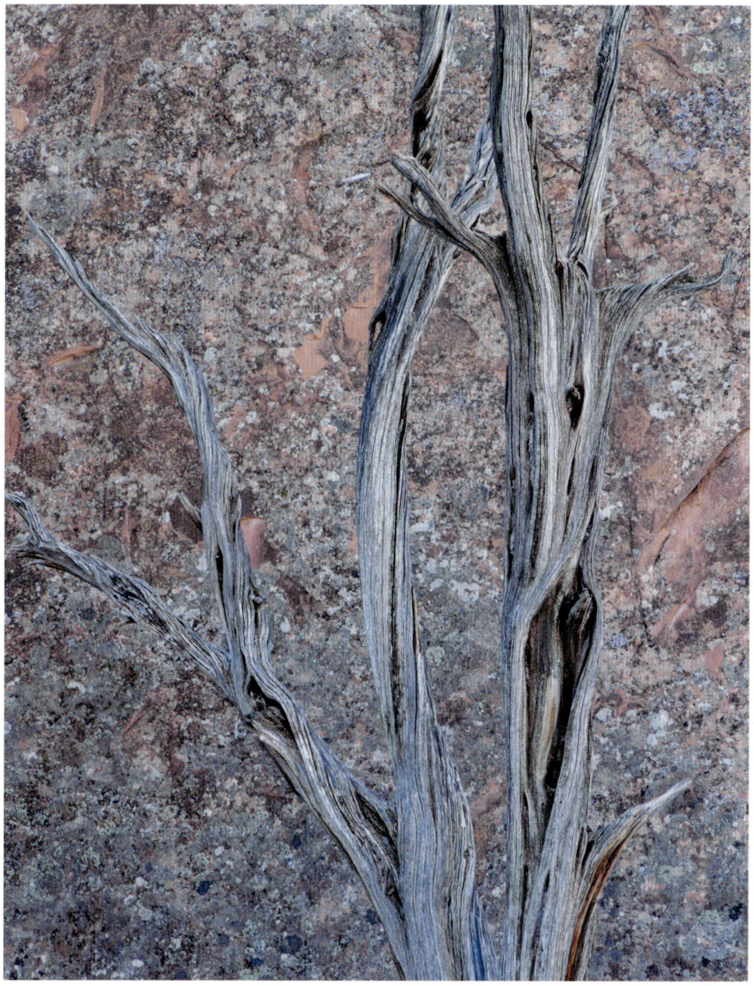

FIGURE 2.5: This tree is located very close to a popular attraction in one of Utah's National Parks. It is likely that thousands of people walk by it every year, unaware of its photographic potential. I have never seen another image of it.

the mind is primed to only seek one specific outcome, it will focus its attention on this outcome and likely miss many other possibilities.

It takes deliberate and conscious training of the mind to shift out of your default way of seeing, and out of sticking only to well-trodden formulas, and to consider a variety of creative possibilities. Even when you possess knowledge of what is possible when processing your images in Photoshop, oftentimes this knowledge is not applied intuitively, and requires deliberate, conscious effort to be useful at the point of decision. Such considerations only become intuitive through practice and repetition.

Knowledge of what can be accomplished by various processing techniques is, of course, very useful in considering your options, but other things that may be helpful are perhaps not as obvious. For example, familiarity with the styles of other artists may inspire you to consider things you like about their work. Knowledge of such things as the science of visual perception or Gestalt psychology may be very useful in knowing how to compose effectively, and which elements to emphasize so your image inspires specific perceptions. Even a general interest in other, seemingly unrelated topics may yield new and unexpected creative associations.

Awareness requires attention, which is a scarce and valuable resource. Your brain is very good at assigning attention to things it considers most important. Alas, the human brain did not evolve to consider the creation of expressive photography as very important; we must consciously train it to do so. Since, by default, the unconscious brain may not consider creative expression very important, we are prone to being distracted when attempting to create visual art. However, we have the ability to override our default circuitry—to consciously focus our attention on the task of making expressive work and to make ourselves aware of as many possibilities as we can think of. When practiced frequently and repetitively, this conscious shifting of attention toward visualizing images will become intuitive.

Perhaps the simplest and most effective advice to becoming more aware is this: slow down—don't rush, don't multitask, consciously ignore distractions, and focus your mind. In doing so, you are freeing up attention resources, allowing them to be reallocated to creative work. Set aside errant thoughts or even social interaction for a bit and focus your attention on evaluating possibilities. Although not specifically a processing technique, the workflow I describe in this book includes a step for such consideration, which I refer to as *Dynamic Visualization* (see chapter 7).

## Evolving Intuition

Photography instructors often attempt to summarize some topics into lists of so-called "rules," tips, acronyms, or clever sayings to make them easier to memorize. Think about such things as the Sunny 16 Rule, the Rule of Thirds, and ETTR (Expose To The Right). It might seem that an experienced and effective photographer is one who consciously and deliberately considers every rule and every bit of knowledge in the process of making an image, but such a conclusion is incorrect. In fact, the more experienced the artist, the more he or she will tend to work out of intuition and instinct—an innate sense for what the "right" approach is in each situation—rather than rely on some memorized term, stepwise process, or other means of recalling information.

To an outsider, such intuition regarding the making of successful photographs may seem the privilege of uniquely gifted individuals (indeed, some ancient cultures even considered artists who possessed such abilities

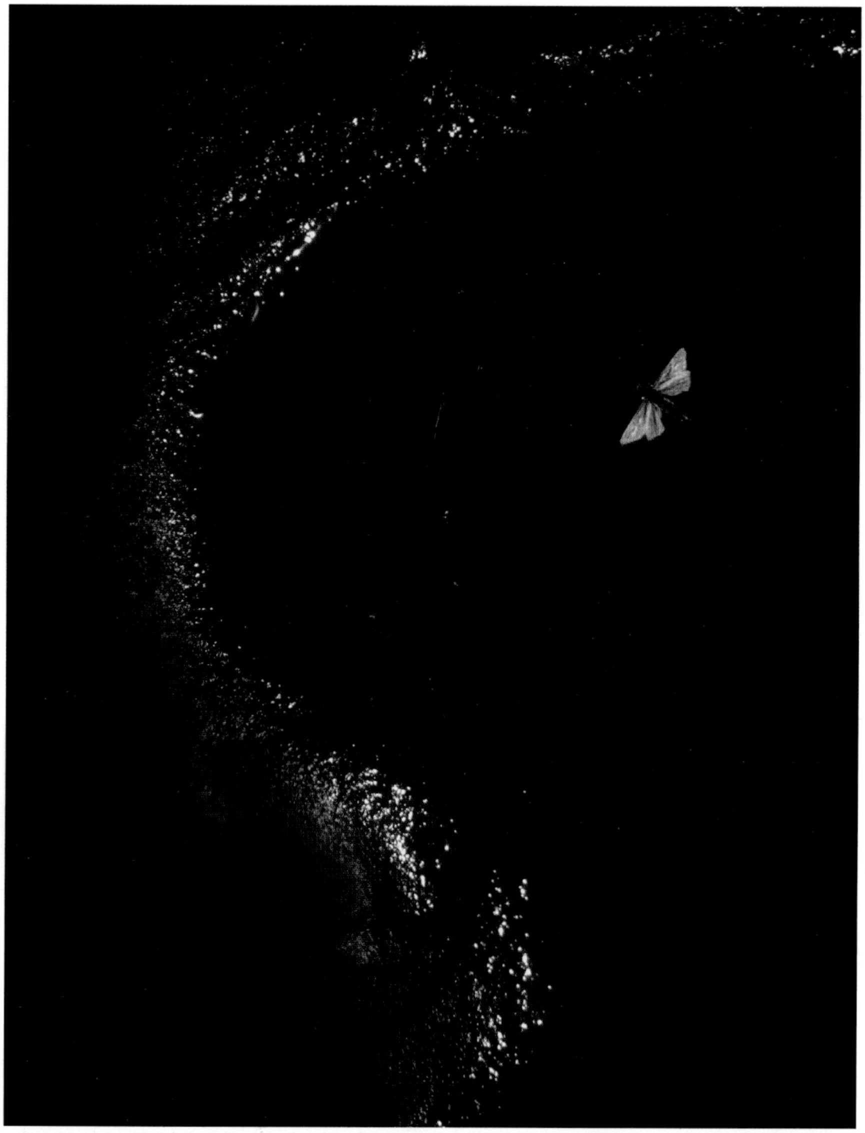

**Figure 2.6:** It is unlikely that I would visualize a high-contrast black-and-white rendition of this little scene, which reminded me of a figure flying into a cluster of stars, if I had no prior knowledge of black-and-white processing, or if I did not have an intense interest in cosmology, or if I was not inspired by the style of photographer Minor White. More important, I would never have made this image if I did not slow down and take the time to consider and contemplate how I might use this interesting little scene that I nearly walked by en route to another destination.

as being divinely inspired). But that is not the case. Consider such skills as driving a car or forming a proper sentence. Nobody is born knowing how to perform such things, but in time and with practice they may seem like second nature, requiring little-to-no deliberate thinking. Repetition is the key to transitioning conscious skilled work that requires cognitive effort and concentration into seemingly effortless intuition. The more you perform a function, exercise a skill, or apply a specific process, the less you will need to consciously think about it.

Psychologist and Nobel Prize Laureate Daniel Kahneman characterized the human brain as having two "Systems"—System 1, which operates intuitively and effortlessly; and System 2, which requires investment of effort and attention to tackle complex problems. When an activity is (or becomes) intuitive, System 1 handles it automatically, whereas anything requiring deliberate thinking and a methodical approach calls upon System 2 to invest the required effort and attention. When tasked with answering simple questions, such as "What is 2+2?" or "What is your name?", System 1 provides an instant, and seemingly effortless, answer. System 1 also handles many common tasks we perform without being conscious of them, such as determining someone's mood based on their facial expression, instantly noticing a little red flower in a green meadow, or diverting attention to the source of an unexpected sound. System 2, on the other hand, performs those tasks that require attention, such as playing a game, performing difficult calculations, choosing the right lens to use for a given composition, or deciding whether an image is best processed in color or black-and-white.

Since attention is a limited resource there is great value in investing time and practice in making common and repetitive tasks intuitive (i.e., repeating them often enough that they end up being handled by System 1), leaving more attention to be utilized by System 2 in considering more creative tasks, such as visualization.

Put in terms of photography, we want to reach a point where we don't have to consciously think about common camera settings and operations, and can instead focus attention on such things as composition and deciding how we wish to capture a given scene. We want be able to subconsciously manage the camera's settings, such as shutter speed, aperture, and ISO. Similarly, in processing images, we want to get to a point of thinking in terms of contrast or color and a desired appearance, rather than which tool is most appropriate for which task. In time and with practice, such mechanical choices as what tool to use and how to perform a selection will become intuitive.

Visualization is not a simple skill. Neither are some of the Photoshop techniques I describe in this book. To hone such skills to a point where they become rich and intuitive (in the sense that you will automatically consider a wide variety of possibilities when encountering a scene and have an innate sense of the most effective way to compose and process an image so it expresses what you have in mind), you should practice them repeatedly and over time. Do not expect to become an instant master. Not only is that impossible, but as I explain below, it is also not desirable. Let your intuition evolve organically and alongside your own sensibilities and personality. It's the only way to arrive at a workflow that is custom-tailored to the things you wish to express and that set your creative mind apart from anyone else's.

**The Importance of Practice**

A friend of mine likes to illustrate the importance of repeated exercise with this joke: A street musician is sitting on the sidewalk of a busy Manhattan street when a shiny limousine pulls to the curb. The tinted window rolls smoothly down and a well-dressed gentleman calls out to the musician, "Do you know how to get to Carnegie Hall?" The musician nods knowingly and responds, "Practice man, practice."

## Creativity

Creativity is one of the great mysteries of the human mind, and despite being the topic of a lot of recent research (by psychologists, neuroscientists, artists, and many others) we still do not understand it completely. A commonly accepted definition of creativity, coined by Dr. Michael Mumford, is this: *the production of novel, useful products*. Novelty means that a creative product should be original—something that did not exist before. But novelty alone is not enough for something to be considered as creative. I can close my eyes and point my camera in some random direction and I'll have a novel image, but such an image will not be creative. As the definition suggests, to be considered creative, the product also must be useful: it needs to serve some purpose. And who gets to decide whether an image, or any work of art for that matters, is useful or not? Or even that it needs to be.

Many readers, I'm sure, have had the experience of visiting an exhibit of modern art, and perhaps of being perplexed by some of the works on display, wondering what, if any, purpose they might serve. The answer is that a work of art can be useful in various ways. Most important, a work of art is useful in different ways to the person *making* it and to the person *viewing* it.

It is no secret that photographs of great aesthetic and popular appeal may be created with no investment of creativity at all. Purchase a guidebook, join a photo tour, or just search the Internet, and within minutes you can find precise instructions for where to go, at what time, and with what equipment to photograph spectacular compositions. Similarly, many automated tools can shortcut much processing work and result in very attractive images with just a few clicks of the mouse. However, such images, no matter how aesthetically pleasing or impressive, cannot be considered creative or expressive.

Why pursue creative, expressive work, which may require great commitment and effort and may well be less productive than pursuing easy trophies? Likewise, why invest the time and effort to process images using an application like Photoshop, rather than reach for easier and more automated tools?

Psychologist Mihály Csíkszentmihályi, in his book *Creativity, Flow, and the Psychology of Discovery and Invention*, offers two good reasons. The first, an objective one:

> *First, most of the things that are interesting, important, and human are the results of creativity.*

Although undoubtedly a noble reason, I suspect that most who pursue landscape photography as an enjoyable hobby or vocation would not voluntarily make their work more difficult and less productive out of a sense of civic duty. But, Csíkszentmihályi offers a second, subjective, reason as well:

> *The second reason creativity is so fascinating is that when we are involved in it, we feel that we are living more fully than during the rest of life. The excitement of the artist...comes close to the ideal fulfillment we all hope to get from life, and so rarely do.*

I think, and I hope you'll agree, that accomplishing "the ideal fulfillment we all hope to get from life" is worth investing some effort in.

The reason creative work is so fulfilling is that it is conducive to a state known as *flow*. And, as it happens, Csíkszentmihályi also wrote the seminal book about it, and defines it as "the state in which people are so involved in an activity that nothing else seems to matter; the experience itself is so enjoyable that people will do it even at great cost, for the sheer sake of doing it." And as it turns out, effort and attention are required to accomplish the state of flow. Csíkszentmihályi explains:

> *Contrary to what we usually believe...the best moments in our lives are not the passive, receptive, relaxing times—although such experiences can also be enjoyable,* ***if we have worked hard*** *to attain them. The best moments usually occur when a person's body or mind is* ***stretched to its limits in a voluntary effort to accomplish something difficult and worthwhile.*** *(Emphasis added.)*

Can you say that your photography, in any of its aspects, makes you feel that your mind is stretched to its limits?

As one who has practiced landscape photography for three decades, I can attest from personal experience that the inner reward—the pride and satisfaction—I experience when making a successful creative, expressive, image eclipses any reward or affirmation originating from an image that is not, no matter how attractive or popular.

But to consider only the end result misses a more important point, which is this: over time, the most rewarding and transformational experiences of making art come from the making—from the process—and not from the art. The times when I experience flow are not when the work is done, but rather during the process of making my work: whether considering compositions in some remote and wild place; or sitting in front of the computer and taking my time to mold the image, a small step at a time, sometimes for hours at a stretch; or contemplating the visualized outcome in my mind, working with my hands, and seeing the image slowly coming into being before my eyes. It is an experience that, once felt and appreciated, is one you will not want to deny yourself by relegating it to automated tools.

## Learning to Visualize

Visualization is a skill built on experience. The more you do it, the better you get. Expect for it to be challenging at first and trust that with dedication and practice, it will yield great rewards.

To form and to exercise those brain circuits that are conducive to visualization, start by acknowledging that it is something you must do consciously and proactively. If you count on expressive images to just be obvious to you in the normal course of seeing, you will (literally) never know how much you are missing.

Avoid preconceptions. Begin visualizing at the point of inspiration—when you get a sense that there is something in your surrounding (or in your mind) that is worth expressing in a photograph.

### Find Word Equivalents, Metaphors, and Connotations

Once you feel inspired to make a photograph, begin by articulating your source of inspiration in words before setting out to decide your composition and processing approach.

Think of your photograph as a metaphor for the things you wish to express—something that will evoke a desired response from your viewer. Visual metaphors and connotations work in much the same way as verbal ones. For example, if I wish for my image to have a romantic feeling, I might opt for soft light rather than harsh light; I might look for colors and color combinations known to be associated with romance—warm, earthy tones; and I might look for graceful, flowing lines rather than straight lines or sharp edges. By consciously coming up with words associated with the feelings I have in mind—words like softness, warmth, grace, and tenderness—I am increasing my chances of identifying visual equivalents for them.

As you begin to exercise visualization, I suggest you carry a notepad and write down the words that come to mind when something inspires you to make a photograph. Then, when sitting down to process the photograph, re-read your words as a way of transporting yourself back into the experience, arousing the same mood and inspiration that prompted you to make the photograph so you can continue where you left off.

Likely the most common form of visualization in landscape photography is aimed at faithfully representing the sense of joy and awe experienced in the presence of impressive geography or some other natural phenomena—and with the goal of making the captured image appear close to what you saw through the camera's viewfinder. Although certainly conducive to the creation of pleasing, even impressive, images, often such intent results from lack of ability to imagine possibilities beyond our default way of seeing.

Before making the image, part of the reason for articulating what you wish to express in words is that it also prompts your mind to think beyond the literal. Consider that your inspiration may not always come from the subject. Your state of mind at a given moment may give rise to something you wish to express, and your choice of subjects may be directed by a particular mood, rather than the other way around. By training yourself to identify photographic possibilities both literal and metaphorical, you are also expanding your visual vocabulary and your range of expressions. You are training yourself to become more creative, to be proactive rather than reactive, and to place yourself in a state that is more conducive to flow—one of the most rewarding experiences you are capable of feeling.

It is quite easy to make a beautiful image of a beautiful subject without much thought, but it is a greater and more satisfying experience (and accomplishment) to engage yourself fully in the creative process, to contemplate, and to express something subjective and personal of your own making.

Once you identify word associations, equivalents, and metaphors, consider whether some of them are conducive to visual expression using things like qualities of light, specific colors, lines, and shapes. With these, you will have a foundation for what to emphasize in your image, both in your composition and in how you later process your image.

## Conduct a Self-Interview

Another useful visualization technique is to pose questions to yourself to ensure that you considered all possibilities and that you are consistent in your approach. This is useful both when composing an image in the field, and when processing an image (in the workflow I describe later, this is best done in the Analysis phase when we pause to evaluate the difference between the image as it is at a point in time and the visualized result).

When visualizing in the field, you may want to ask yourself whether your chosen perspective is the best one or whether you should move to a different spot; whether there are elements in the frame that may distract from, rather than contribute to, the composition and the emotion you wish to express; whether you should include the sky or whether a more intimate composition may be more effective; whether it is worth returning to the scene at a different time of day or a different time of year; etc.

When processing an image, ask yourself such things as whether a different hue of blue will be more effective in the sky, whether the foliage is the most effective shade of green, whether contrast is too high or too low, and whether elements in the composition distract and should be made less prominent (or eliminated completely). I also recommend looking away from

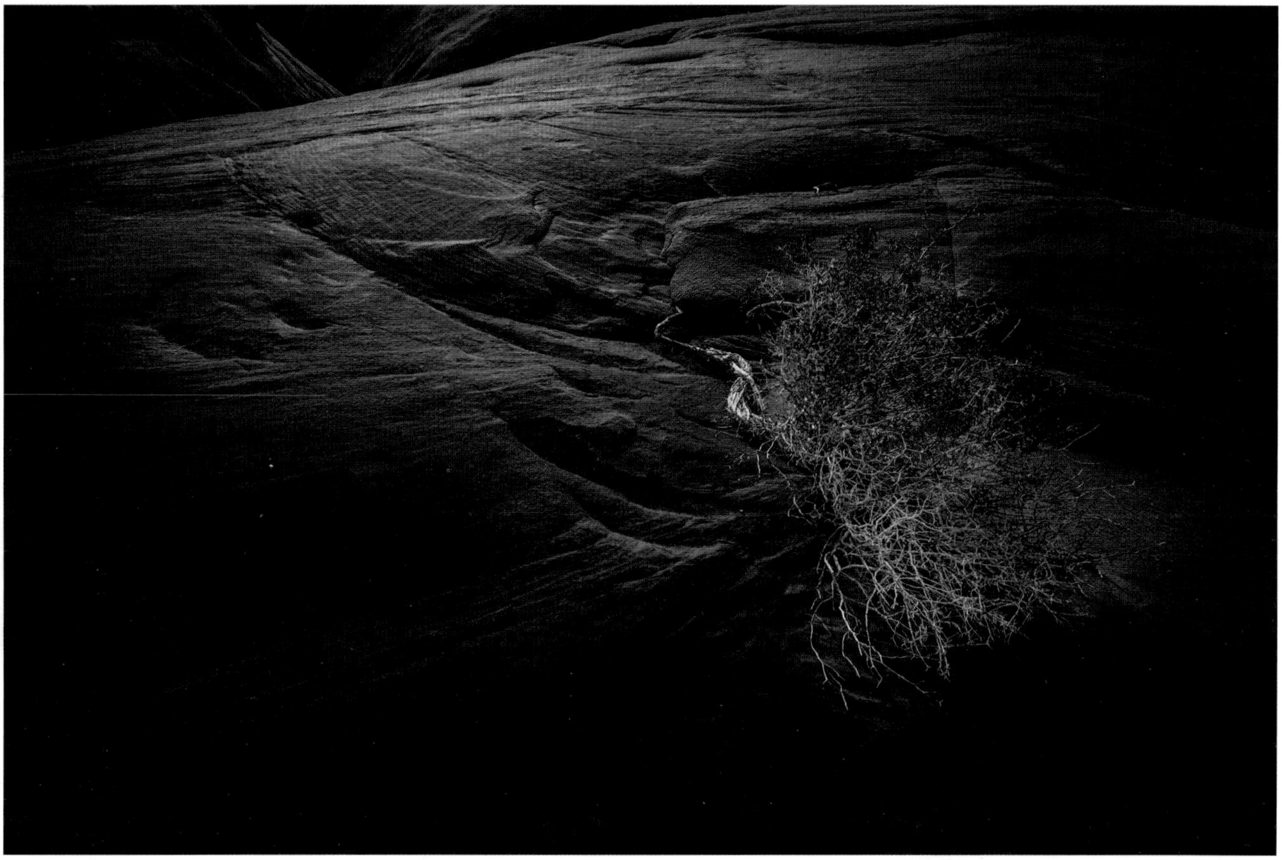

FIGURE 2.7: While this may be considered an image of a buckwheat plant growing out of a crack in the sandstone, I doubt anyone would consider it a particularly good representational image to be used in a plant guide or a location guidebook. The words I had in mind, and that I tried to articulate by use of composition and processing are these: *tenacity, solitude, perseverance,* and *survival.*

the image for a few moments and then returning to it: then ask yourself whether you are on the right track, whether some adjustments need to be revisited, and whether you are making progress toward your desired visualized outcome.

The self-interview is a great way to avoid becoming too focused on some aspects of the image while missing others. This may happen when attention is focused on solving a specific problem and little of it may be left to maintain a general awareness of how the entire image is coming together. You may be familiar with the surprise of returning from a shoot, studying your images, and realizing that an errant branch or tripod leg is peeking into the frame, or that your horizon is tilted, and wondering, "How could I have missed *that*?!"

Also, don't be afraid to ask yourself whether the image ultimately works or not. Nobody wants to give up on a potentially good image, but it may well be that some technical or compositional flaws are too great to overcome, that the light wasn't quite right for the mood you intended to express, or that your skills at a point in time are not sufficient to accomplish exactly what you wish. If you decide to give up on an image, my advice is to not discard it. Save the file for another time. Your skills will get better, your sensibilities will change, new and better tools may become available, and you may realize later that you can accomplish your original visualization after all, or perhaps you may even come up with a visualization you did not think of previously.

## EXERCISE 1

1. Write down five things (objects, qualities, properties, etc.) that you may find in a natural landscape that can inspire a sense of drama; then write down five more that can inspire a sense of intimacy.
2. What dominant color, or colors, would you choose to communicate a sense of joy? How about sadness?
3. What things might you choose to exclude from your composition if you wanted your image to communicate a sense of serenity and peace?
4. What considerations would lead you to choose to convert an image to black-and-white?
5. Choose a landscape image you made and try to imagine it in different permutations, such as:
   a. If it has a sky, what would it look like without the sky? If it doesn't, what would it look like with different kinds of skies added?
   b. What would it look like without one or two of its prominent elements?
   c. What would it look like if you could add new elements? What would they be?
   d. What would it look like if you could move some elements around or change their sizes or colors?
6. Recall what inspired you to make the image; close your eyes and imagine being there again. Can you think of compositions other than the one you chose at the time? Is there anything you would do differently, in the field or in processing, to make your image more effective?

*See Appendix for answer key.*

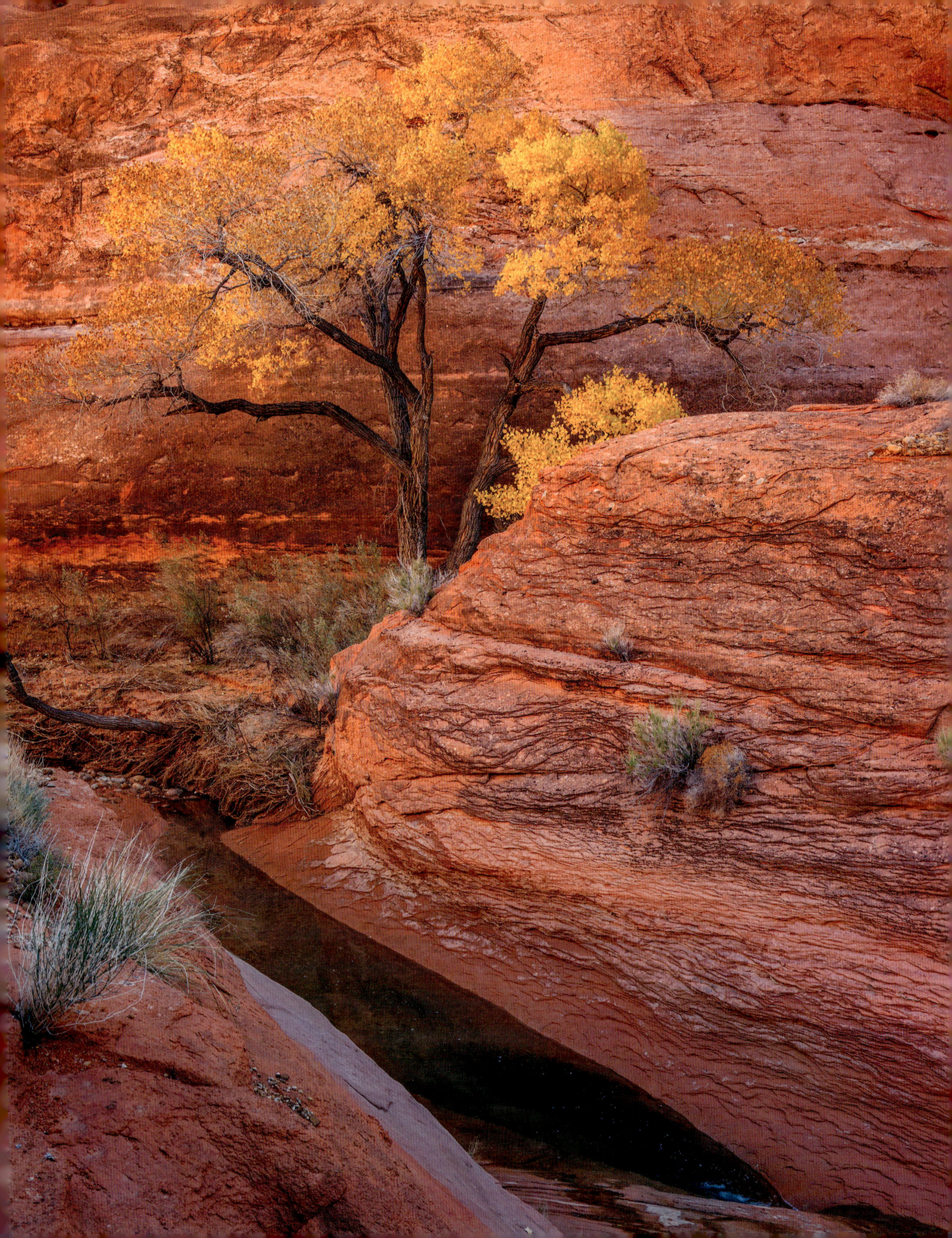

# 3

# The Digital Studio

*I think it's fair to say that personal computers have become the most empowering tool we've ever created. They're tools of communication, they're tools of creativity, and they can be shaped by their user.*

—BILL GATES

Not too long ago, processing and printing photographs required a considerable investment in equipment, dedicated space for a darkroom, and knowledge of photographic chemistry. For several decades, most photographers avoided making such an investment and instead confined their photographic process to exposing film and then outsourcing the tasks of development and printing to commercial providers. In doing so, photographers forfeited much control over the outcome.

While there is something to be said for the convenience of using third parties for tasks that offer little room for creative expression (such as processing color film), it should also be acknowledged that in today's digital world, a much greater array of creative options is available to those who choose to process and print their own work .

Today, we are fortunate to have all the power and control once requiring a traditional darkroom available to us in the form of software applications that may be used just about anywhere we have access to a personal computer. Using affordable desktop printers, we can make quite large prints of exquisite quality. And even when we outsource printing, we can still maintain a great degree of control over the results when we prepare our own files and proof them on a color-calibrated screen.

In this chapter, I review some of the hardware and software components needed in a digital studio capable of supporting a complete color-managed workflow, from capture to print.

## The Creative Workspace

Before delving into technical matters, it is worth considering that just owning the tools and having the skills to use them is no guarantee that these tools will be put to the best and most desirable—and, just as important, the most rewarding and creative—use. Processing images should be an enjoyable activity, and your enjoyment will be very much enhanced by having a workspace that is pleasant and comfortable to inhabit for prolonged sessions, making it more conducive to creative work.

Even such things as a comfortable chair; a way to control the direction, intensity, and type of light (natural and/or artificial); not sitting with your back to the door; and the ability to isolate yourself from distractions for a time (whether working in a dedicated room with a door, or having a privacy screen around your workspace) can have as much of an effect on the quality of your work as any device or software you may purchase.

If your space is uncomfortable, poorly lit, or prone to distractions, you likely will not enjoy spending much time in it, nor will you be able to dedicate your full attention to your work.

Some people may be more prone to distractions than others. Some are fortunate enough to be able to tune out their surroundings at will. If, like me, you are not one of these fortunate people, find ways of isolating yourself. If your space is overly noisy, consider investing in a comfortable set of noise-cancelling headphones; if you enjoy music, consider purchasing a sound system to fit your space; if you wish to have inspiring books or other reference materials within reach, consider installing bookshelves.

Last, don't neglect to tackle what may be the greatest distraction of all: the Internet. If you are in the habit of checking email or social sites frequently, train yourself to do so at longer intervals. In most cases, the world can wait for an hour or two while you immerse yourself in creative work. Think of it as giving yourself a small vacation each time you close those tempting yet

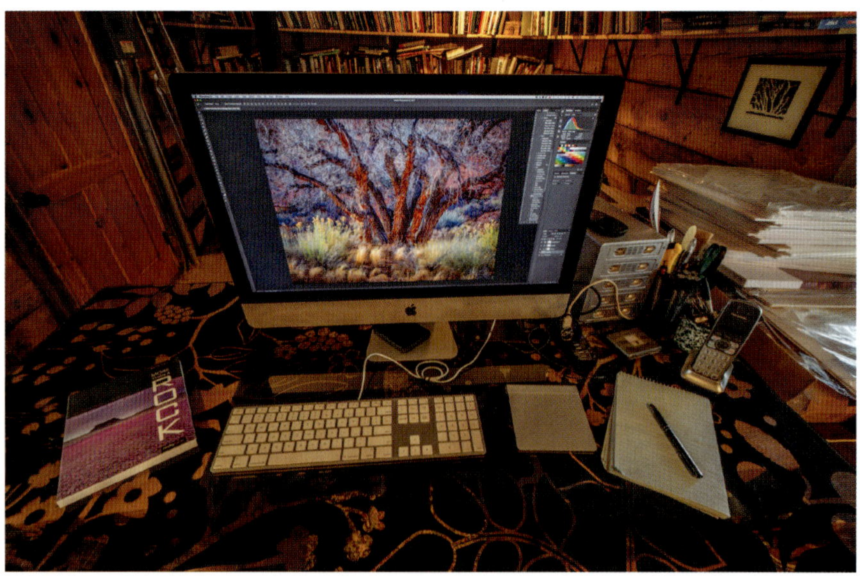

**Figure 3.1:** My (usually much messier) office is a converted century-old wooden shed that had been used as a garage by the previous owner. Having the freedom to design my workspace, I made sure to include large bookshelves, a sound system, and a plethora of dimmable lights so I can adjust the feel of the room to fit my working mood. The design of my workspace was as important an investment in my work as any piece of camera or computer gear I own.

superfluous applications and browser windows. If you are distracted by frequent phone calls and text messages that are not truly urgent, turn off your ringer for a while and only check messages on breaks from creative work. As I mentioned earlier, attention is a limited resource, and we are surrounded by technology specifically designed to hijack our attention (and not always for its most worthwhile uses). Take back control of your attention.

## Software

With Adobe's Creative Cloud Photography Plan (www.adobe.com/creativecloud/photography.html), users are provided access to both Adobe Photoshop CC and Adobe Photoshop Lightroom CC. While overlapping in some functions, these applications are also complementary in many ways, each possessing some powerful features that the other does not. If you choose to subscribe to this plan, I recommend that you take advantage of both.

To have the most power and flexibility in processing and printing your work, following are the capabilities you need covered by software applications (whether one or several):

- **RAW conversion:** I recommend that you capture all images in RAW format, rather than JPEG, for reasons I explain in the next chapter. RAW files require conversion to become viewable digital images, rendered in pixels.

  Adobe Photoshop includes a component called Adobe Camera RAW (ACR) that produces excellent results and is very conveniently integrated. The same RAW conversion capabilities are also part of Lightroom, which is also well-integrated with Photoshop. However, you may also want to evaluate other options, since there may be small variations among products from different manufacturers.

- **Global adjustments:** Most digital imaging applications can perform adjustments to the entire image (i.e., adjustments that are not explicitly restricted to just a portion of the image). These are your "heavy lifting" tools. In my opinion, the tools offered in Photoshop, and to a lesser degree in Lightroom, are among the best available.

- **Local adjustments:** Local adjustments are specifically targeted and restricted to just portions of the image. To be useful, we need accurate selection tools that are capable of isolating the desired area to be affected. Adobe Photoshop's selection and masking tools are, in my opinion, the best of breed. Although Lightroom offers limited local adjustment capabilities, its selection tools are not as robust as those offered in Photoshop.

- **Color profile awareness:** Later in the book, I explain the advantages of a color-managed workflow, meaning that all devices involved in image processing and reproduction (most notably screen and printer) are calibrated to a standard target to ensure that they reproduce colors consistently. Color management is accomplished using color calibration devices that generate device-specific profiles, and software that supports these profiles. Adobe Photoshop and Lightroom are both able to use color profiles in a color-managed workflow.
- **Interpolation (resizing) and sharpening tools:** The image as captured by the camera has the best and purest information as it consists of measurements of actual reflected light. However, different forms of output require different sizes of images (e.g., to produce a web image, most of the information captured by the camera should be discarded; or, if making large prints, the information captured by the camera may not be sufficient and new information may need to be manufactured).

  Enlarging or reducing an image from its native camera-captured size is called interpolation. This process almost always degrades the original data. Most notably, interpolation reduces the appearance of sharpness, requiring additional steps to sharpen the files for best results in different uses.

  Photoshop's interpolation and sharpening tools are excellent, although there are some superb third-party tools that are worth considering as well.
- **Printing and exporting images for specific devices and uses:** For images to be used outside your own studio, processing software should be able to export (or save) images in a variety of formats, as well as send image data to printers and other devices. Photoshop offers rich support for a wide variety of file formats and can communicate with any printer driver installed on your system.

Although not always necessary, additional functions may prove useful as well. Among them:

- **Image catalog management (Digital Asset Management, or DAM):** Photoshop does not offer DAM features such as keywording, storage and retrieval of image data in a database, nor can it keep track of images stored on removable drives when they are not connected.

These functions are supported in Lightroom, which is why I recommend using both Photoshop and Lightroom for what each does best.

- **Specialized niche tools:** Although Photoshop offers excellent tools for practically all image processing needs, some specialized products exist that take different approaches to functions such as noise reduction, sharpening, black-and-white conversion, and stitching together multiple exposures. Although I never found reason to use such products in my own work, it is possible that one or more may better fit your workflow, so I encourage experimentation and comparison.
- **Special effects:** Third-party manufacturers offer a plethora of computerized visual effects that can be easily applied to your images and that would be difficult or impossible to create manually. This is where personal taste should dictate your choices. I do not use such tools in my work. I enjoy my time spent processing images and I don't seek a shortcut for quick results. Also, I don't find such effects, no matter how visually appealing, to be particularly creative or expressive since anyone can purchase the same tools and produce the same effect. Self-expression to me manifests in the things I can control directly, rather than in automated algorithms.

You will find that various software packages overlap in some functions. However, differences among products go beyond whether a particular feature is available, but also in how it is implemented—its user interface, the degree of control and precision it offers, etc. Even similar tools available in both Photoshop and Lightroom differ in the "range of motion" they allow (with Photoshop tools generally allowing for more control but also requiring greater skill).

Processing software should offer nondestructive editing (i.e., allow you to change or roll back adjustments without altering the original image data or other adjustments), the ability to practice an integrated workflow (easy progression and handoff from one application to the next), and the ability to leverage system features such as multiple processors or cores, 64-bit architectures, and graphical processor acceleration, to improve performance and productivity. Photoshop and Lightroom offer all these.

Some may balk at the cost of software, but consider this cost in the context of your overall investment in image making, including what you spend on camera gear, travel, training, etc. Even a multi-year subscription to a service such as Adobe Creative Cloud Photography Plan still costs less than a mid-range camera or a high-end lens, and likely will have as much or more impact on the ultimate quality and success of your images.

## Hardware

Practically any computer made within the last few years will suffice for digital image processing. In the past, processor speed was a limiting factor, but today even entry-level processors offer perfectly adequate performance.

### Computer and Storage

If budget is limited, rather than spending money on the fastest processor available, you may reap more benefit from investing in a memory (RAM) upgrade and/or from switching from a conventional hard drive (HDD) to a Solid-State Drive (SSD) for your main system and application files. Conventional hard drives are still your best bang-for-the-buck option for storing your image files, documents, and other data.

To a computer, a digital image is a large set of data; and the more data the computer can hold in its memory at one time, the faster it can manipulate it. When the image is too large to fit into the available memory, the computer will use a portion of its drive space to temporarily hold the excess data. This is referred to as "swapping." Reading from and writing to a hard drive takes much longer than performing the same operations in memory, therefore swapping can severely degrade performance.

My recommendation is to equip your computer with at least 8GB of RAM, but preferably 16GB or more. Less memory than that is likely to result in a significant amount of swapping, reducing overall performance.

SSDs, which have no moving parts, are much faster than HDDs, which use spinning magnetic plates and a number of moving heads to access data. However, SSD capacity, at least at the time of this writing, is limited and is significantly more expensive than large HDDs. Therefore, I recommend using an SSD as your main system and application drive, as these files are accessed more frequently than data files (images, documents, etc.), giving you the greatest performance improvement. High capacity HDDs, and hybrid drives (which are faster than HDDs but still slower than SSDs) offer an excellent price-performance option for storing large image files.

### Backup and Redundancy

Always store your image files in at least two places. All drives are prone to random failure, and all storage methods are prone to data corruption. To lose your only copy of years-worth of images, or even of one prized image, can be a devastating experience. Don't tempt fate.

My recommendation is to purchase two large-capacity drives, at least one of them external (connected via a USB or other interface); and use one as your main image drive and the other as a live backup (preferably kept in sync using automated backup software). Once a drive pair is filled, purchase another pair and set it up in a similar manner.

If you wish to be even more cautious (as I am), I recommend storing your images in three places. Set up the backup as I mention above, and also keep another backup off-line and off-site (perhaps in the trunk of your car or at a friend's house). Other than just having another copy of the data, this arrangement will also protect you in case of catastrophic disaster such as being burglarized, having your data infected with a computer virus, or losing your house or office in a fire. It will also protect you from data corruption, especially if your primary backup drive is synchronized automatically (if the source file becomes corrupt, the synchronization software may overwrite the good backup file with the corrupt file). Be sure to update your off-site copy frequently.

Some savvy computer users favor a redundant disk array (RAID), which can be configured to mirror drives automatically (i.e., RAID 1) or to accomplish redundancy using parity data (i.e., RAID 5). I generally do not recommend these to photographers. For starters, recovering from a drive failure inside a RAID box requires some technical know-how and if the box itself malfunctions, there may be no recovering the data despite the redundancy. Also, today you can purchase drives of high capacity (6TB or more) for reasonable prices, and it's easy (and relatively inexpensive) to purchase a matching set of drives and to keep them in synch (most external drive solutions actually include free backup software to do so). A RAID solution, on the other hand, is significantly more expensive and does not usually justify the added expense in terms of data protection. Specifically, a RAID will not protect you against data corruption (unless you purchase a system that offers snapshot functionality, allowing you to recover your data at a point in time) or catastrophic events (theft, fire, virus, damage to the RAID device, etc.) So, with a RAID you may be adding a layer of complexity to your setup without significant benefit over a simpler solution.

A RAID can be an effective way to improve storage performance if you are willing to spend the money on redundant striping arrays. But here, again, the cost/benefit ratio is difficult to justify, and interfaces such as USB are becoming progressively faster all the time, allowing for acceptable performance with simple external drives.

## Cloud Storage

An attractive option for storage, which is becoming more available and less expensive as more providers enter the market, is outsourced cloud storage. You pay a subscription fee to rent drive space with a cloud provider, and you can synchronize your data to it, ensuring that it is safe and resides off-site. For me, this is not a very useful solution since I often work in places with no (or very poor) Internet connectivity, and I prefer to back up my images as soon as I download them, rather than waiting until I return to a place where I can synchronize them to the cloud.

There are many ways in which storage technologies can be combined, such as with redundant portable drives for use in the field and cloud storage as a secondary backup. My experience suggests that the simple three-drive setup I describe above (work drive, on-site real-time backup, and off-site backup) has yet to fail me even after more than two decades of working with digital images and documents.

## Card Reader

Images can be downloaded to your computer in multiple ways. If your computer does not already have a built-in slot for your memory cards, I recommend using a dedicated card reader rather than downloading images from the camera (whether directly connected or wirelessly).

Card readers are inexpensive and easy to replace, and can be left permanently connected to your computer, while the camera may require frequent plugging and unplugging, which may damage its data port.

Since card readers are not very expensive, if you use more than one computer (e.g., a light laptop in the field and a desktop in the office), I recommend purchasing a separate reader for each.

I recommend purchasing a card reader that can accept multiple popular formats (you never know when you might want to switch to a different camera, borrow a friend's camera, or download someone else's files). Look for a reader that is compatible with the fastest data interface your computer has (for example, favor USB-C, USB 3.x or Thunderbolt over older USB versions if your computer supports these faster interfaces). Downloading many large image files may take a while and a fast interface can save considerable waiting time. This is also the reason I recommend against downloading a large number of files wirelessly.

## Display and Calibration Device

Since we are editing images visually, a good monitor is every bit as important as a good computer. At the time of this writing, cathodic ray (CRT) monitors are no longer sold for general use, and practically all models on the market use liquid crystal (LCD) technologies. However, not all LCD monitors are equally capable.

LCD monitors come in a variety of panel types. The least-expensive (and most common) panels on the market are of the TN variety, which offer a low-cost option suitable for most users, but they are not ideal for applications requiring accurate color reproduction, such as digital imaging.

Next in line are the VA panels (sometimes marked as PVA or MVA), which offer excellent color rendition, but may suffer from color shifting when viewed from extreme angles.

Monitors using IPS (sometimes marked as S-IPS or H-IPS) or LED panels are generally better suited for photo editing but tend to be pricier. These monitors provide accurate color rendition and a wide viewing angle, and can be calibrated accurately for consistent reproduction.

The best monitors for image processing are those labeled as "wide-gamut." These monitors excel at rendering a wide range of colors (including very saturated colors beyond what consumer models are capable of). They also generally render superior pure blacks, have a better contrast range than consumer models, and offer more precise control over brightness, contrast, and color so they can be calibrated accurately.

Monitor physical size and resolution should be decided based on your available desk space and budget, but with these parameters, generally speaking, more is better.

In the next chapter, I explain the use of a colorimeter (color measuring and calibration device) to profile your monitor. I recommend purchasing one of these devices as a color-calibrated monitor is the cornerstone for a color-managed workflow. Without monitor calibration, there is no guarantee of consistency of color between your monitor and your printer (or your outsourced prints).

**Laptop Screens**

Laptop computer screens often fall short in terms of color capabilities compared with desktop models. While high-end laptop models can be more than adequate for processing images on the move, I recommend that you keep a better-quality monitor on your desk for color-critical work, such as preparing and proofing images for print or publication.

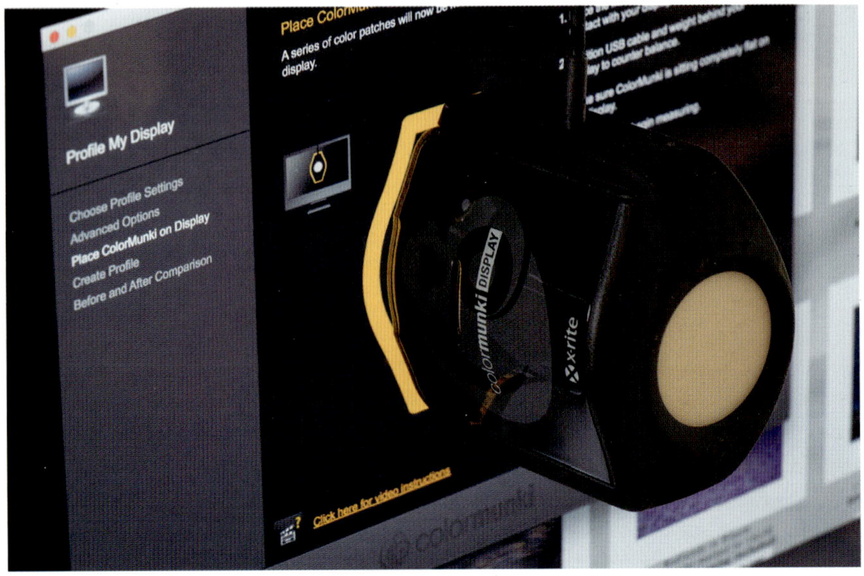


**FIGURE 3.2:** The ColorMunki Display screen colorimeter from X-Rite offers a relatively inexpensive way to keep your screen calibrated, which is essential to a color-managed environment, ensuring consistency among your screen images, prints, and other forms of output.

Colorimeters come in a variety of grades and prices; some are also capable of profiling papers for your printer and more. I recommend starting with a display-only colorimeter since screen profiles (representing a given screen's color, brightness, and contrast capabilities) tend to shift more quickly than printer profiles. It is likely that, if you choose to make your own prints, you will standardize on a small variety of favorite papers and, once you have these profiled (e.g., by a commercial service), you will probably have no further use for an expensive print colorimeter. Your screen, however, may need to be re-profiled every week or two to maintain accuracy.

## Printer

Few things are as satisfying as seeing your image in the form of a beautiful print. I also believe there is great value to artists in having as much control over our entire production process as possible, and, should you decide to sell your prints, also in offering to your customers something created by you and expressing your skills, as well as your vision. For these reasons, I recommend that serious photographers own a photographic printer.

My suggestion is to start with a medium size (17" wide) desktop printer from a leading manufacturer, such as Epson or Canon. Be sure to pick a printer that uses archival pigment inks, especially if you intend to sell your prints, as these prints will maintain their color and contrast for decades or longer.

The reason I recommend a desktop printer, rather than a larger model is that stepping up to a wide-format (24" or wider) model generally implies more than just getting a larger printer. For starters, these printers are *much* larger than desktop models, usually requiring a dedicated stand and quite a bit of floor space. These printers are also optimized for using roll paper, rather than sheets that are more convenient, especially if you don't intend to make a large volume of prints. Desktop models generally offer the ability to stack sheets for easy feeding. While sheet paper can be used in a wide-format printer, it usually needs to be loaded one sheet at a time, and requires removing any previously installed paper roll, which can be inconvenient.

A 17" printer can produce 16"×20" or larger prints, which are impressive to behold. These printers have a much smaller footprint than a wide-format printer and they are much more user friendly and amenable to being used for general printing in addition to photographs. Even if you decide to later purchase a larger printer, I suspect you will want to keep your desktop printer for smaller jobs or when the convenience of sheet paper trumps the small saving in cost of printing the same size image on roll paper.

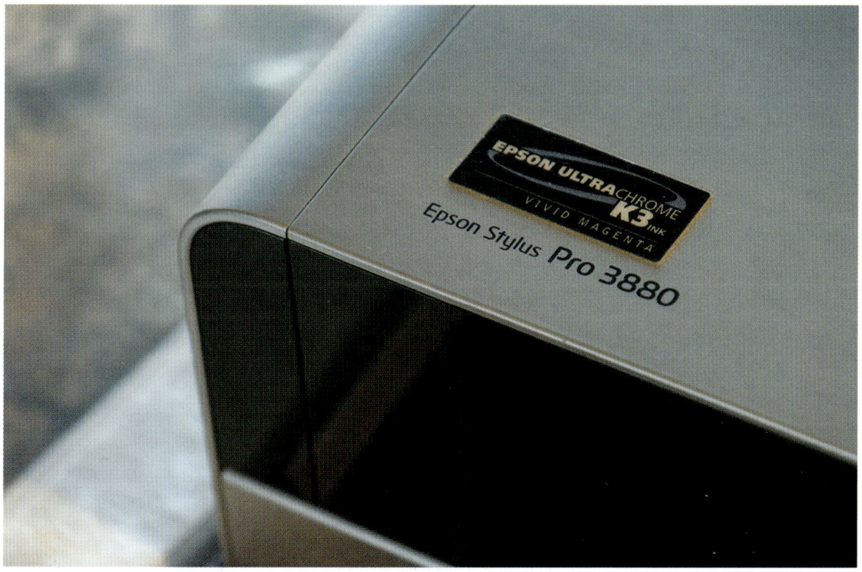


FIGURE 3.3: Epson offers a line of excellent professional photographic printers. My Stylus Pro 3880 has proven to be a reliable workhorse, making excellent prints up to 17" wide, which covers most my needs.

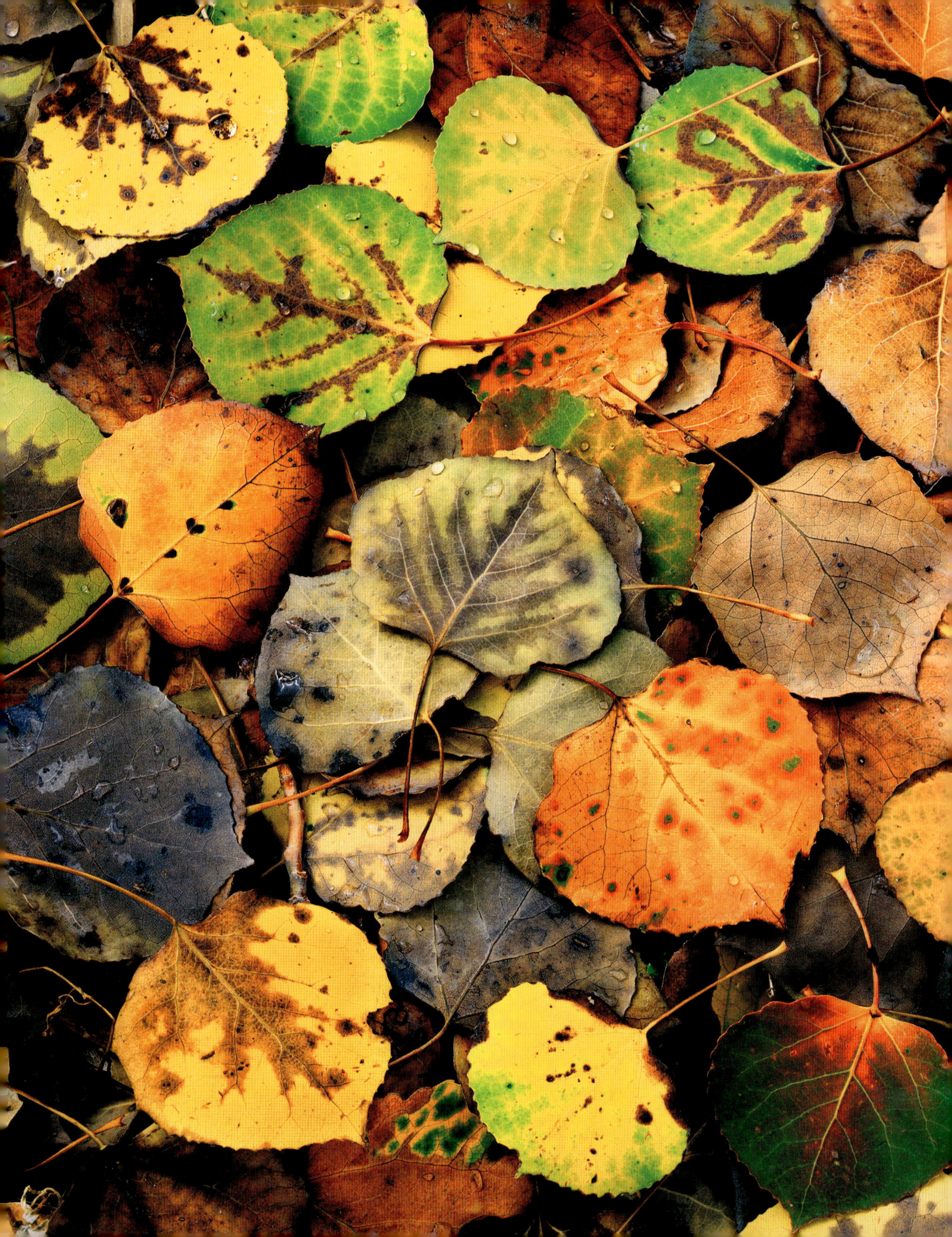

# Speaking Digital

# 4

*I am sure the next step will be the electronic image, and I hope I shall live to see it. I trust that the creative eye will continue to function, whatever technological innovations may develop.*

—ANSEL ADAMS

Computer technology today places immensely powerful and precise tools in the hands of photographers. The same desktop or laptop computer that you use to author documents, surf the Internet, and communicate electronically can also serve as an image processing platform with capabilities matching—and often exceeding—those previously possible only using a state-of-the-art darkroom. Moreover, computers can perform image-processing tasks with greater speed, accuracy, and comfort than what was possible in the analog age.

Both hardware and software manufacturers have made great progress in designing their products so they are intuitive to most users, hiding much of the complexity of digital processing behind user-friendly interfaces and easy-to-use controls, such as buttons, sliders, checkboxes, and plain-language menus. However, those who seek the greatest control over their work will benefit greatly from also understanding some of what happens "under the hood."

In this chapter, I review some of the concepts and terminology associated with digital image processing, both because I believe it is useful to establish a common language that can be used to explain various processing concepts, and because such terms sometimes are used in ambiguous ways and may become confusing.

Before delving into technical terminology, I believe it is important to first place such knowledge in the context of its relevance to creative photographers. We are, after all, here to make art, not to learn to become computer engineers. Much like cameras, computers and software can be thought of as not just tools but as *creative* tools, meaning they can be used to give tangible expression to ideas and feelings, even values and beliefs. And these ideas, feelings, values, and beliefs cannot be conceived by machines; they must come from a human mind. Technology alone may indeed be used to accomplish images of great interest and beauty, but such images—even if popular or profitable—are not likely to result in the same inner rewards as making original, creative, expressive work.

To possess a deep understanding of the tools and technologies that make our work possible is both useful and important. However, as expressed by the great photographer André Kertész, "If you want to write you should learn the alphabet. You write and write and in the end you have a beautiful, perfect alphabet. But it isn't the alphabet that is important. The important thing is what you are writing, what you are expressing. The same thing goes for photography. Photographs can be technically perfect and even beautiful, but they have no expression."

## Understanding Bits

The word *bit* is shorthand for binary digit. It is the smallest unit of computerized data. A single bit can hold a value of either 0 or 1. Two bits can be used to represent a range of four values: 00, 01, 10, and 11; corresponding respectively to the decimal numbers 0, 1, 2, and 3; and so on. Therefore, the more bits are assigned to a given parameter, the greater the range of values it can have. The total number of possible combinations is easily calculated as 2 to the power of the number of bits. So, for example, an 8-bit number can have one of 256 possible values ( $=2^8$), corresponding to the range of 0 (all 8 bits are set to 0) to 255 (all 8 bits are set to 1).

Present-day computers generally process and store data in chunks of 8 or 16 bits. This is why multiplications of eight are commonly used in various digital formats.

A common use for bits in digital photography is in association with color depth—the number of distinct color variations possible within a digital image. Using more bits means having a wider range of possible values and, consequently, smoother transitions from one color to another or, in the case of black-and-white images, more continuous gradations of tone. Most digital image formats represent color using three numbers for the respective amounts of red, green, and blue (also known as the *RGB Model*) which, when blended together, can produce a rich palette of colors (e.g., blending red and green, with no blue, produces yellow). In digital imaging, red, green, and blue are also generically referred to as *color channels*.

Digital images are rendered as arrays of dots, called *pixels* (pixel is short for *picture element*). In the RGB model, which is what we will use for most of our work, each pixel is associated with three numerical values—corresponding respectively to amounts of red, green, and blue that define its color. In 8-bit formats, the value of each color channel can range between 0 and 255. So, for example, the most saturated red possible is represented as 255,0,0 (maximum red, no green, no blue). When all three numbers have the same value, the pixel will be of a neutral color (i.e., gray) somewhere between pure

**A Bit More About Bits**

In some cases, you may find reference to the total number of bits used to represent a pixel rather than just the number of bits used for each color channel. As a result, confusingly, texts referring to "8-bit color" or "24-bit color" may in fact mean the same thing. Similarly, some texts may refer to "48-bit color" rather than "16-bit color."

black (0,0,0) and pure white (255,255,255). Using 8 bits for each of the three channels gives us a total of 24 bits with which to represent color variations, which add up to roughly 16.8 million possibilities (more precisely, $2^{24}$=16,777,216).

When using 16 bits in each channel, values for red, green, and blue can each range between 0 and 65,535 (=$2^{16}$), and the total number of colors that can be represented by combining all three channels is over 281 trillion! This is quite an impressive jump from the 16.8 million possibilities when using only 8 bits per channel.

Digital cameras offering RAW capture capability generally record data in a 16-bit format, although this does not necessarily mean they can truly utilize all 281 trillion possible color variations. In fact, many sensors can only differentiate between color values in ranges of 12 or 14 bits, but since standard file formats support either 8 or 16 bits, the sensor readings are padded with zeroes and stored as 16-bit values.

The user interfaces of some image processing software (including Adobe Photoshop) show the color channels as ranging in value between 0–255, even when working with 16-bit files. This is done to keep things consistent for human users and is useful as a general reference. To know the actual numbers, whether in 8-bit or 16-bit format generally is not as useful as understanding how the ratios of red, green, and blue combine into a discrete color. The 0–255 range is more than sufficient to inform us and to factor into our processing decisions. Some software, such as Adobe Lightroom, use a notation based on percentage, where each channel is represented by a value in the range of 0–100. While perhaps more intuitive within a single application, it is not common.

FIGURE 4.1: RGB values of various pixels in a landscape image. Note how different combinations of red, green, and blue values create a variety of unique colors.

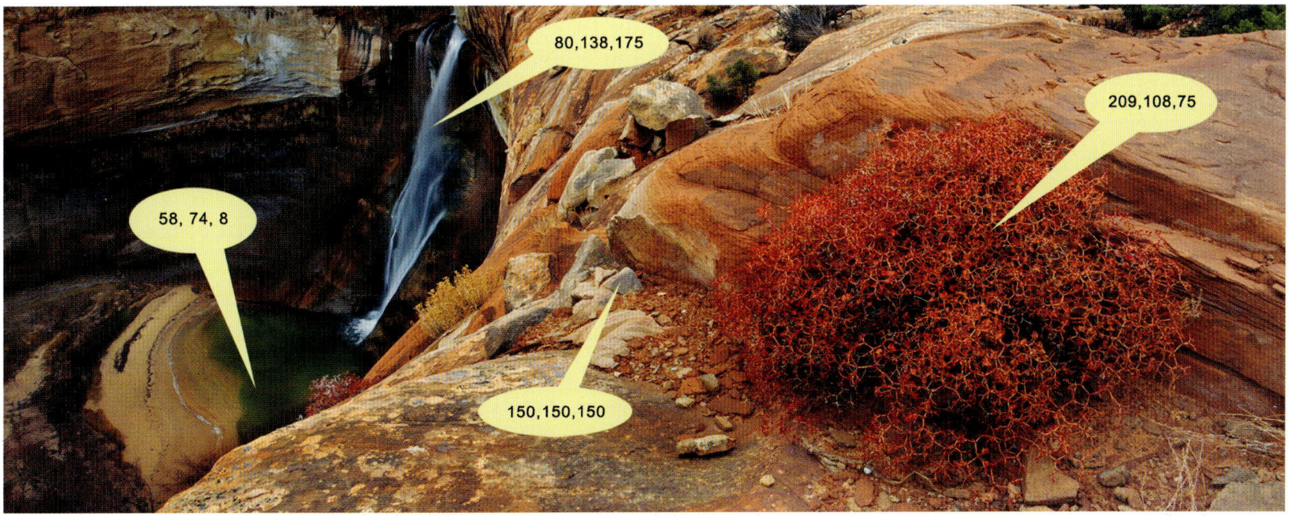

## The RAW File

Most current mid-level and high-end digital cameras, as well as several advanced compact models, offer the option of recording data in one of many RAW file formats, in addition or instead of the ubiquitous JPEG. Before discussing RAW further, it's important to note that RAW files are not image files in the same sense that other file formats, such as JPEG or TIFF, are. RAW files do not contain pixel data. Instead, they contain data about the amount of light measured by each of millions of microscopic light-sensitive detectors in the camera's sensor, and that can be converted into pixels in multiple ways. There is no one "right" way to display a RAW file; in fact, it can be converted into a visible image (made of pixels) in an almost infinite number of ways, depending on the parameters provided to the conversion algorithm. When opening a RAW file using conversion software, such as Adobe Photoshop's built-in RAW converter, Adobe Camera RAW (ACR), the image you see is generated using some default values—a best-guess—chosen by the software manufacturer, and you may decide to change these parameters to other values to better fit your desired outcome. I discuss these parameters of RAW conversion in detail in chapter 8.

To provide a better sense of the difference between a RAW file (containing light measurements) and an image file (containing pixels), think of a RAW file as a pantry containing the ingredients required to bake a cake. It does not, however, contain an actual cake. In order to turn the ingredients into a cake, we need to combine them in various proportions and to bake the mix at a given temperature for a specific amount of time. In other words, just having ingredients is not enough; we also need to apply a recipe and a workflow in order to make something of them. In the digital world, the RAW conversion software is where we mix our ingredients in order to "bake" the sensor readings into a visible image. Just as cake ingredients do not by themselves make a cake, so does a RAW file not make an image until it is converted into one.

Digital sensors use an array of microscopic detectors, called *photosites*, in order to measure light. Each photosite is covered in a tiny lens tinted red, green, or blue. These lenses act as filters, allowing light of their own color to pass through, and blocking light of other colors. This results in individual measurements for each color channel that can later be combined to generate RGB pixels. Photosites are most often arranged in what's known as a *Bayer Pattern*, consisting of two green-filtered lenses, one red-filtered lens, and one blue-filtered lens at each 2×2 section of the array (figure 4.2).

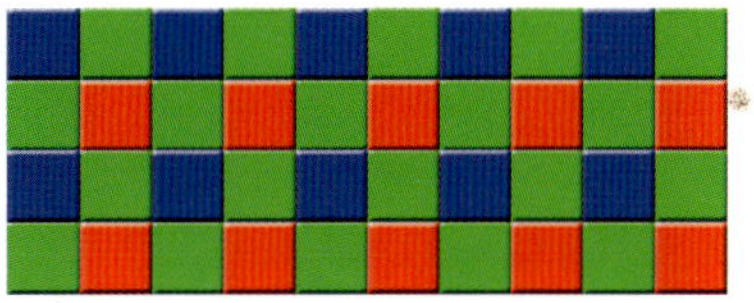
FIGURE 4.2: The Bayer pattern

### The Human Eye and the Bayer Pattern

The Bayer Pattern is designed so it mimics the sensitivity of the human visual system to various color ranges. The human eye contains a layer of photoreceptor cells that convert light into neural activity—electrical signals sent to the brain via the optic nerve. Color is perceived using a type of photoreceptor called a *cone cell*. Human eyes contain three types of cone cells, each sensitive to either short, medium, or long wavelengths, and corresponding roughly to red, green, and blue. Cones sensitive to medium and long wavelengths (green/yellow and red, respectively) are much more abundant than cones sensitive to short wavelengths (blue/violet), making our vision more sensitive to variations of yellow-green light than to other colors, which explains why there are more green photosites than blue or red photosites in a Bayer pattern.

A digital sensor converts analog data (the amount of light measured at each of its millions of photosites) into numeric (digital) values. It is these values that get written into the RAW file. In order for these values to be presented as a viewable image, RAW conversion software uses a variety of parameters and algorithms to map light measurements into pixels. In the most common case of a Bayer pattern sensor, the measurements from each 2×2 array of photosites are used to calculate the RGB values assigned to a given pixel. The software also applies some logic to ensure that transitions from one pixel to the next are smooth, to adjust colors based on characteristics of light, and to apply a desired level of contrast. This process is called *demosaicing* (pronounced de-mosaic-ing) as the mosaic of readings from the sensor is used to calculate pixel values.

You may wonder why a conversion is needed at all if we already have distinct red, green, and blue values measured by the sensor. The reason is that sensors measure light in a linear fashion (e.g., if Point A reflects twice the amount of light as Point B, the sensor will record a value for A that is twice as high as for B). However, human perception of brightness is not linear (mathematicians may think of it as logarithmic). If Point A is measurably twice as light as Point B, the brain may perceive the difference between them as significantly smaller or greater than the numbers would suggest, depending on various factors, most notably color.

As I mention above, there are many types of RAW file formats. In fact, even different camera models from the same manufacturer sometimes use different RAW formats. Most of these formats are proprietary (meaning that their specifications are owned by the manufacturer, who may at their sole discretion change or discontinue them at any time or charge a licensing fee for their use), which creates a significant challenge for software developers who constantly have to keep up with a multitude of RAW variations as new camera models are released. There currently is only one RAW format that is non-proprietary (i.e., not subject to the whims of any manufacturer, remains the same regardless of camera model, and is available freely to software developers): Adobe's Digital Negative (or DNG) format. DNG is natively supported by a handful of camera models. However, Adobe provides a free utility to convert many proprietary formats into it. If you plan to archive your RAW files for long-term storage, with the intent of revisiting them in the future as better conversion software becomes available, I recommend converting them into DNG to ensure they can be recognized by future versions of RAW converters, in the event that your camera's proprietary format becomes obsolete and is no longer supported.

The need to convert images from RAW prior to further processing obviously introduces some amount of additional work, and some may be tempted by the relative ease of capturing images in JPEG format, instead. If you are as particular as I am about maintaining absolute control over your work and maximizing the quality of your image files, my advice is not to cut corners. RAW files give you several distinct advantages over JPEG files as follows:

- The camera always captures RAW data. When set to record JPEG files, the camera's computer converts the RAW file into JPEG on your behalf—using its own built-in conversion algorithm and best-guess parameters—and then discards the original data (unless set to record RAW+JPEG). Some of these conversion decisions cannot be changed or undone later, and may not always be the ones you might choose based on your own sensibilities or expressive intent.
- The JPEG format offered in digital cameras supports only 8 bits of data per color channel, which in some cases may be limiting and may produce unsightly artifacts. RAW files generally use 16 bits (sometimes 12 or 14) for each color channel, resulting in a much greater gradation of colors. This means that, when capturing a JPEG, you are potentially discarding color data (most notably gradations of color) that you may want later. These data cannot be recovered if the RAW file is not available. This is of particular concern in landscape photography, as many natural scenes contain smooth and subtle color transitions such as in the subtle transitions of blue in skies and reflections in water surfaces. And, it is of even greater concern for black-and-white photographers, where each pixel in a black-and-white image is defined not by 3 color channels, but only by 1 gray channel (i.e., allowing only 256 gradations in 8-bit JPEG format).

**Adobe's Digital Negative (DNG Files)**

Users of Adobe Lightroom may choose to convert their RAW files to DNG format as part of the import process, which takes a bit longer than just copying the RAW files but in my opinion is worth the wait. If you're not using Adobe Lightroom, you may download the free DNG Converter utility from Adobe (https://helpx.adobe.com/photoshop/digital-negative.html).

Scenes containing deep shadows or very bright highlights may result in a loss of detail due to under- or over-exposure (also known as *clipping*). These losses, when confined to small areas in the image, may be too subtle to notice on the camera's small screen while in the field and their loss may not be known (or reflected in the histogram) until you process the image. In many cases, RAW files will still contain some or all of the data needed to recover these lost details: JPEGs will not (figure 4.3).

- Standard JPEG files use lossy compression algorithms—algorithms that alter and discard image data in order to achieve a reduction in file size. Once lost, these data cannot be recovered. RAW files, on the other hand, retain all captured data, although the files are usually larger as a result.

**FIGURE 4.3:** The image on the left was converted from RAW using default values. The image on the right was converted from RAW using the maximum values for shadow and highlight details. Notice how much more information is available in the RAW file that can be recovered. If this image had been originally captured as JPEG, both the deep shadows and bright highlights would have been permanently lost.

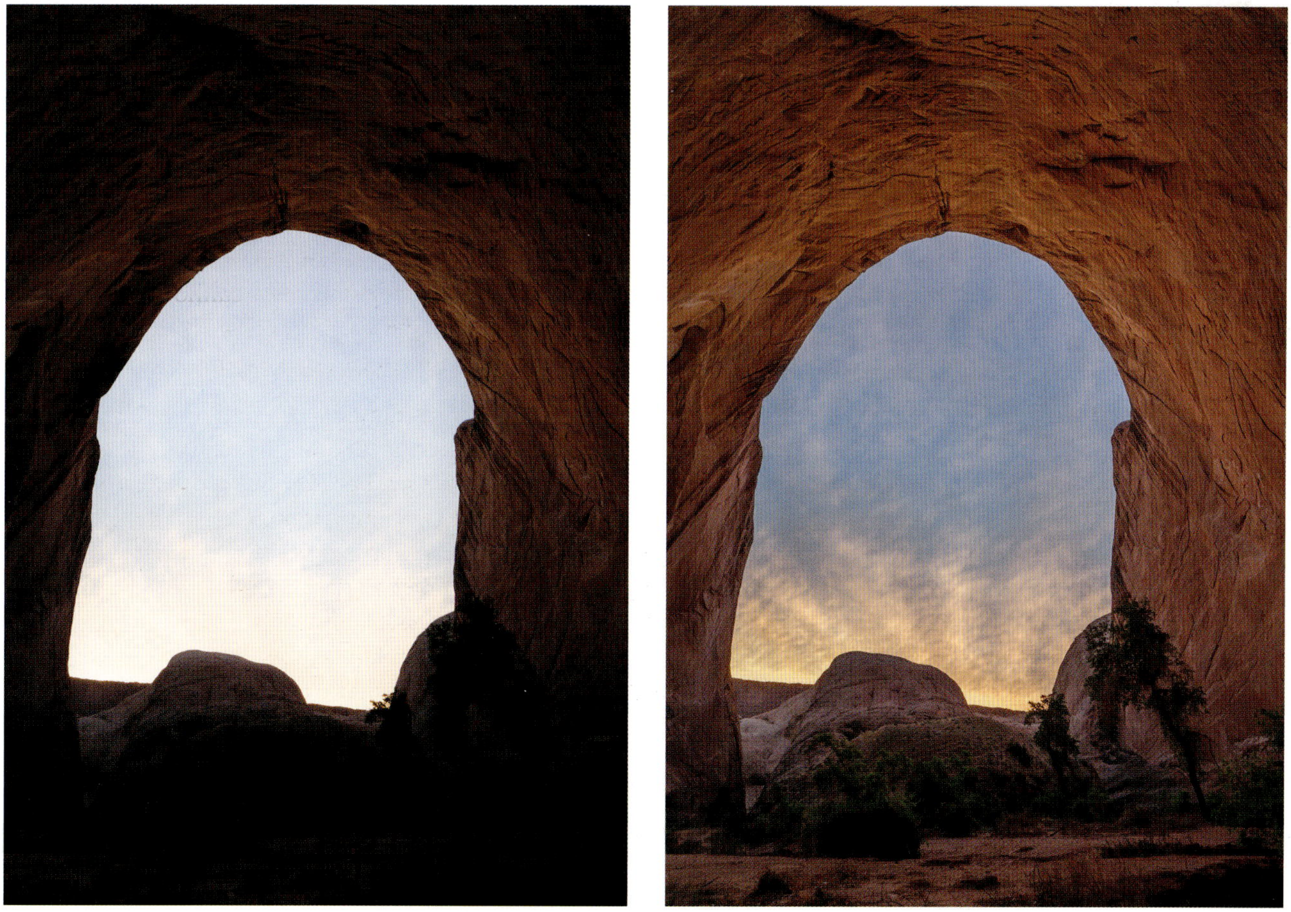

**Compression Options for RAW Files**

As new sensors offer greater resolutions, and correspondingly larger files, some manufacturers now offer both lossy and lossless compression options for their RAW files. I recommend always choosing the lossless option, even if it means having to purchase memory cards and drives of greater capacity. Lossy compression algorithms may offer faster write times, given the smaller files, which may be useful in situations such as sports photography or wildlife photography, where speed is of the essence, but this is rarely the case in landscape photography.

Converting from a RAW file into an image made of pixels is but the first step in the processing workflow, and is done using a specialized RAW conversion software. RAW converters usually also offer some rudimentary tools to adjust color and contrast or to perform local adjustments (i.e., adjustments applied to a portion of the image, rather than globally). Impatient photographers may be tempted to use these to attempt to bring the image as close as possible to the desired end result. While doing so may seem intuitive, in fact it may limit your options later on. Adobe Photoshop offers far more powerful and precise tools for adjusting and fine-tuning such things as color, contrast, and other aspects of the image than those available in RAW conversion software. For best results, I recommend using the RAW converter not to replace the tools available in Adobe Photoshop, but rather to create a good starting point for further processing. I describe what makes for a good starting point in chapter 8.

If your goal is to achieve the highest possible quality for your image files, keep in mind that patience is a virtue. Take your time and use each tool for what it does best.

**RAW vs. raw vs. Raw**

As a matter of convention, RAW is spelled in upper case when referring to a file type even though it is not actually an acronym. This helps distinguish it from the word "raw."

## Image File Formats

I mention above that RAW is not truly an image format and that it requires conversion into pixels to be displayed. Pixel data can be saved in a number of image file formats.

Not all image file formats are the same, and some are better suited for storing photographs than others. In particular, the following considerations are important in order to determine which format is best for a given use. Keep in mind that the same image may be saved in multiple formats for

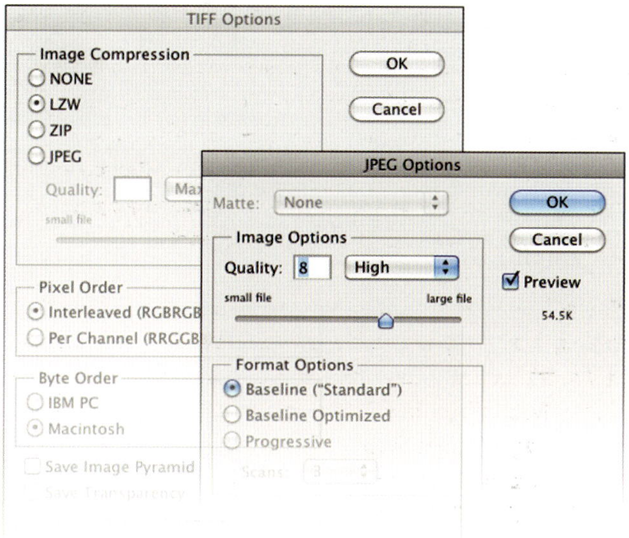


FIGURE 4.4: TIFF and JPEG Options windows.

different purposes; for example, one format may be preferable for archival storage while another may work best for posting to a website.

## Compression

Image files can be relatively large and may use up a lot of drive space. Although storage is consistently becoming less expensive, there is still a cost associated with storing large files, both in terms of price and also in terms of performance, since large files may take considerable time to load, save, copy, back up, or transmit over a network. Compression is a way of reducing the amount of space needed to store a file.

While many image file formats allow for compression, some compression methods, categorized as "lossy," discard image data in order to reduce the file size. Other methods, called "lossless," preserve all the data in the original file but may not achieve the same reduction in size as their lossy counterparts. Lossless formats are obviously preferred for archiving your full-size image files, while lossy formats may be better suited for applications that benefit from small file size and that do not require all image details, for example images used in a slideshow, sent via email, or posted to websites.

Of the common image file formats, standard JPEG uses lossy compression, meaning that every time you save the file, some amount of image data is altered or discarded in order to reduce the file size. On the other hand, formats such as TIFF offer multiple compression methods (or no compression at all), which include both lossy and lossless options. ZIP and LZW are common lossless compression methods that can be used with TIFF files, and therefore are recommended for storing what I describe later in the book as *master files*—files containing the best image data, as opposed to task-specific files.

### Open vs. Proprietary

Most image file formats are "open," meaning that their specifications are standardized and publicly available for anyone without the need to license or otherwise depend on any one vendor in order to use. Among these open formats are JPEG, PNG, and TIFF. Some image formats, however, such as Adobe's PSD, are proprietary. As a rule, it is preferred to stick to open formats since they are more likely to withstand the test of time and can be used by a variety of products from multiple vendors. If you decide at some point to switch to a different software vendor, your non-proprietary files are more likely to be usable in other applications.

### Bit Depth

Some formats, such as standard JPEG and GIF, allow for only 8 bits of data per color channel. As modern cameras are able to capture higher bit counts, choosing an 8-bit format may result in some loss of color gradation. Formats like TIFF and PSD, on the other hand, support high bit counts and are therefore capable of preserving all color information recorded by the camera.

### Indexed Color

Some image formats, such as GIF, are designed to further reduce file size and to speed up image rendition by setting aside part of the file for a pre-selected (and limited) palette of colors. Pixels in such a file can each only have one of the colors options in the palette, rather than being able to utilize the full range of possible colors. This can be a severe limitation for photographic images. For example, GIF files can only contain 256 colors in their palette, compared with millions or trillions of possibilities available in other, non-indexed, formats, such as JPEG and TIFF. Indexed color formats were useful in the days when computing power and network speeds were much more limited than they are today. These formats are generally not recommended for storing photographs.

## Layers, Masks, and Alpha Channels

Later in the book, I explain how to use multiple layers and associated masks in order to apply nondestructive editing and local adjustments to an image. Ideally, such adjustments should be preserved in such a way that they can be changed at a later time without damaging the original image pixels. Your chosen file format should be able to store and retrieve these layers and masks without applying their effects permanently. When used with Photoshop, formats such as TIFF and PSD are capable of storing layer and mask information using a feature known as *alpha channels*. Alpha channels are used to store multiple image layers, which are then blended transparently—or composited—into the final image. Other image formats may only be capable of storing "flat" images, which limit our ability to revisit and adjust editing decisions later on.

## Choosing a Format

So, which format should you use? It depends. The same image can be stored in multiple formats for various uses. For example, images displayed on the Internet will not gain much from high bit depth or from having multiple layers, but will benefit from a small size (high compression) that allows them to load faster. For this purpose, a format like JPEG is a great choice. However, when storing our full-size files for a variety of possible future uses, we want a file format capable of preserving every last bit of information recorded by the camera, as well as our subsequent edits. These files are also likely to be stored on a local drive (or one connected via a fast interface like USB or Thunderbolt), or on a file server connected to a fast, local network, which allows saving and loading large amounts of data much faster than is possible over the Internet. For these files, a format like a 16-bit TIFF meets the desired qualities in every one of the categories listed above.

## Pixels and Dots

A pixel is the smallest unit in an image that can have its own unique characteristics of color and position.

Computers measure image dimensions (height and width) in pixels, although for some uses, such as printing, we need to convert pixels into physical units of length, such as inches or centimeters. In other words, we need to decide how many pixels to cram into a given length of paper. For example, if an image measures 3,000 pixels across and we tell the printer to use 300 pixels per inch, the print will be 10" wide. However, if we tell the printer to use only 150 pixels per inch, the print will be 20" wide.

The number of pixels per inch, or PPI, is meaningful only in the context of printing. When an image is displayed on a screen or projected, only the pixel count matters. The physical size will depend on the screen size and density, the projector's resolution, or the size of the projected area. In other words, an image of a given pixel size will look exactly the same on screen whether it is set to 1 PPI or 1,000 PPI.

**DPI vs. PPI**

Confusingly, the terms DPI and PPI often are used interchangeably, especially in commercial printing, although they are not always the same.

Inkjet printer manufacturers often tout the number of dots per inch (DPI) their printers are capable of (as opposed to PPI). A dot is a measure of the smallest drop of ink the printer is capable of rendering on paper. My Epson printer, for example, boasts a resolution of 2,880 DPI. While an impressive number, it really means that if I print my file at 360 PPI, the printer will use 8 tiny drops of ink (dots) for every pixel in the image (2,880/360=8). I elaborate on choosing the best values for these parameters in chapter 14.

The DPI count is an indicator of an inkjet printer's ability to simulate continuous tone. In theory, the higher the number, the smaller the ink drops, and the smoother the transition appears from one pixel to the next. Still, as an overall indicator of print quality, it is but one of several factors and not a particularly useful one.

## Color

Earlier in this chapter, I describe the RGB color model where a set of three numbers is used to represent the respective amounts of red, green, and blue that determine the color of a pixel. Commonly, these values are presented on a scale of 0–255, corresponding to 8 bits of data per color channel. This standard notation originated in the days before computers handled higher color bit depths, and is often used even with higher bit counts.

While not obvious, an underlying assumption of the RGB model is that pure white is represented by the maximum amount of each color (255,255,255), and pure black is represented by the absence of all colors (0,0,0). In other words, pure white requires adding together all colors. For this reason, RGB is classified as an *additive* color model.

Additive color models are suitable for devices that can generate their own light, such as monitors and projectors. In essence, every pixel on the monitor is rendered by three sources of light (red, green, and blue), and by varying the intensity of each individual light source in order to create variations in color. When all light sources are off, we get the closest thing to black. When they are each at maximum capacity, we get the brightest white the device can generate.

Additive color models do *not* work for media that cannot generate their own light, such as printers. The paper starts off as white as it will ever be, without adding any color to it. In fact, adding the maximum amounts of red, green, and blue inks, as required by the RGB model, will result in a mess rather than pure white. For that reason, printing requires a *subtractive* color model—one where white means the absence of all colors. Similar to additive color models, color inks applied to the paper at various ratios create variations in color. The most commonly used subtractive color model is CMYK, relying on four channels representing the respective amounts of cyan, magenta, yellow, and black. Black is needed since no combination of cyan, magenta, and yellow inks will produce pure black. The letter "K" stands for "Key" since in commercial printing each color ink is applied separately using a plate, and color plates are aligned (keyed) to the black plate, which contains the image details (dots, lines, characters, etc.) CMYK colors are generally represented as a set of four numbers ranging from 0 to 100, denoting the percentage of each of the inks used. In CMYK, pure white means the absence of all ink (0%, 0%, 0%, 0%).

While several other color models are available for specific applications, and except for commercial printing, most digital processing of photographs is done using the RGB color model.

Both RGB and CMYK are device-dependent, meaning that any given device (such as a monitor, scanner, projector, printer and paper combination, etc.) may present them in its own way. Consider, for example, the RGB color 255,0,0, which represents the most saturated red in the model. Any device supporting RGB will display it as some shade of bright red. However, there is no guarantee that it will appear identically on my monitor as it does on yours. The results will differ by the type and quality of monitor used, the age of the monitor, the individual brightness and contrast settings, the video hardware, and even environmental factors such as temperature and humidity.

How then do we ensure consistency among different devices made by different manufacturers and used under different conditions? Moreover, how do we ensure consistency among devices that render color using light, such as monitors, and ones using ink, such as inkjet printers?

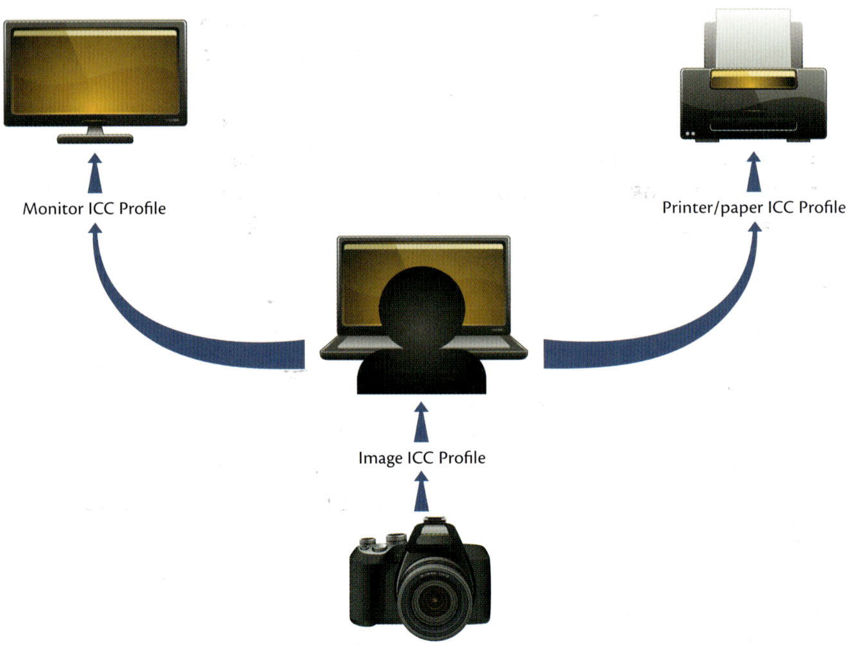


FIGURE 4.5: ICC Profiles represent the color capability of specific devices.

In order to solve these problems, several manufacturers of digital imaging applications came together in the early 1990s to form the International Color Consortium (ICC). ICC produced a standard format, known as an ICC Profile, to describe the color capabilities (known as the *color space*, or *gamut*) of a given device. Software and devices supporting the ICC specifications can use these profiles in order to maintain consistency in color reproduction among various devices (figure 4.5).

Since ICC profiles are device-specific, the profile for my monitor will be slightly different from the profile for your monitor, even if they are of the same make and model. A monitor profile obviously will be different from a printer profile or a scanner profile or a camera profile. Color spaces can also change over time as monitors become older or environmental conditions change. In order to maintain the most accurate color mapping, devices—especially monitors, being our primary viewing devices when processing images—need to be re-profiled with some frequency. The preferred interval for a monitor is once every two to four weeks. Printer profiles generally are more stable since inks and papers are manufactured within strict tolerances, are routinely refilled or replaced with fresh samples, and they tend to maintain their color characteristics for relatively long periods.

The process of creating a profile for a device is known as *calibration*, and usually requires a color-measuring device called a *colorimeter*, as well as a standard target image consisting of multiple color patches with known values. The target is displayed or printed on the device being calibrated, then scanned by the colorimeter in order to compare the colors as rendered with the known values for each patch. Differences between expected and actual colors are then used to generate an ICC profile. It is important to note that the profile represents not only the capabilities of a device, but also its limitations (e.g., not all devices are capable of rendering the same saturation of colors).

Reasonably priced monitor colorimeters are widely available from various manufacturers, and I highly recommend investing in one and recalibrating your monitor every two to four weeks. Print colorimeters tend to be more expensive, and, since printer profiles do not need to be updated very frequently, you may prefer to have a third party produce these profiles for you rather than doing it yourself. This requires downloading and printing a target provided by the third party and sending in the print to have a profile produced.

ICC profiles are stored in files, usually with the extension .icc or .icm. Monitor calibration software will generally install the profile for you once it is produced, although if you ordered a custom profile from a third party or downloaded one from the website of a printer or paper manufacturer, you will need to install it yourself by saving it in the appropriate directory. As of the time of this writing, these directories are as follows:

- For Apple (OS X 10.x or later): /Library/ColorSync/Profiles
- For Microsoft Windows (XP or later): \Windows\system32\spool\drivers\color

  Alternatively, in Microsoft Windows, you may also right-click the file and select "Install Profile" from the menu.

When profiling for printing, since each paper has its own unique characteristics, a separate profile is needed for each type of paper you plan to use with a given printer.

### Custom vs. Canned Printer Profiles

Various paper manufacturers offer canned profiles for each of their offerings that can be downloaded from their websites. These profiles may be quite accurate but are never perfect since they don't account for slight variations between individual printers. Custom profiles, made specifically for your printer, in your work environment, are fairly inexpensive. Compared with the level of investment you likely have in camera and computer equipment, purchasing custom profiles is a small price to pay to achieve optimal results.

With the availability of ICC profiles representing the color capabilities of various devices, software that supports these profiles can perform the calculations needed to ensure that colors are rendered consistently, whether displayed on a given monitor or printed on a given paper. Still, perfect matches may not always be possible. Some devices have larger gamuts and can display more saturated colors than others. For example, digital cameras may support larger color spaces than most monitors can display, and monitors have much larger color spaces than any printer can reproduce.

So, what happens if the particular shade of red I see on my screen is unavailable in, say, the color space of a paper I wish to print to? The unfortunate answer is that converting between color spaces often requires a degree of compromise. The technical term for this compromise is *rendering intent*, and, unless the software insists upon making the decision for you, it is one of the choices you will be asked to make when converting files from one color space to another.

When converting photographs, two rendering intents are particularly useful:

- **Perceptual:** This method "compresses" all colors by the same ratio until they all fit within the capabilities of the target device. A potential advantage to this approach is that it maintains the relationships between colors in the image. This means that overall contrast and gradation is preserved as close to the original as possible, but the actual colors may shift (generally de-saturated) to fit within the destination color space. If the source and destination color spaces are not very different, this method often yields acceptable results without the need for further adjustment. However, if the origin and destination color spaces are very different, the converted colors may appear dull.
- **Relative Colorimetric:** This method preserves all the in-gamut colors (i.e., the colors contained in both the source and destination color spaces), and only changes the outliers: those colors that are out-of-gamut (i.e., that exist in the source color space but not in the destination color space). With this method, if there are large areas in the image that are out-of-gamut, the resulting gradation, contrast, and saturation of some colors may look slightly different from the original. Since devices and software specifically designed to handle digital photographs generally support most, or all, colors likely to be found in natural scenes, out-of-gamut colors are not common, and usually have other in-gamut colors that are very close in appearance. Therefore, this is generally the recommended rendering intent for converting photographs between color spaces (figure 4.6).

Other available rendering intents generally are not useful when working with photographs.

For best results, rather than using a prescribed rendering intent, out-of-gamut colors can be adjusted manually to fit within the destination color space. I explain how to make this adjustment in chapter 14.

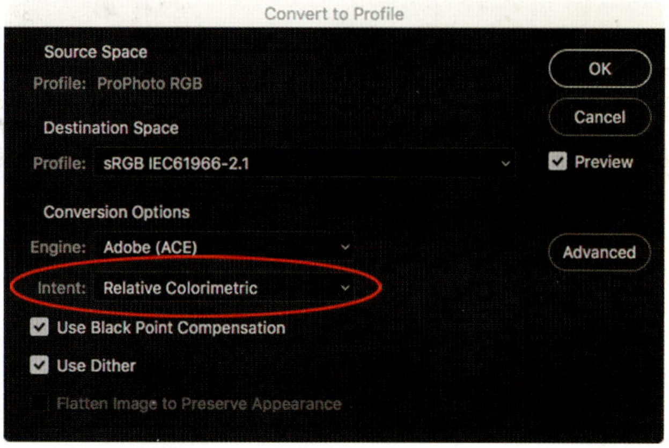


**Figure 4.6:** The profile conversion tool provided in Adobe Photoshop allows choosing one of several rendering intents.

## Standard Color Spaces

In an ideal world, every device would have an associated ICC profile and all software would know how to use such profiles. The reality is very different. While each of us can calibrate and manage the devices that are within our control, we don't always know the properties of other devices on which our images may be displayed or printed.

In particular, images shared on the Internet may be displayed on practically every make and model of monitor, the majority of which are not color-calibrated. More to the point, as a photographer posting images on the Internet, you have no way of knowing the color capabilities of the screens used by those viewing your work.

Another scenario entails images submitted for commercial publication or sent to a third party for printing. While some labs offer the custom profiles for their printers to photographers who wish to proof their work, others prefer to handle the conversion themselves, and the results may be different than expected.

To mitigate these concerns, several standard color spaces exist that can be used in lieu of a custom profile.

Realizing that most consumers do not need very precise color management, several companies collaborated to define the sRGB color space. sRGB is a low-common-denominator standard, meaning that a wide variety of devices, including screens, projectors, consumer printers, and scanners are designed to meet it as a minimum.

sRGB was also adopted as the standard color space for the Internet, meaning that web browsers, in the absence of color space information, assume that any image they encounter is in the sRGB space. Although some Internet browsers do also support custom ICC profiles, if the end user's monitor isn't calibrated (and most aren't), this support is of little value to photographers beyond using it on our own workstations.

Therefore, in the absence of information on how your images will be viewed, converting them to sRGB ensures that they will look as close to the original as possible across a wide variety of devices, whether the devices are

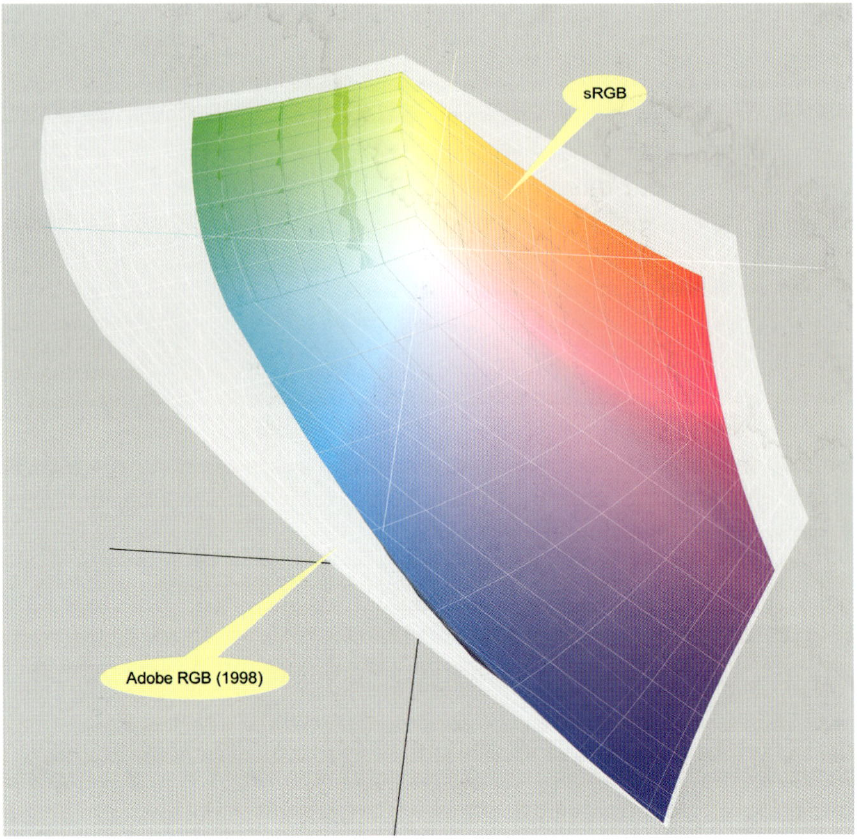


FIGURE 4.7: A graph showing the difference in gamut between a large color space (Adobe RGB [1998]) shown in gray, and a smaller one (sRGB) shown in color. The easiest way to interpret the graph is that colors become more saturated the farther they are from the intersection point of the axes.

explicitly calibrated or not. Keep in mind that "close" is not perfect, and some variation is to be expected.

As seen in the graph on this page (figure 4.7), sRGB is not a very large color space. It is quite possible that many of your images may contain colors that do not exist within its limited gamut. This may be acceptable for some uses such as for posting on the Internet, but when it comes to storing master image files, we want to preserve all colors, without having to compromise. In other words, we want our master image files (as opposed to web images) to use a color space large enough to accommodate every possible color, including very saturated ones (which are at the extreme edges of the color space).

Among the largest and most useful color spaces for this purpose are Adobe RGB (1998) and the even larger ProPhoto RGB, which was developed by Kodak specifically for the storage of photographic images. These color spaces are large enough to contain practically all colors generally found in photographs and they allow for great flexibility in editing and adjusting digital images without fear of losing color information to a limited gamut. Some high-end monitors can reproduce the entire Adobe RGB color space, but no device in existence today can display all colors supported in ProPhoto RGB. While both are good choices, having seen digital technology advance in leaps and bounds within my lifetime, I save my own files in ProPhoto RGB.

## Color Spaces and Bits

Bit-depth and color spaces are often mentioned in the context of the range of colors in an image or the color capabilities of a device. This can get confusing. For example, does a 16-bit image mapped to the (relatively small) sRGB color space contain more or fewer colors than the same image rendered in 8 bits but using the enormous ProPhoto RGB color space?

To put things in perspective, think of the color space as defining the boundaries of how saturated colors can be reproduced by a device, while the bit-depth provides the number of discrete grades within those boundaries.

Consider, for example, an image containing a large area of blue sky. The sky is never a uniform shade and contains subtle variations of blue in different areas. In this example, the color space represents the range from the least saturated to the most saturated shades of blue possible. This range remain the same whether the image is rendered in 8 or 16 bits. What does change is the number of possible shades or gradations within that range. In this example, a large stretch of blue sky likely will appear smoother in a 16-bit file than in an 8-bit file. If the 8-bit file does not have sufficient gradations, the transitions from one shade to the next will become more abrupt and the image will appear pixelated (figure 4.8).

FIGURE 4.8: In this example, both color strips have the same gamut (color space). However, the upper strip shows the smooth transitions possible in a high-bit file, while the lower strip shows the gradation limits of a low-bit file.

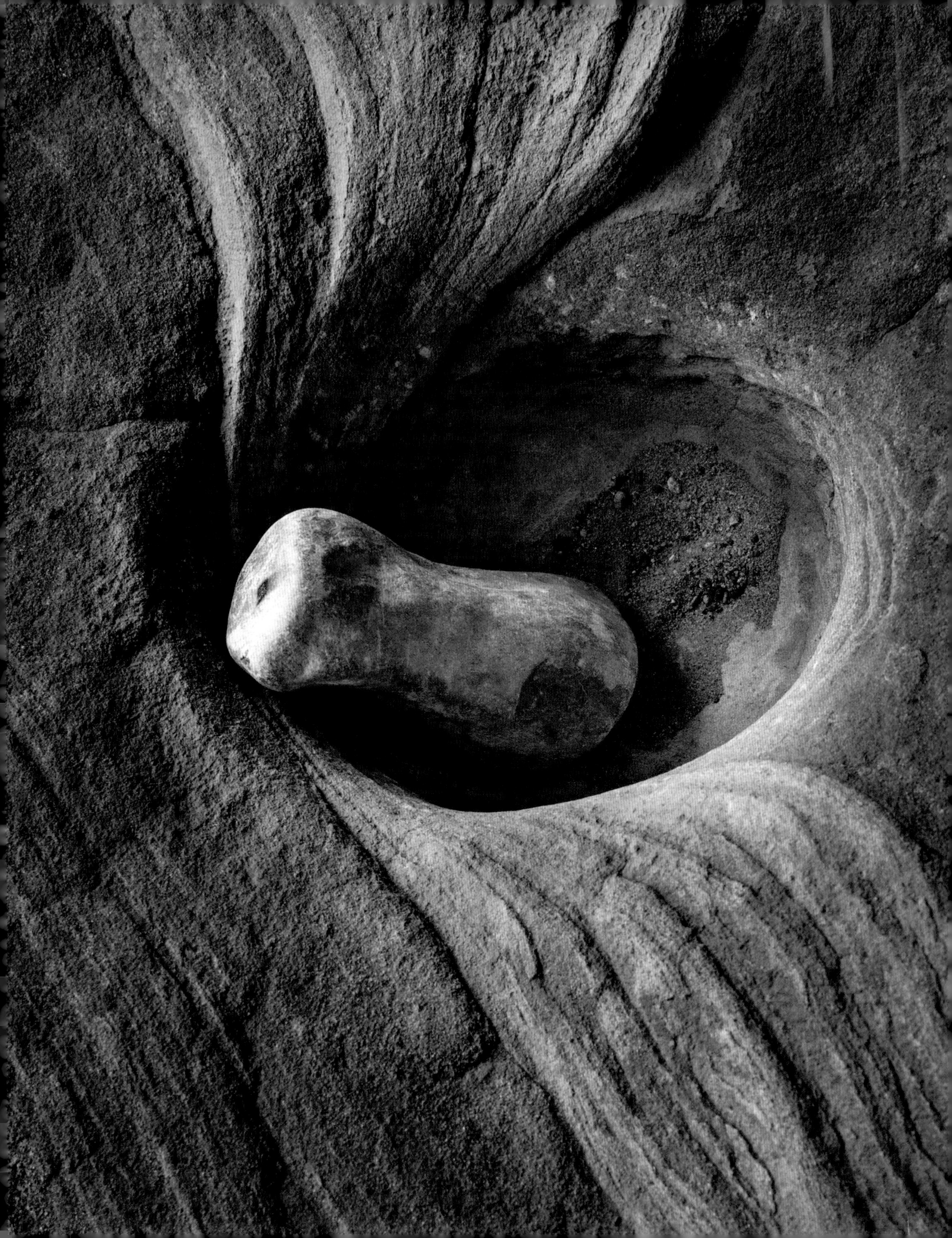

# Understanding Histograms

5

*Different levels of photography require different levels of understanding and skill. A "press the button, let George do the rest" photographer needs little or no technical knowledge of photography. A zone system photographer takes more responsibility. He visualizes before he presses the button, and afterwards calibrates for predictable print values.*

—MINOR WHITE

A histogram is a chart representing distribution of values. In digital cameras and most image-processing software, the most common histograms represent the distribution of brightness or luminance values in an image.

Histograms offer important information at a glance, which can be used to judge the effects of adjustments as we apply them, as well as to avoid undesired loss of image information.

Histograms are displayed along a horizontal scale representing degrees of brightness (or lightness), ranging from dark tones on the left to light tones

### Lightness, Brightness, and Luminosity Are Not the Same

Although linguistically synonymous, *lightness, brightness,* and *luminosity* are not the same. Brightness represents the measurable amount of light reflected off an object; lightness is a perception of how light/dark an object appears compared with other objects under similar light. For example, a white sheet of paper viewed outdoors on a bright sunny day is much brighter than the same sheet of paper when illuminated by a lightbulb, but its lightness—our perception of how light it is relative to other things in our field of view—remains about the same.

To confuse matters more, Photoshop sometimes uses the term *luminosity* to refer to the perception of how light/dark an object appears based on its color. For example, if a yellow object is situated next to a blue object and they reflect the same amount of light, they are equally bright, however, the yellow object will appear lighter than the blue one. The proper term for lightness adjusted for color perception is *luma,* but Adobe chose to use *luminosity* instead.

The important takeaway is not necessarily the accuracy of the terms, but the fact that when we encounter the terms *lightness* and *luminosity,* we should keep in mind they are values calculated to simulate human visual perception rather than values representing the actual amount of light measured by the camera's sensor.

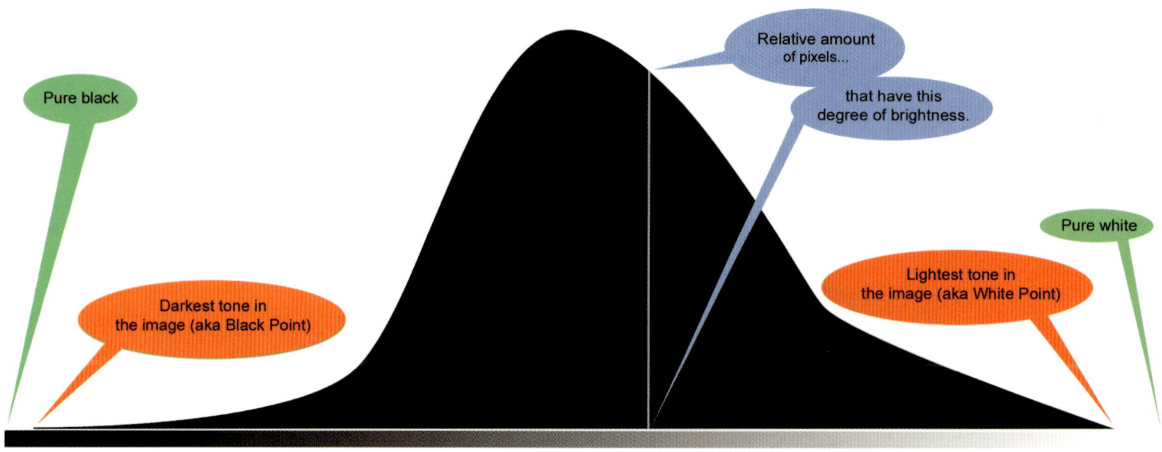


**FIGURE 5.1:** The horizontal axis of a histogram ranges from pure black to pure white; while the vertical axis represents the relative number of pixels at each lightness level. The rightmost tip of the histogram represents the value of the lightest pixel(s) in the image, and is called the *White Point*; the leftmost tip of the histogram represents the darkest pixel(s) in the image, and is called the *Black Point*.

on the right, with the extremes representing pure black and pure white (figure 5.1). The histogram's vertical axis represents the relative number of pixels in the image at each level.

By looking at a histogram we can learn a lot about an image. For example, a histogram biased toward the left side of the scale indicates that the image is predominantly comprised of dark tones, while a histogram biased toward the right side of the scale indicates that the image is predominantly made of light tones. If a histogram has a prominent "hump" at the center of the scale, it indicates that the image is comprised mostly of mid-tones (figure 5.2). And so on.

## The Histogram and Image Detail

Variation in lightness or color creates image details. If adjacent pixels in a given area have the same, or very close, lightness and color, that area will appear featureless. On the other hand, if pixel lightness values span a wide range, representing significant differences in lightness or color, the area will have visible detail.

The broader the range covered by the histogram, or a portion of the histogram, the more details will be found in the image or in that range of tones. For example, the histogram in figure 5.3 indicates a lot of details in the midtones (straddling the middle of the scale), but relatively little detail in the highlights (on the right side of the scale) and in the shadows (on the left side of the scale).

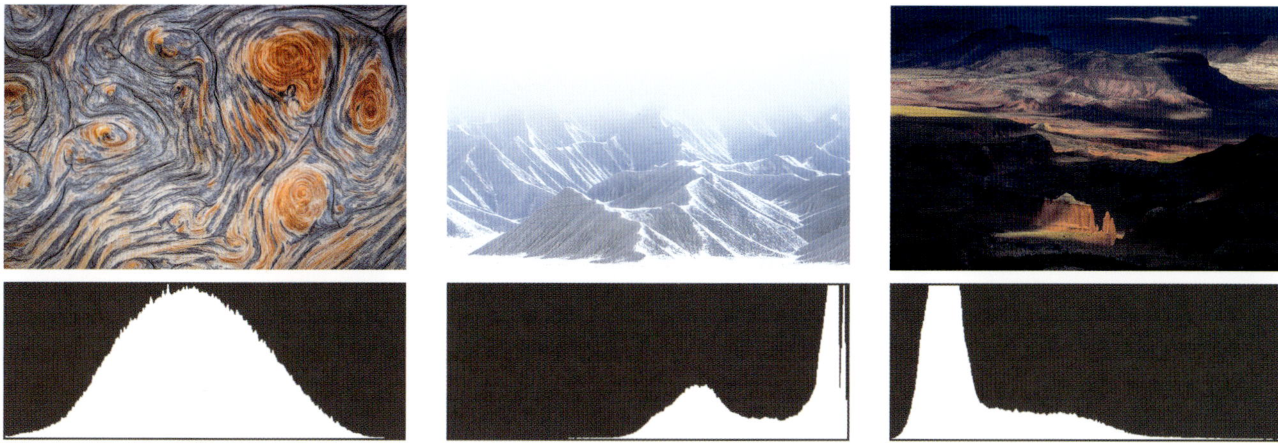

FIGURE 5.2 The image on the left is mostly comprised of mid-tones, reflected in the large "hump" in the center of the histogram. The image in the middle is comprised mostly of light tones, evidenced by the fact that most pixels are found on the right side of the histogram. The image on the right is mostly comprised of dark tones, and most pixels are on the left side of the histogram.

Don't be concerned if the histogram is too tall for the vertical values to fit (as seen in the middle and right histograms). Since the vertical axis represents the relative number of pixels at a given lightness value, it's there to give us a sense of the distribution, rather than an exact representation. If there are very few pixels at some levels, Photoshop might (literally) go over the top to ensure that the thinner parts of the histogram are still represented, if only by a single pixel.

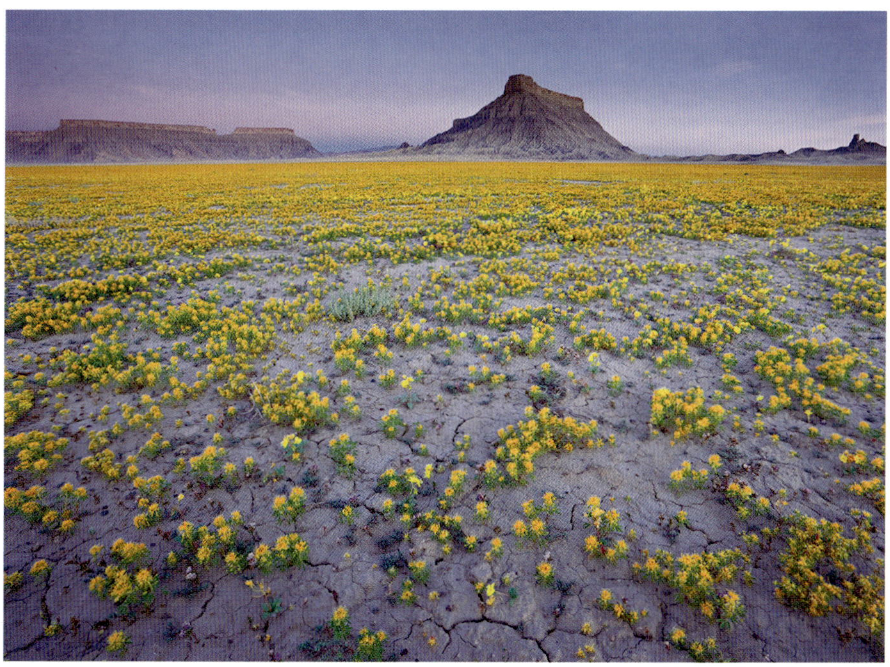

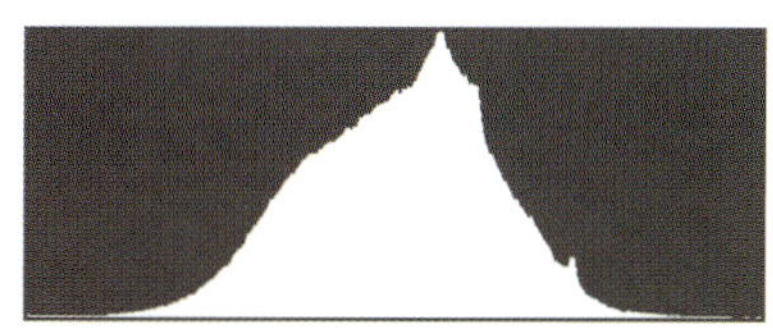

FIGURE 5.3: In this histogram of the image at left, notice that most pixels in the image have lightness values around the center of the histogram, and relatively few in the extreme right (highlights) and the extreme left (shadows), which is to be expected in the soft pre-dawn light.

Lack of detail in the highlights is typical of images that are comprised mainly of light tones (known as high-key images) and/or images with skies, as the sky is generally light and featureless.

## Clipping

The term *clipping* is used to describe the histogram abruptly ending at one or both ends of the scale, indicating loss of detail. A histogram clipped on the left side of the scale indicates that some shadow details that would otherwise be represented by the left "tail" of the histogram were all mapped to pure black. A histogram clipped on the right indicates that highlight details that would otherwise be represented by the right "tail" of the histogram were all mapped to pure white. In cases of images containing very high contrast (very dark shadows and very light highlights), it is possible that clipping may occur on both ends (figure 5.4).

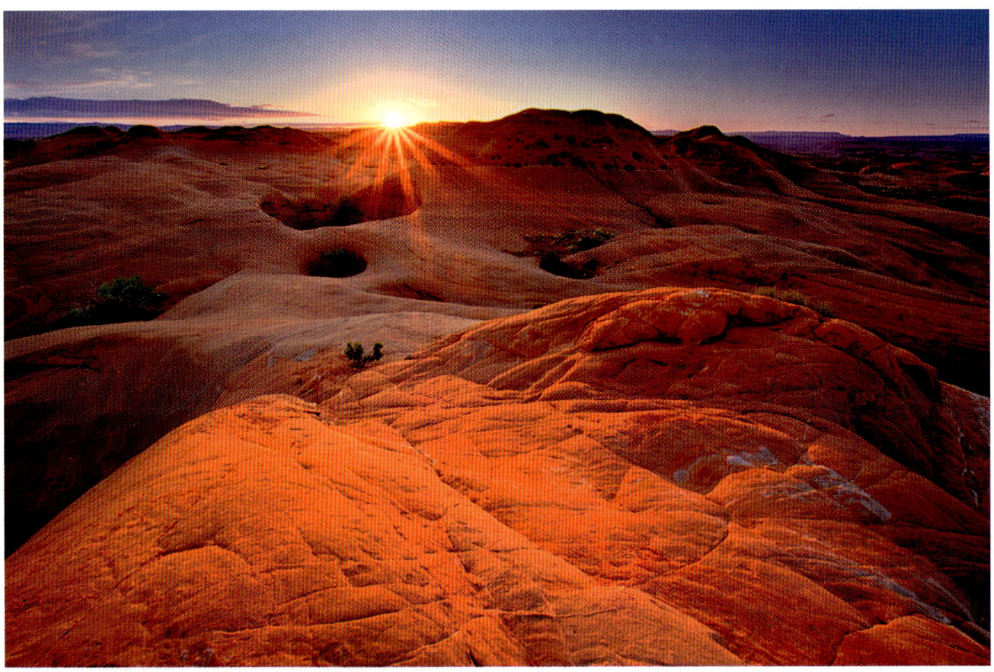

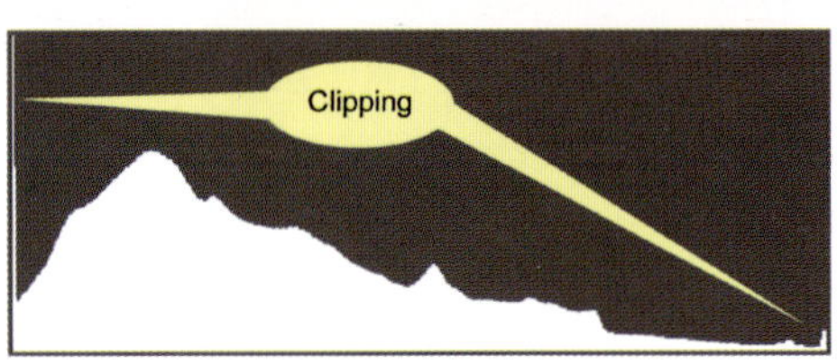


**Figure 5.4:** This histogram shows clipping on both ends. The bright highlights in the sun, and the deep shadows in the crevices exceeded the sensor's capacity to detect fine detail in those areas. These types of clipping are sometimes referred to as *blocked shadows* and *blown highlights*.

## Histogram Types

Photoshop offers a variety of histograms, not all of which correspond to the histograms you may be familiar with from your camera. Each histogram type is useful for some purposes, but not all are equally useful for processing photographic images.

If the histogram panel is not visible in your Photoshop workspace, open the *Window* menu and click on *Histogram*. You may now select any of the available histogram types from the *Channel* menu.

**Refreshing the Histogram**

Refreshing histograms requires a bit of computation and can therefore be taxing on your computer's CPU. To optimize performance, Photoshop calculates the histogram based on cached data, rather than keeping it updated in real time. If Photoshop detects that certain operations may have altered the histogram before the cache was refreshed, it will display a small warning sign next to it. If you wish to force Photoshop to refresh its cache and recalculate the histogram, you may click either the warning sign, or the *Refresh* button (figure 5.5).

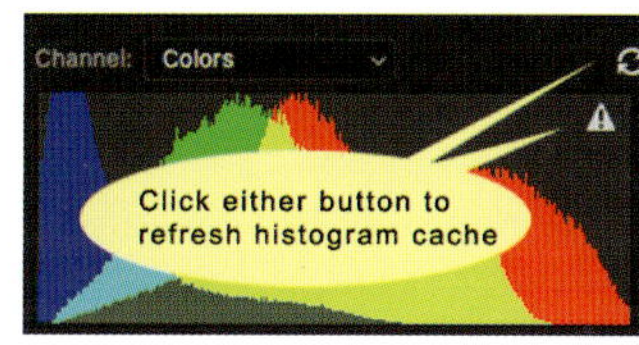


FIGURE 5.5: The histogram may be refreshed using either of the buttons shown here.

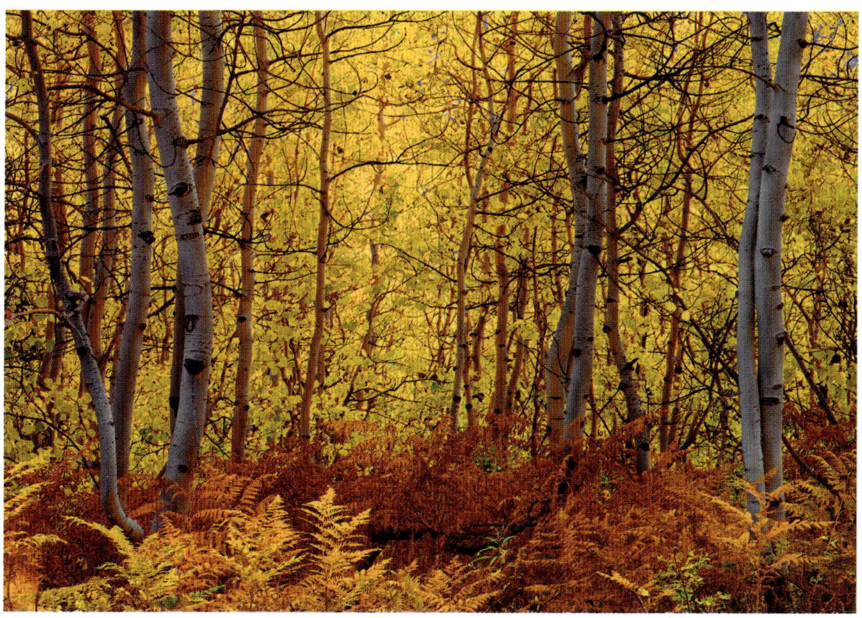

FIGURE 5.6: This autumn scene is useful in demonstrating the differences among various histogram types.

To illustrate the differences among the various histogram types, let's look at different histograms, all calculated based on the image in figure 5.6. For convenience, let's assume the horizontal (bottom) axis ranges in value from 0 (pure black) on the left to 255 (maximum value for the parameter represented) on the right, same as the standard RGB notation.

## Colors and Red/Green/Blue Histograms

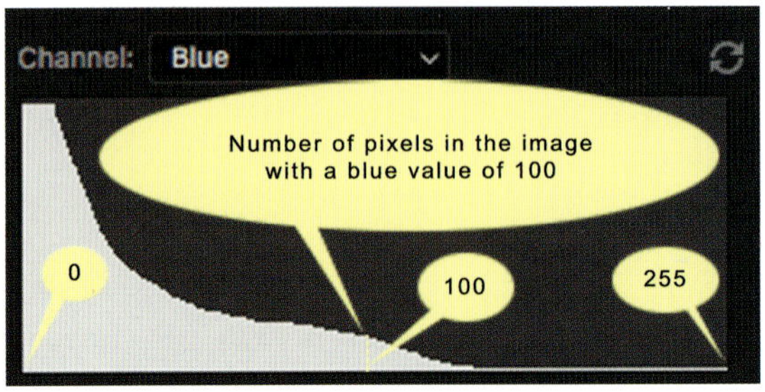


FIGURE 5.7: This histogram shows the distribution of values in the blue channel across the image. Note that because our sample image includes very little blue and a lot of yellow (yellow pixels are made mostly of green and red, and have little or no blue), the blue channel is clipped on the left side as many (yellow) pixels have a blue value of 0.

The *Red*, *Green*, and *Blue* histograms only show the distribution of values in one color channel. The vertical axis shows the relative number of pixels in the image that have a value corresponding to the position on the histogram (figure 5.7).

Individual channel histograms are generally of limited value, especially in color photography. As evident in this example, the image has good details throughout even though individual color channels show clipping. This is because in a color image, detail is rendered by a combination of all three color channels.

Individual color channel histograms may be useful if our intent is to convert an image to black-and-white, as I explain later in the book.

Much more useful than individual color channels histograms is the *Colors* histogram, which juxtaposes the histograms for *all* color channels together (figure 5.8). In the *Colors* histogram, each individual channel (red, green, and blue) is shown in its respective color. Where multiple channels share the same lightness value, the following colors are used:

- **Gray:** all channels (red, green, and blue) have pixels of this lightness level
- **Yellow:** the red and green channels have pixels of this lightness level, but not the blue channel (red + green = yellow)
- **Magenta:** the red and blue channels have pixels in this lightness level, but not the green channel (red + blue = magenta)
- **Cyan:** the green and blue channels have pixels in this lightness level, but not the red channel (green + blue = cyan)

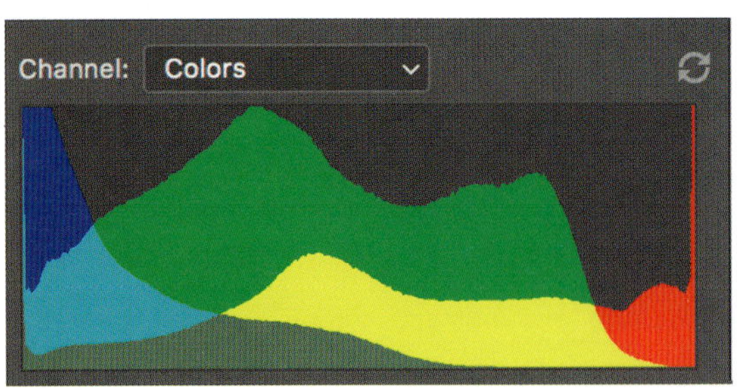


FIGURE 5.8: A *Colors* histogram.

Some photographers suggest that clipping should always be avoided, but I disagree. Even though the *Colors* histogram for our image shows clipping in every channel, I can tell that it still has proper color and detail throughout. Here is how I know this based on matching the histogram with qualities of the image:

All channels are clipped on the left, showing that some portions of the image are pure black and have no details. By looking at the image, I can tell that these black areas include such elements as the thin black branches and portions of the knots in the tree trunks. This is OK. I want these elements to be as black as they can be and clipping in this case does not indicate loss of important shadow detail.

Only the red channel is clipped on the right, which is also OK since the extreme highlights in the image are the yellow leaves and these still have good detail in the green channel (yellow = red + green).

This is an extreme example, where I wanted very deep blacks and very saturated yellows. As I processed the image, monitoring the *Colors* histogram helped me judge how far I could push the blacks and yellows without the risk of losing important details.

The *Colors* histogram provides the most—and most useful—information for making processing decisions, and it is the one I recommend keeping visible in your workspace by default. I explain how to configure the workspace later in the book.

## RGB Histogram

An *RGB* histogram aggregates (adds up) the red, green, and blue values for each pixel (figure 5.9).

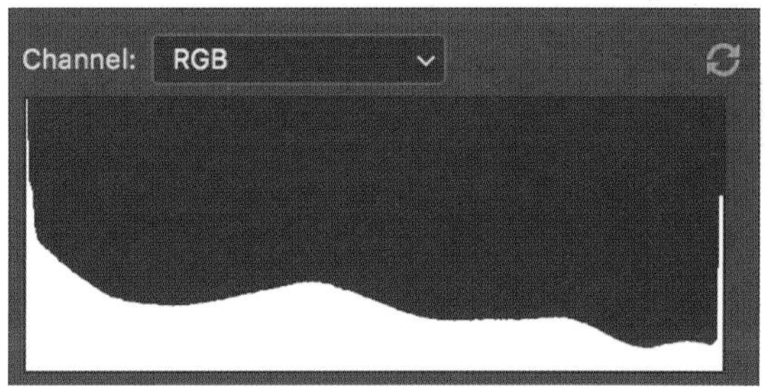


FIGURE 5.9: An *RGB* histogram.

In processing photographic images, I find this type of histogram to be of limited use. For example, in this case it shows clipping on both sides of the histogram, but it doesn't tell me which channels are clipped (which the *Colors* histogram does), making it impossible for me to determine whether the clipping is OK for a given image, or something to be addressed.

Like other features in Photoshop, this type of histogram is a remnant of an older version that had since been surpassed by a better tool but has been kept for legacy users whose workflow may require it.

## Luminosity Histogram

The *Luminosity* histogram offered by Photoshop is similar in function to the default histogram available in most digital cameras. It shows the distribution of degrees of lightness (tones) calculated by applying a formula that simulates the lightness perception of the human eye.

Our perception of lightness varies by color. Most of it (just short of 70%) comes from the green value, followed by the red value (just short of 25%) and the blue value (around 7%). Photoshop uses a formula simulating human perception to assign different weights to the value of each color channel and to determine its lightness level.

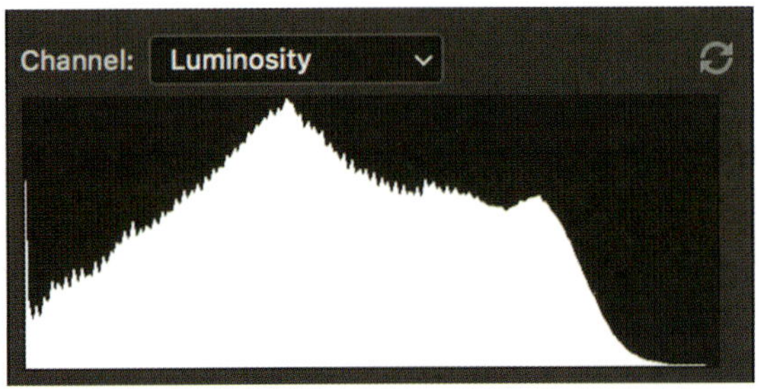


FIGURE 5.10: A *Luminosity* histogram.

The *Luminosity* histogram for our image (figure 5.10) shows the clipping on the left side (blacks), which is to be expected since we have black elements in the image. But, unlike the *RGB* histogram, it is not clipped on the right (highlights). This is because the lightest elements in our image are bright yellow—a combination of green and red—and even though the red channel is clipped, the green is not. This is a truer representation of whether clipping resulted in loss of highlight detail (which is not the case in our image).

While useful for exposure decisions (explaining why they are offered in most digital cameras), *Luminosity* histograms do not tell the whole story. They are useful for cases such as this, to confirm that, indeed, there is no loss of highlight detail, but when processing I still prefer to use the *Colors* histogram so I can see whether individual channels are clipped and then I can decide for myself whether or not such clipping is a problem.

**Clipping in All Channels**

Clipping of all channels on the left side of the histogram (shadows/blacks) is not necessarily a bad thing. There may be cases when we might want to use the deepest blacks possible for elements that are, in fact, black. On the other hand, clipping of all channels on the right side (highlights/whites) is generally not desirable, even if we have pure-white elements. The reason is that if we print the image on an inkjet printer, the printer may not apply any ink at all to these pure-white areas. When such a print is viewed from certain angles, it will be evident that the print is not evenly coated in ink. This is called a *gloss differential*. If your image contains light white elements, I suggest processing the image so these elements are just a bit darker than pure white. The difference in appearance will be negligible, but the risk of a gloss differential will be mitigated. I explain this in more detail in chapter 14.

## Combed Histograms

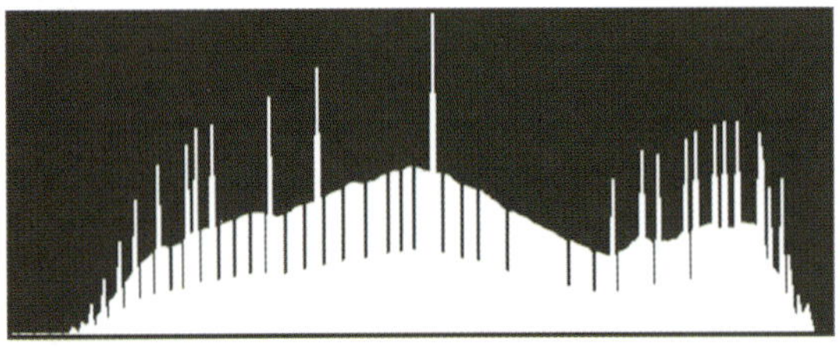

FIGURE 5.11: A combed histogram.

Every so often, when editing an image, you may notice that the histogram displayed in Photoshop has gaps in it (figure 5.11). This effect is known as *combing* (since the histogram appears to have teeth like a comb).

Combed histograms occur when you apply a certain adjustment to the image that requires Photoshop to map pixels to lightness values that did not exist before the adjustment. For example, increasing contrast makes light tones lighter and dark tones darker, creating the need for a new gradation of tones between those light and dark areas, and potentially for values that did not exist prior to the adjustment.

While there is absolutely no reason to be alarmed by combed histograms, it is useful to consider the size of the gaps as an indication of how many values Photoshop had to manufacture to perform a certain operation. If these gaps are large (usually if the original image had a narrow histogram), it is recommended to study the affected area (or the entire image) at full magnification to make sure the change didn't introduce undesirable artifacts, such as pixelation (I explain this and other artifacts in chapter 6).

The need to manufacture gradation values in some cases is another good reason to work in 16-bit color, which gives us a wider range of values to map pixels to. If working in 8-bit color, and more gradations need to be created for a smooth appearance than are possible within the 8-bit range, pixelation and banding will occur.

## EXERCISE 2

1. Explain, based on the qualities of the associated image, why the *Luminosity* histogram in figure 5.12 looks the way it does (two large spikes and a deep trough in the middle).
2. If the histogram for an image shows clipping of all color channels on the left side, is this necessarily a bad thing?
3. If the *RGB* histogram for an image shows clipping on the right side, but the *Luminosity* histogram for the same image does not, how would you explain it?
4. If the *Colors* histogram shows yellow clipping on the left, which channels are clipped? Does it necessarily imply that you lost important details?

*See Appendix for answer key.*

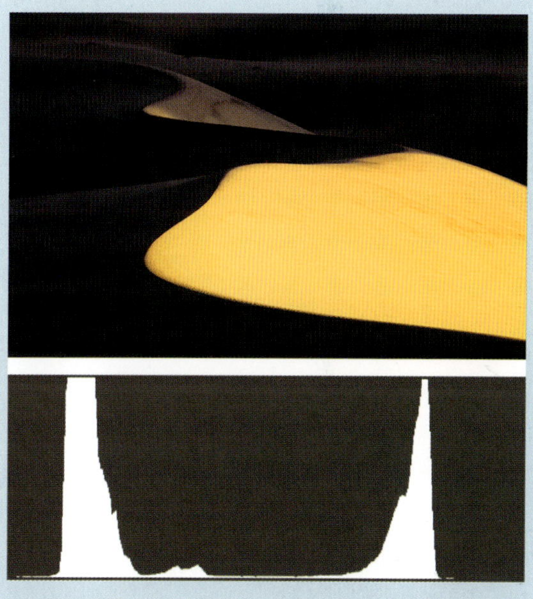

FIGURE 5.12: A *Luminosity* histogram for an image with very high contrast.

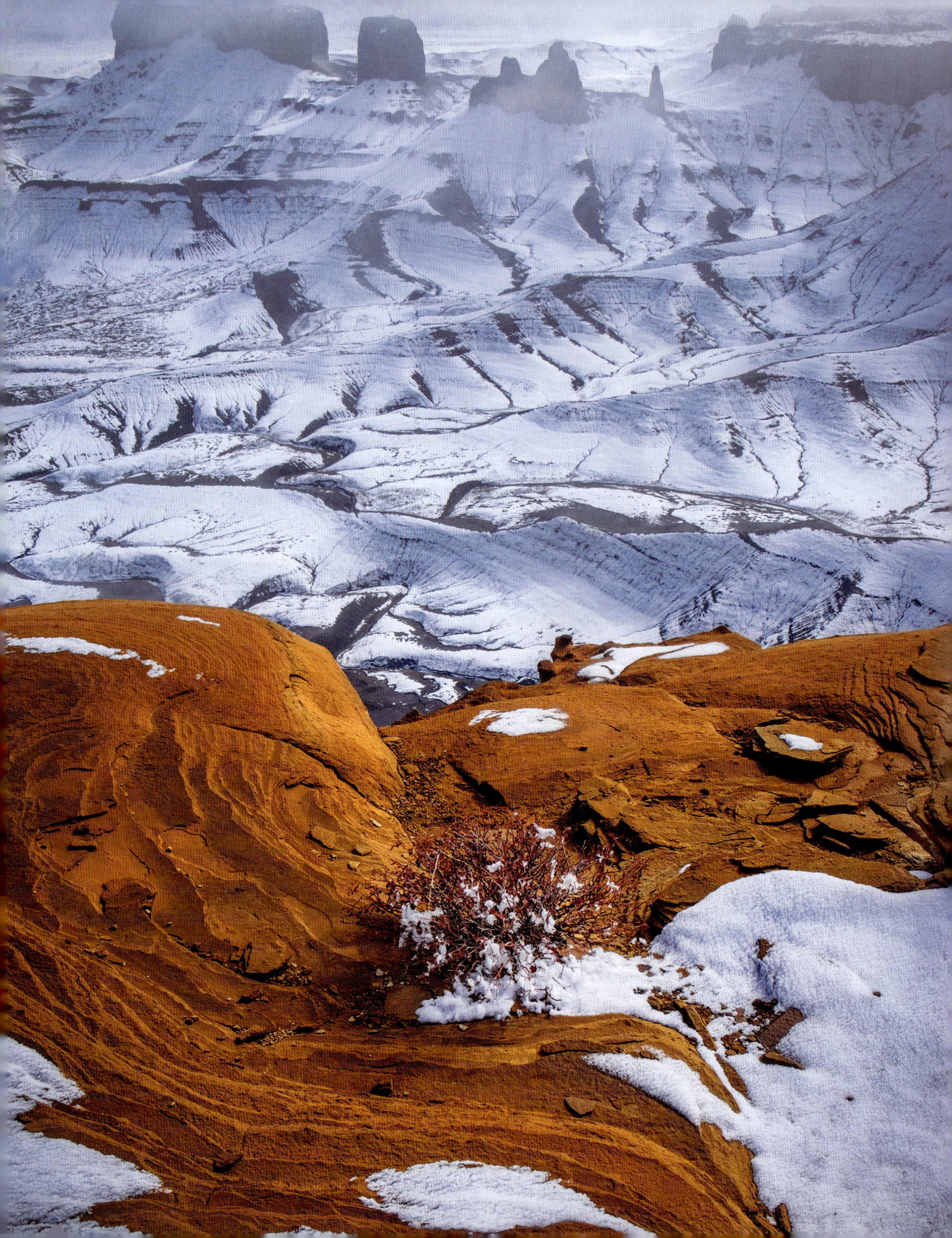

# 6

# Image Analysis

> *Making art provides uncomfortably accurate feedback about the gap that inevitably exists between what you intended to do, and what you did. In fact, if artmaking did not tell you (the maker) so enormously much about yourself, then making art that matters to you would be impossible.*
>
> —DAVID BAYLES AND TED ORLAND

Our goal in processing our work is to transform the data captured by the camera into our desired visualized outcome. Analysis is the process of identifying gaps between the image as it appears at a particular point in time and the visualized image—the way we want it to appear after we process it; and deciding what step(s) to take to close those gaps. Once no gaps remain and the image appears on the screen as the visualized image in our mind, we'll consider it finished.

As we identify gaps, we'll match them with specific actions that will close—or mitigate—them. Those familiar with the discipline of Project Management may know this approach as *gap analysis*.

Working in this fashion, we will not always follow the same succession of steps for every image, but rather will tailor our approach to the unique characteristics of each individual image and to our visualized goal for it.

Unless the image as-captured already appears very close to the visualized outcome, we should not try to identify all gaps and all mitigation techniques in advance, but rather break the work into bite-size chunks: identify a selection of gaps (or one big gap) to address in the next round of processing and then match those gaps with the best means of mitigating them before moving on to the next round.

This method is known as an iterative approach—bringing the image progressively closer to the visualized outcome by repeating a set of steps to close a gap or a selection of gaps in each round. I elaborate on the advantages of this approach in the next chapter.

Effective visualization is critical in the analysis phase. Having a well-visualized outcome in mind enables us to compare it with our work-in-progress, both in the field and when processing. For example, if we visualize our image in black-and-white while in the field, we may also consider our conversion approach at that time, even before making an exposure. Similarly, if we note that some parts of the scene are lighter or darker than we would wish them to ultimately appear, we may note such gaps as "dodge (lighten) shadow under tree" or "burn (darken) highlights in upper-right corner." If you are concerned that you may not remember these gaps later, keep a notepad with you to help remind yourself of them when it's time to process your images. In recent years, I have begun keeping such notes on my smart phone and then I synchronize them to my processing workstation.

### Don't Leave Creative Decisions to the Camera's "Brain"

There are some who maintain a bewildering allegiance to images described as being "straight out of the camera." In fact, to accept images as rendered by the camera's computer is simply to accept someone else's idea of what those images should look like.

A camera's built-in software is designed by engineers who, even when attempting to render the outcome as close to what a random person may have seen (what some who are even more naïve may consider "objective reality"), must make subjective decisions about such things as how to render color and contrast, how to factor in such parameters as color temperature, and what corrections to apply. This is why different cameras aimed at the same subject will rarely produce identical images.

More important, such images simply outsource processing decisions to a computerized brain, rather than the photographer's brain. While computer algorithms may indeed be very good and might produce pleasing results, they are not creative or expressive. To rely on these algorithms is, at best, a labor-saving strategy, but it fails to be a strategy for making expressive art. Expressive art is so named because it expresses something subjective—thoughts and feelings—and as such, it can only be created by human beings who actually have thoughts and feelings, rather than by computer software, which does not.

When considering the image on a larger screen (as opposed to the limited LCD screen on our camera), whether during RAW conversion or when working in Photoshop, we may more easily identify gaps such as "clone out dust spots in the sky" or "reduce noise in shadow under tree" or "change hue in foliage from lime green to forest green."

### Yes, You Are Allowed to Change Your Mind

Don't allow your visualization to become prescriptive. While you were in the field, you may have had an idea of how you wanted the final image to appear, but that doesn't mean it is necessarily the best approach to take. Creative epiphanies may happen at any time, and it is entirely possible that, when looking at the image on your (large, color-calibrated) computer screen, you may realize there is a more effective way (or ways) to process the image. If that happens, update the visualized image in your mind and make the necessary changes to your approach. Tell the better story (or both stories).

To be effective, the gaps we identify should readily match up with processing actions for mitigating them. In other words, they need to be specific and actionable. A good gap may be "darken sky" or "clone out tripod foot in the bottom-left corner." However, gaps identified as "not sure I like that shade of blue in the sky" or "flowers are too close to the edge of the frame" are not very helpful since they do not specifically suggest what needs to be done to address them.

Some gaps may prove impossible to mitigate, so if we encounter one or more gaps such as poor focus or overexposed highlights, and we determine that the visualized image is impossible to accomplish using the captured data, it may be better to move on to another image.

At times, and especially early in the processing cycle, the next round of gaps and mitigations may be obvious and easy to identify. But, as major gaps are addressed, the remaining ones may be subtler or more difficult to correct. The more time you spend looking at, and thinking about, the image as it appears on your screen and comparing it with the visualized image, the more likely you are to notice additional gaps, and the better your results will be. Don't rush.

It is also likely that early in the process the gap between the current state and the visualized outcome will be large enough that it becomes difficult to memorize all the obvious gaps, or to decide which to address first. The best approach in this case is described as "eating an elephant." How do you eat an elephant? One bite at a time. Start chipping away until you have a better idea of what to do next (even if it may require going a few steps back). In time, you will develop an instinct for what operations are best done in what order.

It is also likely that, as you take your first steps with Photoshop, you may encounter gaps that you do not know how to correct. These can provide excellent learning opportunities. Do some research, ask questions on Internet forums, and expand your skills and toolset. If you are unable to find answers, I suggest setting the image aside. In the course of learning, I recommend maintaining a written list of gaps as you find them and then prioritizing them before applying the required actions. The reason is that some adjustments may override others or may make others more difficult to correct if they are not applied in a particular order. In time, as your skills improve, you may wish to do an "archive dive" and rediscover images you gave up on earlier but now have the knowledge to process.

Make a clear distinction between *local* gaps that affect only portions of the image (like cloning out dust spots or changing the contrast in just one part of the image) and *global* gaps that may affect all pixels in the image (like converting to black-and-white, increasing contrast, or correcting a color cast across the entire image). This distinction will help you pick the right tool for the job.

Following is a review of some common gaps to help in your initial analysis.

## Defect Gaps

Defects are unwanted—and usually unexpected—problems that may result from physical limitations of the camera or lens, such as depth of field limitations or dust on the sensor; from flaws inherent in the subject or the scene, such as blemishes on a person's skin or unavoidable distractions; or from human error, such as lack of attention to unwanted elements protruding into the frame or poor camera technique.

Defects are usually the first things we want to correct since their presence, other than being unsightly, may also affect other adjustments down the line. Also, if they are very problematic and impossible to mitigate, we may decide to discard the image before investing a significant amount of work in processing it.

Some defects are best corrected in the RAW conversion phase, although most are better handled after the image has been converted from RAW using the more precise tools Photoshop offers.

When it comes to defects, the adage "an ounce of prevention is worth a pound of cure" holds true: many such defects can be avoided completely with proper technique in the field.

### Capture-Related Defects

Following are some defects that may be introduced in the capture phase, whether because of technical limitations of the camera and/or lens or due to human error. I recommend applying the best possible technique, as well as close inspection of the captured image before leaving the scene. While some of these defects may be unavoidable and/or easy to correct in processing, others may render an image completely unusable.

- **Sensor Dust Spots:** Dust spots are common and generally easy to fix. They come in a variety of sizes and shapes and, in most cases, can be removed using a cloning or healing tool (either in the RAW converter or post-conversion).

  While some spots may be obvious, especially in relatively featureless areas, such as skies or bodies of water, others may be small and difficult to see at a casual glance. I recommend carefully scrolling around all parts of the image at 100% magnification to identify and

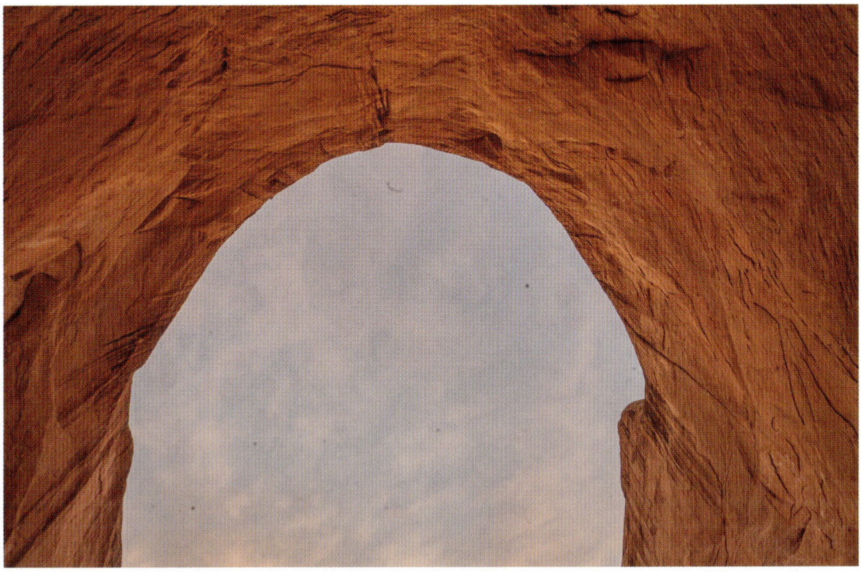

FIGURE 6.1: Dust spots in a portion of the sky in an image captured during a multi-day backpacking trip in the desert. Working in the landscape, and especially in deserts, makes dust spots practically inevitable.

remove all dust spots before proceeding to other adjustments (figure 6.1).

I also recommend having your sensor professionally cleaned at regular intervals. Changing lenses exposes the sensor, and dust will inevitably find its way in, but frequent cleanings will help keep it in check.

- **Lens Flare:** Flare is usually caused by reflections between glass elements inside the lens or by specks of dust on the lens's front element or filter. Lenses of poor quality and/or lenses with many internal elements are more prone to flare, although flare may occur with almost any lens under some conditions (figure 6.2).

  Flare is one of the hardest defects to correct. If the impacted area is large enough that it cannot easily be removed, your only remaining choices may be to completely crop the impacted area, to accept flare as part of the image, or to give up on the image altogether.

  Some measures, such as sampling and de-saturating the specific colors that make up the flare, can reduce the flare's appearance and make it less distracting, but they are unlikely to remove it completely. Flare is best identified and addressed in the field by examining the image carefully on the camera's screen. To prevent flare, make sure to clean your lenses and filters regularly and, when composing an image looking toward bright light sources (such as the sun or an area close to it), make sure to shade the front element of your lens while being careful not to let the shade intrude into the frame.

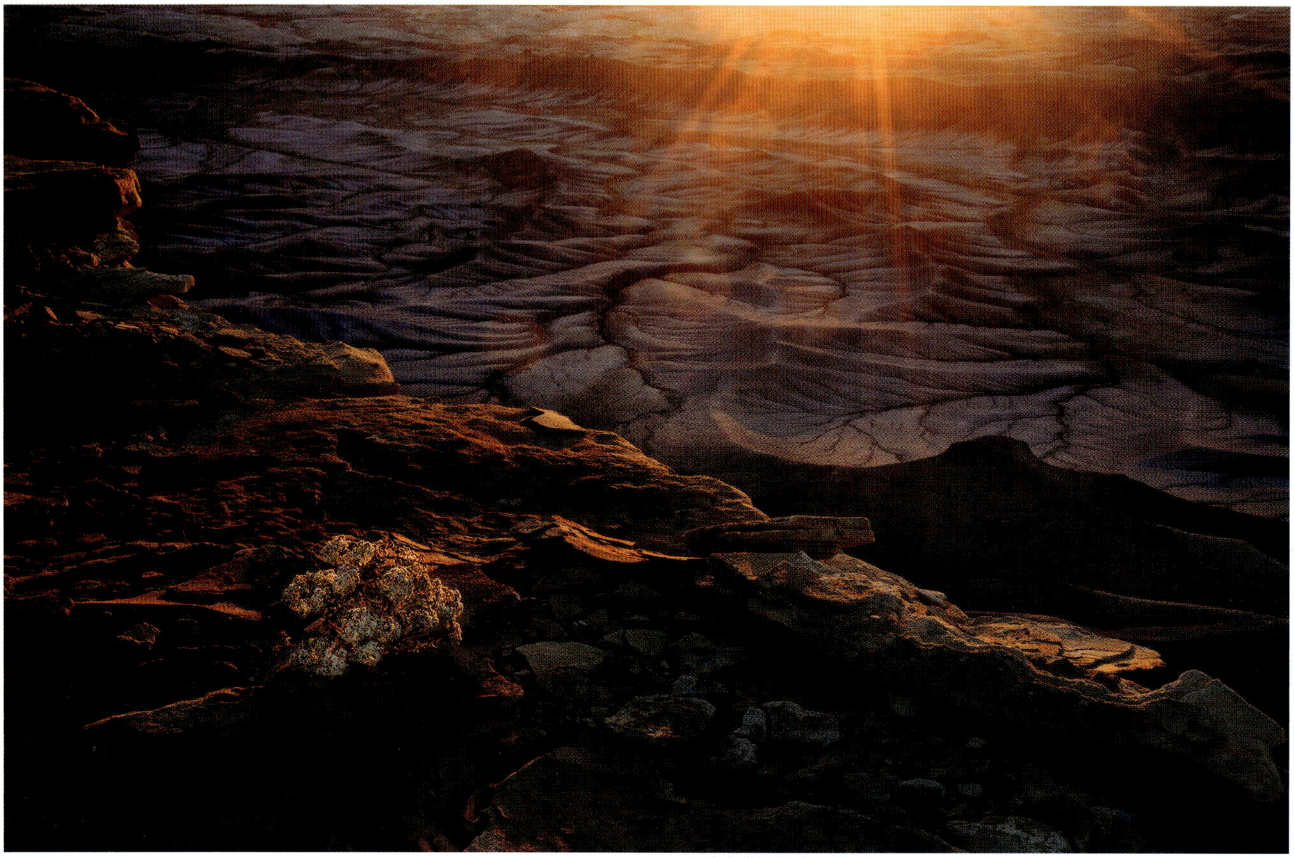

FIGURE 6.2: Try as I might, I could not capture this image without flare, as my camera was aimed directly toward the rising sun. In processing the image, I first attempted to eliminate the round flare spots by cloning them, but could not achieve a satisfactory result. Rather than discard the image, I decided to leave the flare spots intact as the image still accomplished my desired mood.

- **Distractions:** The enemy of good composition, distractions come in many forms: a contrail in the sky, an overly bright element drawing attention from your main subject, a pesky branch, or even the tip of a tripod leg peeking into the frame.

  While usually unintentional, there are also times when we may knowingly include distracting elements for lack of choice, with the intent of removing them later.

  Ideally, distractions should be identified and kept out of the frame while still in the field, but every so often they do sneak into images. Photoshop offers powerful cloning and healing tools that in many cases can eliminate distractions. However, in those cases where the tools fall short, your choice may come down to accepting the distraction or giving up on the image—or, if possible, returning to the scene and recapturing the image.

- **Under- and Over-Exposure:** In many cases, even if exposure is accurate overall, some portions of the image, such as extreme highlights or deep shadows, may be under- or over-exposed, resulting in loss of detail in those areas. Examples may include small bits of sky among tree branches, specular highlights, and areas of deep shadow in an otherwise brightly lit scene.

Although, in some cases, recovery of highlight and shadow details is possible, it is risky to assume this will be the case in every situation. If you suspect that some areas in your image may be overexposed or underexposed to a point of having no details, I recommend bracketing exposures while still in the field. If needed, you can then blend details from these bracketed exposures to fill in where they are lacking. There is no cost to capturing a couple of extra files, and it is a good insurance policy.

I also recommend bracketing exposures in scenes containing deep shadow areas even if the histogram suggests they are properly exposed, as such areas are more prone to noise and you may want to recover cleaner details from an over-exposed frame.

- **Motion Blur:** Wind, water, and other factors may induce motion in plants or other elements where sharpness is desirable, making them appear blurry. Hand-held captures are also prone to undesirable blur because of camera shake.

  Examining the captured image at high magnification on the camera's screen may reveal where such blurring occurs (which may be on select elements or across the entire image).

  Mitigation strategies include mounting the camera on a sturdy tripod, waiting for a lull in the wind, increasing sensitivity (ISO), and using the largest possible aperture that still yields sharp details where needed.

  In cases where only some elements appear blurry but others (mountains, trees, or other solid objects) are not, it may be better to capture one low-ISO image and one high-ISO image, and later blend the sharp details from both exposures into the final image.

  If missed in the field, Photoshop's *Shake Reduction* filter may be used to alleviate the appearance of blur, or at least reduce it to a point where the image can still be used for such purposes as Internet presentation, projected slide shows, or small prints.

- **Improper Focus:** Some images may be deliberately captured out of focus for creative blurring. If, however, the image is intended to appear sharp but suffers from poor focus, there is little you can do to fix it.

  In the best of cases, if focus is just slightly off, the image may still be usable for Internet presentation, projected slide shows, or small prints. However, poorly focused images will not yield acceptable prints past a certain size.

It is extremely important to verify proper focus while still in the field where focus corrections can be made. Review the image on the camera's screen at the highest magnification available before leaving the scene.

- **Lacking Depth-of-Field:** Like focus, there are times when limited depth-of-field is desirable to separate sharp (in-focus) objects from their surroundings, and we may want to deliberately blur extraneous background detail.

  The optical blurring of out-of-focus areas is called *bokeh*, and when properly used, the effect is prized for such things as portrait and close-up photography. However, if our intent is to maintain sharp focus throughout the frame, insufficient depth of field is a defect that is impossible to correct after the fact. Make sure to use the appropriate aperture setting and capture multiple exposures at varying focus distances that can later be blended, if needed.

- **Chromatic Aberration:** Chromatic aberration (also referred to as *fringing*) may occur along high contrast edges where one area abuts a significantly darker/lighter area (figure 6.3). Chromatic aberration manifests in vibrant red, cyan, magenta, or green fringes.

  A common cause of chromatic aberration is the lens not accurately focusing all colors on the same plane. Low-quality consumer grade lenses are more prone to it than high-end models, but there are exceptions to the rule on both ends.

  Even if not immediately apparent, you should always examine high contrast edges at high magnification to look for these fringes. If not corrected early, they may become more visible with subsequent adjustments and will become more difficult to correct if not addressed early.

  The most common type of chromatic aberration is best corrected in the RAW converter since the software can more effectively align color data found in the RAW file to eliminate the undesirable fringes. Once converted from RAW, correction is more difficult. If using ACR or Lightroom to convert your RAW files, be sure to check the *Correct Chromatic Aberration* box found under *Lens Corrections*. I recommend doing so for every image; I have yet to see any cases where this is a detriment.

- **Noise:** Digital noise occurs because of sampling (measuring) errors, meaning that the sensor did not accurately measure the amount of

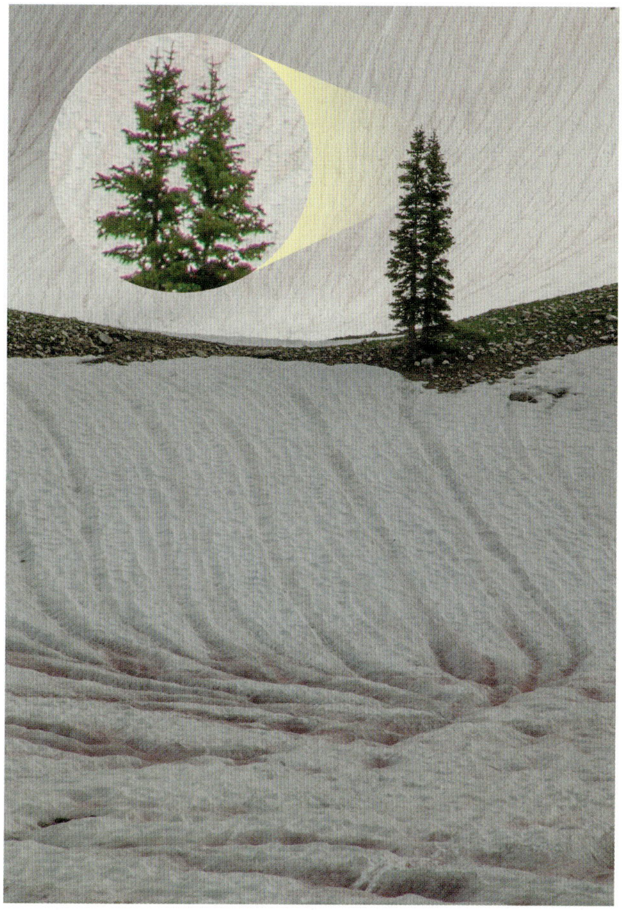

**Figure 6.3:** Chromatic aberration (aka, fringing).

light at a given location, making it appear slightly different from its surroundings. Very dark conditions such as deep shadows and night exposures are especially prone to sampling errors for various reasons: there is less light to be sampled, heat and electronic interference affect measuring accuracy during long exposures, and values on the dark end of the tone scale have less gradation than those on the light side. Readers may be interested in researching the Expose-To-The-Right (ETTR) rule for more information that is relevant to image capture.

In digital photography, we distinguish between two types of noise: *chroma noise* resulting from errors in measuring color, which appears as colorful specks; and *luminance noise* resulting from errors in measuring brightness, which appears as dots or small areas of differing lightness where smooth transitions are expected (figure 6.4).

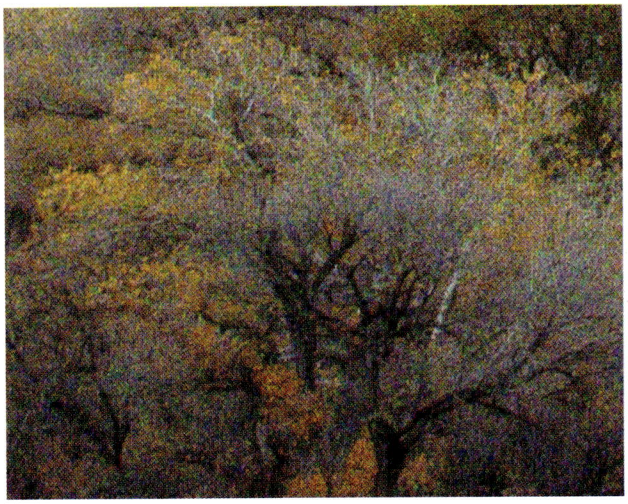

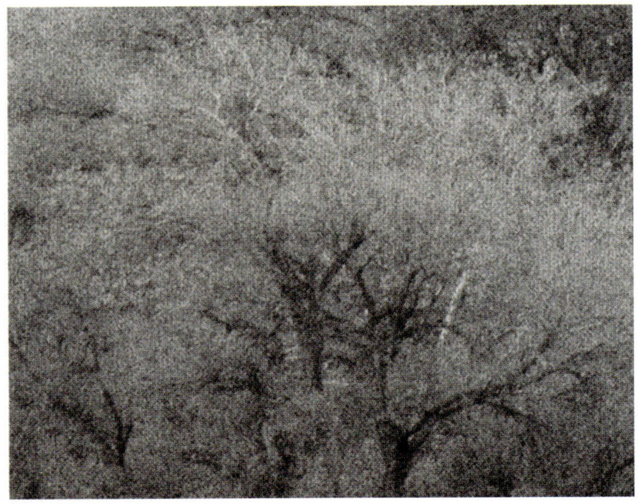

**FIGURE 6.4:** Examples of Chroma Noise (*left*) and Luminance Noise (*right*). When processing this image, both types will need to be corrected.

The best way to deal with noise is to avoid, or reduce, it when capturing the image: use the lowest ISO setting appropriate for the scene, avoid under-exposing, remove unnecessary filters (e.g., a polarizer) from the lens if its effect is not needed, and apply the ETTR rule. Noise reduction can be applied in ACR/Lightroom when converting from RAW, or from within Photoshop. Both offer separate settings for correcting chroma noise (referred to as *Color noise*) and luminance noise (referred to as *Detail*). I recommend doing it in Photoshop since it has better tools to apply noise reduction in various amounts to specific parts of the image, rather than applying the same settings to the entire image.

Noise reduction should always be applied with caution since it is difficult for the software to distinguish between noise and image detail. When applied carelessly, noise reduction may also unintentionally "clean up" image detail.

- **Vignetting:** Vignetting is the visible darkening of the corners and edges of an image. The term originates from the old practice of decorating the corners of books and documents with ornamental illustrations of vines.

  Vignetting can sometimes be caused by light falloff, which occurs when a lens's image circle is not large enough to cover the sensor area, therefore the effect is more pronounced at large aperture settings. In some cases, vignetting may be deliberately added to an image to help focus the viewer's attention toward the center of the frame.

Even when the effect is subtle, viewers will instinctively gravitate to the lighter areas in your image.

Vignetting can be corrected (or added) very effectively in ACR or Lightroom when converting an image from RAW. Photoshop also has a tool for correcting vignettes, but at the time of this writing it is not as effective as the tools offered in ACR and Lightroom.

Even if desirable, I suggest avoiding vignetting introduced by the lens, and adding the effect digitally later. If your lens introduces pronounced vignetting, I suggest using small apertures or getting a better lens.

## Processing-Related Defects

Some defects may be innate to digital technology or they may be introduced in the application of various digital processing techniques. These undesirable effects are often referred to as *artifacts* and most can be avoided by proper technique and by using tools such as the histogram to ensure that we become aware of potential problems as we go along and can avoid or correct them before they degrade the image. Following are examples of various types of artifacts:

- **Color Casts:** A color cast is a consistent bias of *all* colors in the image toward a specific hue. Color casts may be real and natural, resulting from qualities of light (particularly color temperature) under certain conditions. For example, in open shade, at dawn, or at dusk the color cast may be biased toward blue; during sunrise or sunset the color cast may be biased toward yellow/orange.

  Color casts shouldn't always be "corrected" and at times may be desirable and useful to convey a certain mood. There are, however, cases when certain operations may introduce undesirable color casts. For example, using various *White Balance* settings when converting an image from RAW may profoundly shift all colors in the image when we intend to only affect a subset of them, and increasing overall contrast may saturate existing color casts to a point of making them unsightly.

  Later in the book I discuss various strategies for correcting color and for preventing certain adjustments, such as contrast correction, from affecting color.

- **Posterization and Banding:** Posterization occurs when there are not enough gradations of color or tone to render smooth transitions, causing areas that should appear as smooth gradients to be "bunched" into the few available values, making these areas appear patchy rather than smooth. In cases of consistent gradation in a given direction, posterization may appear as bands of distinct shades or tones that do not transition smoothly into each other—an artifact referred to as *banding*.

The most effective strategy for avoiding posterization is to select a large color space, such as ProPhoto RGB or Adobe RGB 1998, when converting an image from RAW (which will ensure a large range of available colors), and working in 16-bit rather than 8-bit (which will ensure sufficient gradation within the color space).

Even if editing an image in a large color space and in 16-bit, posterization and banding may occur when the image needs to be targeted to a form of output with more limited capabilities than a screen (for example, a printer). I will discuss strategies for mitigating this effect in chapter 14.

- **Pixelation:** Various operations may result in pixel edges becoming visible. Pixelation is also sometimes referred to as *stair stepping* when diagonally arranged pixels appear as a staircase, or "*jaggies*," due to the jagged appearance of pixelated edges.

  Pixelation may occur under similar conditions as posterization (limited color space and/or gradation). It can also happen when an image is improperly enlarged and pixels are "stretched" until they become visible, or when an image is over-sharpened. It may also occur along very thin lines that the sensor didn't have sufficient resolution or sensitivity to resolve accurately.

  Current generations of sensors and RAW conversion algorithms are less prone to producing pixelation artifacts than older ones, and pixelation is generally easy to avoid when working in a large color space and 16-bit.

  Later in the book I discuss proper techniques for resizing images in a way that will not produce visible pixelation.

  If pixelation artifacts do exist in your image and the image was originally converted with older software, you may want to re-convert the original RAW file using a current generation converter. Pay attention to whether any sharpening is applied in the conversion process and reduce if necessary.

  Other means of mitigating pixelation may require deliberate blurring of an affected area, or healing the area using the *clone stamp* tool or the *spot healing brush* tool.

- **Inaccurate Selections/Masks:** At times, we may wish to apply an adjustment to just a portion of the image (known as a *local* adjustment). Selections and masks, which I cover later in the book, offer a powerful way of isolating portions of the image so that a given adjustment only affects pixels in that area. Photoshop also offers tools for refining the edges of selections and masks so they transition smoothly into unaffected areas.

  If selections or masks are not accurately drawn, or if the transition along their edges is too abrupt, the effect applied to the selected areas may have an unsightly edge, or perhaps "spill over" beyond the area we wish to affect.

  When selections need to be drawn accurately, I recommend taking the time to ensure that they are as perfect as possible, including working at high magnification and manually adding or removing individual pixels until the transitions appear seamless.

  At times, we may start a selection using an automated tool, which may capture the bulk of what we wish to select, but I recommend not trusting these tools to be perfectly accurate every time. Always view the selection edges at high magnification to ensure they are accurate.

- **Compression-Related Artifacts:** Some forms of data compression (most notably the compression used to create JPEG files) are considered "lossy," in the sense that they degrade the data to achieve a smaller file size. Lossy compression algorithms are useful in situations where bandwidth is limited and/or loading speed is crucial, such as Internet sites (viewers likely will not want to wait for your full-size image files to download when visiting your web page).

  However, when it comes to saving your master files—the files converted from RAW and edited to match your visualized image, and from which you will later derive different forms of output (such as Internet images and prints)—you should *never* use lossy compression. Disk space is relatively inexpensive, and loading files from a hard drive is relatively speedy (and even if a bit sluggish, is still better than sacrificing image data).

  If starting with a JPEG file, such as a file captured using your phone camera or an older file you only have in JPEG format, I recommend first switching it to 16-bit and a large color space (ProPhoto RGB or Adobe RGB 1998) before applying adjustments in Photoshop, and then resaving the file in a *lossless* format, such as TIFF. This will not bring back data that was already lost, but will avoid degrading the file further.

## Aspect Ratio

It would be silly to suggest that any camera's native aspect ratio is ideal for every composition and subject. In fact, I recommend training yourself to not even use the camera's viewfinder when composing an image in the field—learn to draw imaginary frame lines in your mind and free yourself from becoming locked into the camera's native aspect ratio.

Some images work best at a ratio of 2:3 (the ratio used in full-frame 35mm and APS cameras), but others may work better as 3:4, 4:5, square, panoramic, or any other ratio. The simplest way to accomplish an aspect ratio different from that of the sensor is to crop the image. With current high-resolution sensors, you likely will still have sufficient data to make excellent large prints. In my opinion, using the most effective aspect ratio to accomplish a balanced composition is more important to the ultimate success of an image than sacrificing a couple of megapixels. Alternatively, if you feel you must have as many pixels as possible, you may wish to stitch multiple exposures to produce a larger file at the desired aspect ratio.

## Color

Color and contrast, in various contexts, are the two areas we'll usually spend most of our processing time adjusting.

Remember that our goal in identifying gaps is to match them with specific actions to correct them. Photoshop's most effective color correction tool—the *Hue/Saturation Adjustment*—separates color into three components: *Hue, Saturation,* and *Lightness* (HSL). This is a particularly useful way to think about color correction since each of these components can be adjusted separately, and for a given range of colors. Learning to think about color in terms of HSL will serve us well when it comes to specifying color gaps, and correcting them using the appropriate controls.

Following is an explanation of the HSL components and how they can be used to adjust color:

- **Hue:** Scientists quantify hue as the degree to which a color relates to the four "basic" hues: blue, green, red, and yellow. For our purposes, hue can be thought of as the answer to the question: "What color is it?" For example, blue, green, purple, orange, and pink are all hues. And, of course, hues may be distinct variations of colors, such as cherry red, chartreuse green, sienna yellow, or navy blue.

  Changing hue values is especially useful in fine-tuning colors to a particular shade. For example, you may shift the sky color from

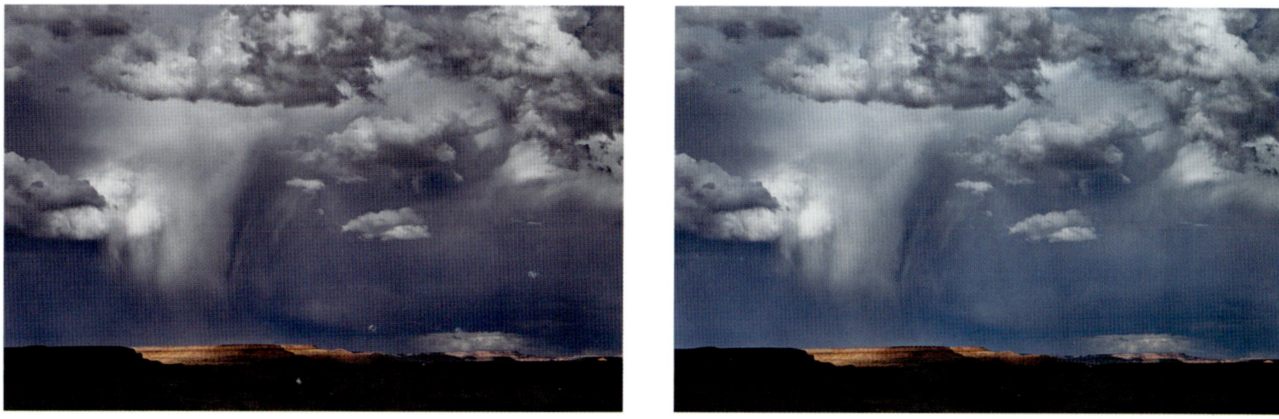

FIGURE 6.5: Note the difference in the overall mood of the image as different Hue, Saturation, and Lightness settings are used for blues.

cyan blue to a cerulean blue, or shift the colors of bright green-yellow leaves to a richer shade of forest green (figure 6.5).

The hue setting can also be used to map one color (or a range of colors) into another. Want to turn your green foliage purple? Hue is the parameter to tune. Exercise good taste.

- **Saturation:** Saturation refers to the intensity (or vibrance) of a given hue. In our analysis, we may decide, for example, that all or part of the image should appear more (or less) vivid. Photoshop allows us to control the saturation of separate color ranges. For example, we can make greens more saturated, but reds less saturated. And, the ability to target adjustments to just parts of the image allows us to saturate a given color in some portion of the image (say, the main subject) and to de-saturate the same color in other parts of the image so they don't compete for attention with the more vibrant ones.

  Saturation is an area where many tend to go too far in an attempt to give the image more visual impact. When adjusting saturation, be very careful not to get carried away. An over-saturated image may indeed draw attention initially, but upon closer inspection may be dismissed as overdone or even "kitschy."

- **Lightness:** As I mentioned earlier, lightness refers to our perception of how light or dark a color appears. Since lightness is a subjective perception, when adjusting the lightness of a given color, Photoshop will attempt (and will usually fail) to hold the hue and saturation constant. A common result of adjusting lightness is that colors will appear more or less dusky (depending on whether lightness is added or subtracted), rather than lighter or darker. This can be a useful effect, especially in landscape photography, when we wish to render such things as a dramatic gray-blue sky (accomplished by reducing the lightness of blue) or when we want to maintain the appearance of earth tones in such things as colorful rocks (rather than having them appear unnaturally vibrant).

Despite the definition, making a portion of an image lighter or darker may be better accomplished in ways other than adjusting color lightness. For example, by using techniques such as dodging (making a portion of the image lighter), and burning (making a portion of the image darker). I describe these methods in greater detail later in the book.

## Contrast

Contrast is the degree of separation—or, the difference—in lightness and/or color between adjacent elements in the image (figure 6.6). The greater the difference, the higher the contrast. Note that the reverse is also true.

Differences in lightness and color can be exaggerated or reduced using a variety of tools in Photoshop. In identifying gaps, we may identify such things as "increase global contrast" or "reduce contrast in water."

Other than perhaps a small initial bump in global contrast, if needed, I recommend thinking about contrast in local, rather than global, terms. This is especially true in landscape images that contain varied scenery and lighting.

## Color, Contrast, and Subjective Sensibilities

Traditionally, nature photographers tended to favor images exhibiting high contrast, partly due to aesthetic reasons but also for increased visual impact,

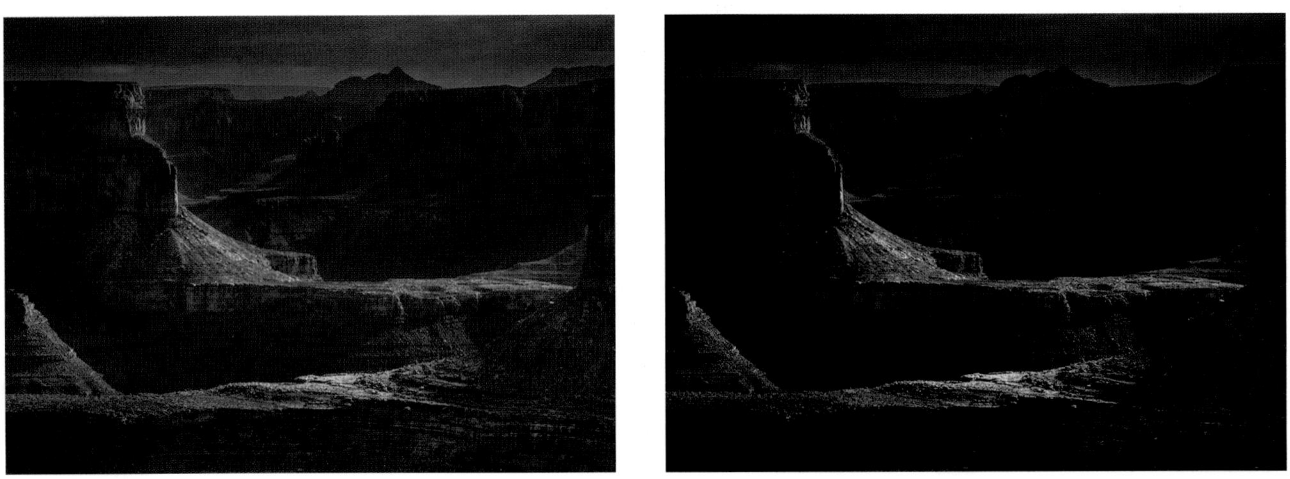

FIGURE 6.6: Low- and high-contrast versions of the same image express different moods.

particularly with photo editors and buyers in the days when slides were examined on a light table. Photographs are often submitted for publication in large batches, and, unromantic as it may sound, those that "scream the loudest" often get the most attention. These days such tendencies are driven by the nature of presenting images on social media sites where it is becoming increasingly difficult for an image to stand out from a very large crowd. Still, this trend has reversed somewhat in recent years as more photographers develop their sensibilities in more creative and artistic ways and choose to shed the convention in favor of personal taste rather than competition.

Do not assume that high contrast and over-saturated color are always the best choices for your expressive purpose. Before all else, consider what you wish for your image to express—how it should make your viewers feel—and then consider all your options before settling on the right look for a given work.

Images with high contrast and saturated colors may be seductive as they draw attention and make a more powerful first impression, but they don't always have "staying power" if bold color and some generic "pretty scenery" is all they have to offer. On the other hand, nuanced, complex, and subtle images, when presented in the right context, often invite closer inspection and result in a more extended, contemplative, and memorable viewing experience for those willing to invest the time to study them.

## Black-and-White

Despite its traditional origins, black-and-white photography is very well suited for digital capture and processing. Traditional (film) black-and-white photographers are required to make critical decisions while in the field, such as push-processing or the use of color correction filters, without immediately seeing the effect of their choices and with limited ability to revisit or reverse their decisions later. Digital capture enables making these same decisions in the studio, seeing and fine-tuning the effect of such choices in real-time, on a large screen, and using tools with greater precision than are available to film photographers.

Some decisions related to black-and-white are best made during conversion from RAW. At this step, our goal is to map as much detail as possible from the red, green, and blue channels into the one channel we later want to be dominant when converting to black-and-white. For example, if we determine that most of the detail in the image resides in the red channel, but the visual effect we are after requires using the green channel, we may decide to adjust the white balance setting toward the far green end of the scale. The result may look very unnatural in color, but will yield the most detail when later converted into black-and-white. If you are not already a black-

and-white photographer and this makes little sense to you at this point, don't worry—I cover these concepts in detail later in the book.

Once converted from RAW, many creative options can be applied to further enhance image detail; to establish and adjust tonal relationships; and, if desired, to add a hint of color such as sepia or platinum to tint the image for a specific look or mood.

Black-and-white photographers who are familiar with traditional darkroom tools and techniques can readily use familiar terminology when identifying gaps—such as push/pull, dodge/burn, and Zone System terminology. Almost any effect possible in the chemical darkroom—color filtration, dodging and burning, zone placement, and toning with precious metals for specific looks—can be achieved in Photoshop, as well, and with very precise control over the outcome.

Furthermore, in Photoshop, effects can be combined in ways not possible with traditional film/chemical methods. For example, the same image can blend the effects of both a red and a blue color correction filter in various ratios. With actual glass or resin filters, only one or the other can be used with any degree of predictability, and the photographer is limited to the grades he or she happens to have available.

The digital studio also allows us to separate the look we're after from the limitations of specific films, papers, or chemicals. For example, if you like the look of a platinum print but dislike matte papers, you can digitally apply platinum toning and then print on a wide variety of papers, including ones with glossy surfaces.

The most obvious gap when working on a black-and-white image is the initial conversion from a color capture. I describe this process in detail later in the book. Other gaps, such as lightness and contrast, should be noted the same as with a color image, and for the most part they will be mitigated using the same tools.

## Dodging and Burning

If you have ever worked in a traditional darkroom, you may be familiar with the terms dodging and burning. These refer, respectively, to techniques for lightening (dodging) or darkening (burning) specific areas in the image in various degrees.

Among other things, dodging can be very effective in recovering shadow details or lightening the main subject so it stands out from its surroundings; burning can be used to tone down highlights or to darken the area around a subject we wish to stand out more (figure 6.7).

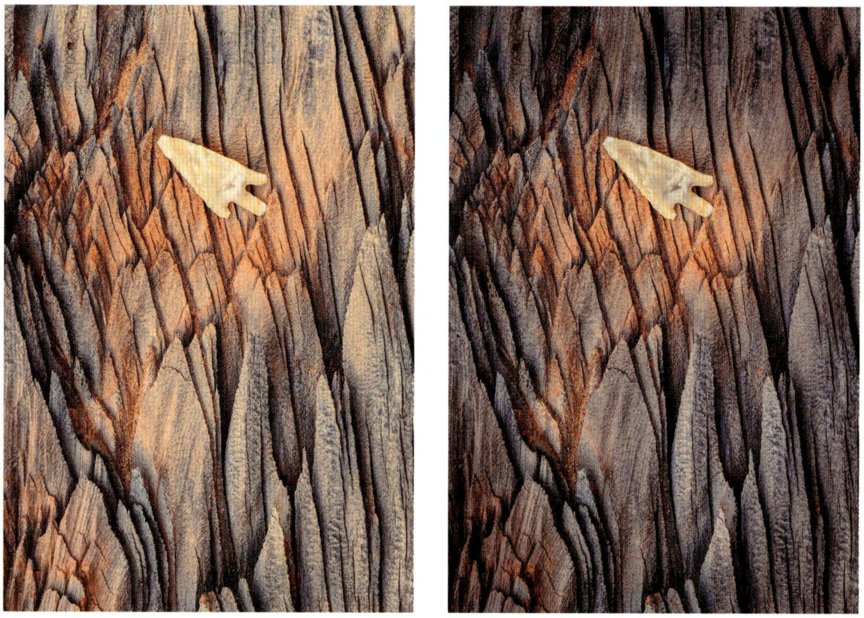

FIGURE 6.7: Notice the subtle but undeniable effect of dodging (lightening) and burning (darkening) of various areas in the image.

## Blurring

While viewers tend to gravitate toward the lighter areas in the frame, even if only slightly lighter than their surroundings, the same is also true for areas that are significantly sharper than their surroundings. We can draw attention to those elements we deem most important by blurring unneeded details around them. This effect is commonly used in portrait and wildlife photography, generally by using lenses of relatively high magnification and selecting large aperture settings to reduce the depth of field.

Selective blurring can be applied digitally in processing as well. As part of our analysis, we may identify those less important areas that can be blurred to divert attention away from them.

While such blurring often will be applied locally to portions of the image, some types of blur can also be applied globally for a variety of effects. One common technique is named after photographer Michael Orton, who originally combined two exposures (one sharp, one intentionally out of focus) to create subtle blurry halos around sharp elements without sacrificing important image detail. In Photoshop, where we can create a duplicate frame and apply any amount and type of blur, the Orton effect is easy to apply and can create ethereal, dreamy-looking images (figure 6.8).

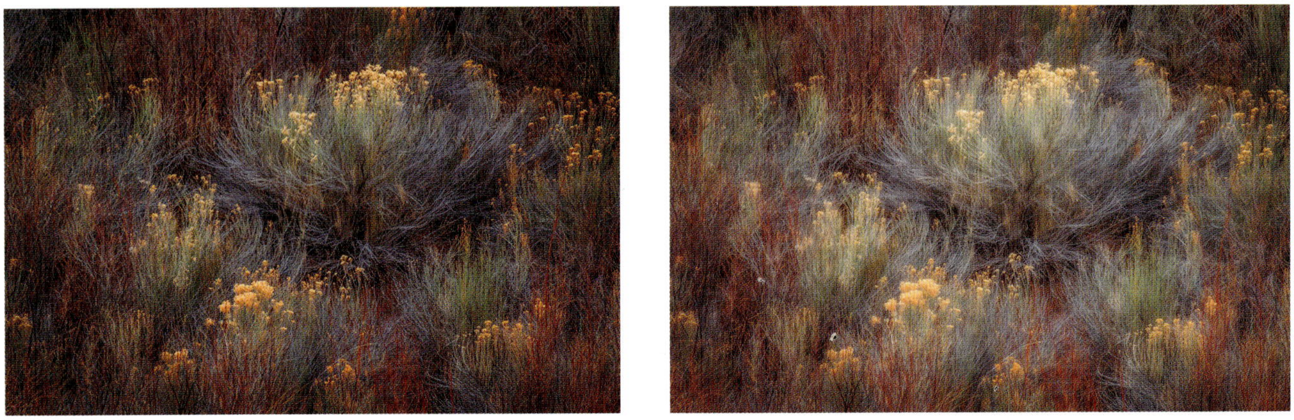

FIGURE 6.8: The Orton blurring effect (*right*).

## Blending and Stitching

There are situations in which the camera's abilities fall short of capturing all the information needed to arrive at our visualized image in just a single exposure. These situations may include limitations of dynamic range, which means the range of tones between the darkest and lightest portions of a scene exceed the sensor's ability to capture both highlight and shadow detail. Other situations may include insufficient depth of field to maintain sharp detail in all areas of the image front-to-back, or insufficient resolution to meet large print requirements. In these cases, we may need to combine multiple exposures into a single image (figure 6.9).

Following are some common scenarios for blending exposures:

- Blending bracketed exposures, combining the highlight details from one exposure with the shadow details from another. This technique is sometimes referred to as High Dynamic Range (HDR).
- Blending an exposure focused on foreground elements with one focused on distant ones, resulting in greater depth-of-field than is possible in a single exposure.
- Stitching multiple exposures to create a larger and more detailed file.

Blending exposures opens the door to various creative uses, for example, making one exposure at high ISO to freeze fast-moving elements (such as a flower swaying in the wind) and another made at low ISO to reduce the risk of noise in those areas not prone to movement, and then blending the sharp elements from each exposure into a single image. Blending techniques can also be used to blend an attractive sky from one scene with an interesting foreground from another, for example.

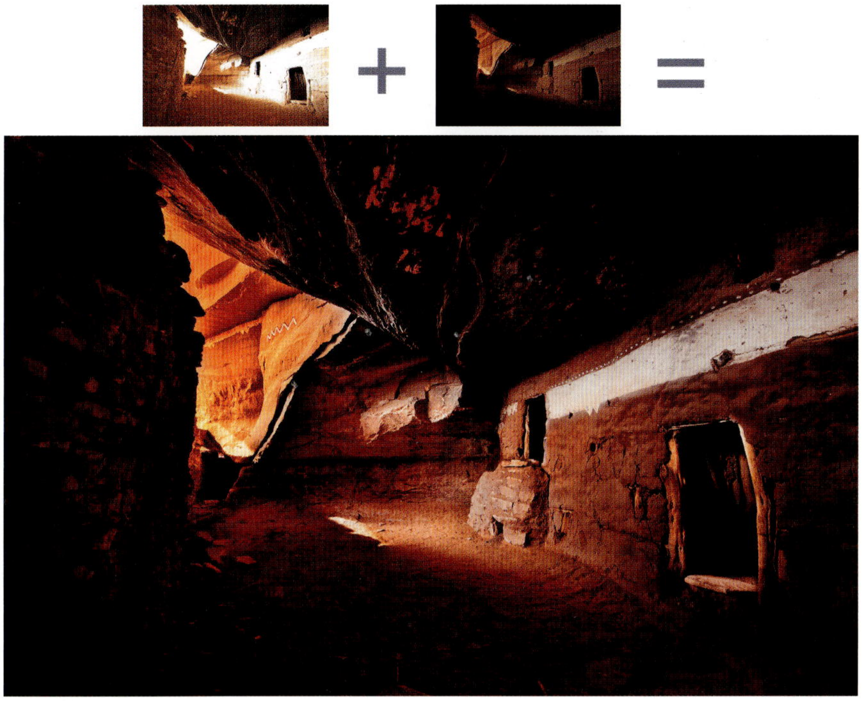

FIGURE 6.9: Blending two exposures—one metered for the highlights and one for the shadows—can be used to expand dynamic range and to avoid the risk of featureless highlights/shadows, and of excessive noise.

Keep in mind that just because something is possible doesn't mean you should do it. Exercise good judgment.

Blending can be accomplished by using automated tools or by manually selecting those portions in each frame we wish to retain in the final image. I demonstrate some blending methods later in the book.

## Image Analysis Example

In this section, I provide an example of how I approach my work on an image. Pay attention to the way gaps are turned into actionable items that readily translate into specific adjustments at each iteration. Although I describe the tools applied, do not be concerned with them at this stage. I explain them in detail later in the book. Instead, focus on the analysis and thought process I use to guide the RAW file toward the visualized outcome.

The tabular format I use to record gaps is designed to articulate the results I'm after and to link them with the specific tools I'll later need to address them. This method of documentation may help as you process your first images. With sufficient practice, and as your skills evolve, you may reach a point when you will no longer need these written descriptions and instead will work from memory.

## Preparation

Before applying any adjustments to the image, you should first have a visualized goal in mind. It's not enough to have a vague idea of the outcome; you need to clearly see it in your mind's eye!

Two techniques I find especially useful in visualizing images are as follows:

- Open your RAW file, examine it on your screen and make a conscious effort to recall the moment you first came upon the scene and decided to photograph it. Walk through your composition decisions and capture process. Try to remember not only the visual qualities of the place but what it felt like to be there: the smells, temperature, sounds, whether it was windy or breezy, the thoughts you had, and so on. Be there!

  Now close your eyes and remember what you wanted your image to look like as you were working. Project it on the inside of your eyelids until it is clear and vivid in your mind. This is your initial visualization. You may choose to keep or revise it later.

- Articulate in words what it felt like to make the image, the feelings and sensations, your state of mind, and the things that inspired you to stop and make a photograph. While this is certainly more time consuming, you may be surprised to learn how much information remains hidden in your memory, unavailable to you until you make a deliberate effort to access it.

  As you tell your story, highlight nouns, verbs, and adjectives that drew your attention the most and that you wish for your viewers to feel and pay attention to. These are the things that make the image

FIGURE 6.10: The image as originally rendered by Adobe Camera RAW (*left*) and my final outcome (*right*).

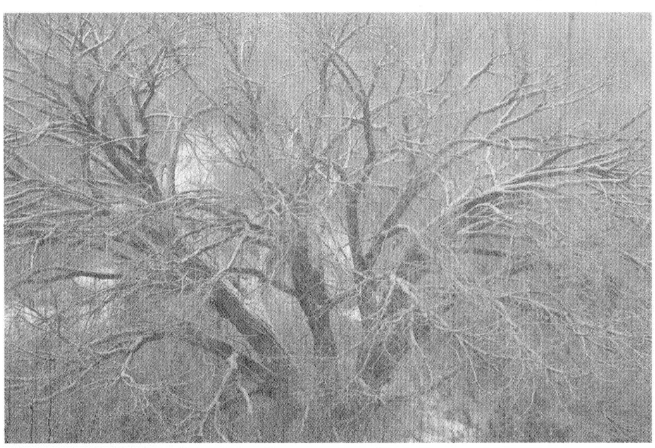

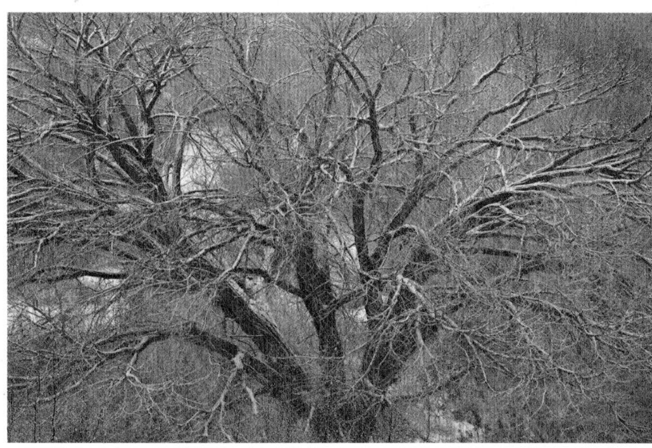

personal and expressive, and that you will want to emphasize in processing.

Here's the story I wrote about this image (figure 6.10):

*I remember looking out the window at the dreary, cloudy sky as I prepared a quick breakfast before heading out to my beloved canyons for the day. A light snow began to fall just moments before. To most photographers, these conditions may be far from ideal, but I was looking forward to the silence and solitude of a winter day on the Colorado Plateau. I drove slowly. The road had not been plowed and no tracks appeared in the fresh snow, suggesting I was the first to travel this route since the snow started. Even from the high mountain overlooks, little was visible of the desert and canyons below. The sun, a pale white circle in the sky, could not pierce the* ***veil of slate blue and gray*** *blotting out the sky. The air was almost completely still. As I arrived at my destination and began hiking into the wilderness along the cottonwood-lined creek, the snow continued to fall. I remember how crisp and clear everything was and how* ***the light snow accentuated every tiny detail in every tree and every rock.*** *Then I saw it: an old cottonwood tree, its limbs erupting in all directions. I stood there looking at it for a few moments, in awe of* ***its majestic size and the intricate patterns of its branches,*** *the heavy limbs splitting over and over and tapering into an infinite complex of tiny tentacles. I looked around to find the best vantage point. A high ledge on one side of the canyon caught my eye and I scrambled up to it. From here, I could take in the tree in all its ancient beauty. I worried about* ***the red birch branches*** *within my line of sight but then recognized the interesting effect of their subtle color,* ***so different from the otherwise monochromatic setting,*** *and I decided to include them in my composition.*

By recalling the story and highlighting those things most representative of the visual elements I found most interesting (notice the bold passages above), the image formed itself in my mind.

Here is how these highlighted points translate into visualization (and later, processing):

- An overcast sky means diffused lighting. Under these conditions all things are evenly illuminated. There are no extreme highlights or deep shadows. In practical terms, it means I will need to keep the contrast low to convey the mood of the scene.

- A cloudy sky also means a high ambient color temperature (i.e., biased toward blue), which is also consistent with the cold temperature. The dominant color in my visualized image will therefore need to be a cool faint blue, just strong enough to set the mood and avoid the dreary look of a completely monochromatic scene.
- Since it was the intricate details in the branches accented by snow that fascinated me, I will need to enhance edge contrast (using slight sharpening) to better define every line and detail.
- My decision to include the birch branches was based on the way their unique red/magenta hue added a subtle splash of color to the scene. When processing, I will make sure their color is clearly visible yet doesn't distract from my main subject—the cottonwood tree.

I now have a clear visualized image in mind. Can you see it, too? While it may not seem obvious, knowing what the image should ultimately look like is more important to its success than any technical consideration or skill.

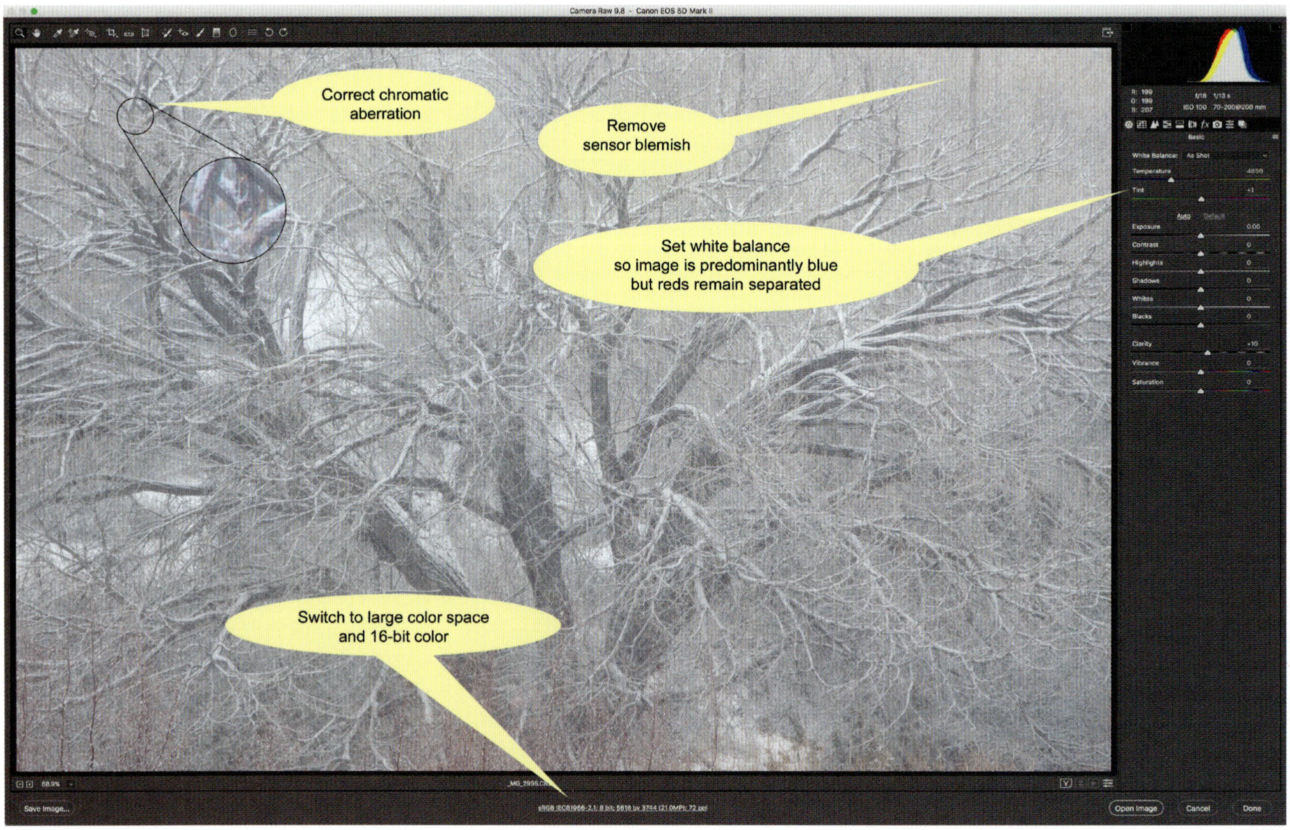


**FIGURE 6.11:** The gaps I found relevant to address in the RAW conversion phase.

Processing techniques can be learned and applied in the same way by anyone, but the way we respond to the world—and consequently, the way we visualize our images—is unique to each of us.

### Converting the RAW File

Although I may find any number of gaps by merely examining the image in the RAW converter, my main concern at this early stage is to identify those gaps that are best addressed in the conversion phase (for technical reasons explained in chapter 8).

Some gaps, such as the large dust particle in the upper-right area of the image, are almost too obvious to miss, while others, such as the subtle chromatic aberration, require careful inspection at high magnification to identify. Gaps such as finding the appropriate color balance directly relate to the visualization analysis in the previous section, while others such as the need to use a larger color space are of a more technical nature.

Let's examine the list of gaps I have so far and what can be done to mitigate them:

| | Description | Location | Possible Mitigation |
|---|---|---|---|
| 1 | Color space and bit depth setting too restrictive | Global | Select new settings |
| 2 | Chromatic aberration | Global | Use ACR Lens Corrections to eliminate |
| 3 | Color balance incorrect using default settings. Need to ensure blues dominant overall, and separate the reds | Global | Use *Temperature* and *Tint* sliders to bring the image close to desired balance, fine tune in Photoshop later |
| 4 | Need to remove sensor blemish | By upper-right corner | Use *Spot Removal* tool in ACR, or, if unsuccessful, use *Clone Stamp* tool in Photoshop |

Note how each of the gaps translates into adjustments and corrections I can readily apply. This helps break what may be a daunting task into manageable chunks, and greatly reduces the need for trial and error. This is not to say that you shouldn't experiment. While some corrections, especially defects, may be straightforward to mitigate, others may present opportunities for new interpretations. Do not be afraid to pause, ask yourself "What if?" and try those things that pique your curiosity.

One of the most powerful aspects of digital editing is the freedom to pursue creative ideas as they come to mind without fear of damaging the image.

In the worst of cases, you may have to return to the RAW file and reconvert, which is far less ominous than the potential consequence of making errors in a traditional chemical process and ruining the film.

With this list of gaps, I am now ready to apply the first round of mitigation techniques in ACR.

Certainly, if I were to continue, I could list many more gaps, such as areas requiring a contrast adjustment, areas I may want to darken (burn) or lighten (dodge), a change in aspect ratio (crop), and areas where individual colors may need fine-tuning. The list may grow and shrink as I go along. When all gaps have been mitigated, the image should appear on the screen identically to the visualized image.

## EXERCISE 3

1. Select a favorite image you made on a memorable trip. Write down its story. Highlight key parts that may help define the visualized image and that you wish to emphasize in processing.
2. Open the RAW file for your image in ACR or Lightroom, set the magnification to 100% (1:1) and identify at least five gaps using the tabular format described earlier.
3. What are some cases when blending multiple exposures may be desirable? If unsure, the answer is on page 106.
4. Is chromatic aberration best corrected during RAW conversion or in Photoshop? If unsure, find the answer on page 94.
5. The term "medium vibrant orange" describes the three properties (hue, saturation, and lightness) of a specific color. Which word matches which property? If unsure, see page 100 for the answer.
6. Why do some photographers intentionally add vignetting to their image? If unsure, find the answer on page 96.
7. What are the two types of digital noise? If unsure, find the answer on page 95.

*See Appendix for answer key.*

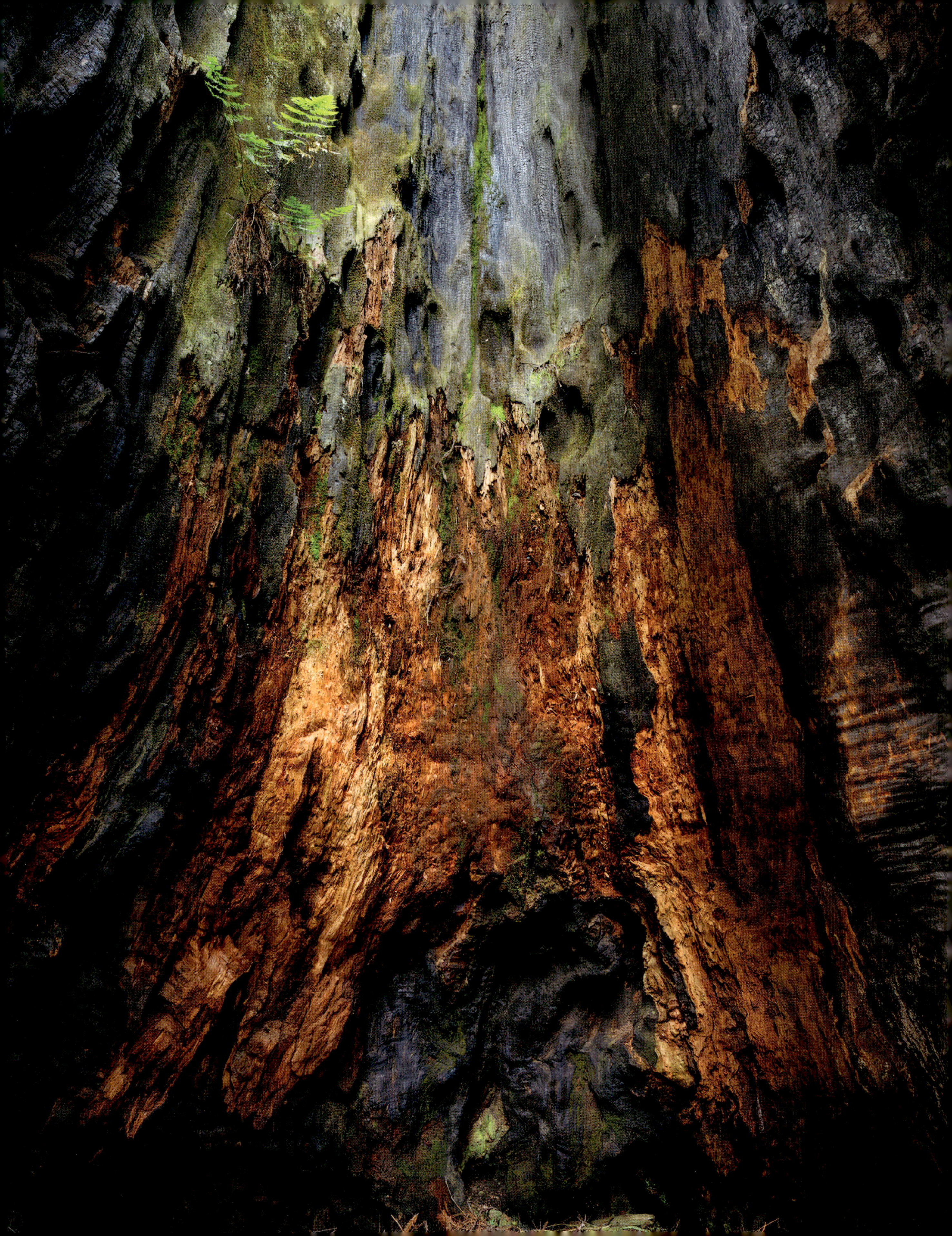

# 7

# Workflow Overview

> *Most creative photographs are departures from reality and it seems to take a higher order of craft to make this departure than to simulate reality.*
>
> —ANSEL ADAMS

The workflow I describe here is designed to benefit creative photographers in making expressive photographs. As such, I prioritize accomplishing your expressive goal and producing the highest quality results possible, rather than efficiency and minimizing processing time. Indeed, this workflow may be ill suited for applications that require processing a large quantity of images in a short amount of time, or for applications where the resulting images are only required to meet some baseline criteria to make them usable for such purposes as publication, reportage, slideshows, or some other use where consistency is important and expressive intent is not necessarily the primary goal.

There are many ways to automate image processing, such as batch-processing many photographs using identical settings, or using various "smart" products to minimize the amount of personal, manual, skilled involvement required from the photographer. Such approaches are completely valid for a variety of photographic applications, but in my opinion are limiting when it comes to creating expressive art.

The approach I take here is conducive to creative work, and offers the advantage of being adaptable to the unique characteristics and intent of each image.

Earlier in the book, I mention the difference between convergent and divergent thinking. Convergent thinking is useful for many "cookie cutter" tasks that may require some skill but not creative on-the-fly decision making. Divergent thinking—considering many possible solutions in real time, and avoiding preconceptions—is better suited for creative work. It is the nature of creativity that the proverbial lightbulb over the head can light up at any time, with entirely unpredictable ideas. As such, a workflow that is too rigid, repetitive, and formulaic, and that does not allow for creative epiphanies to dictate new directions, is not ideal when the goal is creative expression.

Too much automation, which circumvents direct decision making by the artist, may reduce the range of possibilities to be consciously considered.

This is not to say that automation and other laborsaving solutions are necessarily a bad thing; far from it. Rather, I am making the distinction between automating operations that do not require creativity, and placing manual control and deliberate decision-making with the photographer when creative choices are possible.

Think of driving a car, for example. Most of us have no idea what happens between the moment we turn the ignition and when the engine comes alive, or how pushing the accelerator results in the wheels turning faster. But that knowledge is not nearly as important as deciding where we want to go and what route we want to take, or whether we want to deviate from the original plan (if we even had one) to explore a side road, which requires conscious decision-making and control.

Some photographers prefer to follow what is known in project management as a "waterfall approach," where the same set of steps is followed in every case and each step logically follows another until all boxes are checked and the project is complete. The waterfall approach is best suited when a singular path is known to work and/or if there is risk in deviating from that path. While quicker and easier than other approaches, a waterfall workflow leaves little room for fine adjustment and experimentation and may be better suited for stock, editorial, or commercial photography where time is of the essence and quality should meet a certain bar, but where creative expression is not the ultimate goal.

In contrast, a non-linear, iterative approach—which is what I describe here—is one that relies on progressive refinement and course correction; where a small set of actions is taken in each iteration, and then goals are re-examined to inform the next iteration. This approach has the advantage of being effective when we don't know everything in advance and when we have the freedom to adapt our approach (or we might even change our desired outcome) as we go along. With each iteration, we get progressively closer until we arrive at a final iteration that results in the image on the screen looking like the one we visualized, at which point we declare it finished. At least temporarily. As your skills improve and your sensibilities evolve, you may no longer be satisfied with the way you originally processed a given image and you might want to revisit some of your earlier decisions.

The circular workflow I describe is the result of my experience over many years of processing and reprocessing my images. It allows for adaptations and leaves ample room for creative decisions. While it provides a structured approach to tackling the specific tasks at hand, it also leaves much room for customization to meet a desired, visualized outcome or even to change that visualization midstream and to make the necessary corrections (figure 7.1).

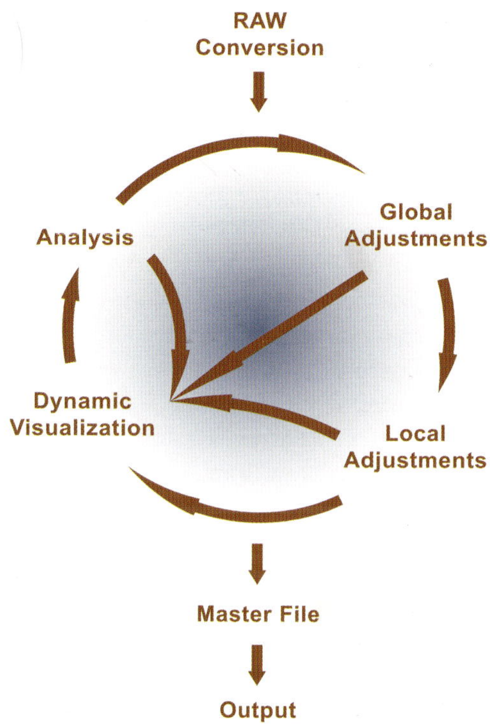


FIGURE 7.1: A visual representation of the phases involved in processing an image.

Not all activities in this workflow require technical skills or specialized software. In fact, the Analysis and Dynamic Visualization phases require no hands-on work at all, although they are critical to the ultimate success of the finished image.

Following is an overview of each process phase. Each phase is then discussed in greater detail in the following chapters.

## RAW Conversion

Converting a RAW file into pixels before importing it into Photoshop for further processing can be thought of as a global adjustment (affecting the entire image). Still, I prefer to consider RAW conversion as a separate and distinct step in the workflow. The reason is that, while we may revisit various adjustments applied in Photoshop, RAW conversion is something we likely want to do just once. An exception to this rule may be if improved RAW conversion software comes along that may give us a better starting point, but even in that scenario it is quite easy to swap out the initial converted image for a new one without having to reprocess the image from scratch. The reason I prefer to do as much as possible in Photoshop, rather than in the process of RAW conversion, is that adjustments made in the RAW converter do not take advantage of Photoshop's nondestructive editing features such as layers and masks.

There is a tendency among photographers to use the tools provided in the RAW converter to attempt to make the image appear as close to the visualized result as possible, and then fine-tune it further in Photoshop. I recommend that you resist this urge. The tools provided in most RAW conversion software, including ones that overlap with similar tools in Photoshop, are almost always not as powerful or precise. Also, making significant changes to the image in the conversion phase may limit your options later.

In our workflow, the goal for RAW conversion is to produce the best starting point for further editing in Photoshop. This starting point may not look much like the visualized image. In fact, it *should not* look too much like it. A good starting point is generally one of low contrast, muted color, and the greatest amount of detail possible.

## Analysis

As I explain in the previous chapter, before making any changes to an image it's important to assess the gaps between its current state—the way it appears at a point in time—and the desired, visualized outcome. This will ensure that processing decisions are driven by both the unique qualities of the image and the visualized outcome, rather than being a succession of arbitrary, prescribed adjustments.

Consider that there are practically infinite ways in which an image can be visualized and processed. Rather than assume that all images are intended to accomplish the same goal (most commonly, aesthetic appeal), analysis allows us to shift our attention—if only for a short time—to considering possibilities and identifying the most effective expressive direction possible, beyond just making a pretty picture.

Analysis is also useful in identifying preemptive steps that may not be obvious. For example, we may wish to increase saturation before fine-tuning specific colors so we can better see the effect of our adjustments and then we can dial the saturation back down after the desired hue has been achieved. Another example may be increasing contrast significantly so that blemishes, noise, and other defects become more visible and easy to identify, and then restoring the proper contrast once these defects have been corrected.

## Dynamic Visualization

Remember that visualization is the ability to see in our "mind's eye" the finished image before it is created—whether visualizing in the field before making an exposure or visualizing a desired outcome while working on an image in Photoshop.

The visualized image will be our guide at each iteration as we decide what to do next. Not only will it help us tailor our processing decisions to the desired outcome, but it will also serve as a reminder of what we are creating and the emotional effect we wish to evoke in our viewers, rather than becoming mired in technicalities, which is always a risk when working with complex applications such as Photoshop.

Creative ideas and revelations may emerge at any moment, especially when our attention is focused on the image, allowing us to notice nuanced and less obvious things we may have missed while in the field or when we looked at the image on the camera's little screen. At times, new ideas may prompt us to rethink our initial visualization. This is a good thing! Give new ideas due consideration as they may well lead us down a path that is better than the one we originally intended. Or, if these new ideas fail to improve on our original visualization, they will help validate it.

This process of constant refinement and re-consideration is what I call *Dynamic Visualization*. Rather than assume that your initial visualization is the absolute best outcome, make a conscious effort to remain open to new creative ideas.

## Global Adjustments

As the name suggests, global adjustments may potentially change the value of every pixel in the image. Put another way, they are adjustments that are not deliberately targeted to just a portion of the image.

For example, a global adjustment may be conversion to black-and-white, lightening or darkening the entire image, changing overall color saturation, or adjusting overall contrast.

Global adjustments should be applied with care, as sometimes an adjustment that may improve the appearance of most of the image may introduce problems in small areas where the adjustment was not appropriate. On the other hand, if an image is already looking close to the desired visualized outcome, a handful of global adjustments may be all that is needed to accomplish the visualized result.

## Local Adjustments

Local adjustments often use the same tools as global ones, but are deliberately restricted to affect specific parts of the image (like specific areas, colors, or tonal ranges). For example, a local adjustment can be used to darken a sky or to increase the saturation of only one flower without affecting other elements.

Local adjustments are also useful in cases where a global adjustment may degrade parts of the image that do not require it. For example, operations such as noise reduction or sharpening may impact fine image details and to the extent possible should only be applied to specific areas where they are needed, rather than globally, as might be the case when wanting to make adjustments to a sky. It is usually beneficial to reduce noise in the sky since fine details are usually not important there, but sharpening should *not* be applied to the sky for the same reason: there is no important detail worth sharpening, but sharpening may make such things as noise more visible. Applying noise reduction and sharpening as local, rather than global, adjustments offers us the freedom to apply them selectively, where and when they are needed.

## Master File

The master file holds the best data we have for an image as well as information about the adjustments we made to it in a nondestructive format; meaning we may decide later to change or discard any given adjustment without affecting the original image pixels while preserving other adjustments we may wish to keep.

The master file should look on screen like your visualized image while providing the highest degree of flexibility so it can later be targeted to a variety of outputs, such as web presentation, publication, or fine art prints.

## Output

While master files hold *all* the information we have about a given image, most practical uses for the image do not require all of it. Some forms of output, such as images for a website, may need to discard data to produce smaller versions of the image, and others may need to manufacture data if there is not enough (e.g., to produce a very large print).

Practically any form of output requires some degradation of the original data to fit within the capabilities and limitations of the output device.

## Working Iteratively

In an iterative workflow, some or all activities may be repeated more than once before processing is complete. Rather than thinking in terms of going from point A to point B, think of your activities as gradually funneling and converging toward the visualized image (or possibly a newly visualized image). With each iteration, our path to the next set of adjustments will become clearer and the gaps fewer until the image finally matches our visualized goal.

After each iteration, we return to the Dynamic Visualization point where we revisit our visualized image and consider whether to keep our current goal or vary from it. We then analyze the current state of the image, determine what gaps to tackle in the next iteration, apply the appropriate global and/or local adjustments, and repeat this cycle as needed (figure 7.2).

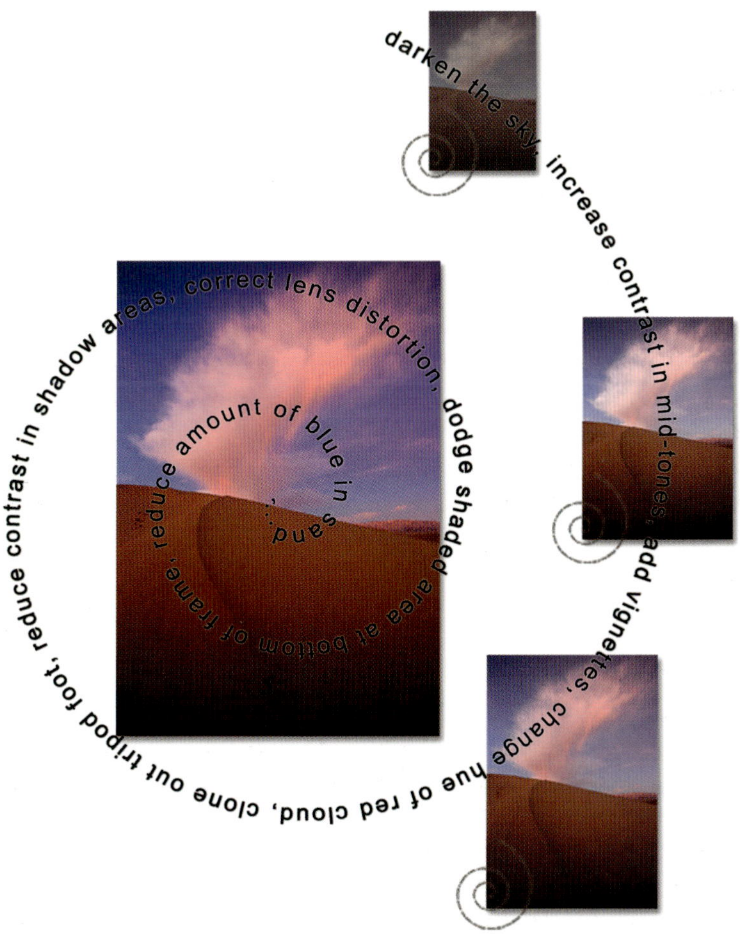


FIGURE 7.2: An image takes shape in iterations. At each step, a few adjustments are made and an analysis of the remaining gaps takes place before the next round of adjustments until the image appears as we visualized it.

## Monotasking

It may seem contrary to the hurried way many of us conduct our personal lives and professional work, but multitasking is not conducive to creative activities. Much like a good composition, image processing is greatly enhanced by the absence of distractions—do one thing at a time, give it your undivided attention, and do it well.

Beyond just creative benefits, the focusing of attention is also conducive to the psychological state of *flow*, described by psychologist Mihály Csíkszentmihályi as "...the state in which people are so involved in an activity that nothing else seems to matter; the experience itself is so enjoyable that people will do it even at great cost, for the sheer sake of doing it." Csíkszentmihályi explains further, "One of the most frequently mentioned dimensions of the flow experience is that, while it lasts, one is able to forget all the unpleasant aspects of life. This feature of flow is an important by-product of the fact that enjoyable activities require a complete focusing of attention on the task at hand—thus leaving no room in the mind for irrelevant information."

More and more, the demand for greater automation, larger batches, do-it-at-the-click-of-a-button visual effects, and faster turnaround times is forcing creative minds into a mode of monotonous repetition that is more appropriate for machines than for intelligent, creative beings, and this crowds out the innovation and experimentation needed to create not just good work but meaningful, expressive work.

I often hear my colleagues bemoan being behind on their processing, having to crunch through hundreds of RAW files from a recent shoot, or just wanting to be done with an image to get to the next one. Is this really what we want from practicing our photographic work?

Certainly, the need to process large volumes of images for commercial or editorial use may justify the need to minimize the amount of attention given to any one image, but the same justification does not apply to creative work or to the making of expressive art, or if the state of flow is among the rewards we wish for from pursuing our work.

We do not think of Ansel Adams "crunching through" processing *Moonrise, Hernandez, New Mexico* (in fact, it took him a couple of decades to find the look we are familiar with today), or of Picasso "just wanting to be done" with *Les Demoiselles d'Avignon*. Creative work requires time and attention. It is a pursuit of quality rather than quantity, substance rather than volume, depth rather than superficiality. It is the pursuit of finding joy in the process of making creative work rather than in just the outcome. Creative work, when pursued intently as a goal in itself, not only deserves a slow and mindful approach, but also richly rewards those who are willing to invest time and effort in it.

# Part II:
# Practice

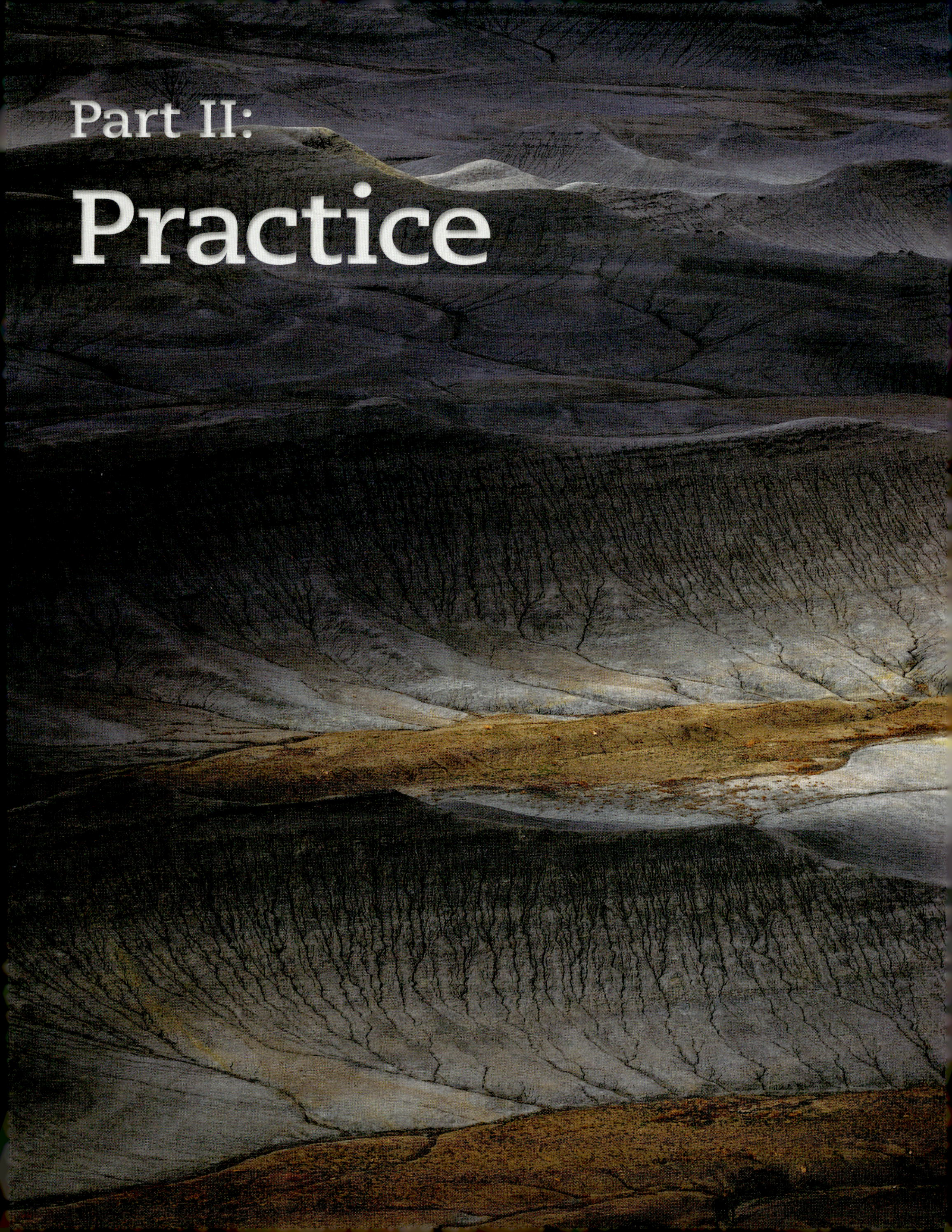

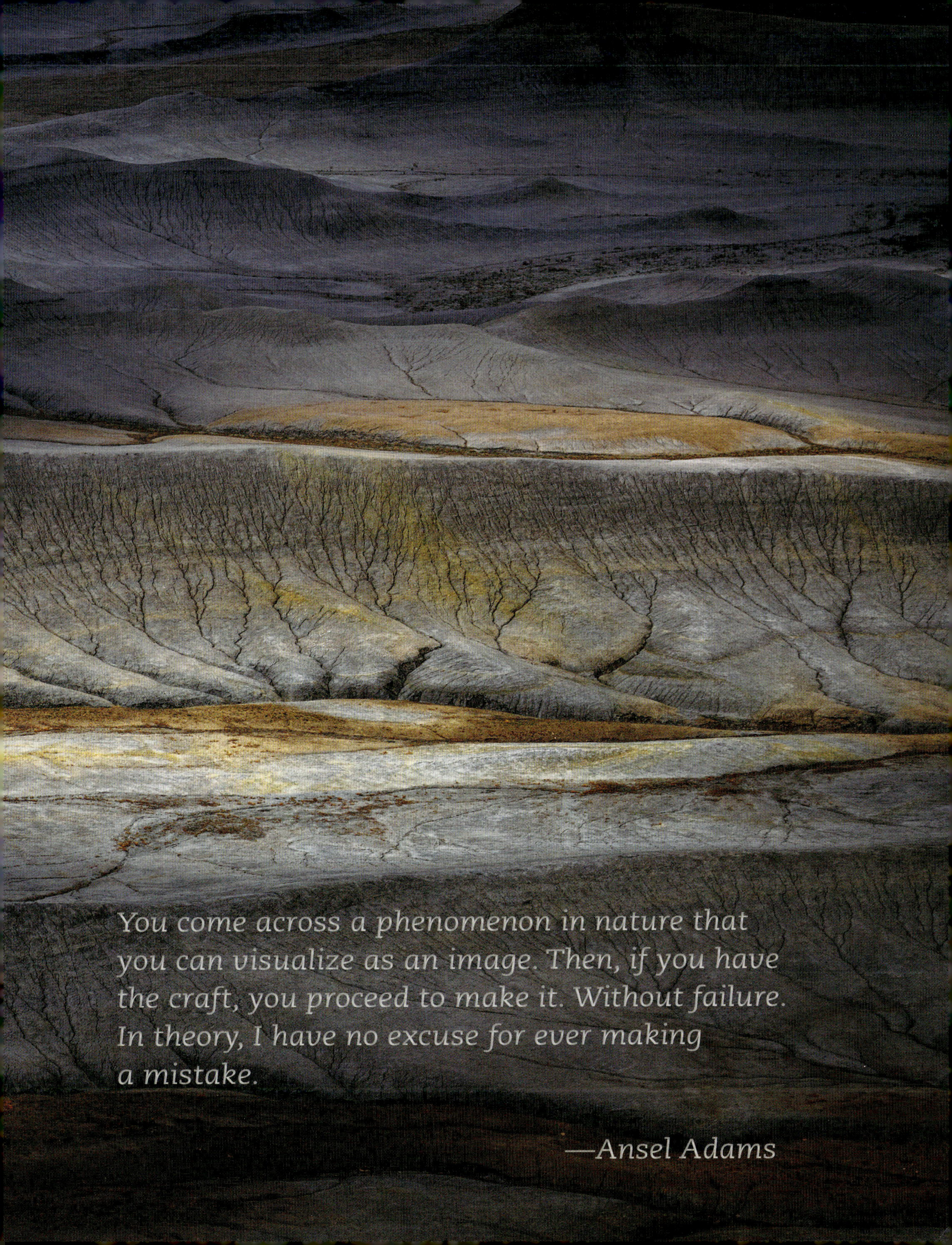

*You come across a phenomenon in nature that you can visualize as an image. Then, if you have the craft, you proceed to make it. Without failure. In theory, I have no excuse for ever making a mistake.*

—Ansel Adams

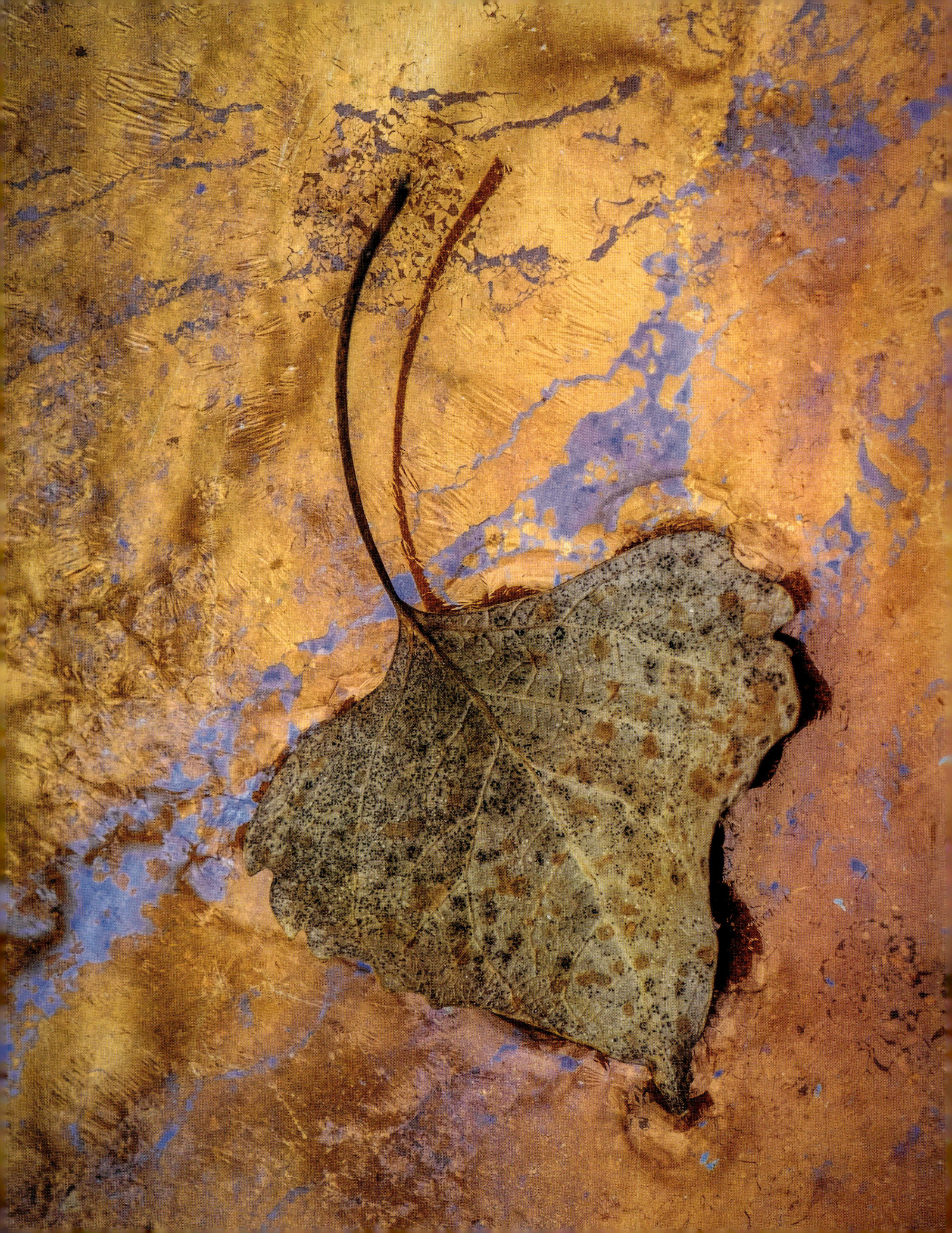

# 8 RAW Conversion

*Though I may not distinguish at exposure, I can distinguish later in leisure those images given by Spirit from those given by the wisdom of my psyche, from those forced out by suppressed forces demanding attention.*

—MINOR WHITE

The process of converting a RAW file into a viewable image made of pixels is often compared to the development of film. In both cases, impressions of light recorded using a light-sensitive surface are converted into a visible image. However, this is where the similarity ends.

While similar in principle, RAW conversion and film development are quite different. Color film development generally relies on standardized processes such as E6 for transparencies and C41 for color negatives. These processes leave very little room for image-specific adjustments and they offer practically no control over color balance and contrast, which are determined by the film's chemistry. Also, any shortcomings of the film or technique are carried over to the developed image without any ability to introduce corrections. Black-and-white film development is not quite as strict as color film development and does allow for some customization of contrast. However, with film such customizations should be predicted in advance, and, once applied, cannot be undone or fine-tuned. For example, to correct for exposure using push/pull processing, you'll need to know exactly how much to correct based on your decisions in the field. If you are unaware of exposure mistakes, you won't know they need correcting or by how much, and you may end up with an unusable image.

On the other hand, when converting a digital image from RAW, the conversion process can be varied and optimized to the unique needs of each individual exposure, and the effects of conversion settings can be seen instantly, changed, or rolled back if needed. The range of parameters within our control in RAW conversion is far greater than what is possible in the chemical darkroom, precision is much higher, and the process does not change the originally captured information, allowing an image to be converted and reconverted any number of times, in any number of ways, without degrading the original captured data.

**Converting with ACR or Lightroom**

Although examples in this chapter are demonstrated using Adobe Camera RAW (ACR)—the RAW converter that comes bundled, and is integrated, with Photoshop—all functions demonstrated are also available in Adobe Lightroom, which uses the same underlying engine.

## The Right Tool for the Right Job

RAW files are not the same as image files. RAW files contain measurements of the amount of light sampled by each of the millions of photosites making up the camera's sensor. There are virtually infinite ways to map these values into image data that can be displayed digitally. Specifically, to translate these measured values into a viewable image, they need to be mapped into pixels—dots of a specific color and lightness—in a process called *demosaicing* (referring to the fact that the photosites in a sensor are arranged in a mosaic-like pattern).

RAW conversion applications usually contain a variety of demosaicing algorithms to accommodate different RAW formats, as well as a visual interface consisting of tools that allow the user to control various parameters that govern how RAW readings are mapped into pixels.

It is important to keep in mind that the RAW converter, concerned with mapping RAW data into pixels, is not the same as an image editing application, such as Photoshop. Photoshop provides tools that operate on pixel values rather than on sensor readings. Although ACR and other RAW converters offer tools that are similar in function and appearance to some Photoshop tools, those are generally offered for convenience, or for users who are not interested in editing their work in Photoshop. They are not as powerful (in terms of precision or range) as the ones offered in Photoshop.

When working on a digital image captured in RAW format, the logical progression of data is this:

- Sensor converts analog light measurements into digital (numeric) values at each of its photosites and stores those readings in a RAW file.
- Sensor readings from the RAW file are mapped into pixels by the demosaicing algorithm in RAW conversion software (ACR, in our case).
- The resulting pixels are imported into an editing application (Photoshop, in our case) where further adjustments to their values can be applied with more precision and using a variety of tools.
- Pixels are saved in a common image format, such as TIFF or JPEG.

Applications like ACR and Lightroom in fact do more than just convert RAW data into pixels, and also offer some tools for controlling the resulting pixel values (color, contrast, etc.). This blurring of the lines can be helpful in streamlining some processes, such as when the goal is to reach an acceptable result quickly or to automate batch processing. However, for the purpose of making expressive images, the primary role of RAW conversion is to generate pixels, not to attempt to match the visualized outcome.

While, in some cases, matching the visualized outcome is possible using just the tools provided in the RAW converter and without going into Photoshop, I still recommend performing all color and contrast work in Photoshop and not in ACR (or Lightroom). This is because the tools offered in Photoshop are generally more powerful and precise, and because they can take advantage of Photoshop's ability to use layers and layer masks, which I explain later in the book.

In the workflow I describe here, our goal in the RAW conversion phase is to produce the best starting point for further adjustment using Photoshop.

## What Makes a Good Starting Point?

In converting from RAW, our goal is to provide Photoshop with an image that offers as much detail and flexibility as possible. Such an image may not look much like our visualized outcome, but that's OK. In fact, in most cases it is even encouraged.

A good starting point will generally have the following characteristics:

- **Low contrast and low color saturation:** As tempting as it is to wish to see our visualized image as early as possible, it is best to resist the urge to pursue shortcuts. There are distinct advantages to applying color and contrast adjustments using the accurate tools provided in Photoshop, rather than the crude sliders offered in ACR.
- **Large color space:** Other than converting sensor readings to pixels, the RAW converter also maps the colors in the image to a color space of your choice. As I explain in chapter 4, using a narrow color space, such as sRGB, may result in loss of color data, as out-of-gamut colors will be compressed into the limited range of options available. Large color spaces, such as Adobe RGB (1998) or ProPhoto RGB, can accommodate practically all colors found in a photograph.
- **16-bit color depth:** Like the color space consideration above, the more bits we use for each color channel, the finer the possible gradation of colors and tones. Although some sensors, in fact, capture only 12 or 14 bits of color data, there are no common file formats

that accommodate these possibilities. Therefore, it is preferable to use a 16-bit format (realizing that a couple of bits may not be used), rather than an 8-bit format, which may cause some color data to be discarded. At the time of this writing, even the most advanced camera sensors available do not exceed 16 bits of data per color channel, although it is worth mentioning that Photoshop already has the ability to support 32 bits per channel in some operations.

- **Adjustments best done in ACR:** Although most adjustments can be applied with greater precision in Photoshop than in ACR, there are some notable exceptions. One such exception is the correction of chromatic aberration—under some circumstances it is much easier and more precise using RAW data than pixel data.

## Converting from RAW Using ACR

Following is an overview of the essential tools offered in ACR (some of these are found in Lightroom as well). Similar tools may be found in other conversion software, although they may appear under different names.

Although ACR offers a wide array of powerful tools for adjusting color and contrast, and for making a variety of corrections, practically all these tools are superseded by Photoshop's better, more powerful tools. Recall that our goal in converting the RAW file is to provide Photoshop with the best possible starting point, rather than to attempt to match the visualized image. Therefore, I will only touch on a small number of controls that are useful in accomplishing the qualities I describe above for a good starting point.

### Default Settings

Before we begin using the various tools available in ACR, it is useful to configure some default settings to be applied to every image.

To set your defaults, start with a RAW file that has never been converted before. (If you don't already have one, click off a random image with your camera. The content of the image doesn't matter here.) This is because anything we change prior to saving new default settings will become part of these defaults, and we want to change *only* those things we want applied to all images.

Since ACR doesn't have its own standard menu system, the locations of some settings are not always obvious. Most notably, the settings for color space and bit depth are hidden behind the line at the bottom of the window

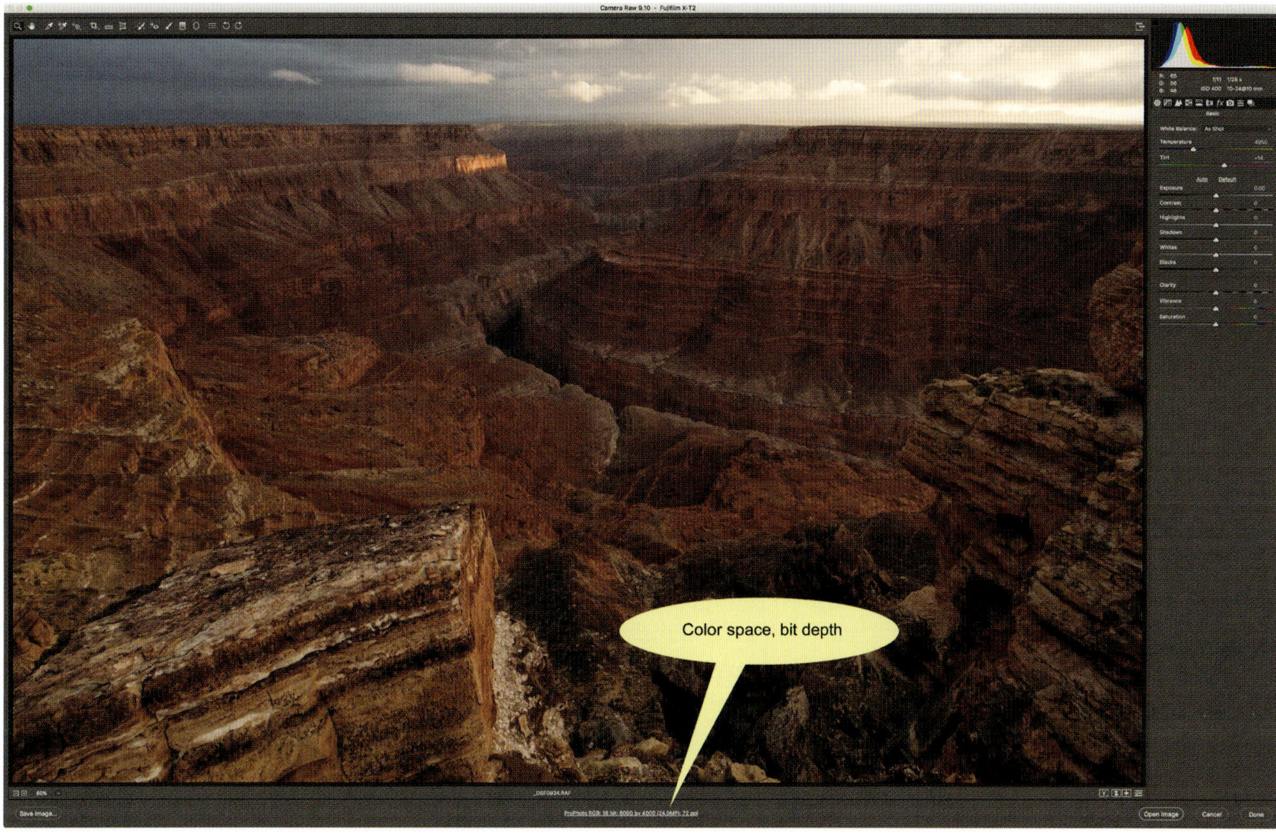


**Figure 8.1:** ACR window, when opening a RAW file. Note the line on the bottom indicating, among other information, the color space and bit depth. To change these settings, click on this line.

(figure 8.1). Click on this line to change these values. I recommend selecting *ProPhoto RGB* as your default color space and *16-Bits/Channel* as your color bit depth, as shown.

The resolution value (shown in figure 8.1 as 72 PPI) has no effect on the file but will become useful later when we derive various forms of output, such as prints. You can leave it at the default value (300 PPI) or select a different value if you already know what your most commonly used setting will be. This is not an important setting at this time, but is really just a laborsaving setting—you can change it later if a different setting is required.

### Why I Use 72 PPI

I set my default resolution to 72 PPI since, at this setting, text point size appears as we expect it. This is the setting we are used to seeing in word processors or other applications, so it's useful to me in generating a text watermark for my web images, which I do more often than other operations that require a different resolution setting.

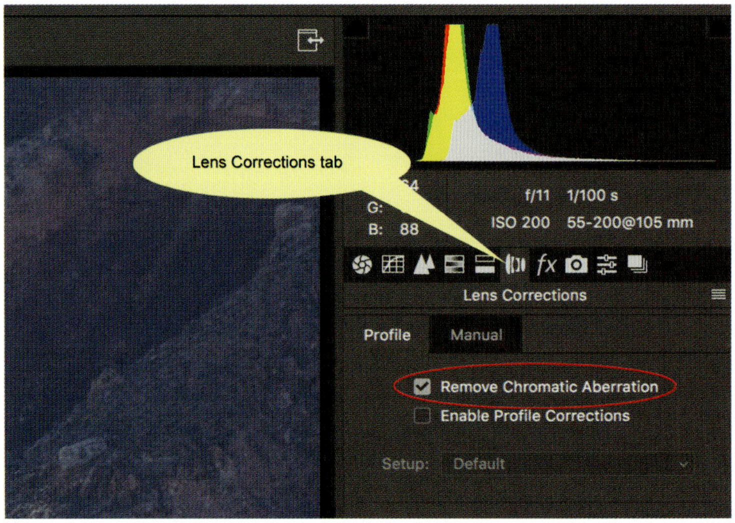


**FIGURE 8.2:** The setting for automatic removal of chromatic aberration in ACR.

Next, click the *Lens Corrections* tab and check the *Remove Chromatic Aberration* box (figure 8.2). This will enable the excellent automatic chromatic aberration removal function in ACR. I have used this option since its introduction and to date have not found a down side to leaving it activated for every image.

Now, save these settings as default by opening the *Settings* menu and selecting *Save New Camera Raw Defaults* (figure 8.3).

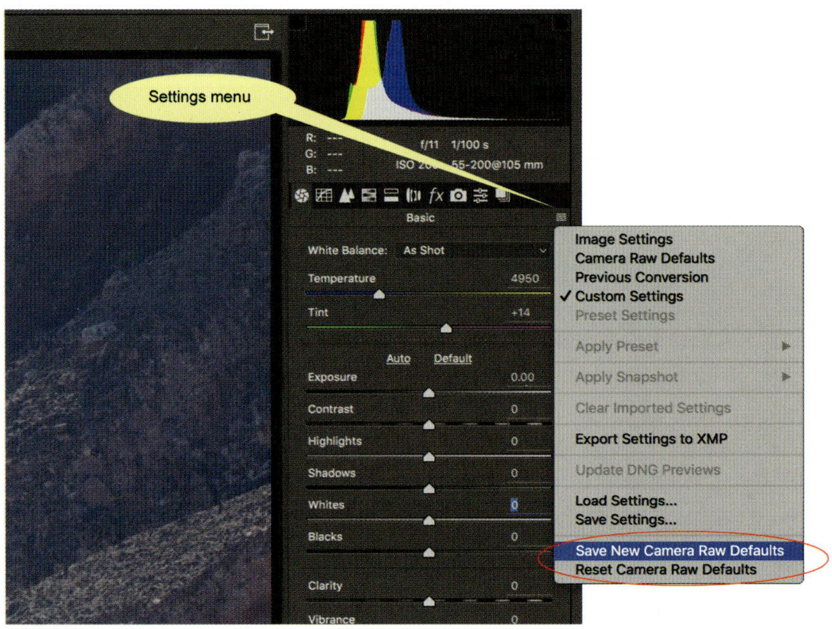


**FIGURE 8.3:** Saving the current settings as default.

These are the most common settings you likely will want applied to every image. In time and with experience you may realize there are other settings you use very frequently and want to make default. At that point you can update your default settings using the methods described here.

## White Balance (WB)

White Balance controls, shown in figure 8.4, are primarily used to compensate for color casts caused by various lighting conditions, although they are also useful in achieving a desirable color balance for a given image.

It used to be that color casts of any kind were considered undesirable and always had to be "corrected." While this approach may be useful for a variety of evidentiary images, it makes little sense when it comes to creative, expressive photography. Remember, our goal is to communicate not only appearances but also emotions, and color can be an extremely powerful means of evoking emotions (figure 8.5).

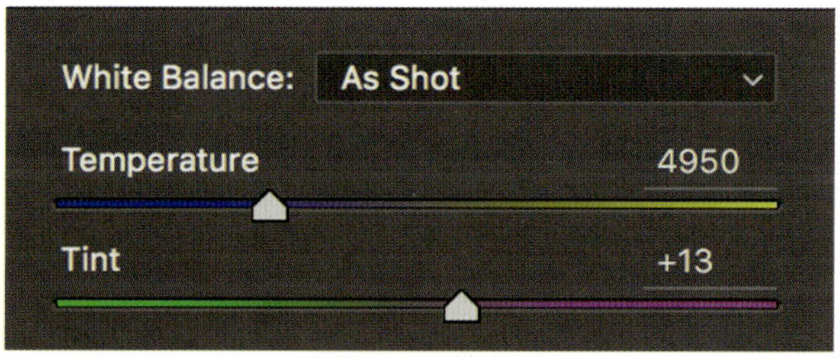


FIGURE 8.4: *White Balance* controls in ACR.

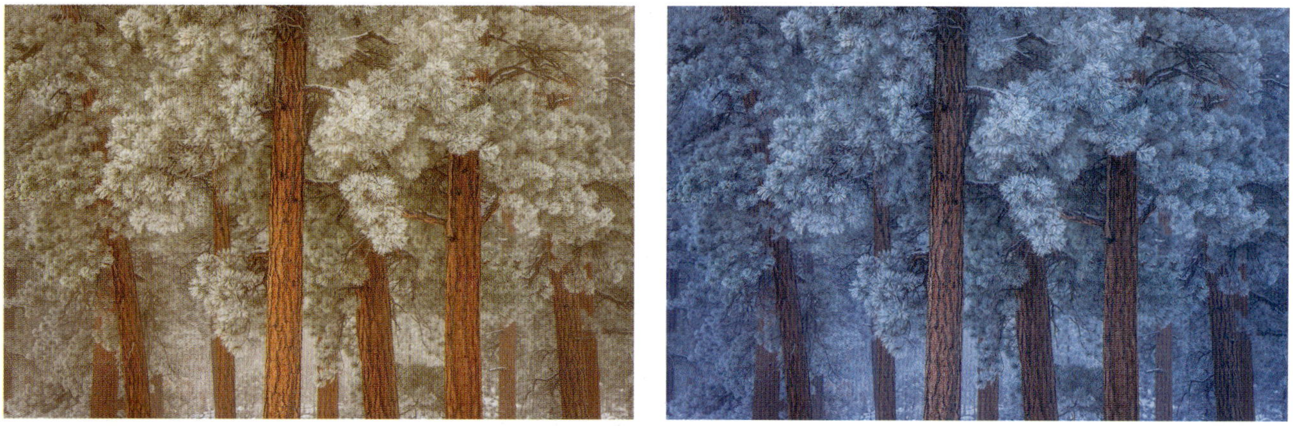

FIGURE 8.5: The image on the left was converted using the *Auto* setting, which automatically neutralizes color casts. It selected a color temperature of 6900°K, making the image appear very warm. However, obviously, the scene is a cold, wintry one—a feeling I wanted to communicate and emphasize. To do so, I manually set the color temperature to 5050°K (*right*), which added the blue tint I was after (and that I later enhanced further in Photoshop).

## Temperature and Tint

The *Temperature* slider (ranging from yellow to blue) uses a scale denominated in degrees Kelvin; and the *Tint* slider (ranging from green to magenta) has units arbitrarily ranging from –150 (on the green end) to +150 (on the magenta end). The combination of the two allows correction of color casts introduced by variations in the light's color.

You may wonder why photographers should care about degrees Kelvin, or why these two strange sliders are useful, rather than Adobe allowing us to choose a desired color from a color wheel containing the entire spectrum. The reason is that these controls allow traversing the range of possible colors of natural light. This is a useful distinction to keep in mind. We can use these controls to simulate the appearance of a variety of natural light conditions, however, if our expressive goal requires colors that fall outside the range of natural light, we will want to use other tools to further adjust colors.

### Measuring the Color of Light

The *Temperature* and *Tint* scales in ACR—ranging from yellow to blue and from green to magenta—correspond to the sensitivities of different types of cone cells in our eyes, which enable us to see color. Measuring color in terms of temperature comes from the discipline of quantum physics, and refers to the color of light emitted by a device called a *black body radiator* when heated to a given temperature. The black body radiator is a perfectly black piece of metal, meaning that it does not reflect any light. When heated, light measured from the black body radiator is a direct result of the amount of energy fed into it, rather than ambient light reflecting off it. For many years, it was unclear why, when a black body radiator is heated, the light it emits not only becomes brighter with more energy (which is to be expected), but also changes color (which is where the term *color temperature* comes from). It was the great physicist Max Planck who explained the changes in color by suggesting that light can behave as a particle, and not just as a wave, setting the foundation for the current science of quantum mechanics.

What does this have to do with photography? Not much. It's like knowing the number of RPMs (revolutions per minute) your car engine is spinning at while driving, when in fact all you really need to know is that your engine is working and how fast you are moving. Still, many cars offer tachometers, showing the driver the number of RPMs in case the driver is skilled enough (and interested enough) to make use of such information to optimize performance.

The proper way to use *Temperature* and *Tint* is to arrive at a more-or-less correct color cast that best fits the mood you wish your image to have. Once in Photoshop, we have far better tools for adjusting and fine-tuning individual colors with far greater precision than these controls allow.

Note that ACR gives you a variety of presets to choose from in order to correct an image for specific known lighting conditions (*Daylight*, *Cloudy*, etc.).

I suggest ignoring these. Not only are they inaccurate, but if our goal is an expressive (rather than documentary) one, we can use color casts to attain a specific mood, rather than to neutralize all color casts or to be constrained to the color of light detected at the time of capture.

The *Auto* option will attempt to simulate the *Auto White Balance* (AWB) setting on your camera to automatically neutralize color casts. This option is entirely useless in expressive photography.

ACR also provides a *White Balance* tool (figure 8.6). This tool is useful in cases where absolute color neutrality is needed, such as when photographing products and the logo colors must exactly match the client's specifications, or when photographing a wedding and the bride's dress must appear perfectly white. This tool is only useful when there is a neutral reference point in the image that can be sampled. Some product photographers intentionally place a neutrally colored object in the frame for that purpose, and then reshoot the scene without it. The frame with the neutral object is then used with the *White Balance* tool to determine the precise *Temperature* and *Tint* settings, which can then be applied to the frame that does not have the neutral object in it. While it may be a nifty function to have it serves no expressive purpose.

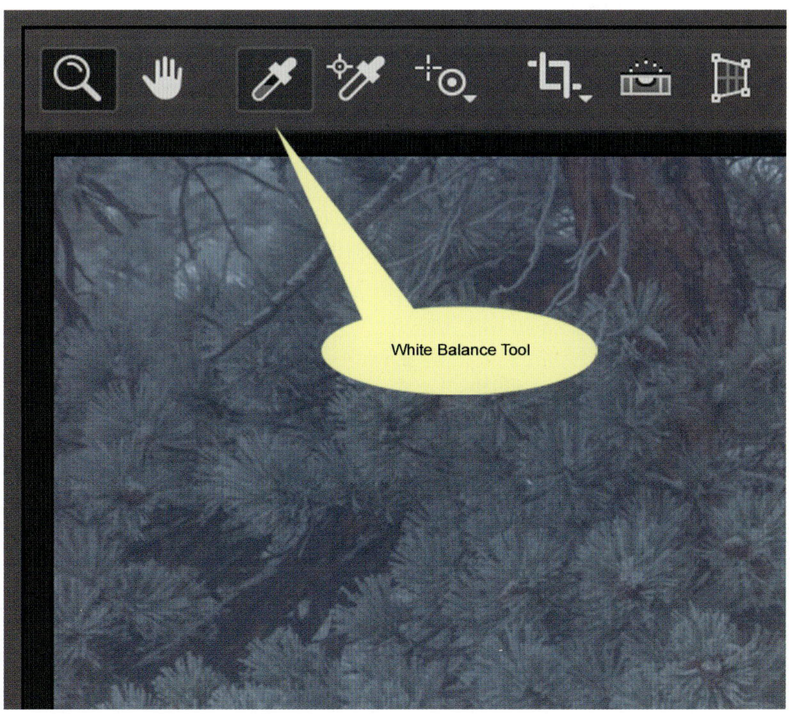


FIGURE 8.6: The White Balance tool in ACR.

## Exposure, Highlights, and Shadows

The *Exposure, Highlights,* and *Shadows* sliders control the lightness of specific ranges of tones. *Exposure,* despite its name, does not control exposure, but rather the lightness of the midtone areas. *Highlights* controls the lightness of the lightest tones in the image and can be useful in recovering over-exposed areas (assuming the data is available in the file). *Shadows* controls the lightness of the darkest tones in the image and can be useful in recovering details in under-exposed areas (again, assuming the data is available in the file).

To gain a deeper understanding of what these sliders control, consider a histogram divided into four equal sections, or blocks. Values on the rightmost 25% of the scale are generally considered the highlights; values on the leftmost 25% of the scale are generally considered the shadows; and the middle 50% contains the mid-tones (figure 8.7).

When one of the *Exposure, Highlights,* or *Shadows* sliders is moved, values in the corresponding section of the histogram are shifted to lighter or darker tones; however, the histogram section within the block remains the same. Put another way, tonal relationships (the distribution of values within the block) are preserved. Other tones are preserved when possible, but may be compressed or expanded to accommodate the new placement of the block being moved.

## Contrast

Contrast is defined as the difference in either lightness or color between adjacent elements. The greater the difference, the higher the contrast—and vice versa. The *Contrast* slider in ACR (and Lightroom) controls differences in

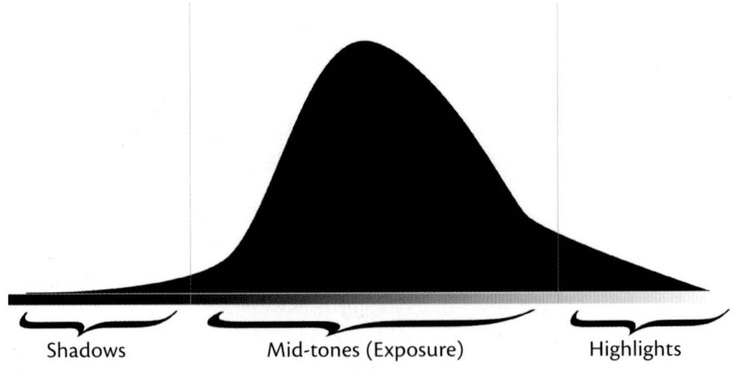


FIGURE 8.7: Blocks of tone corresponding to the *Exposure, Highlights,* and *Shadows* sliders.

lightness. When moved, tones are either pulled apart from each other (contrast is increased) or brought closer together (contrast is decreased).

I recommend *not* using this slider to affect the final appearance of the image. It is a crude tool and we'll have much better tools to manage contrast later when we bring the image into Photoshop.

That said, the *Contrast* slider can be useful in cases when we may want to *temporarily* increase contrast so we can have better visual feedback when performing other adjustments, especially if the image as-captured has inherently low contrast. Increasing the contrast temporarily allows us to see the effects of other tools more clearly. Once these effects are tuned as we like them, we can move the *Contrast* slider back to its neutral position.

## Whites and Blacks

The lightest tone in an image, marked by the point at which the histogram ends on the right, is called the *White Point;* the darkest tone in an image, marked by the point at which the histogram ends on the left, is called the *Black Point* (figure 8.8).

The *Whites* and *Blacks* sliders allow shifting of the white and black points, and then stretch or contract the rest of the tones in the image to accommodate the new values. This can be useful in a couple of ways:

- If the histogram is still clipped even after adjusting the *Highlights* and/or *Shadows* sliders to their maximum settings, shifting the white or black point(s) can be used to avoid clipping. It is important to keep in mind that doing so will not bring back values that are lost due to over- or under-exposure. Therefore, I suggest only using this technique to bring overexposed highlights into the histogram (to eliminate pure whites, which may be problematic in printing, as I explain

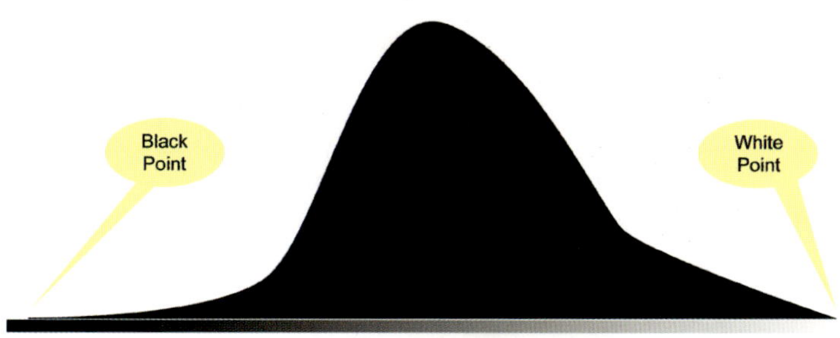


FIGURE 8.8: Locations of the white and black points, as reflected in the histogram. These points can be moved using the *Whites* and *Blacks* sliders.

later in the book). Moving a clipped black point into the histogram may push other tones closer together and result in loss of detail, especially in the shadows.

- If we want to deliberately clip the shadows to create silhouettes, moving the black point can be useful, realizing that the farther we push the black point, the more dark tones will be mapped to pure black, and assuming that this is desirable.

Use these controls with caution. Keep in mind that if you're expanding the tonal range (stretching the histogram to be wider than its original breadth), new gradations of tone will be manufactured. And, if you're contracting the tonal range (making the histogram narrower than its original breadth), tones will be bunched together into fewer values. Either one, if taken far enough, may result in noticeable loss of detail.

## Clarity

The *Clarity* slider uses a proprietary algorithm to sharpen details, particularly in the midtones. As I explain later in the book, sharpening really is a form of contrast adjustment applied to edges (the lines separating visual elements). When we increase *Clarity,* lines become more defined (the difference—or contrast—between one side of the line and the other is stretched out), making the image appear more detailed.

I recommend not using this slider, except in small doses and when detail is difficult to see. The reason is that sharpening is a destructive operation—although it may give the appearance of the image being more detailed, it may in fact degrade very fine details.

If you like the effect of *Clarity,* my suggestion is to simulate it in Photoshop, and apply it more precisely where needed using a local adjustment (i.e., using a layer mask, which I explain later), rather than as a global adjustment.

## Vibrance and Saturation

As the name suggests, these controls affect the visual impact of an image by making colors appear more or less vivid. Despite the two names, both sliders control color saturation. The difference is that the *Saturation* slider affects all colors to the same degree, while the *Vibrance* slider is proportional. Increasing *Vibrance* applies more of the effect to less-saturated colors, which may help avoid over-saturating colors that already appear saturated enough, and vice-versa.

Here, again, it is worth keeping in mind that Photoshop offers better tools for adjusting color than do ACR or Lightroom, so I recommend not attempting to use these sliders just to make the image look better at this point—we can do that more precisely later.

These sliders can be useful when we wish to *temporarily* increase color saturation so we have a better idea of what the different hues in the image look like as we adjust other settings, such as the *Temperature* and *Tint* sliders. To do so, increase saturation until colors become easy to discern. Then, adjust the desired settings (e.g., *Temperature/Tint*) until overall color balance appears correct (keeping in mind that you can still adjust and fine-tune colors later, and with greater precision, in Photoshop). Then dial saturation back to its neutral position.

Another good use for these sliders is when we wish to equalize color saturation across the image (i.e., bring all colors to the same level of saturation). To do so, use the following method:

- Use the *Vibrance* slider to increase saturation. Since this slider applies more of the effect to the least-saturated colors, keep moving until these colors appear correct and ignore already-saturated colors, which may become oversaturated.
- Use the *Saturation* slider to *decrease* overall saturation. Since this slider applies its effect to all colors, the previously less-saturated colors will remain relatively more saturated than they were originally.
- Repeat this process a couple of times until colors appear evenly saturated.

## RAW Conversion Example

In this example, keep in mind our goal of producing a good starting point for further processing in Photoshop, rather than to make the image match our visualization.

The image in this example was captured during a cold winter trek into the famous Subway in Zion National Park, and I wanted the image to reflect not only the icy conditions but also the sense of awe I felt being by myself in this magical place, frozen yet glowing in the warm light, the polished red sandstone, the emerald pools, and the crystalline waters flowing at my feet.

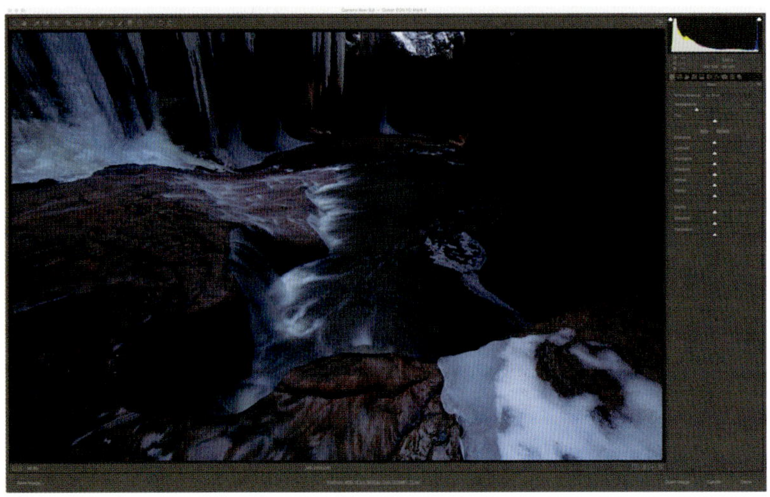

FIGURE 8.9: The image as initially displayed when opened in ACR using the default settings.

FIGURE 8.10: The image as visualized and processed.

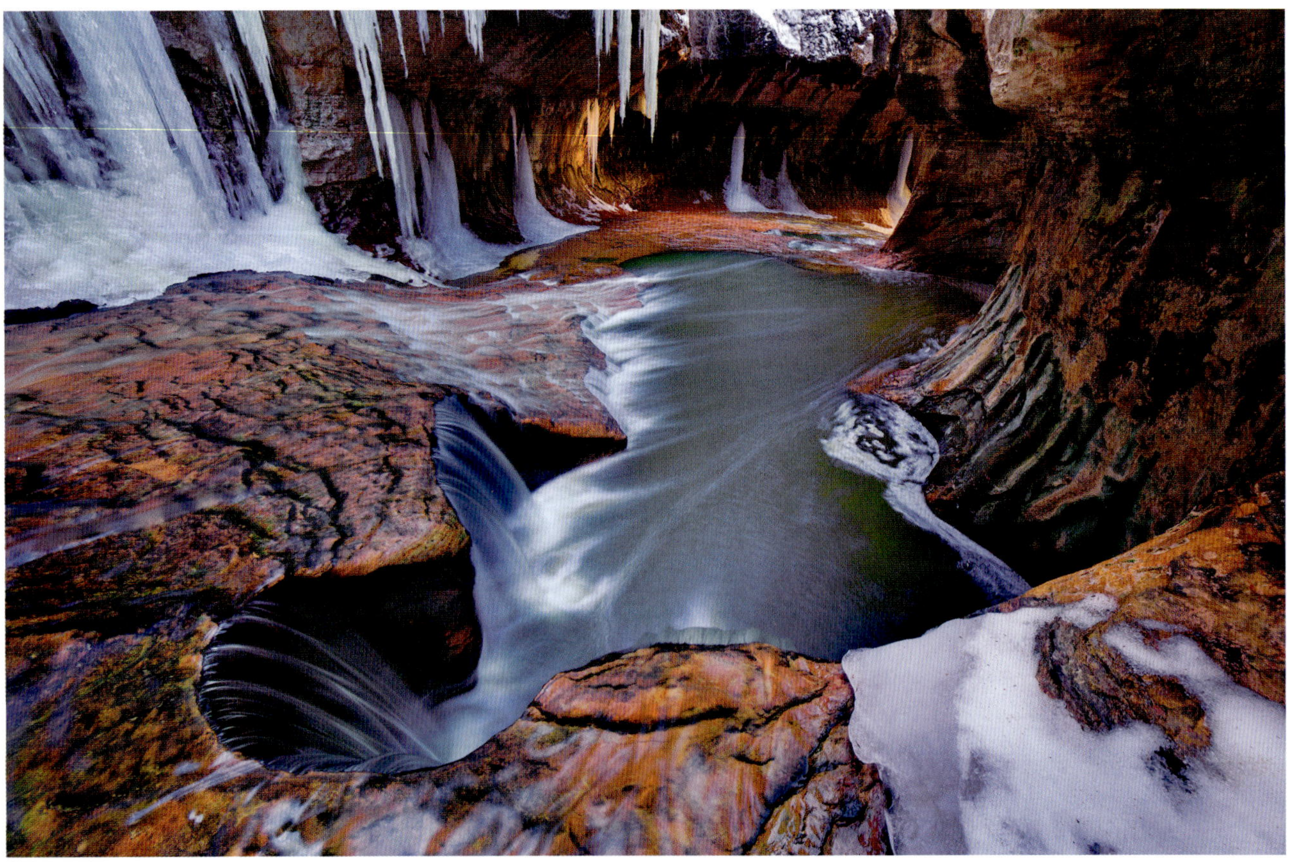

I started with a RAW file and a visualized outcome in mind (figures 8.9 and 8.10).

As before, I began with an analysis of the RAW file. I will spare you the steps already described in chapter 6, "Image Analysis," and will provide you with the following list of gaps I came up with:

| | Description | Location | Possible Mitigation |
|---|---|---|---|
| 1 | Clipped highlights | Upper edge, right of center | Use *Highlights* slider to recover missing details, or<br><br>Use a burn layer in Photoshop, or<br><br>Clone out completely |
| 2 | Clipped shadows | Right and rear walls | Use *Shadows* slider to recover missing details, or<br><br>Use a dodge layer in Photoshop, or<br><br>Leave as-is |
| 3 | Chromatic aberration | Along edges of icicles | Examine image at 100% magnification, correct aberration in Lightroom or ACR |
| 4 | Color cast too blue; need to better separate reds from blues and greens | Global | Adjust *Temperature* and *Tint* in Lightroom or ACR to ensure reds and emerald greens are well separated |
| 5 | Contrast too high | Global | Adjust *Highlights* and *Shadows* for more even contrast |

Before proceeding, it is important to determine the best order in which to address these gaps. In this case, I decided to first work on gaps 1 and 2. If I could not recover the clipped details, my approach may need to change. If these details are critical, I may decide to discard the image altogether, or, if I did my job properly in the field, I may turn to other bracketed exposures to recover missing details.

Using the *Blacks* and *Whites* sliders I was able to regain the clipped details, although doing so compressed the remaining tones a bit (figure 8.11). To retain *all* tones and to control noise, blending bracketed exposures would likely still be a preferred option in this case, as I explain later in the book.

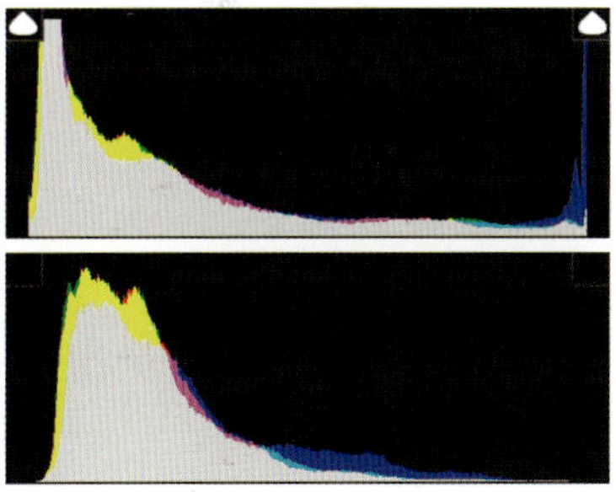

**FIGURE 8.11:** The initial, clipped histogram (top) and the corrected version, using the *Blacks* and *Whites* sliders (bottom).

Next, I used the *Highlights*, *Shadows*, and *Exposure* sliders to achieve a better balance between highlights and shadows (figure 8.12).

Although the image may appear correct at the screen size, it is always good to review it at 100% (1:1) magnification after corrections have been made. The compressed histogram (compared with the original) suggests that new artifacts may have been introduced as a result of the extreme val-

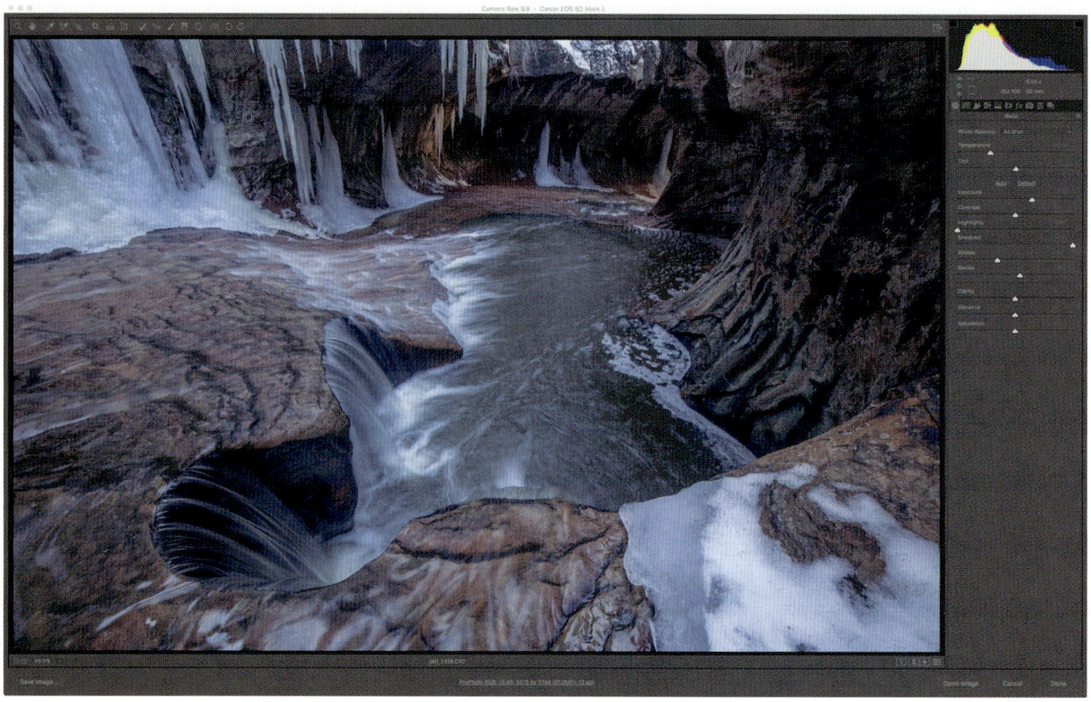

**Figure 8.12:** The image after tonal correction using the *Highlights*, *Shadows* and *Exposure* sliders.

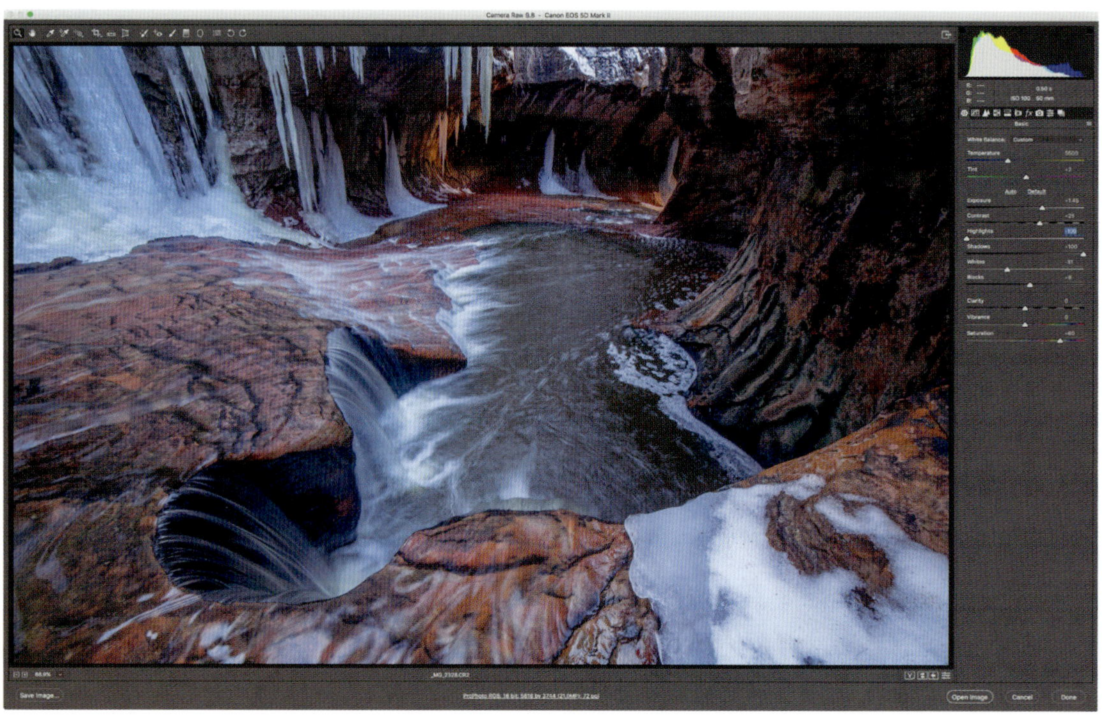

**Figure 8.13:** The image after temporarily increasing *Saturation* and *Contrast*, and fine-tuning the *Temperature* and *Tint* sliders.

ues needed to achieve the desired tonal balance. Indeed, the small patch of bright light on the upper right now appears posterized (lacking smooth, continuous tone), as seen in figure 8.14.

This introduces an interesting conundrum: I could pull back on some of the previously-applied corrections to regain smoother tones in this small area, but this would have meant going back to a non-optimal tonal balance in the rest of the image. This is a shortcoming of global adjustments. What was needed was a local correction, which could be applied more precisely in Photoshop later, rather than in the RAW converter. Realizing this, I noted it as a new gap to be addressed later. Jumping ahead, I'll reveal that I ended up making a second conversion of the same RAW file using different values tailored to just this one small area, and I then blended the two versions to achieve the visualized result.

At this point—prior to tackling the color cast (gap 4) and chromatic aberration (gap 3)—I set the *Saturation* slider to +60 and the *Contrast* slider to +25 (these are arbitrary values arrived at by pulling the sliders while looking at the image on the screen. Other images may require different settings). My goal was to temporarily simulate the colors and contrast I wanted in my final image, as closely as possible. This had the effect of making colors more vibrant so I could better assess their balance, and the chromatic aberration became more visible, making it easier to correct.

With the increase in saturation and contrast, I went back to my *Temperature* and *Tint* sliders and adjusted them to 5500°K and –2, respectively, to achieve the ideal color balance to my eye (figure 8.13).

Note that while the image may have appeared on screen very close to my visualized outcome, I still preferred to roll back the Saturation and Contrast settings so that I could apply them more precisely, and with better tools, later in Photoshop.

Last, correcting chromatic aberration is best done at high magnification. Setting the magnification to 300% (3:1), the subtle fringes along the icicles became clearly visible (figure 8.14). Using the simple check box for correcting chromatic aberration eliminated gap 3.

I then return to the *Saturation* and *Contrast* sliders to their default settings, and my image was ready for further processing in Photoshop.

Remember to first define your desired (visualized) outcome and perform an analysis of the gaps before jumping into the RAW converter. Practice both the workflow and your conversion skills!

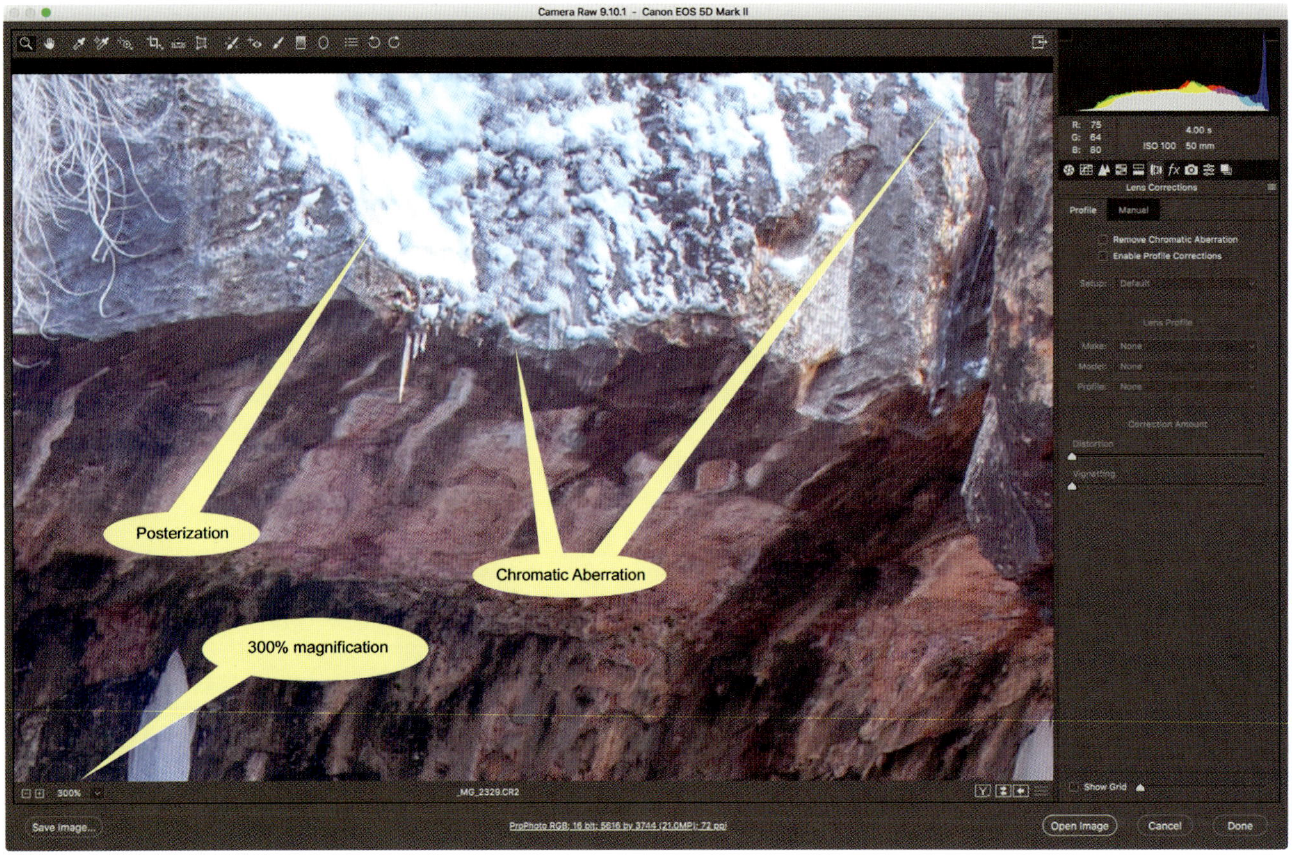


FIGURE 8.14: Studying this image at high magnification (300%) revealed that this small area exhibits both posterization and a small amount of chromatic aberration.

## EXERCISE 4

1. List some of the desired characteristics of a good starting point for post-processing. If unsure, the answer can be found on page 129.
2. While clipping is not generally desirable, there may be cases when it is actually OK. Can you think of any? If unsure, the answer can be found on page 82.
3. Explain how the *Saturation*, *Vibrance*, and *Contrast* tools, although not recommended in the conversion phase, can be used to optimize other settings. If unsure, find the answers on pages 136 and 139.
4. Why is it worth reviewing the image at 100% magnification both before and after making adjustments in the RAW converter? If unsure, the answers can be found in the Image Analysis chapter and on page 141.
5. Select one of your RAW files (or capture one for the sake of this exercise) that exhibits high contrast. Use the tools and processes described in this chapter to convert it to meet the criteria for a good starting point as described on page 129.

*See Appendix for answer key.*

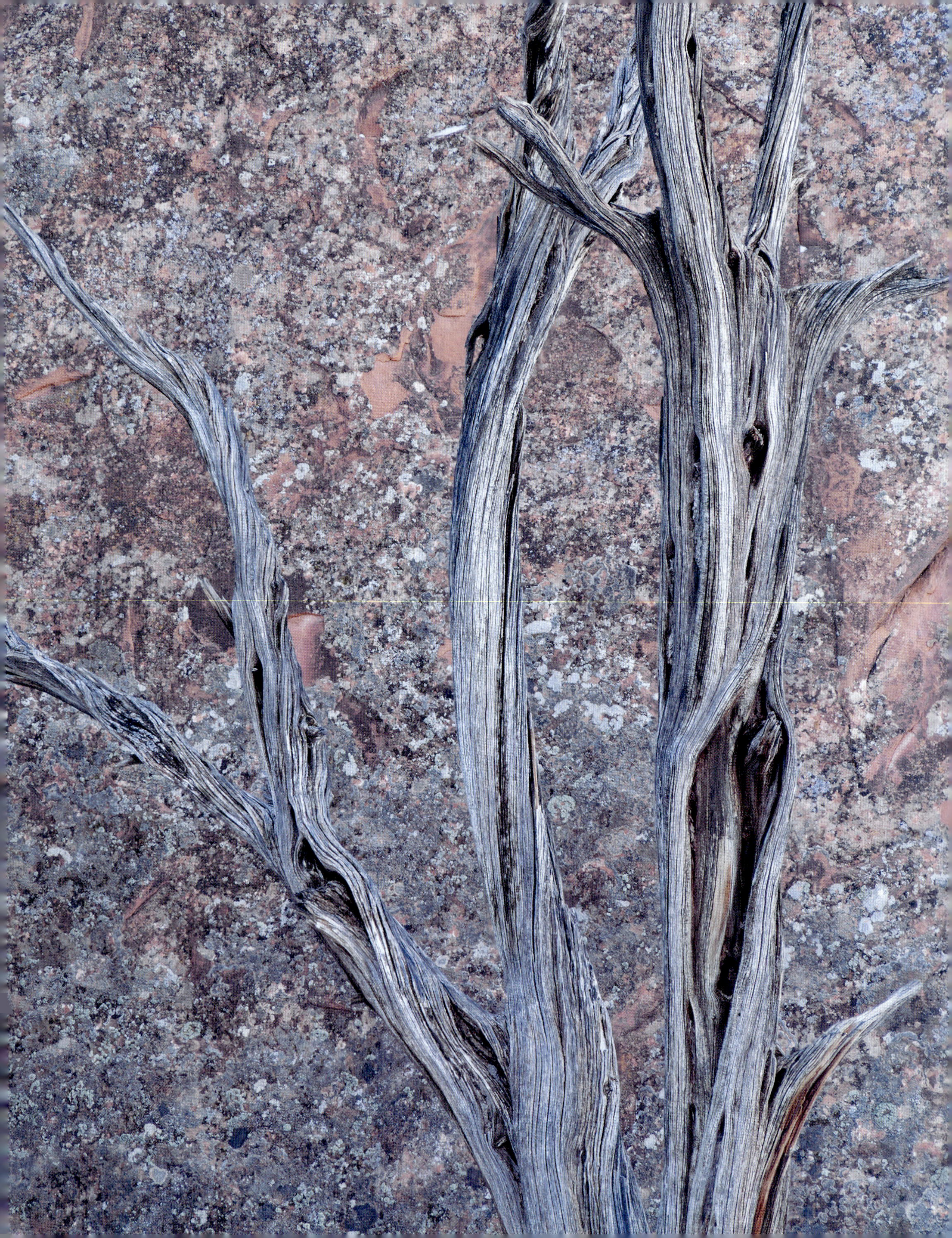

# Photoshop Basics

9

*Craftsmanship is the fundamental basis which you can learn and develop provided you start with absolute respect for your materials, which, as students of photography, are a machine called camera and the chemistry of light and other agents upon metals. The living element, the plus, you can also develop if it is potentially there. It cannot be taught or given you. Its development is conditioned by your own feeling which must be a free way of living. By a free way of living I mean the difficult process of finding out what your own feeling about the world is, disentangling it from other people's feelings and ideas.*

—PAUL STRAND

In the nearly three decades since Photoshop was introduced, digital imaging has become progressively more popular and affordable, computers have become more powerful and accessible, and Adobe has continued to add countless features to Photoshop. Some of these features are relevant and useful to landscape photographers, while others are less so or not at all. As Photoshop evolved, Adobe, for the most part, did not remove older functions and tools even when replaced by newer and better ones, so as not to disrupt users' existing workflows and automated scripts. This abundance of features not only makes Photoshop an extremely powerful application, but also is responsible for Photoshop's reputation for being somewhat complex and difficult to master, especially when compared with more targeted and less feature-rich applications, such as Lightroom. Also, since Photoshop's user interface largely remained consistent throughout its history, it might seem somewhat dated when compared with more recently designed applications that take advantage of more contemporary features and design paradigms.

Becoming acquainted with, and skilled at using, Photoshop's myriad features (even just the subset relevant to landscape photographers) takes time, and Photoshop will almost always offer more techniques and possibilities than any one user can know or have use for. On the other hand, once you become familiar with Photoshop's features that are relevant to your own type of work, you will be rewarded with unprecedented power: the power to shape images with great control and precision down to the individual pixel level, if needed.

As you learn to use Photoshop, keep in mind that while the process of learning may require an investment of time and practice, and may even be a bit frustrating at times, it is an investment well worth making. Consider that, as photographic artists, Photoshop gives us the most comprehensive, powerful, and precise set of software tools available to process our images—our art. Think about the time and effort that a violinist, a painter, or a sculptor needs to invest in mastering their instruments. As photographic artists, making a similar investment in becoming proficient with the best tools available is, I believe, not only justifiable but also necessary.

It is impossible to cover all the features of Photoshop in a single book. Also, given Adobe's design methodology, you may often find there are multiple ways to accomplish the same result in Photoshop. What I share in this book are those tools and techniques I find most useful in my own work.

As we delve into technical details, it's easy to become focused on technical considerations, and to inadvertently lose sight of the bigger picture—our expressive intent manifested in the visualized image. Always keep in mind where you are in the process. Use the workflow chart found in chapter 7 as a roadmap while you guide the image toward your desired outcome. Work in small, incremental iterations, focusing on a few gaps (or one large gap) at a time; pause to re-visualize and analyze after each iteration and then decide on the next adjustment.

While the computer may represent your image as a set of pixels, numbers, graphs, layers, and masks, don't be tempted to think of your image in these terms; don't lose sight of the emotional and aesthetic values you are working to express, and the viewers whose hearts you wish to touch. The goal is not to become a computer operator who is mindlessly pushing buttons and moving sliders like a mad alchemist hoping something magical will emerge from a jumble of bubbling beakers, vials, and instruments. We are artists, here to create visual art. One of the things I love most about Photoshop is that it is not all about numbers and computerized interfaces; it also allows us to work with our hands, using virtual brushes, creating selections manually, and receiving instant visual feedback, allowing us to feel much as a painter might feel when stroking the canvas with a brush. Processing images can be a visceral and tactile experience, not just a technical one.

While some instructors preach the approach of editing "by the numbers," minding numerical values for colors, lightness, and other properties of the image, my belief is that this approach is more appropriate for such things as balancing your checkbook or preparing your taxes, rather than creating expressive art. Always edit visually, no matter what the numbers say. The primary goal is to get your images to look the way you want them to. Only then should you worry about numbers to fine-tune the image to the best possible technical qualities.

I strongly recommend working with a color-calibrated display. As I mention earlier in the book, colorimeters for screen calibration are relatively inexpensive and they ensure consistency among the various devices used to reproduce your image (e.g., printers and other people's screens). Without a calibrated display you are "flying blind" and can't be certain that the image you see on your screen will appear the same way in a print or on another person's screen.

## A Word about Attitude

A common quip I hear from novice photographers—and especially nature photographers who often wish to spend their time in the field rather than working at the computer—is that image processing is a necessary evil and as such should be automated and simplified as much as possible. I suggest making a conscious effort to transcend such an attitude. It is within your power to consciously choose to approach processing as an enjoyable, creative, and satisfying experience, which it absolutely can be.

Not only can the time spent processing be enjoyable and deeply intimate, but also, seeing your visualization coming to life, out of the recesses of your mind, transformed into a luminous and beautifully crafted image, whether on screen or in print, is a wonderful feeling.

To repudiate such inner rewards is not only to rob yourself of the joys that are to be found in processing, but also to ignore the possibility that investing time in processing can be essential to your success as an artist. As we speak, there may be untold numbers of would-be masterpieces sitting in photographers' files that may never earn the recognition they deserve if not properly processed and presented so they fully convey the genius and creativity that went into their making.

Don't quit before the finish line.

## Arranging Your Photoshop Workspace

Let's first get comfortable within Photoshop's workspace, which I like to refer to as the *digital studio*. You'll be much more productive when your most frequently used tools are within easy reach, the most important information is in prominent view, and any excessive or distracting items are tucked away out of sight.

To address the inevitably complex task of making a staggering number of features and options accessible without undue clutter, Adobe developed a clever method of arranging tools and information so workspaces can be customized to a given user's needs. Tools and adjustments are grouped into panels, which are small windows that can be dragged and placed around the screen. Panels can also be pinned, stacked so they are accessible using tabs within the same container, appear at the click of a button using the flyout menu, or hidden from view completely.

The workspace I use is shown in figure 9.1. This arrangement provides a clean workspace with easy access to the things we will use most frequently. Let's review what's on the screen:

- **Tools panel:** This panel contains a variety of selection, painting, correction, text, and other tools.
- **Control panel:** This panel's contents change based on which tool is selected, and provides options and settings relevant for that tool.
- **Histogram panel:** This panel can show a variety of histogram types. Like the histogram available in your camera, the Photoshop histograms provide invaluable information about your image at a glance.
- **Properties panel:** This panel's contents change based on which adjustment is selected. It shows the various options and controls relevant to that adjustment.

FIGURE 9.1: My Photoshop workspace.

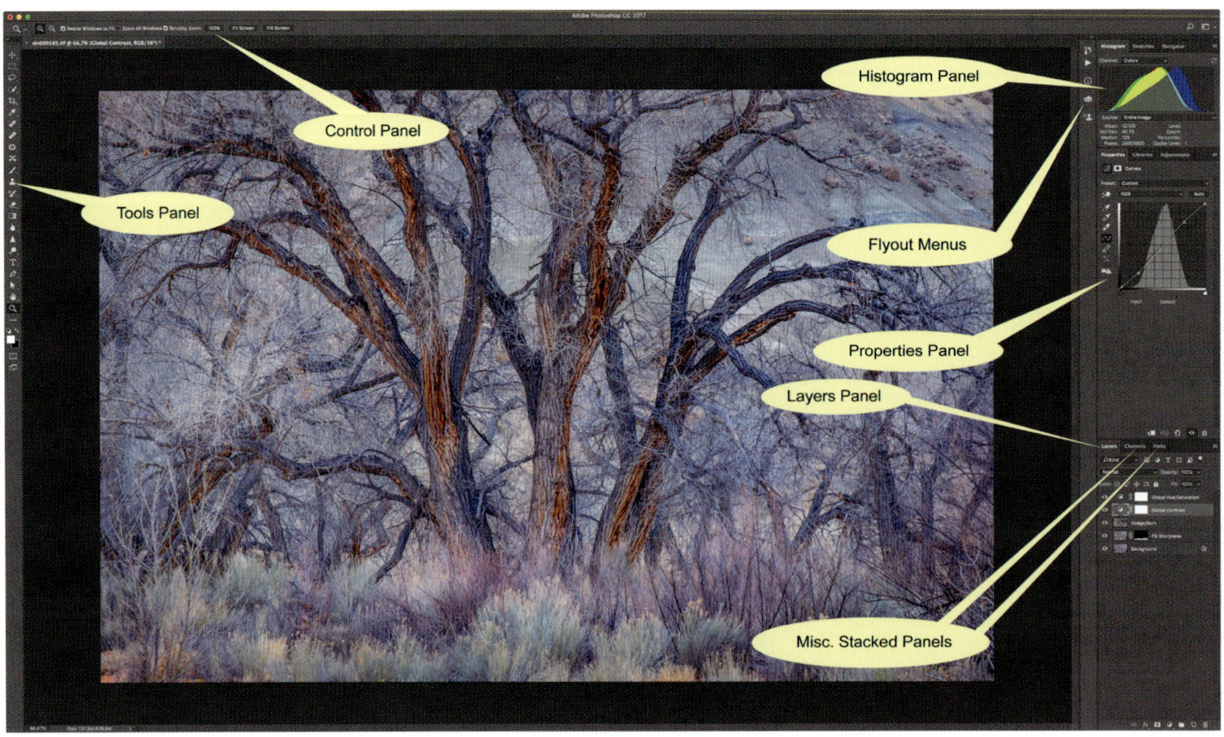

- **Layers panel:** This panel shows the layers making up the current image so they can easily be selected, adjusted, rearranged, masked, made visible or invisible, etc.
- **Miscellaneous panels:** Other panels can be accessed as tabs in containers by clicking them or by selecting them from the flyout menu.

**Missing Panels?**

If you are unable to find a given panel within your Photoshop workspace, chances are it is unchecked in the *Window* menu. Selecting the desired panel from this menu will make it pop out of wherever it is hiding. If you wish to pin this panel to an existing container, or even to have it float over the image, you can drag it by its title and place it where convenient.

## Keyboard Shortcuts

Photoshop offers a multitude of keyboard shortcuts to activate various functions. In time, you'll memorize many of them that correspond to your most used operations.

At this point, I suggest setting aside a clean sheet of paper or starting a new text document where you can keep track of keyboard shortcuts as I mention them. Keyboard shortcuts not only save labor when it comes to moving around the screen or navigating through menus, they also make processing more viscerally intuitive.

Below are a few initial keyboard shortcuts worth memorizing:

- **Command/Ctrl+Space** activates the *Zoom In* function. While holding down both keys, click anywhere in the image to magnify it. Repeated clicks will increase magnification.
- **Option/Alt+Space** activates the *Zoom Out* function. Hold down both keys and click anywhere in the image to reduce magnification.
- **Command/Ctrl+0** zooms in or out to fit the image in the available screen space.
- **Command/Ctrl+1** zooms the image to 100% (1:1) magnification.
- **Holding down the Space bar** activates the *Hand* tool, which, when the image is larger than can fit in the Photoshop window, allows you to pan around the image by dragging it with your mouse or other pointing device. Keep the Space bar pressed and drag the image around to view different areas.
- **The Tab key** toggles between hiding and revealing the tools and panels. If your screen becomes too cluttered with tools and you want to see just the image, click the Tab key once to hide the clutter and again to bring everything back.

## EXERCISE 5

1. Reset your workspace to the default *Photography* workspace by opening the *Choose a Workspace* menu in the upper right corner and selecting *Photography* (figure 9.2). If *Photography* is already checked, select *Reset Photography*.

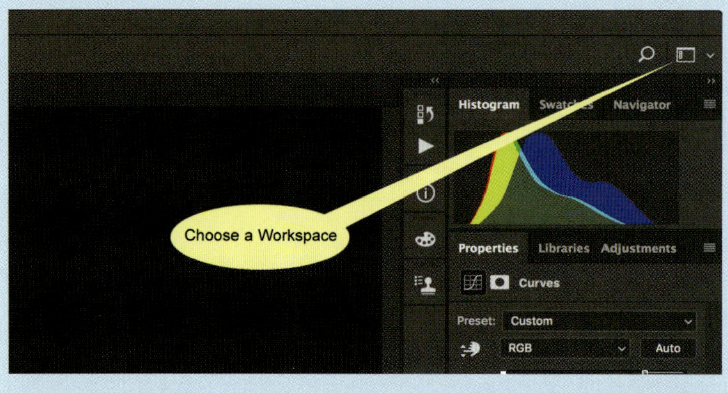


FIGURE 9.2: The *Choose a Workspace* menu.

2. From the *Window* menu, select *Properties* to bring out the *Properties* panel, which by default is tucked into the flyout menu.

3. Drag the *Properties* panel (by clicking on the word "Properties" and dragging it), and place it in the same container that by default has the *Libraries* and *Adjustments* tabs. Keep holding down the mouse button and hover over the word "Libraries" or "Adjustments" until the container border flashes blue, then release the button. The container will now have the *Properties* panel as a new tab (figure 9.3).

4. Save this as your default workspace by opening the *Choose a Workspace* menu and selecting *New Workspace*. Name your workspace as you wish, and be sure to check the *Keyboard Shortcuts, Menus,* and *Toolbar* boxes. This will ensure that you can always reset your workspace to this configuration, if things go awry.

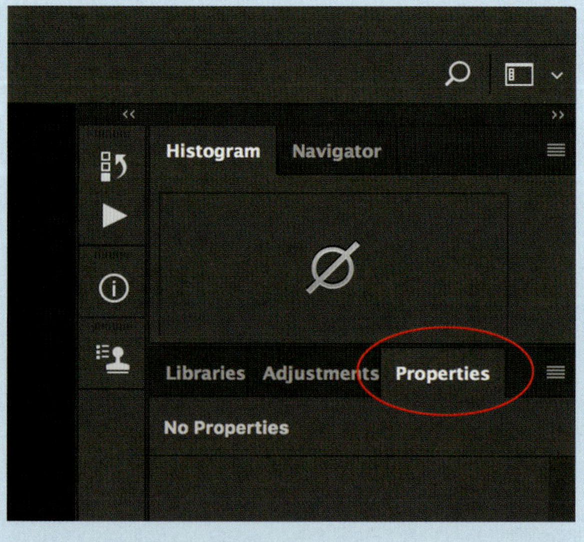


FIGURE 9.3: The *Properties* panel as part of the same container that originally only had *Libraries* and *Adjustments*.

**PC vs. Mac Modifier Keys**

While keyboard shortcut letters and numbers are consistent between PC/Windows and Mac/OSX, the modifier keys are unique to each platform: the Ctrl key on a PC keyboard is equivalent to the Command key on a Mac keyboard, and the Alt key on PC keyboard is equivalent to the Option key on a Mac keyboard. For convenience, I use the notation "Command/Ctrl" and "Option/Alt" to indicate use of the relevant keys for each platform.

## The *Tools* Panel

The tools in the *Tools* panel (figure 9.4) can be used to perform a variety of operations on the currently selected layer. When first opening an image, it will appear as a layer in the *Layers* panel titled *Background*. I'll describe other types of layers later in the chapter. For now, I'll just point out some of the features associated with the *Tools* panel.

Tools that have a small triangle in the lower-right corner offer multiple options or variations. To toggle through the various options, hold down the Option/Alt key and click on the button to rotate through the options. When a tool is selected, the *Control* panel at the top automatically changes to show any options that may be associated with the selected tool.

Toward the bottom of the *Tools* panel, you'll notice two overlapping squares showing the current foreground (top) and background (bottom) colors. These are used to determine the colors used by multiple tools (e.g., the *Brush* tool). You can always set the default for the foreground and background colors to black and white by clicking the D key. You can switch the foreground/background colors using the X key. These shortcuts will become very useful in the discussion of layer masks later in the book.

Note that this panel also includes the *Hand* and *Zoom* tools, which allow you to pan through and magnify/reduce the current image. Since these are functions you will probably use often, I recommend learning to use the keyboard shortcuts, as I describe above, rather than using them directly.

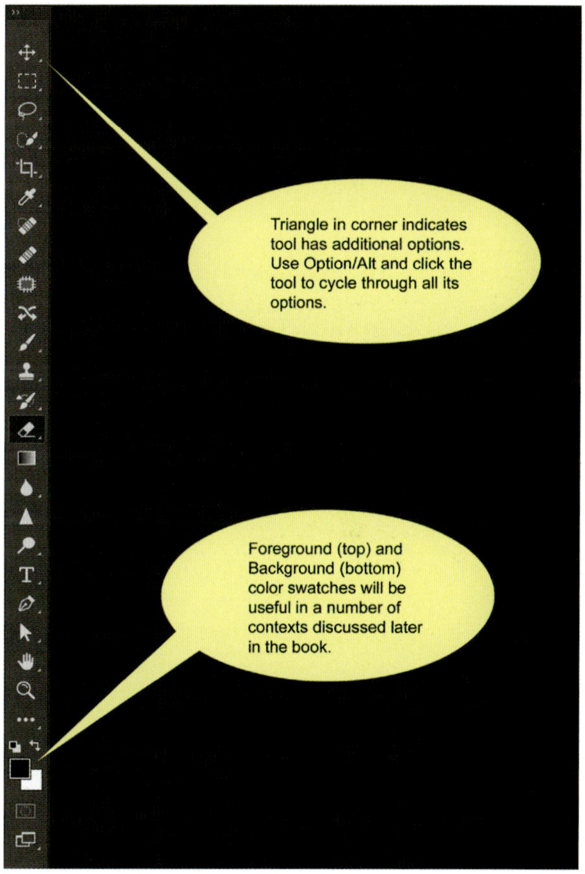


FIGURE 9.4: The *Tools* panel.

## The *Control* Panel

By default, the *Control* panel is a strip at the top of your Photoshop workspace (figure 9.5). This panel is context-sensitive, meaning that its contents change depending on the tool in use. Although it can be moved around, I suggest leaving it where it is for convenience.

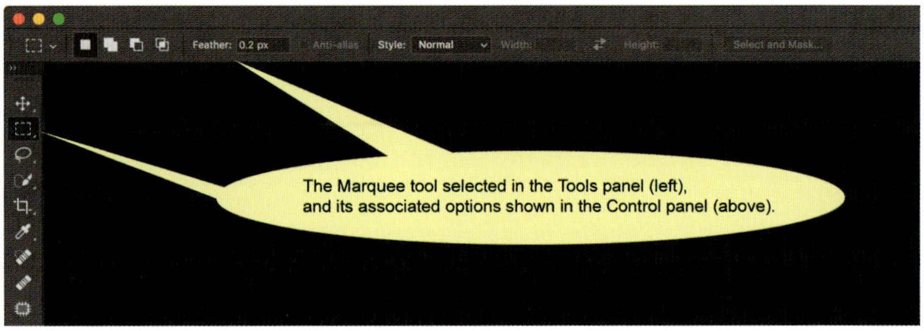


FIGURE 9.5: The *Control* panel.

## The *History* Panel

The *History* panel allows you to move backward and forward several steps with a single click (figure 9.6). If it isn't visible, you can find it in the *Window* menu, or in the flyout menu.

This panel can be thought of as a more powerful version of the Undo/Redo functions common to many types of software, although Undo/Redo for the last operation performed is still available in Photoshop using the common Command/Ctrl+Z keyboard shortcut.

The number of history states available can be configured under *History States* in the *Performance* tab of the Photoshop Preferences. Keep in mind that maintaining these history states uses up memory and the number should not be set too high.

In addition to being able to click on a desired previous state, you can also step through the list by using the following key combinations:

- **Command/Ctrl+Option/Alt (together) + Z** to step backward to a previous state
- **Command/Ctrl+Shift (together) + Z** to step forward to a next state (after you stepped backward, of course)

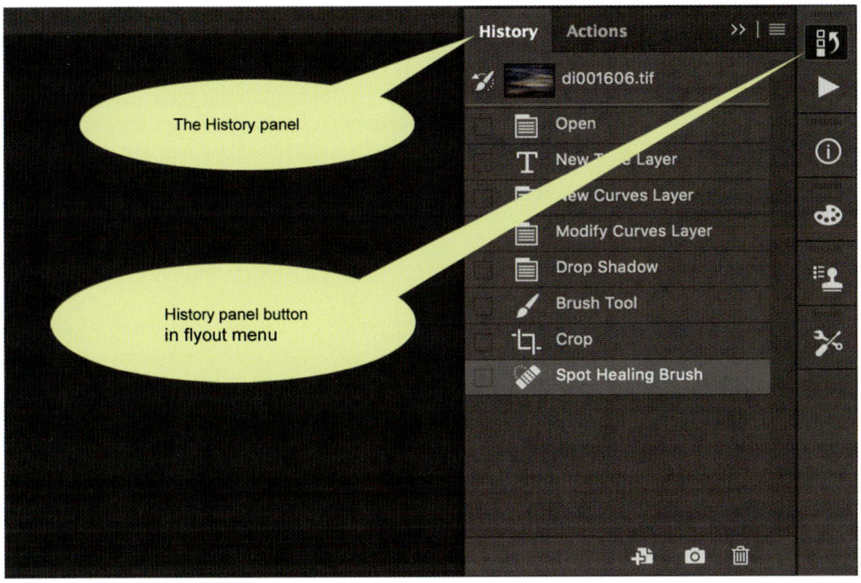


FIGURE 9.6: The *History* panel.

## The *Histogram* Panel

Much like the histograms available in most digital cameras, the Photoshop histogram can display the distribution of tones in your image and can help identify clipping.

Photoshop provides histogram types not usually found in cameras. By selecting the *Expanded View* from the little menu on the top right corner of the *Histogram* panel, several *Channel* options become available, including the ability to see each of the individual color channels as well as a consolidated view (*Colors*), which is the most useful for our purpose.

In addition, Photoshop also provides the option to view a *Luminosity* histogram, which is similar to the one available on most cameras. This histogram is based on the relative number of pixels at each lightness level, and although useful for identifying highlight or shadow clipping, it will not show when just one or two channels are clipped. The same is true for the *RGB* histogram, which is calculated by aggregating the Red/Green/Blue values. I recommend configuring your workspace to show the *Colors* histogram.

Photoshop updates the histogram in near real-time, meaning that it will show the effects of various adjustments as you go along, although for performance reasons, the histogram may be updated only at given intervals. When the histogram is not updated, a small warning sign (exclamation point in a triangle) will show in the upper right corner of the histogram. If you want to manually force Photoshop to update the histogram, you can click this triangle or use the *Uncached Refresh* button.

For a more detailed explanation of Photoshop's histograms, refer to chapter 5, "Understanding Histograms."

## The *Info* Panel

The *Info* panel can be activated under the *Windows* menu by checking the *Info* option (figure 9.7). It can then be accessed from the flyout menu in certain configurations.

This panel can be configured to show a variety of useful data. By clicking the menu button in the upper-right corner and selecting *Panel Options*, you can select the information you wish to display.

This is also a convenient way to switch units of measurement on the fly. For many uses, pixels are the most useful unit, but when preparing a document for print, the ability to see information in inches or other units can be helpful.

As I often prepare documents for commercial printing, I like to see both the RGB and the calculated CMYK values at the cursor's position. The *Info* panel allows me to display these side by side.

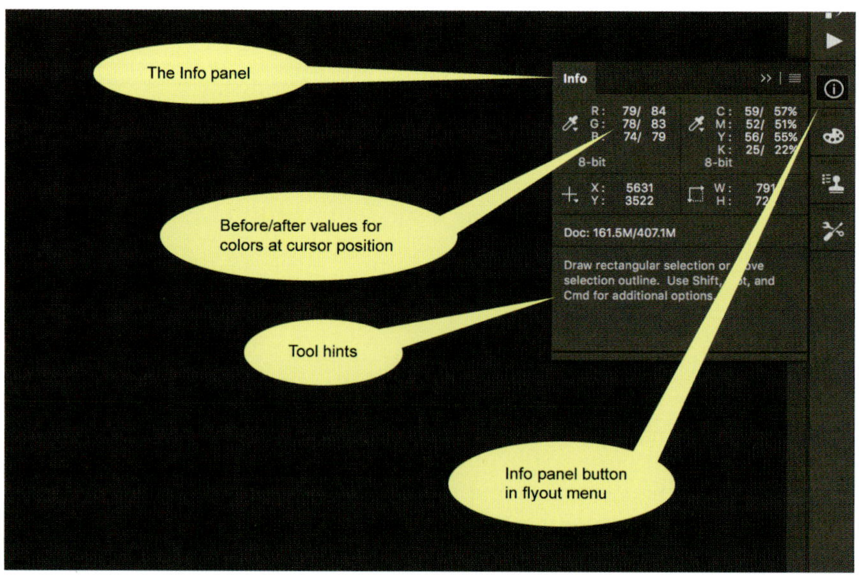


FIGURE 9.7: The *Info* panel.

When the current active layer is an Adjustment Layer (more on layers below), color information is shown in an A/B format, where A is the "before" value and B is the "after" value, making it easy to see the effect of the adjustment on color.

If you are just starting out, you can check the *Show Tool Hints* option, which will configure the *Info* panel to show a short description of the tool you currently have selected. I have the *Rectangular Marquee* tool selected in figure 9.7 and you can see its description at the bottom of the *Info* panel window.

## Layers

One of the most powerful features distinguishing Photoshop from Lightroom and other image-editing software is its ability to organize processing operations in the form of layers. When opening an image in Photoshop for the first time, the original pixels generated by the RAW converter form the base (or *Background*) layer, while subsequent adjustments, as well as other images, can be applied as separate layers on top of it. This approach offers multiple advantages, such as the following:

- **Nondestructive editing:** Layers can be added, adjusted, made invisible, or completely removed without affecting the original image pixels, or the effects of other layers.
- **Blending:** Each layer adds its effect to the sum of all layers below it (which is referred to as the layer's base). A layer's effect can be blended into its base in multiple ways and with varying degrees of strength (called the layer's *opacity*).
- **Masking:** Layers can be associated with masks, which limit their effect to specific portions of the image, as well as allowing the effect of the layer to be applied only to a certain degree (percentage) in various areas. These abilities make masks a superb tool for making local adjustments, as well as for operations that need to be applied in different degrees to different parts of the image, such as sharpening or noise reduction.

Layers come in various flavors, two of which are especially useful for our processing purposes:

- **Image layer:** Often referred to simply as "Layer," this is a pixel-containing layer. Think of it as another image overlaid on top of the original image pixels, and that can be blended into the base in various ways. For example, the lighter tones from one layer can be combined with the darker tones from another layer for dynamic range blending.

- **Adjustment layer:** A layer that calculates new pixel values to accomplish things such as adjustments to contrast and color, and black-and-white conversion. Examples of adjustment layers include *Levels, Curves,* and *Hue/Saturation*, which I describe in detail in the next chapter.

Layers, masks, and various tools for managing them can be found in the *Layers* panel (figure 9.8).

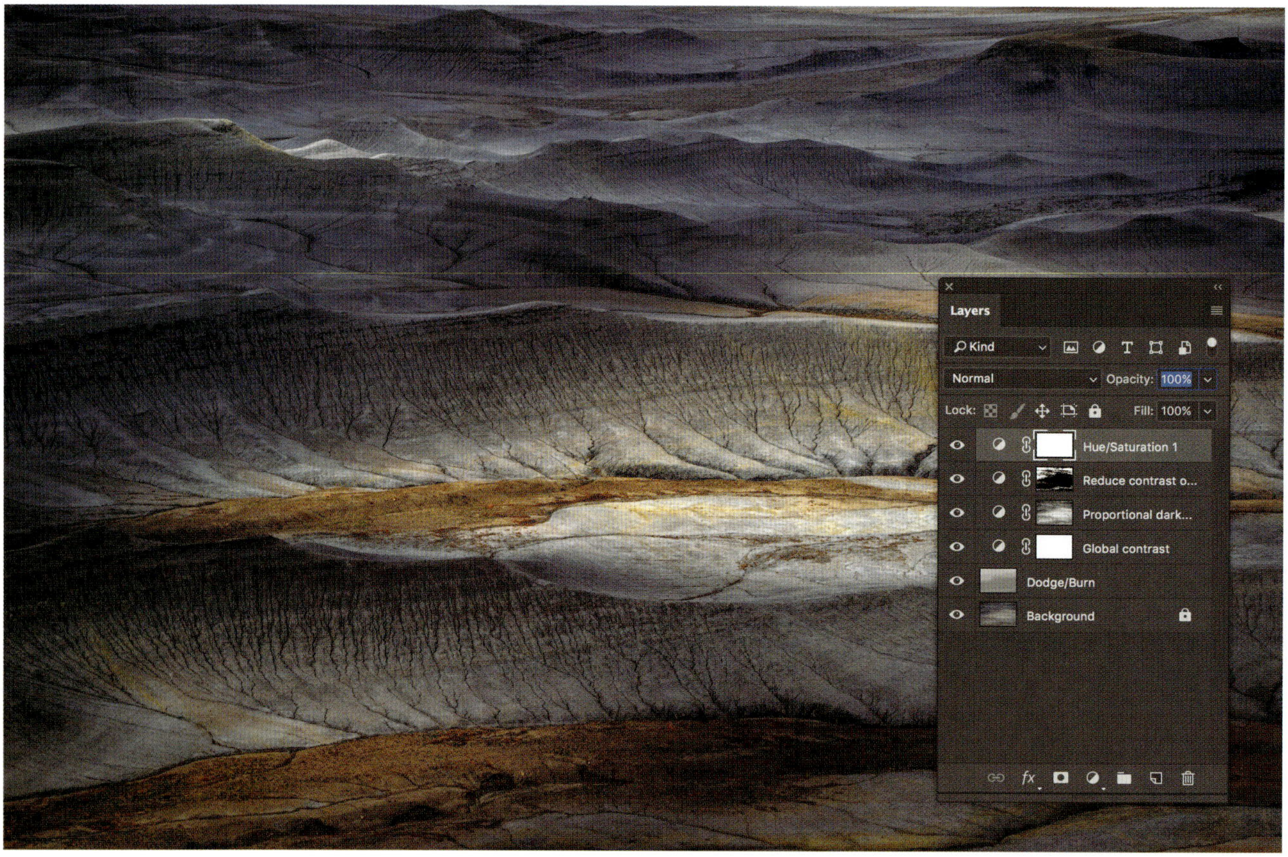


FIGURE 9.8: The *Layers* panel shown overlaid on top of the image that was edited using these layers.

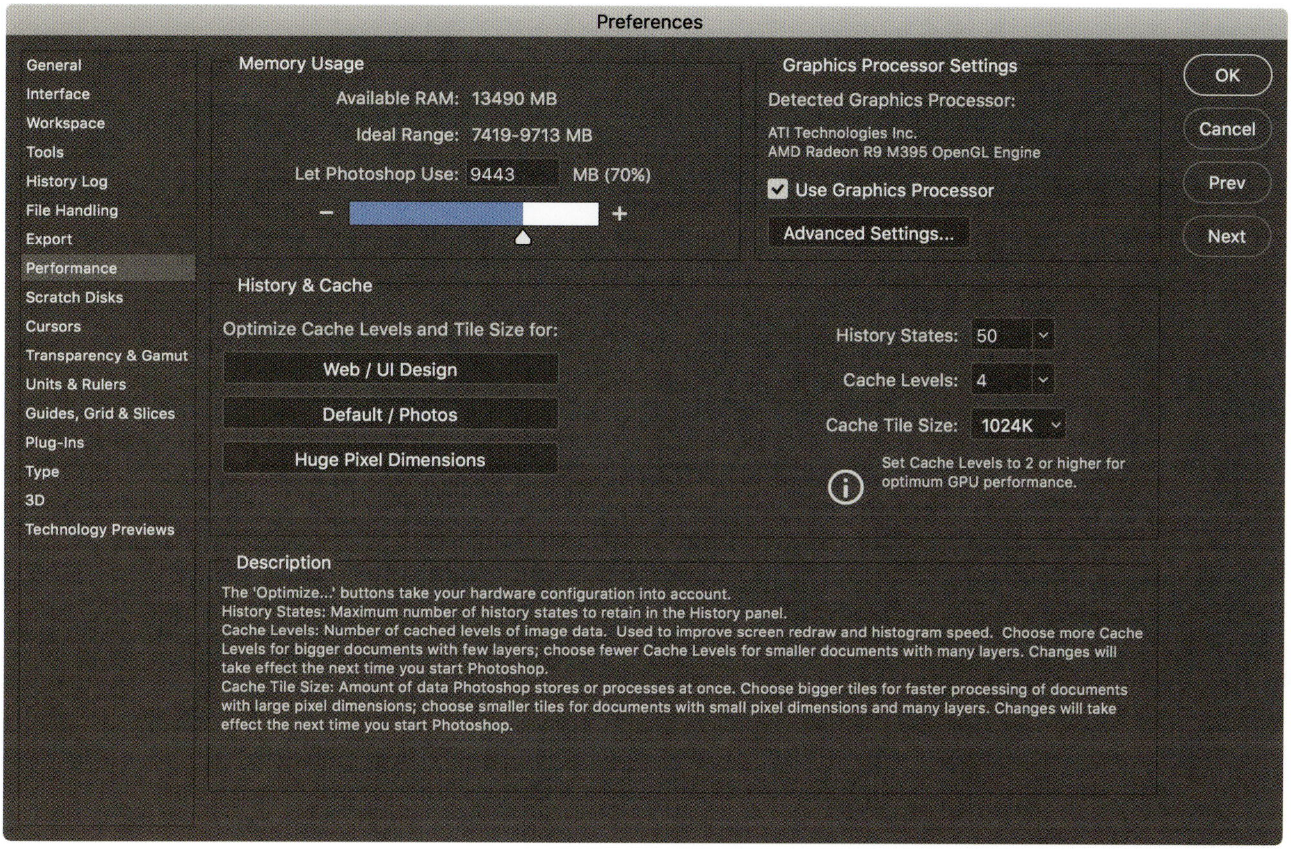


FIGURE 9.9: The *Performance* tab.

## Useful Preferences

Many customizations and settings can be configured in Photoshop's *Preferences* dialog. To start out, I recommend the following settings:

- In the *Performance* tab, set Photoshop to use 70–80% of your available memory (figure 9.9). If you later discover this is not sufficient, I suggest closing other applications while working in Photoshop and/or investing in a memory upgrade.

- If you have more than one physical drive in your computer (i.e., not an external drive connected with a cable, which may be slower to access), click on the *Scratch Disks* tab (figure 9.10) and then configure your secondary drive as *Scratch*, rather than the primary drive that

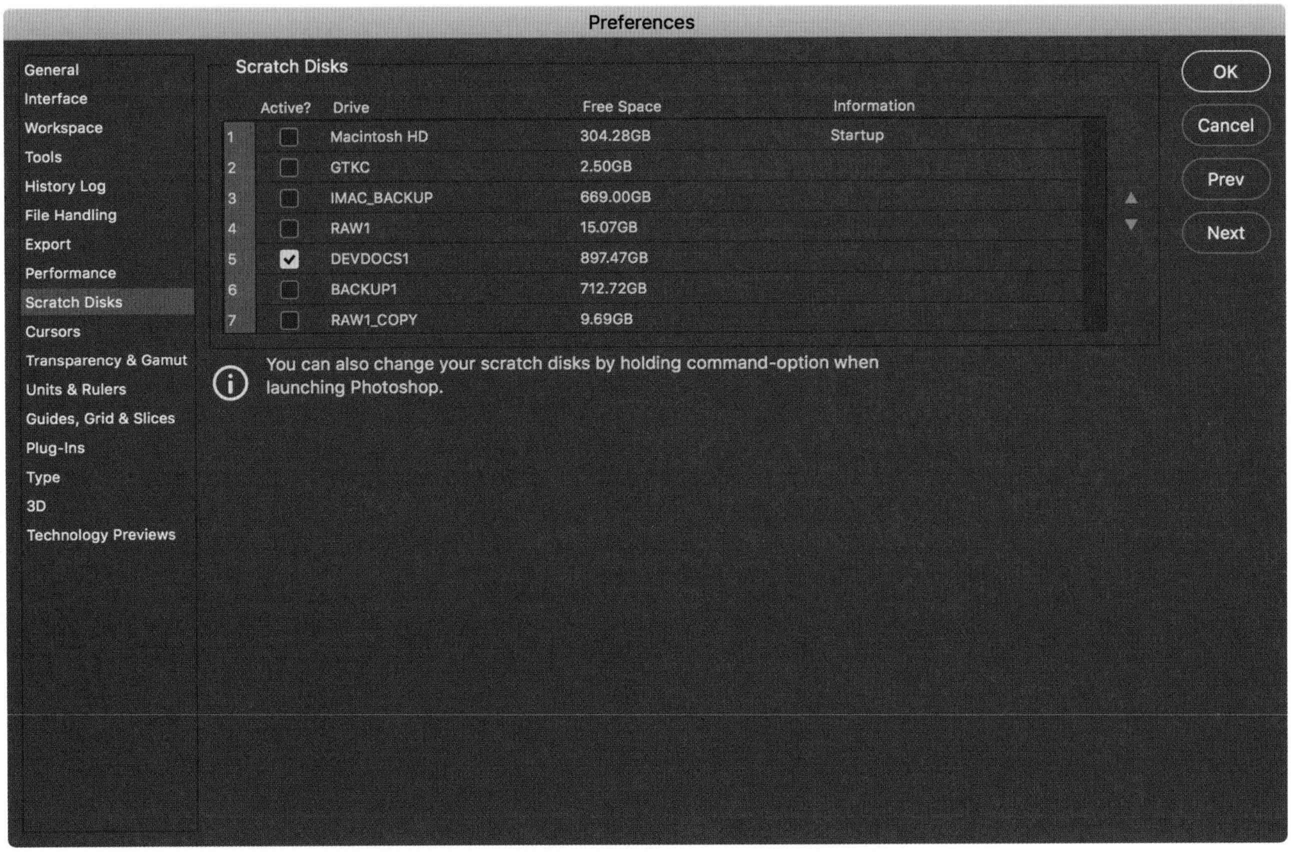


FIGURE 9.10: The *Scratch Disks* tab.

contains your operating system. This will speed up operations that require swapping (using part of your drive space as RAM memory). If you find that swapping greatly impacts performance, also consider a memory upgrade and/or replacing your hard disk drive (if that is what your computer is using) with a Solid State Drive (SSD).

- In the *Cursors* tab (figure 9.11), set the *Painting Cursors* to "Normal Brush Tip" and check "Show Crosshairs in Brush Tip." Set *Other Cursors* to "Precise." These settings will make it easier to visualize where brush edges are and where various effects will be applied.

- In the *Units & Rulers* tab set *Rulers* to "pixels" and set *Type* to "points" (figure 9.12). These are default values you are likely to want more than others, however you may switch these units to others, when needed, either temporarily for a given operation (via the *Info* panel, as I describe above) or permanently by returning to this setting.

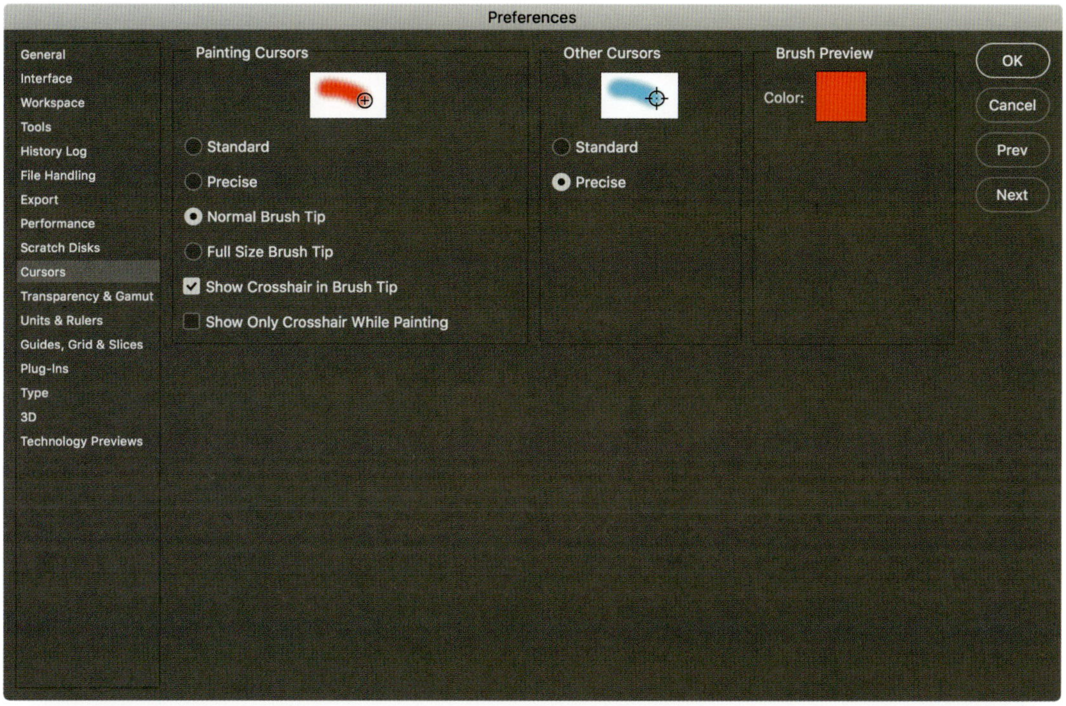


FIGURE 9.11: The *Cursors* tab

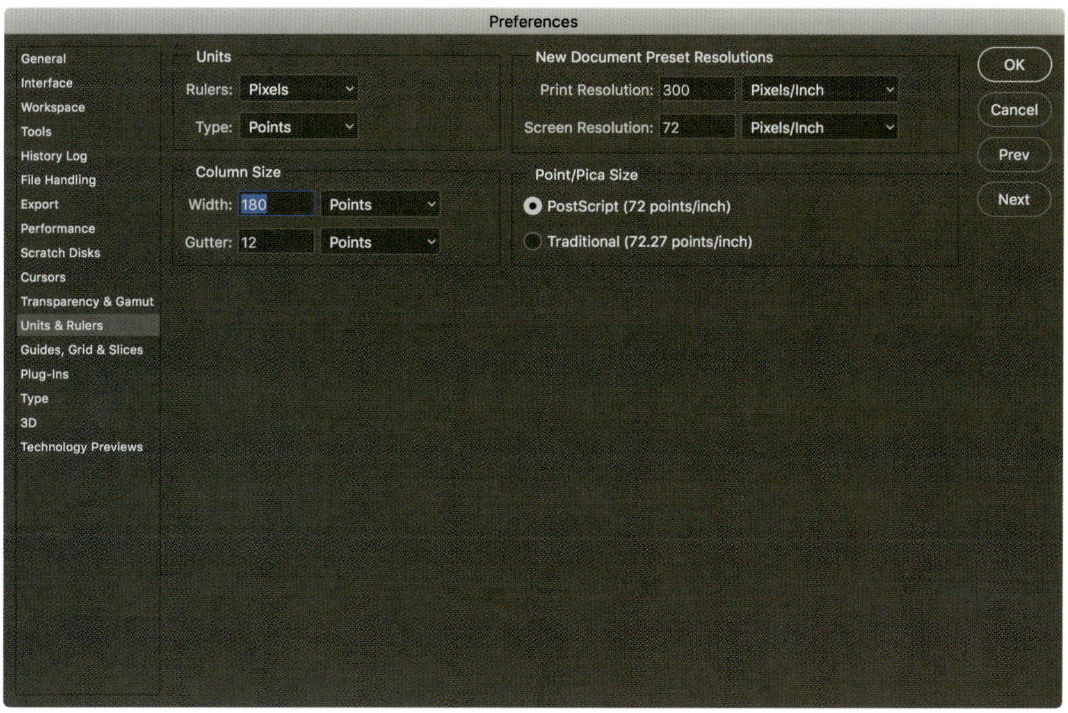


FIGURE 9.12: The *Units & Rulers* tab.

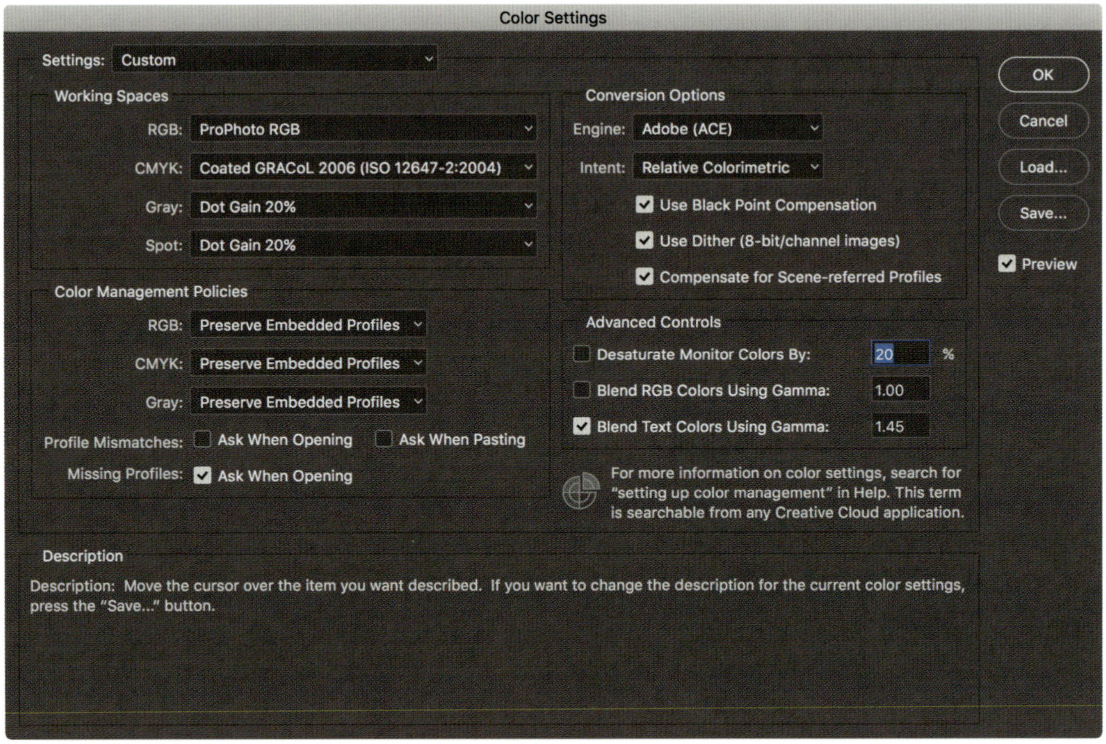


**FIGURE 9.13:** The *Color Settings* dialog.

Last, in the *Edit* menu click on *Color Settings* and configure the following (figure 9.13):

- Set your RGB color space to *ProPhoto RGB*.
- Set all color management policies to *Preserve Embedded Profiles*.

## Your Screen (ICC) Profile

If you used a colorimeter or other mechanism to calibrate your screen, you may see your screen profile any time a list of available profiles is displayed. Do not select this profile as part of your Photoshop color settings. Your screen profile is used by the operating system, not directly by Photoshop.

In Photoshop, we want to work in the largest color space available (ProPhoto RGB), even if your screen is unable to display all colors in the space (at the time of this writing, no screen does). The screen profile is used behind the scenes to ensure colors are appropriately and consistently displayed on your monitor, just as your printer profile ensures that the same colors are consistently rendered in print. These are device-specific profiles and not generic profiles to be associated with an image master file, which is our goal in processing. Other profiles may be useful when we prepare our master files for output.

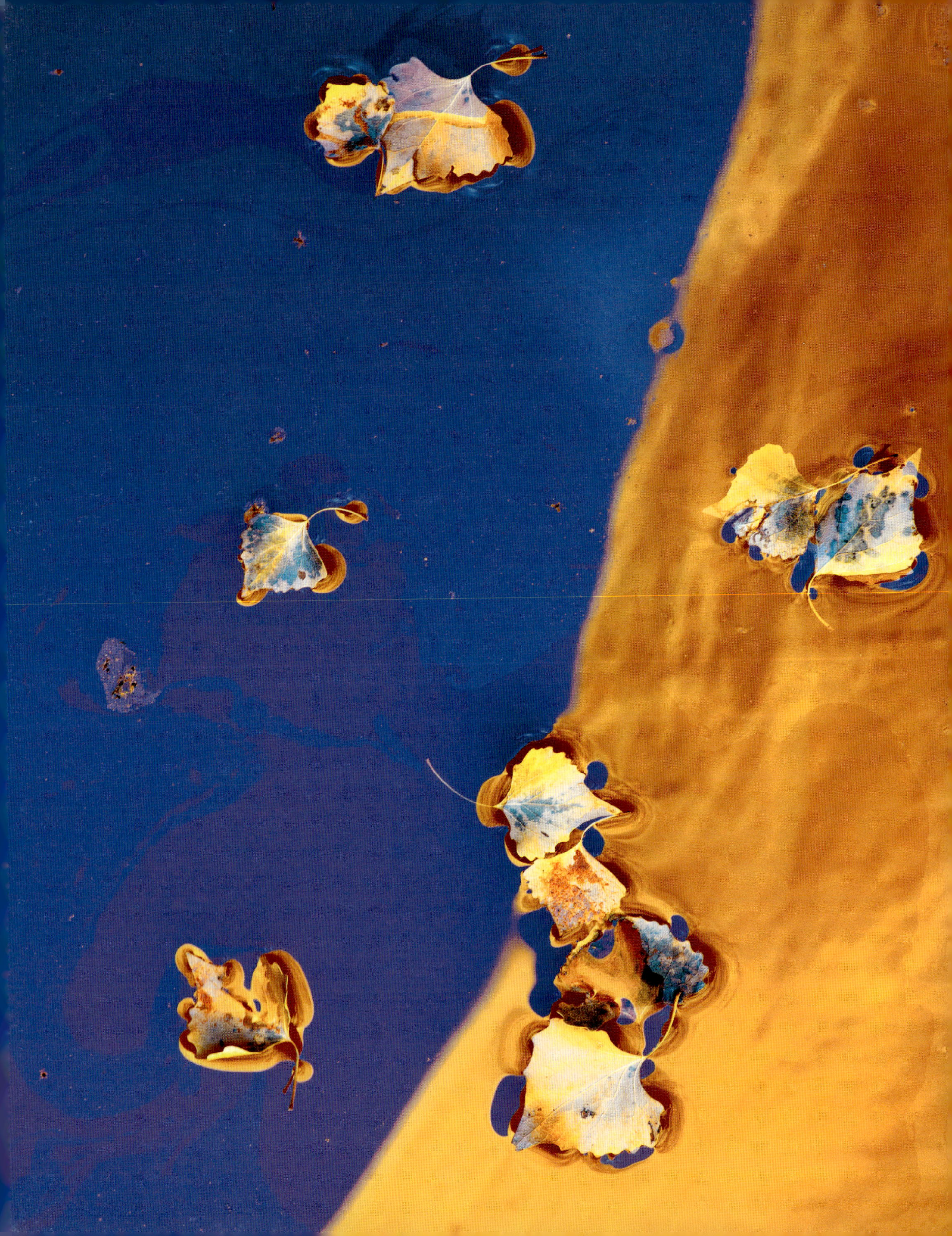

# 10

# Image Editing Techniques

*An artist must first of all respond to his subject, he must be filled with emotion toward that subject and then he must make his technique so sincere, so translucent that it may be forgotten, the value of the subject shining through it.*

—ROBERT HENRI

Now we come to the core of editing our images in Photoshop: applying adjustments. There are two complementary ways to think about adjustments: either as operations that change visual qualities of the image, such as color or contrast, or as operations that change the RGB values of pixels. Both are correct, and I recommend considering both when thinking about matching gaps identified during the analysis phase with the tools needed to address them.

While Photoshop can apply changes directly to the image pixels, to do so is considered destructive in the sense that once the image is saved with the new pixel values, individual adjustments become impossible to revisit or undo. A better way to approach editing is in a nondestructive fashion. Photoshop accomplishes nondestructive adjustments using a mechanism called *layers*. Working with layers takes some getting used to, but I believe it is better and easier to learn good habits from the start rather than to change bad habits later.

Layers come in various flavors. Most of the adjustments I review here are accomplished using *adjustment layers*, which are layers that calculate new pixel values. Photoshop offers a variety of adjustment layers designed to control qualities of color, contrast, and other visual characteristics of an

**Finding the *Layers* Panel**

The *Layers* panel should be visible on your desktop as part of the workspace we configured in the previous exercise. If it is not visible, and assuming you saved your workspace as suggested, you can return to that workspace by selecting it from the *Choose a Workspace* menu in the upper-right corner. Or, if you do not wish to change your workspace, you can make the *Layers* panel appear by selecting it from the *Window* menu.

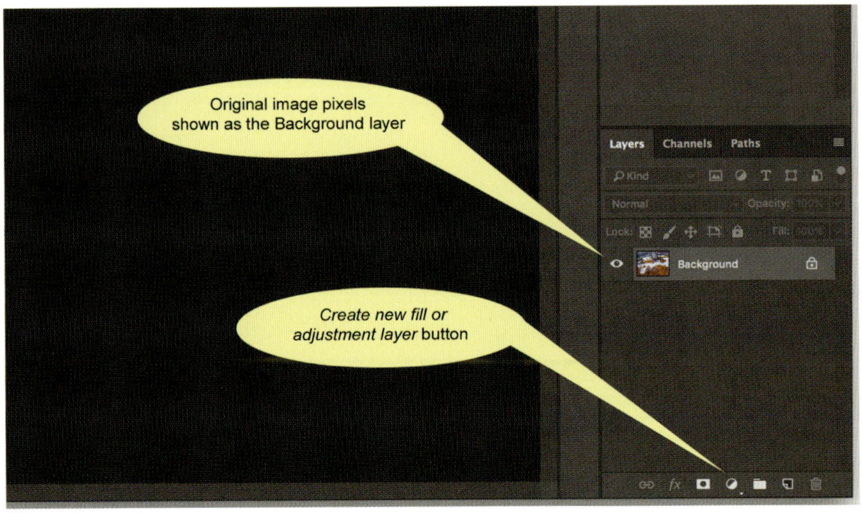


**Figure 10.1:** The *Create new fill or adjustment layer* button, and the original image pixels (shown as the Background layer) in the *Layers* panel. Subsequent adjustments will appear as additional layers on top of the Background layer, and we can later modify or remove layers without affecting the original pixels. This allows for nondestructive editing.

image (or a portion of an image). Adjustment layers can be added in several ways. My preferred way is to use the *Create new fill or adjustment layer* button at the bottom of the *Layers* panel, which opens a menu of adjustment layer options (figure 10.1).

Other ways of adding adjustment layers are: using the buttons provided in the *Adjustments* panel (which can be made visible by selecting it from the *Window* menu); or, by selecting one of the options under *Add New Adjustment Layer* in the *Layer* menu. I suggest picking the one method that is most intuitive to you and sticking with it.

## Global Adjustments Using Layers

Global adjustments are operations that have the potential to affect every pixel in the image. Put another way, their effect is not deliberately restricted to just a part of the image.

In some cases, global adjustments may be all that's needed to reach the visualized outcome. This is perfectly acceptable. There is a tendency among new Photoshop users to experiment with every technique during the learning process, which is a great way to gain and practice skills. However, don't assume that you must use every tool in your arsenal on every image. Each image is unique and each requires a tailored approach. Some images may be processed to meet your visualized goal within minutes and with just a few simple global adjustments, while others may take hours or days of meticulous work.

In the following sections, I describe the workings of some of Photoshop's most useful adjustment layers. When initially applied, a layer's effect is always applied globally. Later, I explain how to target a layer's effect to a specific part of the image to make a local adjustment using a mechanism called *layer masks*.

## Levels Adjustment

The *Levels* adjustment is a simple and powerful way of adjusting the black and white points in the image as well as the lightness of midtones. A *Levels* adjustment can also be used to adjust contrast and color; however, there are better tools for these, which are covered below.

Remember that the white and black points represent the lightest and darkest tones in the image, respectively. It's considered good practice to map the white and black points as close to pure white and pure black as possible early in the editing process. The reason is that doing so stretches the tones in the image across the entire available tone scale (from black to white), resulting in the largest number of discreet levels possible between the darkest and lightest parts of the image. Some operations, such as increasing contrast, increase the differences between light tones and dark tones and may need to create new grades of tones between them. By moving the white and black points out toward the extremes of the tone scale, more tonal values become available for such operations, making transitions smoother and reducing the risk of pixelation.

Setting the white and black points close to pure white and pure black early in the editing process increases contrast and changes the overall appearance of the image, meaning that additional adjustments may be needed later to restore the desired contrast. This is OK. In fact, you will find there are several situations where taking such preemptive steps sets a better starting point for further editing.

To add a *Levels* adjustment layer, use one of the methods mentioned above. For example:

- Click the *Create new fill or adjustment layer* button, and select *Levels* from the menu.
- Once a *Levels* layer is added, the *Properties* panel will change to show the *Levels* controls, allowing you to work on all color channels (RGB) or on each of the individual Red, Green, or Blue channels separately.

When selecting the RGB option, adjustments can be made to the overall black and white points as well as to overall contrast. When individual color channels are selected, color balance can be adjusted by proportionally adding or reducing the amount of each color. I recommend staying in RGB mode rather than working on individual color channels. There are better tools than *Levels* to adjust color balance.

The *Levels* adjustment provides three "input" points on the slider for setting the black and white points, as well as the midtone level.

You will also find two "output" sliders, which can be used to change the absolute value of the input white and black points (figure 10.2). When left at their default position (0 for black point, and 255 for white point), these are the values that the white/black point sliders under the histogram will map to. However, the output sliders can be used to change these values. For example, if I set the output white point to 250, instead of 255, and then move the input white point to the edge of the histogram, the white point will be set to 250 (a bit less than pure white), rather than 255 (pure white). This may be useful when we want to make sure to avoid pure whites or pure blacks.

Note that values for each of the five parameters can be entered numerically or set visually by using sliders. Since we are practicing expressive art, rather than accounting or engineering, I suggest using the numeric values to inform your decisions, but not to dictate what your image should look like. Use the sliders. Similarly, ignore the "Auto" button. There is nothing creative about substituting the computer's guesswork for your own judgment.

Let's review how the five parameters we can tune in *Levels* translate into real-world image adjustments:

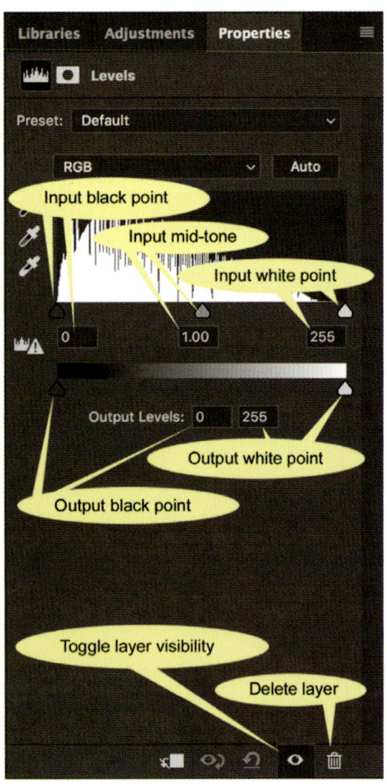


**Figure 10.2:** The *Levels* adjustment properties.

- **Input Black Point:** The black point represents the darkest tone in the image. If it is touching the left edge of the histogram, the image will contain true blacks (RGB 0,0,0). If it is within the histogram, all tones to the left of it will be mapped to pure black (or, to the output black point, if different from 0). This is generally not recommended, with the exception of cases such as silhouettes, where the black point can be used to map more of the darker tones to featureless black. If you want to set the black point exactly at the edge of the histogram (mapping your darkest tone to pure black), hold down the Option/Alt key while dragging the slider until you see pixels appear. These are your darkest tones. I suggest pulling back from this position just a bit to avoid pure blacks, unless needed.
- **Input Midtone:** The midtone slider works by biasing the mid tones toward either the dark or light ends of the scale. It can be used to adjust overall lightness of the image. Tones at the position of the midtone slider will be mapped to exactly midtone (50% lightness).
- **Input White Point:** The white point determines where the lightest tones in the image fall. If it is touching the right edge of the histogram, the image will contain pure whites (RGB 255,255,255). If it is within the histogram, all tones to its right will be mapped to pure

white (or to the output white point, if different from 255). This is generally not recommended, even if the intent is to create high-key images. The reason is that when printing pure-white areas using ink-jet printers, no ink will be used in those areas, which may result in an artifact known as a gloss differential.[1] To determine exactly where to set the white point, hold down the Option/Alt key as you drag the white point slider until pixels appear. I suggest pulling back just a little from this position to avoid pure whites.

- **Output Black Point:** This parameter determines the absolute value for the input black point. For example, if you want the black point in your image to be something other than pure black (0), you can set a new value for it here.
- **Output White Point:** This parameter determines the absolute value for the input white point. If set lower than the default (255), it will ensure that the image will not have pure whites.

The *Levels* properties also contain three eyedropper buttons. These can be used to select the input black, white, and midtone points from within the image. I do not recommend doing so, since the results can be inaccurate.

At the bottom of the *Properties* panel for *Levels* (and some other adjustment layers), note these buttons (figure 10.3):

- **Clip layer toggle:** Limits this layer's effect to the areas affected by the layer below it. (Think, for example, about situations where you may wish to use multiple layers to adjust color or contrast to the same part[s] of the image.)
- **View previous state:** Toggles between the previous state and the change you just made (this option becomes active each time you make a change to the layer properties).
- **Reset to adjustment defaults:** Allows you to undo all changes to the layer properties.
- **Toggle layer visibility:** A great way to see a before/after view (with and without the effect of the layer).
- **Delete layer:** Get rid of the layer if it doesn't accomplish the desired effect (perhaps to start over with a different adjustment).

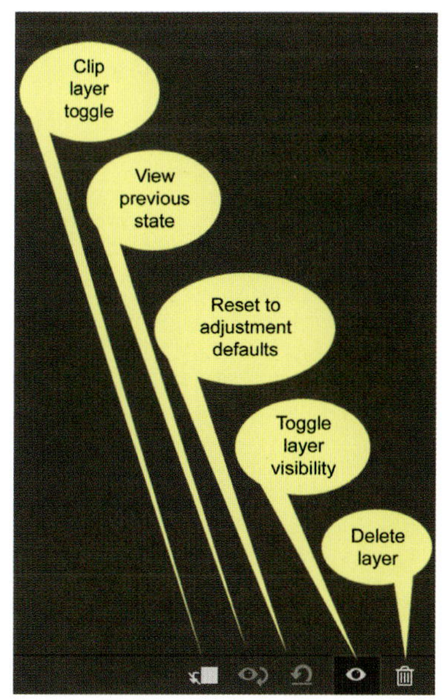


**FIGURE 10.3:** The buttons at the bottom of the *Levels Adjustment Properties* panel.

[1] Some printers can compensate for such situations by using a "gloss optimizer" translucent ink; however, this function is not common.

After this introduction to using an adjustment layer, it is worth coming up for air to again consider the big picture. Remind yourself of your visualized image, and consider whether a *Levels* adjustment may be one of the steps toward getting there, and what other steps may be needed.

As you will soon see, there is some overlap between the capabilities of various adjustments. In this case, although the *Levels* adjustment is quite intuitive to use, I generally recommend not relying on it too heavily, or at all, because the more powerful *Curves* adjustment, described in the next section, can be used to the same effect but with more accuracy. However, *Levels* is a good adjustment to start with, since it touches on many useful controls and concepts, some of which are found in other tools as well.

## Curves Adjustment

The *Curves* adjustment is arguably Photoshop's most powerful means of adjusting contrast. And, like *Levels*, it can also do a few other things.

To add a *Curves* adjustment layer, click the *Create new fill or adjustment layer* button and select *Curves* from the menu; or use one of the other methods I mention above, if you prefer.

The *Curves* properties use a graph (figure 10.5), where the horizontal (input) axis represents tonal values in the current image, and the vertical (output) axis represents the new values they will be mapped to as we move the curve.

The 45° diagonal line dividing the graph indicates where input=output, meaning that for points where the curve intersects with this line, those tones will be unaffected by the curve.

As a starting point, the curve matches the 45° line (meaning it leaves all values as they are). Pulling parts of the curve above or below the line will map input values to new output values (figure 10.6).

When the curve is pulled above the 45° line, input tones will be mapped to higher (lighter) values; conversely, when the curve is pulled below the line, input tones will be mapped to lower (darker) values.

Like *Levels*, and some other adjustments, *Curves* can be applied to all channels (RGB) or to each of the individual color channels, allowing *Curves* to be used not only for contrast and tonal adjustments, but also, in a limited way, for color balance adjustment. Despite this ability, I recommend using *Curves* only to adjust contrast; there are better tools for color adjustments that I describe below.

To position specific tones above or below the line, simply click on the curve and, while holding the mouse down, drag the curve up or down. You'll notice that wherever you click, an anchor point is added to the curve. These

## EXERCISE 6

In this exercise, we'll practice useful techniques for setting the black and white points. I recommend doing this early in the editing process as these operations optimize the range of tones available for upcoming adjustments to use.

1. Select one of your images that includes both light highlights and dark shadows, and open it in Photoshop.
2. Add a *Levels* adjustment layer.
3. Hold down the Option/Alt key and drag the *Input white point* slider slowly to the left until you see pixels appear in the blank frame. Now back off to the right slowly until the warnings disappear. Release the Option/Alt key.
4. Hold down the Option/Alt key again and drag the *Input black point slider* slowly to the right until you see pixels appear in the blank frame. Now back off to the left slowly until the warnings disappear. Release the Option/Alt key.
5. Drag the *Input midtone* slider to adjust overall lightness to taste.
6. Drag the *Output black point* slider to the right until shadow details are visible.
7. Drag the *Output white point* slider to the left until highlight details are visible.
8. Open the *File* menu and select *Save as*, then save the image to a folder of your choice in TIFF format. Make sure to preserve the layers and color space by checking the appropriate boxes (figure 10.4).
9. Click the *Save* button.
10. In the next window, leave the TIFF options at their default settings.
11. Click OK.

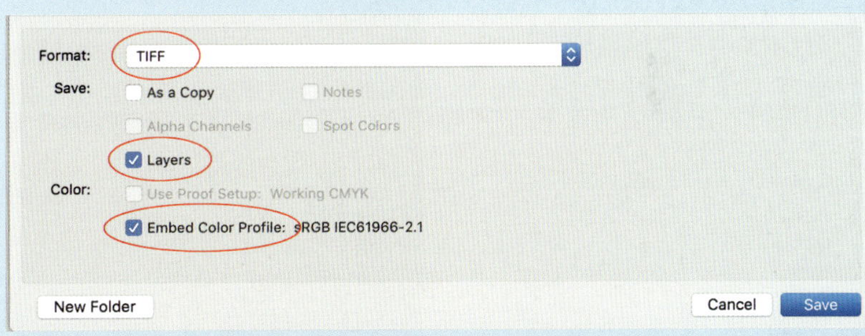


FIGURE 10.4: The options at the bottom of the *Save as* dialog.

This will be the first version of your master file.

**Freedom with Photoshop**

One philosophical difference between Photoshop and such applications as Lightroom and others, is that Photoshop doesn't try to protect you from yourself but gives you a wide degree of latitude to adjust anything in any way you want, assuming you know what you're doing. However, until you actually know what you're doing, it is all too easy to get carried away and to make a mess, especially with a powerful tool such as *Curves*. Feel free to experiment but, if things go awry, you can roll back any number of steps using the *History* panel (if not visible, select it from the *Window* menu), or just delete the layer and start over.

anchors can later be repositioned by dragging them or, if needed, removed by holding down the Command/Ctrl key and clicking them.

*Curves*, like *Levels*, also offers sliders that can be used to set the black and white points, as well as the same three eyedroppers for setting white point, gray (midtone) point, and black point by selecting the tones directly from the image. You can already see that the *Curves* adjustment can be used to achieve a similar effect to that of the *Levels* adjustment, and more. In fact, once you are comfortable with the *Curves* adjustment, you may find *Levels* unnecessary.

FIGURE 10.5: The *Curves* adjustment properties.

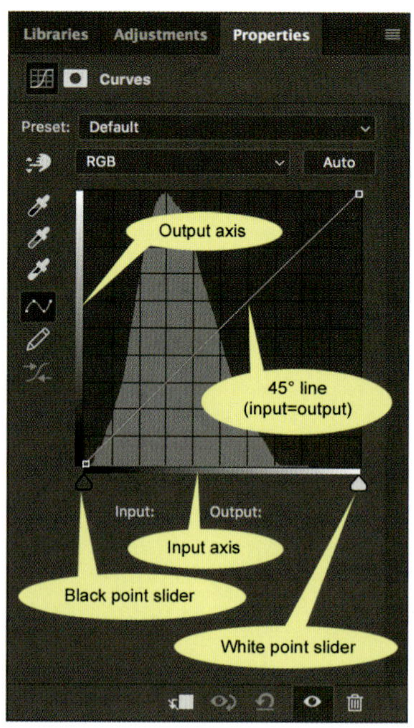


FIGURE 10.6: In this example, the curve maps most of the light tones in the image to higher (lighter) ones, and most of the dark tones to lower (darker) ones. In other words, this curve will make the light areas lighter and the dark areas darker, which is another way to describe an increase in contrast.

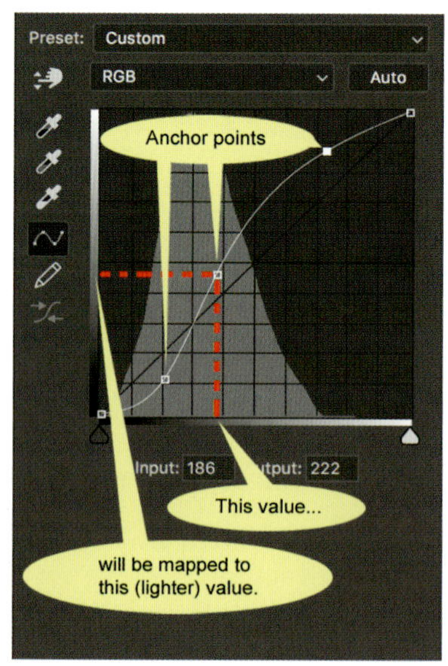

For ease of identifying midtones, shadows, and highlights, a grid is provided behind the curve. If you need greater granularity, toggle between a 4×4 grid and a 10×10 grid by holding down the Option/Alt key and clicking anywhere on the graph.

By placing various anchor points on the curve, we can control specific tonal ranges within the image, making changes to lightness (and, consequently, contrast: the steeper the curve is between two points, the greater the contrast within that tonal range, and vice versa). We can also make multiple adjustments to different tonal ranges using a single curve, making *Curves* much more powerful for contrast adjustment than other methods.

To accurately adjust the lightness of specific areas within the image, it is useful to know where they fall on the tone curve. For this purpose, Photoshop provides the *On-Image Adjustment Tool*, located in the upper left side of the *Curves* properties panel (figure 10.7). Clicking the button toggles the tool on or off. When activated, the cursor will change to an eyedropper, and you will be able to hover over the image to see where different values fall on the curve. To adjust the values at any specific location, click the image at that location and drag either up or down to place an anchor point on the curve at the appropriate location and to pull the curve up (lighten) or down (darken).

Keep in mind that moving any anchor point on the curve will also shift other parts of the curve, so if you wish to protect some tones from changing you may need to add a few more points to the curve to pin parts of it back to the original 45° line (figure 10.8).

A common and useful configuration for *Curves* is an S-shaped curve—referred to as an *S-Curve*—as seen in figure 10.15. The S-Curve has the distinction of increasing contrast between the two anchors (note the angle of the curve in that area is steeper than the 45° line, suggesting that values are stretched farther apart from each other than they were originally) while slightly lowering contrast at the extreme edges (shadows and highlights), which often natively have a high contrast, and where such a decrease may help avoid clipping and loss of detail.

### Curves and the Zone System

The 10×10 grid may ring a bell with photographers experienced with the Zone System. The Zone System divides the range of tones corresponding to the sensitivity of black-and-white film into 11 zones. A 10×10 grid gives us 11 points where the curve intersects with the grid (white point, black point, and 9 intermediate points). These intersections can be thought of as corresponding to Zone System zones, and they enable using Zone System principles in processing images. I describe this ability in more detail in chapter 12, "Black-and-White."

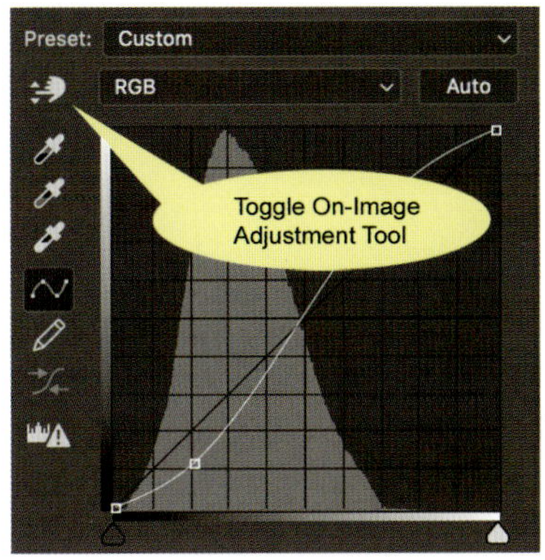


**FIGURE 10.7:** *The On-Image Adjustment* tool button in the *Curves* properties panel.

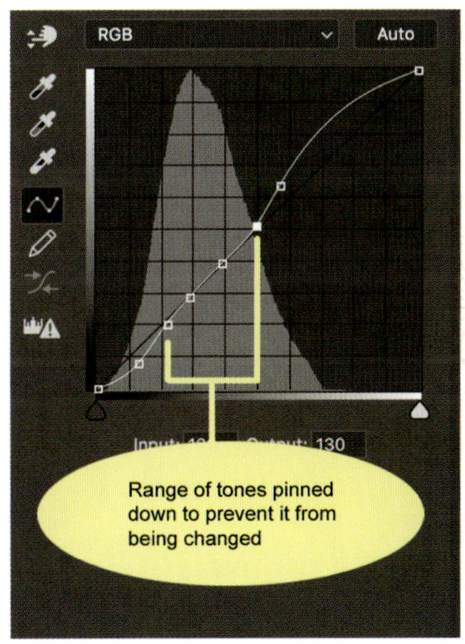


**FIGURE 10.8:** A curve with anchor points pinning it to the 45° line to prevent changes where they are not desired.

## Hue/Saturation and Vibrance Adjustments

When discussing *Levels* and *Curves*, I mentioned their ability to work on individual color channels. This ability can be useful in making rudimentary adjustments to specific colors. Put in context, these tools primarily affect the hue and lightness components of color. (If you need a quick reminder of these terms, see page 100.) Changes in contrast—for example, increasing contrast using a *Curves* layer—may also affect saturation, although the degree of the effect is difficult to control using tools like *Curves*. Adjusting saturation and other color components is best done using the *Hue/Saturation* and *Vibrance* adjustments.

### Hue/Saturation Adjustment

The *Hue/Saturation* adjustment is a feature-rich tool offering control over the HSL (hue, saturation, and lightness) properties of color, and the ability to target adjustments to specific color ranges.

The *Hue/Saturation* adjustment is Photoshop's most powerful tool for fine-tuning color properties to accomplish the precise shades you are after. For example, you can use this tool to change your sky from cyan blue to cerulean blue or to midnight blue. Or, if you want to experiment with surrealism, you can change your blues to purples, your greens to reds, and so on.

When *Master* is selected (which is the default), the sliders affect all colors in the image. I recommend *not* making such adjustments, as various colors almost always require unique settings. For greater control, Photoshop provides a set of pre-defined color ranges, which are selectable from a menu, as well as shown visually (figure 10.9). You may use these ranges as-is, or you can fine-tune them using the sliders along the color spectrum scales at the bottom of the *Properties* panel. When an individual color is selected in the dropdown, note that four sliders will appear: the inner ones define the range that will be most affected and the outer ones define where the effect is tapered off for smooth transitions into other colors.

**Figure 10.9:** The *Hue/Saturation* adjustment *Properties* panel.

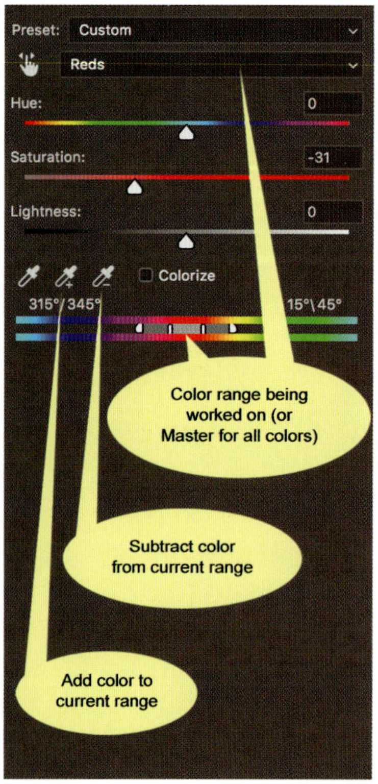


Also provided are three eyedroppers, allowing you to sample colors from the image that you wish to modify. When a range of colors other than *Master* is selected, the left-most eyedropper allows clicking on any color within the image. This color then becomes the center of the range being modified (and will therefore receive most of the effect). The other eyedroppers (with the +/– signs next to them) can be used to add colors to, or remove colors from, the range being modified. For example, if the range of greens you are trying to modify has a warm hue that reaches into the yellows, use the eyedropper with the plus sign to click on the yellowest green you wish to modify to add it to the range.

Keep in mind that color ranges are contiguous, so including multiple colors in the range will also include all the hues between them. For example, if you include both blue and yellow hues in your range, the adjustment will also affect magentas and reds, since they are included between the two extremes. As a rule, it is preferable to adjust small ranges at a time. When you are done working in one range, select a different menu option (other than *Master*) and apply adjustments to it.

Another useful tool for visual editing is the *On-Screen Adjustment* tool (the small hand icon in the upper left corner of the *Properties* panel, under the word "Preset"), which is similar to the one we've already seen in the *Curves* adjustment. After activating this tool, simply point to any color in the image, and then click and drag right or left to increase or decrease its saturation. Notice that when you click on a color, the range name corresponding to it will be automatically selected.

The *Colorize* function is intended to colorize monochromatic images. Checking the box (to the right of the three eyedroppers) will remove all color information from the image (desaturate it) and allow you to use the *Hue*, *Saturation*, and *Lightness* sliders to add a color tint. While the effect is interesting, I recommend avoiding this option, as there are better ways of producing tinted monochromatic images, as I explain in chapter 12, "Black-and-White."

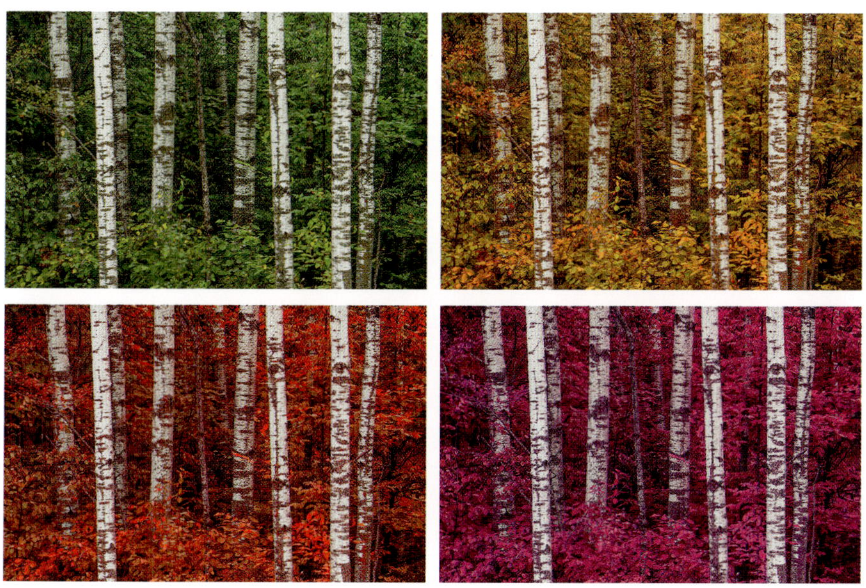

FIGURE 10.10: This woodland image was captured on a visit to Minnesota at the end of summer. I hoped for a hint of autumn color in the woods, but as it turns out I arrived just in time for a 60-year-record heat wave and these trees had not turned yet. But, using Photoshop's *Hue* and *Saturation* controls I was able to convert the summer greens into autumn golds and reds, and even to acid-trip purples. It's easy to go overboard, so remember to exercise good taste.

**The Best Time to Apply Hue/Saturation Adjustments**

As a rule, it's best to apply the *Hue/Saturation* adjustments last, since other adjustments may also affect color. There is one useful exception to this rule: if colors in the original image are muted and difficult to discern, adding a *Hue/Saturation* adjustment and bumping up the saturation with *Master* selected can be used as a temporary measure to make colors more visible when applying other adjustments. Once these adjustments are applied, set the saturation back to its original level. Then, after all other adjustments are in place, return to the Hue/Saturation adjustment and fine-tune the individual color ranges to taste.

## Vibrance Adjustment

The *Vibrance* adjustment is rudimentary and applies only to the saturation component (meaning it does not modify hue or lightness), but it offers the unique ability to increase or decrease saturation in a proportional fashion: increasing vibrance results in greater boost to less-saturated colors, and a smaller one to already saturated colors (figure 10.11).

In practice, *Vibrance* is useful when colors in the image are not evenly saturated (and assuming we want them to be). In this case, we'll want to add a *Vibrance* adjustment layer before adding a *Hue/Saturation* layer. Then, use the *Vibrance* control to saturate the least-saturated colors, before applying more precise changes using the *Hue/Saturation* adjustment.

In some cases, you may notice that *Vibrance* saturates some colors (particularly blues) more than others. This is where the color-specific adjustment capabilities of *Hue/Saturation* can be used to fine-tune individual colors.

The *Saturation* slider provided below the *Vibrance* slider can be useful in accomplishing even saturation. Here's how I recommend using these sliders:

- Increase *Vibrance* until the least-saturated colors in the image are as saturated as you want them to be.

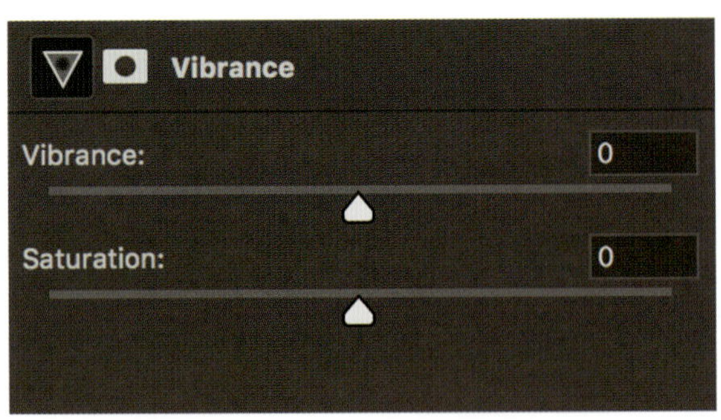


**FIGURE 10.11:** The *Vibrance* adjustment *Properties* panel has just two sliders: *Vibrance*, which affects color saturation proportionally (less saturated colors get a greater boost than already saturated colors); and *Saturation*, which affects all colors by the same amount.

- If already-saturated colors become over-saturated as a result of the *Vibrance* adjustment, use the *Saturation* slider to reduce overall saturation a bit.
- Repeat until you find the ideal balance.

## Color Balance Adjustment

The *Color Balance* adjustment uses sliders to offer a simple interface for controlling the relative amounts of red, green, and blue, and their reciprocal colors. With a combination of the three available sliders, color balance can be adjusted separately in the highlights, midtones, and shadows.

Those familiar with a color wheel know that reciprocal colors are on the opposite side of the wheel for any given color. In the RGB model—where colors are represented by relative amounts of red, green, and blue—the reciprocal color for each color channel is a combination of the other two. For example, reducing the amount of red increases the relative proportion of green and blue, which together make up cyan. To gain a better understanding of the sliders provided in the *Color Balance* adjustment see table 10.1 and figure 10.12.

| Color Channel | Reciprocal Color |
|---|---|
| Red | Cyan (=Blue+Green) |
| Green | Magenta (=Red+Blue) |
| Blue | Yellow (=Red+Green) |

TABLE 10.1: Reducing the color in the left column results in increasing the color in the right column, and vice versa.

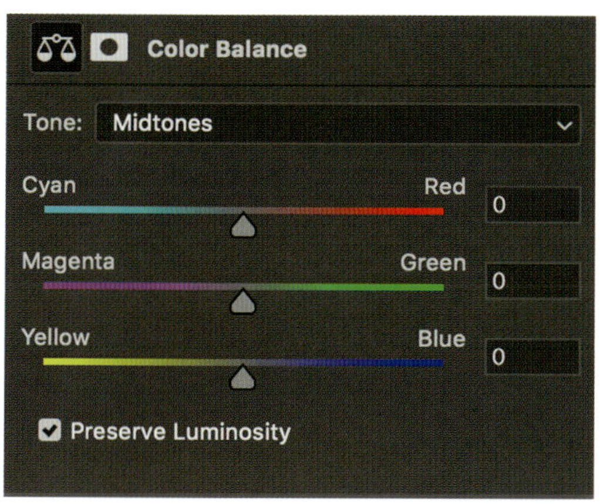


FIGURE 10.12: The adjustment sliders provided in the *Color Balance* adjustment *Properties* panel.

The *Color Balance* adjustment is very useful for such things as controlling overall color balance and adding or eliminating color casts. You can also think of it as a more elaborate version of the *White Balance* (*Temperature* and *Tint*) controls provided in ACR and Lightroom.

Note that adding or correcting color balance using *White Balance* (*Temperature* and *Tint*) simulates properties of natural light, while correcting color using such tools as the *Color Balance* adjustment allows you to set the color balance any way you want, rather than be bound to properties of natural light.

The *Preserve Luminosity* checkbox, as its name suggests, ensures that as colors change, they appear as light/dark as the original. Remember that luminosity is a perception of brightness. Our perception of luminosity is affected by color: for example, a very bright red will appear much more luminous than a blue of the same measured brightness. Checking this box automatically compensates for the way we perceive brightness by color.

The ability to target color adjustments to shadows, midtones, and highlights offers another degree of control. For example, if I want to add a tinge of blue to the shadows, and to make the highlights appear warmer and more yellow, I can accomplish it using the *Color Balance* adjustment in the following way:

- Select *Shadows* from the drop-down menu.
- Use the yellow-to-blue slider to add blue to taste.
- Select *Highlights* from the drop-down menu.
- Use the yellow-to-blue slider to add yellow (while reducing blue) to taste.
- If the above adjustments caused midtone colors to shift to an unwanted hue, select *Midtones* from the drop-down menu, and correct as needed.

## Other Adjustments

In the sections above, I introduced those adjustments and methods I find most useful in my landscape work. Note that the *Black & White* adjustment layer is discussed in detail in chapter 12.

As you undoubtedly noticed, several of the adjustments covered so far offer a variety of menus, tools, sliders, and buttons that I did not touch on. In addition, there are many more adjustments, options, and settings than I can cover within the scope of this book. Indeed, any book attempting to describe every function of Photoshop would span hundreds if not thousands of pages and would not be very practical for any one type of use.

Should you encounter a need not met by what you've learned here, don't assume a solution isn't possible. Photoshop is an incredibly versatile application, and there is a large volume of knowledge online and in other books to address most any imaging challenge. Particularly, Adobe's own staff often respond to questions posted to https://forums.adobe.com and may provide insight not available in other places.

## EXERCISE 7

The purpose of this exercise is to fine-tune colors using the *Hue/Saturation* and *Vibrance* adjustments.

1. Open one of your images containing a blue sky.
2. Add a *Vibrance* adjustment layer. Adjust the *Vibrance* slider until your least saturated colors appear sufficiently saturated.
3. If already-saturated colors have become over-saturated, use the *Saturation* slider to de-saturate them a bit, then increase *Vibrance* a little more. Repeat this process in small increments until all colors appear evenly saturated.
4. Add a *Hue/Saturation* adjustment layer.
5. Select *Blues* from the drop-down menu. Make slight adjustments to the *Hue* slider and pick the shade of blue you find most pleasing (note: moving the *Hue* slider to the right will make your blues more purple/magenta; and moving it to the left will make them more cyan).
6. With *Blues* still selected, adjust the *Saturation* and *Lightness* sliders to taste.
7. Select another color range that is present in the image from the drop-down menu and experiment with different *Hue*, *Saturation* and *Lightness* settings until you are pleased with the result.
8. Repeat the above with every color present in the image.
9. Save your image.

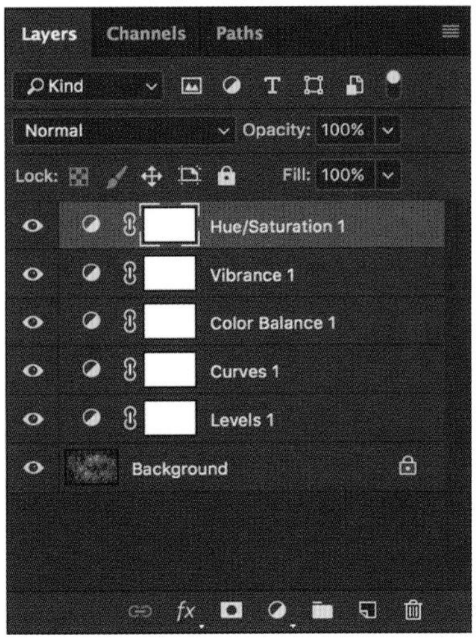


FIGURE 10.13: The *Layers* panel, showing a variety of layers.

## Working with Layers

In the previous sections and exercises, you had the opportunity to add layers and to see them stacked in the *Layers* panel (figure 10.13). This panel offers various functions for working with layers and applying their effects in different ways.

Before proceeding to other uses for layers, let's review a few of the more useful features and functions of the *Layers* panel.

### Active Layer

Note that the layer you are currently working on is always highlighted in the panel. This may take getting used to, especially if you think you are adjusting one layer while another is selected. If you feel like your actions are not having the desired effect, or if some tools appear to be unavailable, make sure you have the correct layer selected.

### Layer Visibility

Notice the eye icon next to each layer in the panel. Clicking it toggles between making the layer's effect visible or invisible. This can be used effectively for a quick before/after view.

### Layer Name

By default, Photoshop names each layer with the layer type and a number (e.g., "Levels 1," "Curves 3," etc.) Layers can be renamed by double-clicking the name and typing in a more descriptive one. Naming layers is useful in order to keep track of what each one does, so if you want to return to an image and fine-tune it at a later time, you will not have to memorize how you processed it. Having layer names such as "Global contrast," "Darken sky," or "Noise reduction" makes it easy to recall what you did and why.

## Layer Order

Layers are arranged such that each one adds its effect to the sum of the visible layers below it—its base.

Layer order can be very important. For example, we want to set the white and black points first to allow our subsequent adjustments a broader range of tones in which to work. Or, if converting an image to black-and-white, we'll want to convert the image to shades of gray before applying additional adjustments.

Layers can be moved up or down the list by dragging them. Be sure to grab the layer by its name or by its icon (to the right of the eye tool). If you accidentally grab the layer's mask (the white rectangle between the icon and the name) you will not be able to move the layer. If you accidentally placed a layer in the wrong place or decide to add a layer between two existing ones, simply drag it to where it needs to be.

## Removing Layers

If a layer is no longer needed and you want to remove it permanently (rather than temporarily make it invisible using the eye button), drag it to the garbage bin icon at the bottom right corner of the *Layers* panel. Alternately, you can right-click on the layer and then select the option to delete it.

## Opacity and Fill

At the top of the *Layers* panel are two fields labeled *Opacity* and *Fill*, which become accessible when a layer is highlighted. These fields can accept numeric percentage values. Clicking on the small arrow next to each will open a slider allowing you to set the values visually, which is my preferred way.

*Opacity* and *Fill* both control the strength of a layer's effect. For example, if I create a *Curves* layer that increases overall contrast and then reduce either its *Opacity* or *Fill* to 50%, the contrast will change only by half as much as it would if left at 100%. Setting either of these fields to 0% will effectively eliminate the layer's effect completely.

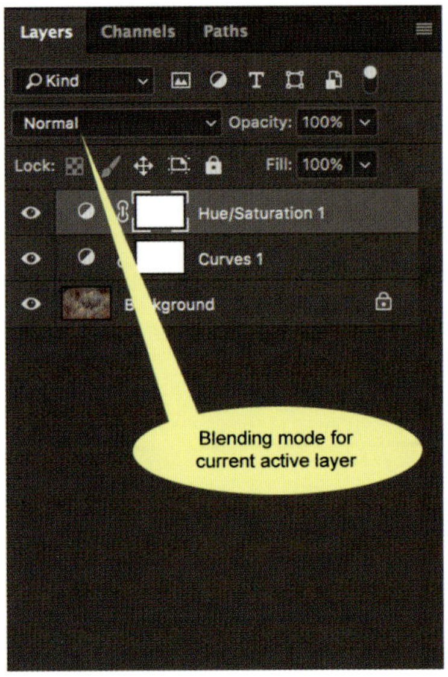


FIGURE 10.14: The blending mode drop-down in the *Layers* panel.

Although both fields seem to accomplish the same purpose, they are slightly different. Photoshop provides ways of changing a layer's style for various visual effects, such as drop-shadow or bevel. These effects are only relevant to some types of layers and can be selected from the *Layer Style* sub-menu in the *Layer* menu. *Opacity* changes the strength of both the content of the layer and its style, while *Fill* changes only the layer's content. For example, if I choose for my layer to have a drop shadow, *Opacity* will change the appearance of both the layer and the shadow, while *Fill* will leave the shadow fully visible regardless of its setting.

## Layer Blending Modes

At any point, the image displayed on the screen shows the combined effect of all visible layers. By default, adding a new layer simply enhances or replaces the value of its base. This is known as *Normal* blending. However, there are times when we may want the effect to be applied more selectively.

Photoshop offers several blending mode options to control how a new layer is blended into its base.

When any layer other than the Background (image) is selected, the blending menu in the upper-left corner of the *Layers* panel becomes active (figure 10.14).

To better understand blending, consider that for each pixel, Photoshop examines the existing (base) value and the new (blended) value introduced by a given layer, and determines the new value for the pixel based on the two. In *Normal* blending mode, the blended value simply replaces the base value. However, Photoshop offers other means of deciding what the new value will be based on the value of the base and that of the new layer.

You may remember, for example, that the *Curves* adjustment is particularly useful in modifying contrast. However, as you adjust the curve you might notice that it modifies not only contrast but also color saturation, even if individual color channels are left untouched. This is often an undesirable effect. We can use Photoshop's blending modes to ensure that an adjustment layer affects only some aspects of the base and not others. In this case, setting the blending mode to *Luminosity* tells Photoshop to apply the new layer's values only to lightness (tone) but not to color. In other words, it will keep colors as they exist in the base, even if the new layer tries to modify them.

Following are other useful blending modes:

- **Darken:** This mode changes only those pixels where the blended layer (or its effect) is darker than the base.
- **Multiply:** Unlike *Darken*, which simply replaces pixels, *Multiply* darkens tones proportionally. Photoshop takes each of the RGB values in the base and multiplies them by the values in the blended layer, then divides by 255 to compute the new value. This means that if either the base or blended values is pure white (255,255,255), the pixels will not be affected because the multiplication and division will cancel each other out. Similarly, if one of the pixels is pure black (0,0,0), the resulting pixel will be black since anything multiplied by zero equals zero. All other tones will be proportionally darkened based on the values in the base and blended layers. The practical effect is that the image will be darker overall; however, the dark areas in the base will be darkened more than the lighter ones.
- **Lighten:** This is the opposite of *Darken* and changes only those pixels where the blended layer (or its effect) is lighter than the base.
- **Screen:** Lightens tones proportionally by using the inverse of each RGB value (by subtracting it from 255). This mode uses the same calculation as *Multiply* and inverts the result. In a sense, this is the opposite effect of *Multiply* and will lighten the image proportionally.
- **Hue:** Changes colors in the image by applying the hue of the blended layer while preserving the lightness and saturation of the base.
- **Saturation:** Applies the saturation of the blended layer but preserves the hue and lightness of the base.
- **Color:** Applies the hue and saturation of the blended layer but preserves the lightness of the base.
- **Luminosity:** Applies the lightness of the blended layer but preserves the hue and saturation of the base.

While several more blending options are available in the menu, they are not often used in photographic applications, as their effects can be quite dramatic and decidedly not photo-like. I mention one other mode—*Soft Light*—when I discuss dodging and burning below.

## EXERCISE 8

The purpose of this exercise is to practice working with layers.

1. Open an image.
2. Add a *Levels* layer and adjust the black and white points as practiced in exercise 4.
3. Add a *Curves* layer and increase contrast by adding an S-Curve (figure 10.15). Explain why this curve increases contrast.

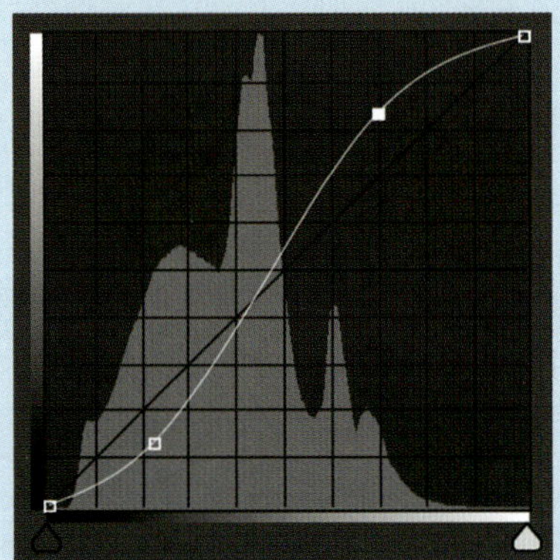

**FIGURE 10.15:** Increasing contrast using an S-Curve.

4. Adjust colors using *Vibrance* and *Hue/Saturation* layers as practiced in exercise 7.
5. Double-click on the *Curves 1* layer name and rename it to Global Contrast.
6. Double-click on the *Hue/Saturation 1* layer name and rename it to Global Color.
7. Change the blending mode of the Global Color layer to *Luminosity*. Explain what happened and why.
8. Change the blending mode of the Global Color layer back to *Normal*.
9. Click the eye icon next to the Global Contrast layer. Explain what happened and why. Click the icon again to undo the effect.
10. Save your file.

*See Appendix for answer key.*

## Cropping

Determining the best aspect ratio for your image is an important decision most often made in the field as part of the composition process. However, there is no rule that says you can't change your mind. When the time comes for another iteration of Dynamic Visualization, evaluate the image and consider whether it might look better in a different crop, and if so mark it as a gap to be addressed by Photoshop's *Crop* tool (figure 10.16).

Cropping sometimes is considered anathema among purists and among those who may experience discomfort about reducing the pixel count of the image. While I don't know of a remedy for such painful conditions, I hope they may be overcome with the consideration that, when it comes to the aesthetic appeal and expressive powers of an image, composition is more important than file size or image detail. Painful as it might be, if cropping the image improves its compositional balance, I say don't think twice.

Cropping can be applied when converting from RAW, or at any point when processing the image in Photoshop. Unlike the simple crop tool provided in applications such as Lightroom or ACR, Photoshop's *Crop* tool offers some useful cropping features that make it a superior choice, including the ability to not actually delete the excess pixels, but rather make them invisible in case you change your mind and want to recover them later. Photoshop's *Crop* tool also allows cropping to specific aspect ratios and/or size (either in pixels, or in physical units, such as inches and centimeters, which will be applicable later when we produce prints).

The *Crop* tool also offers an easy way to rotate your images, which can be done by hovering the cursor just outside any corner of the crop-area wire frame (note, the cursor's shape will change to a 90° double-headed curved arrow). Click on the arrow and, while holding down the mouse button, drag to rotate the image to your liking.

The *Crop* tool also offers the *Straighten* option which, when activated, allows you to trace a diagonal line on your image and automatically tilt the image so that line becomes perfectly horizontal or vertical. To do this, click on one

**Figure 10.16:** The *Crop* tool and its various options.

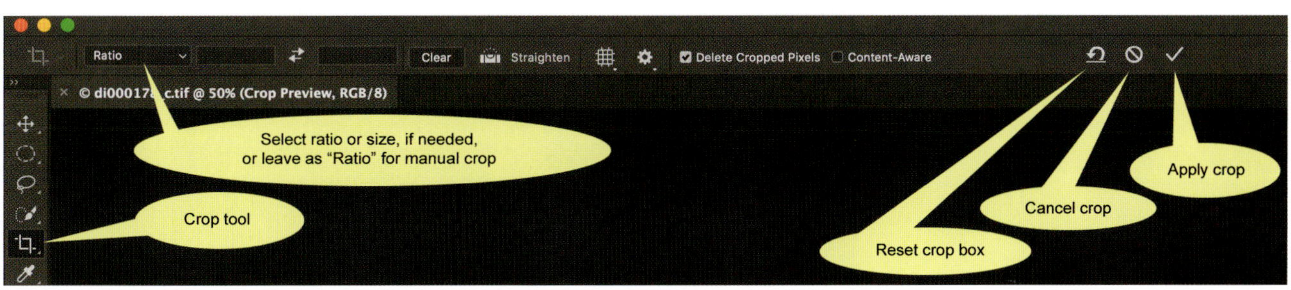

side of the line and, while holding down the mouse button, drag the cursor to the other end of the line. This is a useful way to correct images having tilted horizons or other situations where the camera was accidentally not level.

When rotating an image, inevitably, some areas around the perimeter of the frame will be missing data. Checking the *Content Aware* box tells Photoshop to attempt to fill these areas using its powerful content-aware fill algorithm. I recommend trying it to see if the results are satisfactory, which may save you from having to settle for a smaller file. Still, don't expect it to work perfectly every time. If the manufactured details appear unsightly, undo the operation (Command/Ctrl+Z) and repeat the rotation without the *Content Aware* box checked, and then crop to eliminate the blank areas.

**A Word about Bugs**

Note that the crop tool is notorious for being buggy. At the time of this writing, after persisting for a couple of releases, it seems that most of the previous bugs have been worked out. Still, if the tool doesn't behave as you expect, consider searching Adobe's support forums to see if the problem is, in fact, a new or reintroduced bug.

## Actions

Some operations requiring multiple steps can be tedious to apply from scratch each time. For that purpose, Photoshop provides a way of recording a workflow for later playback. A recorded set of steps is called an *Action*.

FIGURE 10.17: The *Actions* menu button.

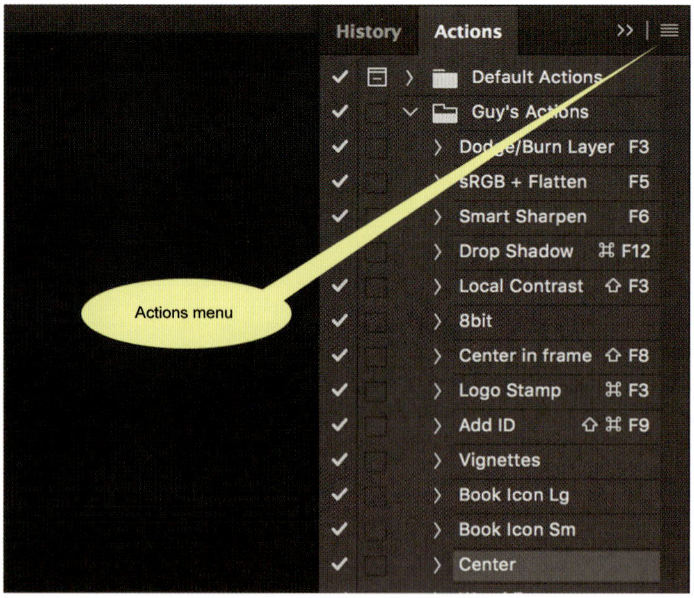

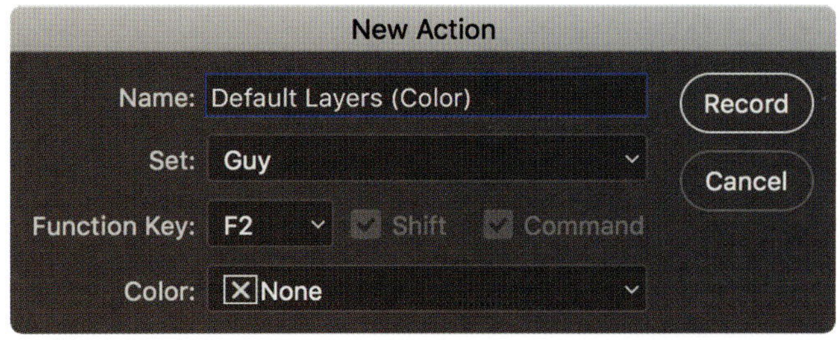


**Figure 10.18:** In this example, the new action will be saved to the set named "Guy," and be activated by the Shift+Command+F2 function key (other keys were not available as I assigned them to other actions).

To begin working with actions, make sure the *Actions* panel is visible by selecting *Actions* from the *Window* menu.

Photoshop also allows grouping actions into sets (which can also be saved and shared with others). I suggest creating your own set upfront so you can keep your actions separate from Photoshop's default action set, and back them up in case you need to reinstall Photoshop and recreate your work environment at some future time, or if you run Photoshop on multiple computers and want to have your actions available on all of them.

To create a set, click the menu button on the upper right corner of the *Actions* panel (figure 10.17) and select *New Set*. Name your set for easy reference (e.g., "Jane's Actions") and click *OK*.

To record a new action, select *New Action* from the same menu (figure 10.18). Name your action and place it into your set by selecting its name from the menu. You can also assign a function key and/or color to your action for easier activation and identification. Next, click *Record*. Anything you do from this point on is being recorded. Note the red *Record* button at the bottom of the *Action* panel indicating that recording is active. To its left is a *Stop Playing/Recording* button (figure 10.19), which allows you to end the recording when needed.

Once an *Action* is recorded, you can play it back by selecting it from the *Action* panel and clicking the *Play* button at the bottom. (Or, if you assigned a function key to it, simply click it to start the action.)

To share your action set with others, or to make a backup of it, click the set name in the *Action* panel and select *Save Actions* from the menu. This will save a file with a .atn extension at your chosen location.

To import a set of actions, whether one you created or one you downloaded online, select the *Load Actions* option from the *Action* panel menu and select the appropriate action file.

### My Actions

In my workflow, I always use at least one *Curves* layer, one *Dodge/Burn* layer (explained below) and one *Hue/Saturation* layer for color images. For black-and-white images, I also require a *Black & White* layer and a standard warm-tone tint layer (both covered in chapter 12). To streamline my workflow, I created actions that add these basic layers at the click of a function key, which I run first thing before editing an image.

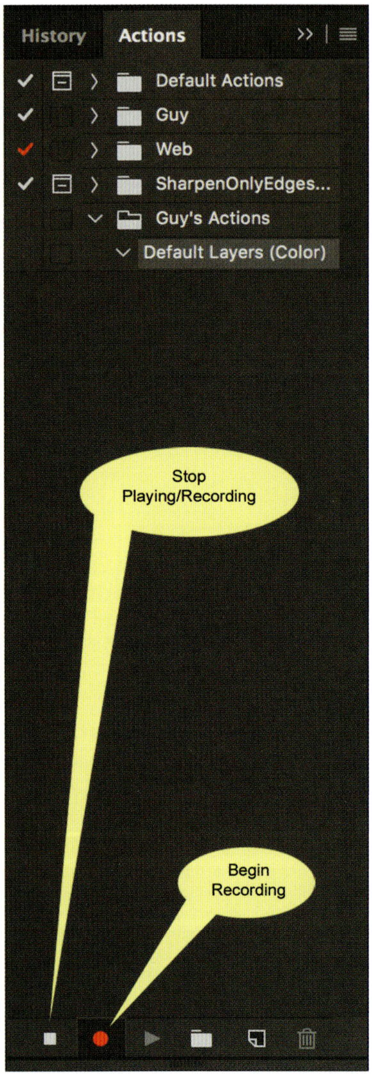


**FIGURE 10.19:** The buttons used to begin/end recording an action.

## Image Layers

Photoshop supports various types of layers. Up to this point, I focused the discussion on *Adjustment* layers—layers that calculate new values for pixels based on various parameters. Another type of layer—an *Image* layer (sometimes referred to as just "layer")—is a layer that contains pixels. The Background layer holding our image is an obvious example of an image layer.

Photoshop allows multiple image layers to exist in a file, which can be useful for a variety of purposes.

Placing an image layer over existing layers using the default *Normal* blending mode will obscure everything below it. However, Photoshop provides various other methods of blending image layers into their base in order to composite portions of them into the final image. This ability will serve us later when I explain how to do such things as combining the highlight details from one image and the shadow details from another to create a high dynamic range (HDR) image and blending images focused at various distances to retain only the sharp portions of each (known as focus stacking).

### EXERCISE 9

1. Open a new image with no previous layers.
2. Create a new action set and name it for easy identification (e.g., "John's Actions").
3. Add an action called Default Layers and select an available function key to attach it to (figure 10.18), and then click *Record*.
4. Add a *Curves* layer and name it "Global Contrast." Do not change any of the properties.
5. Add a *Hue/Saturation* layer and name it "Global Color." Do not change any of the properties.
6. Click the *Stop Playing/Recording* button (figure 10.19) at the bottom of the *Actions* panel.
7. Open another new image with no previous layers.
8. Click the function key you selected in step 3 above to ensure the action works as expected.

*See Appendix for answer key.*

## Local Adjustments

As the name suggests, local adjustments are applied selectively to specific areas of the image. The greatest challenge to performing local adjustments is the accurate isolation of the area(s) we want to apply the change to. The selection should not only be precise, but the effect should also be blended seamlessly into its surroundings so it's not obvious or distracting.

You may recall that some of the adjustments we covered previously, such as *Curves* and *Hue/Saturation*, already allow some ability to target changes to specific ranges of tones or colors. However, these ranges may still be present in multiple areas in the image. Local adjustments are explicitly restricted to well-defined portions of the image, and *cannot* affect other areas.

### Cloning and Healing

Perhaps the most obvious use for local adjustment is to address some of the defects mentioned in the chapter 6.

Photoshop provides various tools for eliminating distracting elements such as sensor dust spots, rogue elements peeking into the frame, contrails in the sky, or undesirable artifacts.

Cloning means copying part of the image over another part; and healing means replacing an area with texture generated to match its surrounding as closely as possible.

The most effective way to use these tools is to work at 100% magnification and slowly pan around the image to identify and correct defects.

The easiest tool to use for removal of small distractions is the *Spot Healing Brush* tool (figure 10.20).

If you added layers to your image, before applying the brush, be sure to select the *Background* layer, where the image pixels are, since *Spot Healing*

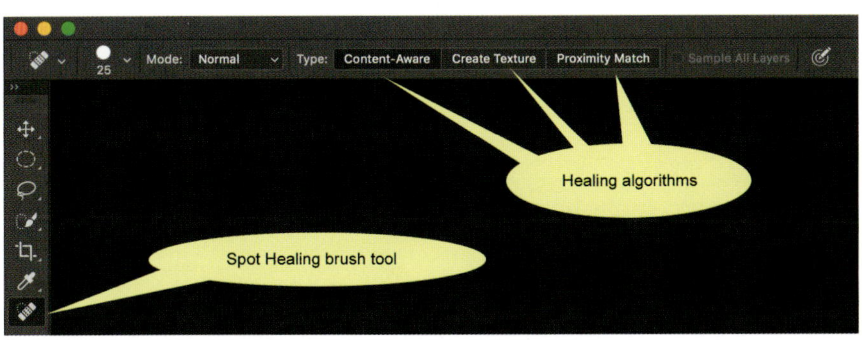


**Figure 10.20:** The *Spot Healing Brush* tool and its options.

### Exceptions to a Rule

Note that Cloning and Healing are the only exceptions we'll make to the nondestructive editing approach. I am quite certain you will never want to bring back dust spots and other distracting elements, once corrected.

*Brush* is a destructive tool: it changes the values of pixels and, once saved, those values cannot be restored short of reconverting the image from the original RAW file.

With *Spot Healing Brush* selected, simply paint over the object(s) you wish to eliminate. Photoshop will sample the areas immediately adjacent to them and attempt to match the patterns and textures so it appears seamless.

### Changing Brush Size on the Fly

When using brushes in Photoshop, an easy way to change the brush size on the fly is to use the square bracket keys, [ and ].

Note that *Spot Healing Brush* provides various healing algorithms. *Content-Aware* is the "smartest" and most recent addition, and usually produces the most desirable results. I suggest starting with it. If *Content-Aware* produces undesirable artifacts, undo the operation (Command/Ctrl+Z) and try the other algorithms to see if they do a better job, or try to paint over multiple small sections of the area to be healed, rather than trying to do it in one step.

While the *Spot Healing Brush* tool works well in most cases, especially when the distracting element is well separated from its surroundings, it may be challenging to use in very tight quarters, such as when a dust spot is in an area of important image detail we want to preserve.

If the *Spot Healing Brush* fails to adequately remove the distracting element, it may require manual removal using the *Clone Stamp* tool (figure 10.21). This tool samples one area of the image, and then clones it over the element

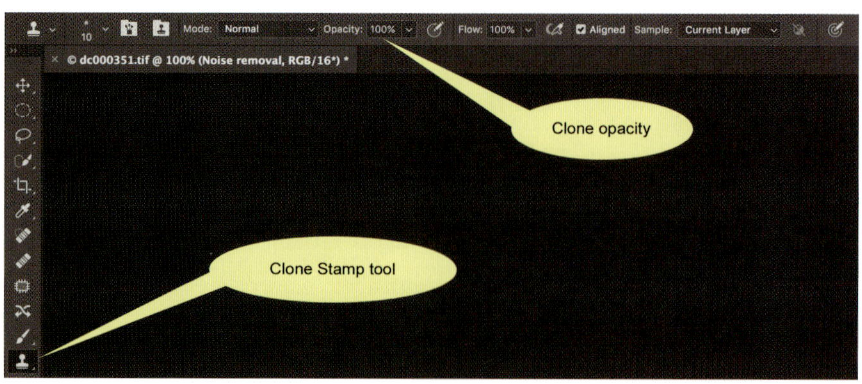


FIGURE 10.21: The *Clone Stamp* tool and its options.

we wish to eliminate. Once the *Clone Stamp* tool is activated, hold down the Option/Alt key (note the cursor shape will change) and click on the area you want to sample (copy from), then release the Option/Alt key and paint over the area you wish to replace (clone over).

Of the various options available for the *Clone Stamp* tool, a useful one is the ability to set *Opacity*. At 100% opacity, the source area will be copied over the destination area and replace the destination pixels completely. When *Opacity* is set to a lower number, some of the original pixels' appearance will be maintained (i.e., not a complete replacement). This is useful to blend the effect more seamlessly: use 100% opacity to clone out the undesired element and then, if the transitions around the edges are too abrupt or unsightly, reduce the opacity (50% is a good starting point, although you may need to fine-tune it for a given situation) and paint over the transition areas to make them less abrupt.

If the area you wish to clone is very small or is in a particularly tricky spot, you may want to work in magnifications larger than 100%. Remember, you can hold down the Command/Ctrl and Space bar keys together, then click the specific area in the image you wish to magnify. Repeated clicks will increase magnification. You can then zoom back out by holding the Option/Alt and Space bar keys together and clicking the image.

## Dodging and Burning

Dodging and burning refer to lightening or darkening specific areas in the image, respectively. In my experience, almost every image stands to benefit from the use of these techniques to some degree, even if applied subtly.

While Photoshop offers dodging and burning tools, I do not recommend using them. These tools date back to older versions of the software before it supported layers, and they change the values of the original image pixels (i.e., destructive editing). Instead, I suggest the following approach, which takes advantage of an image layer (not an adjustment layer, as we used previously) and a blending mode named *Soft Light*:

1. Add a new image layer by selecting *New Layer* from the *Layer* menu. You will be prompted with the dialog box shown in figure 10.22.
2. Name the layer "Dodge/Burn" or some other descriptive name.
3. Set the blending mode to *Soft Light*.
4. Check the box next to: *Fill with Soft-Light-neutral color (50% gray)*.
5. Click *OK*.

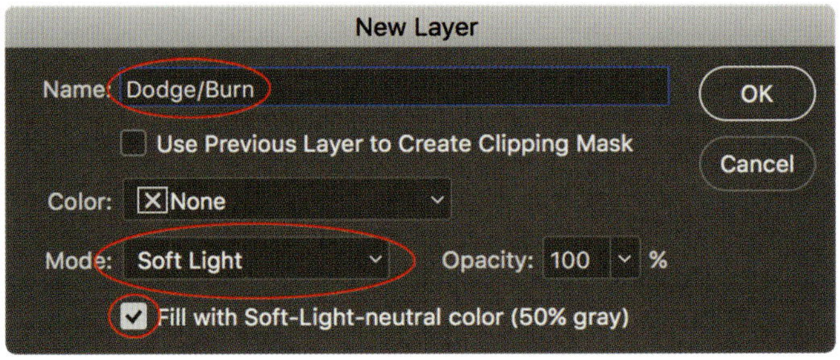


FIGURE 10.22: The parameters for a Dodge/Burn layer.

The *Soft Light* blending mode subtly lightens or darkens the base in proportion to the lightness of the blended layer. Any areas where the blended layer is darker than 50% will subtly darken the image, and any areas lighter than 50% will lighten the image. By choosing to pre-fill the layer with neutral (50%) tone, we essentially create a layer that does not change the image at all. However, we can now paint over this layer in either black or white to lighten or darken (i.e., dodge or burn) specific areas. The subtle blending in *Soft Light* mode will ensure the effect is not abrupt.

Next, we paint over this layer in either black or white to lighten or darken specific areas (refer to figure 10.23 to help identify the various tools and buttons mentioned):

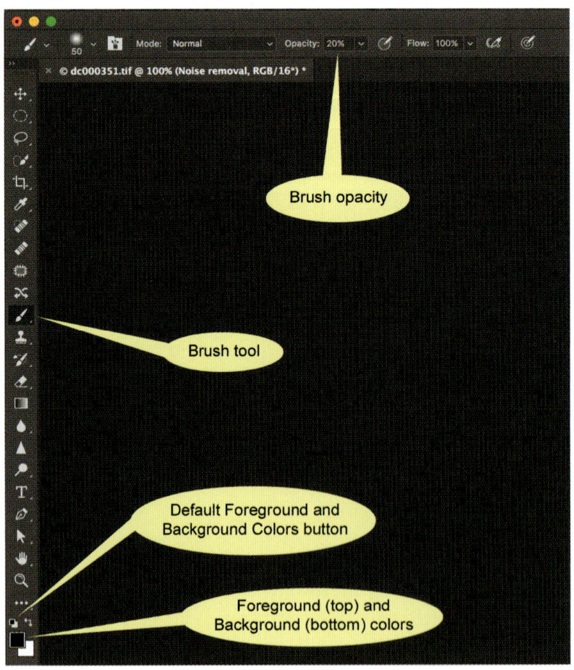


FIGURE 10.23: Tools and buttons used for the Dodge/Burn method described above.

1. Select the *Brush* tool (either from the *Tools* panel or by clicking B).
2. Reset the foreground and background colors to their default black/white settings by clicking the *Default Foreground and Background Colors* button, or by clicking the letter D.
3. Select a brush size appropriate for the area you wish to lighten (dodge) or darken (burn) by using the bracket keys, [ and ].
4. Set the brush *Opacity* in the *Control* panel to 20% as a starting point.
5. Paint over the area you wish to dodge or burn.
6. Switch between black and white as needed by clicking the X key to flip the foreground and background colors.

The approach to dodging and burning described above has the following advantages over Photoshop's built-in tools:

- Dodging and burning is accomplished in a layer separate from the original image so that the effect can be applied in a nondestructive way and can be removed or modified at a later time.
- Using the soft (20% *Opacity*) brush, the effect can be applied incrementally: each additional brush stroke makes the area just a little bit lighter or darker.
- It's easy to see the before/after effect by using the eye icon next to the layer name in the *Layers* panel. This is especially helpful where the difference may be subtle.

If the 20% *Opacity* setting is either too subtle or too bold for what you have in mind, try other settings. Keep in mind that the effect is cumulative, so you may paint over the same area multiple times to gradually darken or lighten as needed. However, the total effect is limited by the brush *Opacity*, so after a few strokes you may no longer see a difference. In this case, either increase the *Opacity* or add another *Dodge/Burn* layer (figures 10.24 and 10.25).

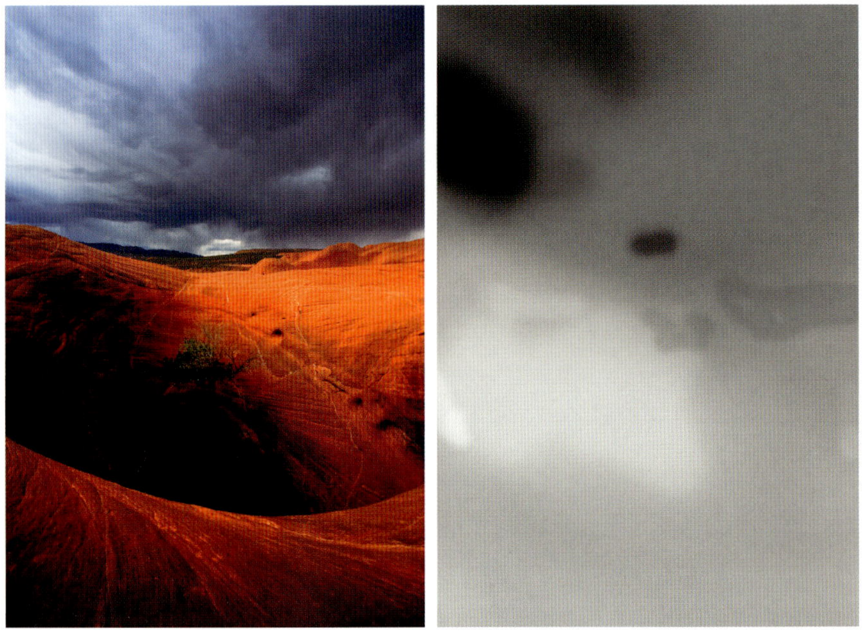

**Figure 10.24:** The image on the left clearly required a significant amount of dodging and burning to even out the tones across the frame. On the right is the Dodge/Burn layer I created in order to accomplish the balance I was after (see its effect in figure 10.25).

## EXERCISE 10

1. Open an image.
2. Record an action within the set you created in the previous exercise that adds a Dodge/Burn layer using the steps listed on page 193 (I recommend also attaching it to a function key as it is an action you may wish to use frequently). Remember to stop the recording once the layer is added.
3. Use a 20% *Opacity* brush to dodge and burn areas of your image, as needed using the steps described on page 193.

### Layer Masks

Earlier in this chapter, I reviewed the powerful features of Photoshop's adjustment layers, such as *Levels*, *Curves*, *Hue/Saturation*, and *Color Balance*. When an adjustment layer is added, by default its effect is applied globally. These same layers can also be used for local adjustments, targeted explicitly to just a portion of the image, without the ability to affect other areas. This is accomplished using layer masks.

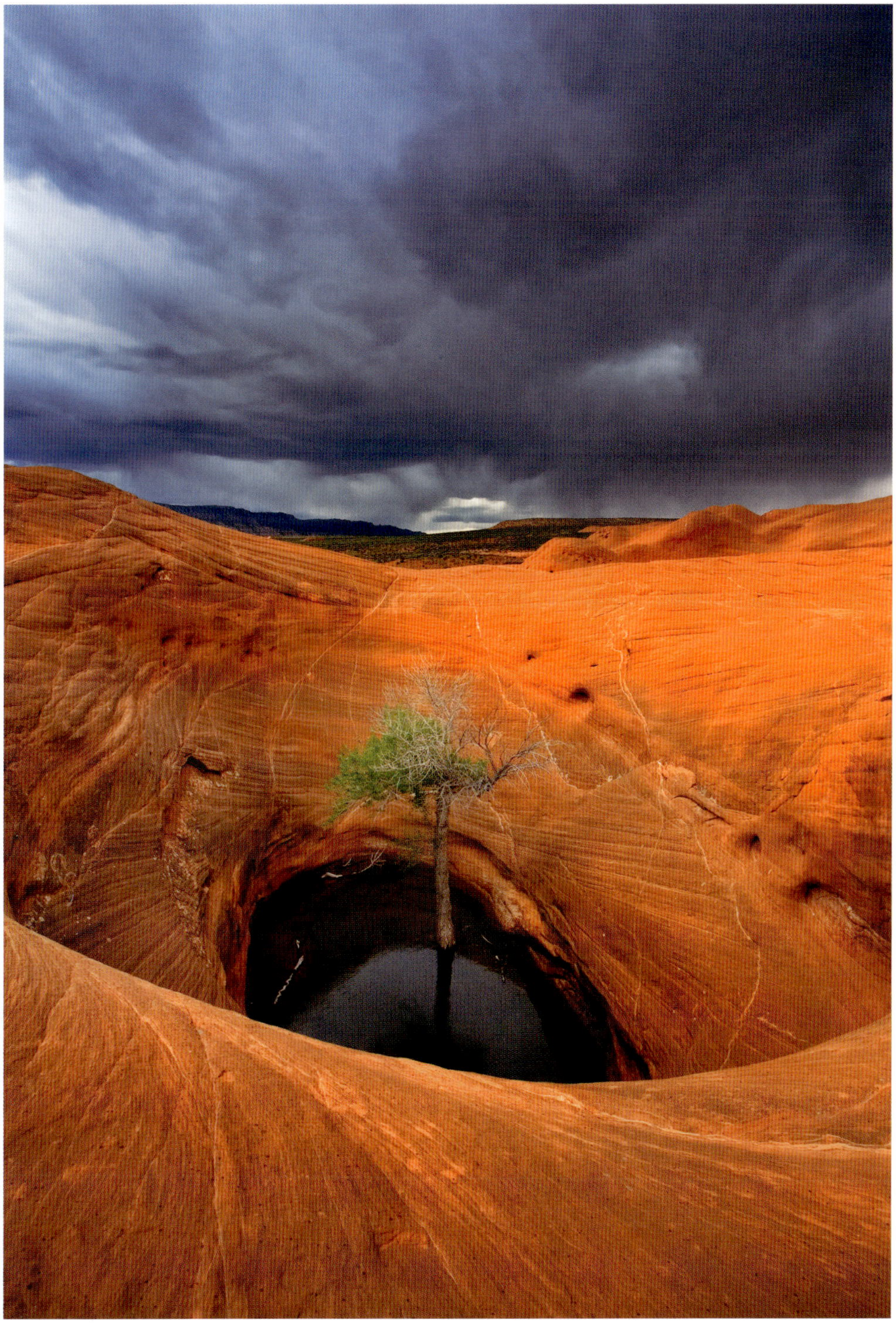

FIGURE 10.25: The image shown in figure 10.24, showing the effects of the dodging and burning applied.

### White Reveals, Black Conceals

An easy way of remembering the mask's effect is this: white reveals and black conceals (referring to the effect of the layer associated with the mask).

A mask is a black-and-white image that can be associated with an adjustment or image layer. A mask acts as a filter, determining where the layer's effect will be visible and where it will not, and to what degree. In areas where the mask is black, the layer will have no effect. In areas where the mask is white, the layer's full effect will be applied. In areas where the mask is gray, the layer's effect will be partially applied, depending on how dark the gray is. For example, at 50% gray, the layer's effect will only be half as visible as it is in areas where the mask is white.

By default, when adding an adjustment layer, it is created with a white mask attached, meaning that its effect is not restricted and may affect any part of the image. If we want the effect to be blocked from (or reduced in) any portion of the image, using the *Brush* tool, we can simply paint over the mask in black (to block it completely) or some shade of gray (to block it partially). Painting in different shades of gray is accomplished most easily by using black as the foreground color, and varying the brush *Opacity* setting. For example, when the brush *Opacity* is set to 50%, areas painted will only show half the effect; when set to 75%, areas painted will only show a quarter (25%) of the effect (75% will be blocked).

FIGURE 10.26: Layers and associated masks in the *Layers* panel.

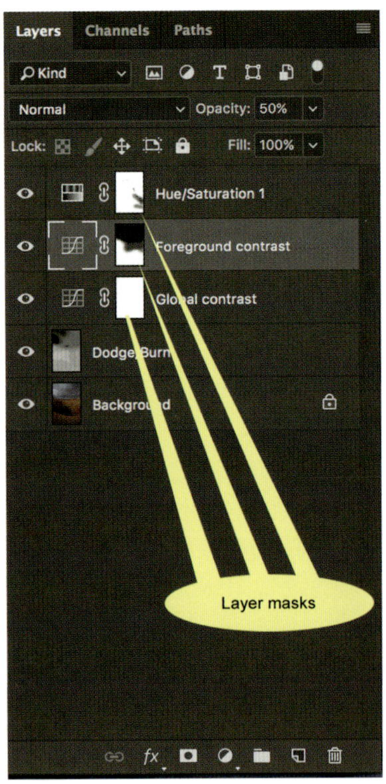


Masks are shown in the *Layers* panel next to the layers they are attached to (figure 10.26). Note the *Curves* layer named "Global contrast" having a completely white mask, meaning that its effect is applied globally, as opposed to the second *Curves* layer named "Foreground contrast," with the effect limited to the lower-left portion of the image (white portion of the mask), applied partially to the center-right portion of the foreground (gray portion of the mask), and blocked from affecting the upper part of the image (black portion of the mask).

To paint your own mask, first add an adjustment layer (such as *Curves* or *Hue/Saturation*), and then make sure its mask is selected in the *Layers* panel. A selected mask shows small outlines outside its corners (figure 10.27). If the mask you wish to paint is not selected, simply click on it once.

With the mask selected, proceed as follows:

1. Set your foreground color to black (remember the shortcuts: D to set the foreground and background colors to their default black and white settings, and X to flip between foreground and background).
2. Select the *Brush* tool (click B).

3. Set the brush opacity as needed (100% blocks the layer's effect completely; anything lower than that blocks the effect partially).
4. Paint over the image areas you wish to apply the mask to. Note how the mask icon changes with each brush stroke (when you release the mouse button).

If you need to fine-tune the mask, flip the foreground color to white (using the X key), set the brush *Opacity* to 100% (or lower, for a subtler effect), and paint over any masked areas you want to unmask.

Remember that you can adjust the brush size using the square bracket keys, [ and ].

## EXERCISE 11

The purpose of this exercise is to practice the use of layer masks.

1. Open an image that has both low-contrast and high-contrast areas.
2. Add a *Curves* adjustment layer.
3. Add an S-Curve to increase contrast across the entire image. Focus only on the appearance of the low-contrast areas and don't worry if the high-contrast areas become too contrasty.
4. Make sure the mask next to the *Curves* layer is active (designated by the outlines outside its corners, as seen in figure 10.27).
5. Select the *Brush* tool (click the B key).
6. Make sure you are painting in black (remember you can reset the foreground and background colors to black and white using the D key, and flip them using the X key).
7. Set the brush *Opacity* to 50%.
8. Paint over the areas of the image where contrast has become too high as a result of the *Curves* adjustment.
9. If brushing once (blocking half of the layer's effect) is not sufficient to make the high-contrast areas appear correctly, brush over them again until you achieve a good balance between low-contrast and high-contrast areas.

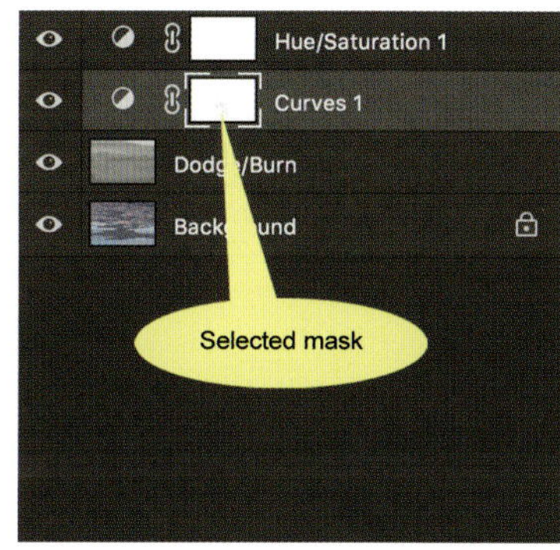


**Figure 10.27:** Note the lines outside the corners, which indicates the mask is selected. When a mask is selected, painting over the image in fact paints over the mask.

When painting a mask, I like to start with a large brush and medium (50%) *Opacity* to draw the rough mask, doing my best to stay away from small areas and transition zone. After I have the larger areas painted over, I then begin refining by reducing the brush size, magnifying (zooming in to) the area I wish to fine-tune, and carefully painting the fine portions of the mask.

## Selections

Masks, as we've seen, offer a way to isolate parts of the image for various purposes—whether to restrict the effect of an adjustment, or to hide portions of an image layer. Another mechanism for isolating parts of an image is selection. Photoshop offers various selection tools that can be used to demarcate portions of an image. Photoshop marks selections using an animated dashed line, dubbed by some "marching ants."

Since masks and selections serve similar purposes, Photoshop treats them as interchangeable: masks can be converted into selections and selections into masks. If you hold the Command/Ctrl key and click on a layer mask, Photoshop will show you the marching ants outlining the area selected by the mask. Since masks may be painted with various degrees of gray that cannot be shown using the single "marching ants" line, the visible selection shows only those areas that are more than 50% affected; however, the actual selection does cover areas that are less than 50% selected, even if not shown.

A useful way to take advantage of Photoshop's ability to treat selections as masks (and vice versa) is this: if you used one of Photoshop's selection tools (described below) to outline an area, and then added a new adjustment layer while the "marching ants" are visible, the layer will automatically be created with a mask matching to the selection. In other words, if it's easier to use one of Photoshop's selection tools to isolate the area you wish to work on, rather than drawing a mask by hand, you may use the selection tool, then simply add an adjustment layer, and this layer will be targeted to just the selected area.

The simplest of Photoshop's selection tools are the *Marquee* selections, which can be rectangular or elliptical. The *Marquee* tool can be selected using the M key or from the *Tools* panel (figure 10.28). You can switch between a rectangular and elliptical marquee by clicking the tool while holding the Option/Alt key to cycle through the various options.

To select a rectangle or ellipse, depending on the *Marquee* tool chosen, click one corner of the desired area and, while holding down the mouse button, drag the cursor to the opposite corner. If you wish to select a perfect square or circle, also hold down the Shift key.

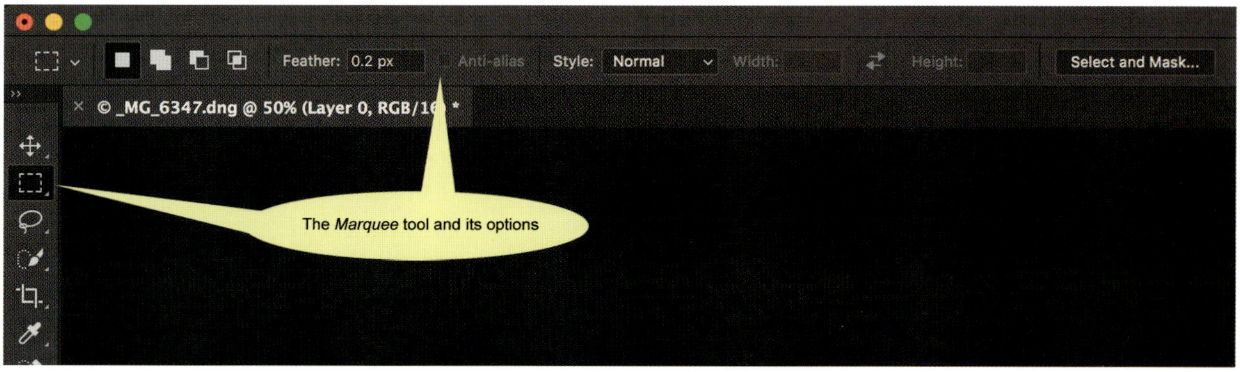


FIGURE 10.28: The *Marquee* tool and its options.

Note that you may also restrict the selection to a given aspect ratio or physical size using the various options in the *Control* panel at the top of the screen.

The *Marquee* tool is useful for various publication-related uses, such as adding a shaded rectangle behind text or creating the ovals used in the illustrations in this book. Natural subjects do not usually follow the limited geometry of rectangles, ellipses, and circles, so they almost always require more complex selections to isolate.

Slightly more useful when selecting portions of an image is the *Lasso* tool (figure 10.29), allowing manual selection using the mouse or other pointing device, and its smarter version, the *Magnetic Lasso* (one of the options under the *Lasso* tool), which allows clicking on various points along the outline of the subject. The *Magnetic Lasso* applies a smart selection algorithm to connect the dots into a selection. The more dots (clicks), the more precise the selection will be. The *Lasso* tools can be selected using the L key or by selecting them from the *Tools* panel. Like the *Marquee* tools, use the Option/Alt key to cycle through the various *Lasso* tool options.

FIGURE 10.29: The *Lasso* tool. To use other variations (e.g., *Magnetic Lasso*, etc.), hold the Option/Alt key and click the tool to cycle through its options.

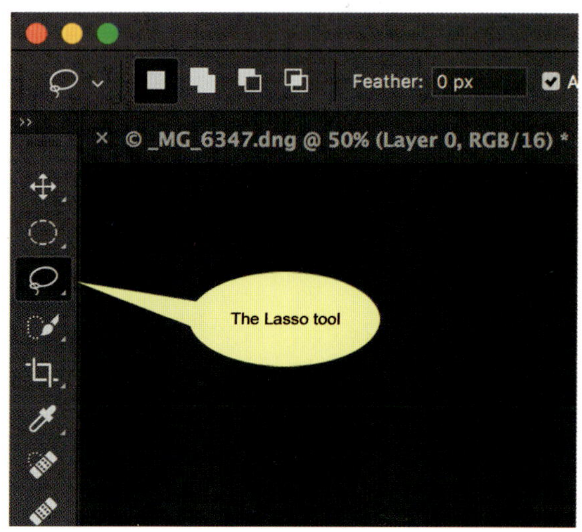


While more useful than *Marquee*, the *Lasso* tools are not very efficient in selecting entire elements in a photograph. Rather than a primary selection tool, I prefer to use the *Lasso* to fine-tune selections made by smarter tools, such as the *Quick Selection* tool described below. These smart tools do a great job of selecting most of the desired areas, but often they miss by including or excluding small portions of other areas. The *Lasso* tool can then be used to surgically add or remove these small areas, right down to individual pixels.

The smartest and most versatile selection tools available in Photoshop are *Quick Selection* and *Magic Wand*, which can be selected using the W key or from the *Tools* panel (figure 10.30).

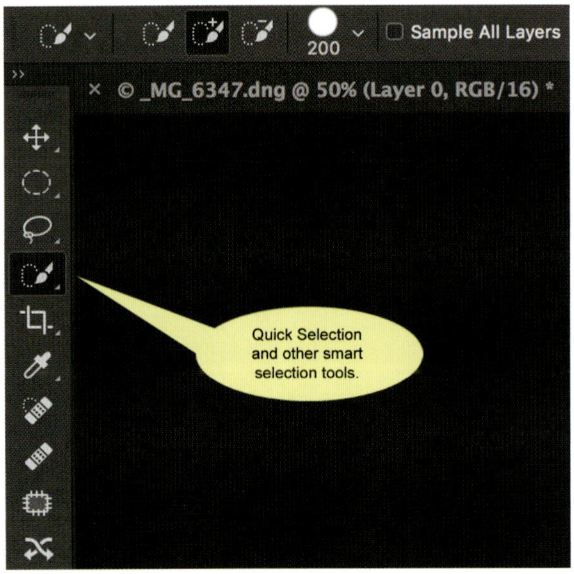


**Figure 10.30:** The button for *Quick Selection, Magic Wand,* and other smart selection tools. Use the Option/Alt key and click the button to cycle through its various options.

The same button is used for all these selection tools, and you may cycle through its options by holding the Option/Alt key and clicking the tool.

Smart selection tools use various algorithms to identify the boundaries of the element you are attempting to select. The *Magic Wand* is used by clicking inside the element you wish to select, and its effect can be fine-tuned using the *Tolerance* setting in the *Control* panel. The higher the *Tolerance*, the more tones and colors will be considered part of the object.

The *Quick Selection* tool allows us to use a brush-like cursor to guide the selection by painting inside the area we wish to select. The algorithm will guess what we are attempting to select and show us the boundaries using the "marching ants." Like other brush tools, you may use the [ and ] keys to set an appropriate brush size.

Whichever tool you choose, you can always add to an existing selection by holding down the Shift key, or subtract portions from an existing selection by holding down the Option/Alt key. You will notice a small + or – sign next to the selection cursor when these keys are pressed. By using these techniques, you can also combine various selection tools in defining the precise boundaries.

For example, you may begin by roughly selecting an area with the *Quick Selection* tool and then switch to the *Lasso* tool. Zoom in so you can inspect the selection's edge closely, and then add to or subtract from the selection using the Shift or Option/Alt key until you select exactly what you want.

As mentioned, once a selection is defined, and with the "marching ants" visible, you can add any adjustment layer and have the selection automatically become its mask.

Selections made using these tools will usually have a hard, well-defined edge to them. In almost all cases, you'll want to feather (or soften) the edges to ensure that any changes you make will blend smoothly into the selection's surroundings. The best way to do so is using the *Select And Mask* button, which will become visible in the *Control* panel whenever a selection tool is active.

When you click on *Select And Mask*, Photoshop will show you the selection and allow you to make the non-selected areas transparent (use the *Transparency* slider to set the transparency level so the demarcation line is clearly visible). You may now use the various fine-tuning options to smooth, feather, expand, or contract your selection for a more precise fit.

When a selection is no longer needed, it can be cleared by using Command/Ctrl+D (de-select). This is important to do before adding further adjustments, to ensure that the selection doesn't accidentally mask their effect.

## EXERCISE 12

1. Open an image containing a well-defined area of sky.
2. Activate the *Quick Selection* tool, use the square bracket keys—[ and ]—to set the brush size so you can easily paint within the sky area.
3. Brush within the sky area until it is selected.
4. Zoom in to 100% magnification or higher so you can clearly see where the "marching ants" selection edge is.
5. Activate the *Lasso* tool.
6. Use the Shift key or the Option/Alt key along with the *Lasso* tool to add or remove areas to fine-tune the selection, as needed.
7. Click the *Select And Mask* button.
8. Zoom in very close to the selection edge and set a *Feather* value to create a slight transition zone along the edge.
9. Click *OK*.
10. Add a *Curves* layer. Notice how the selection automatically becomes the mask for this layer.
11. Pull the curve up or down to make sure it only affects the sky.
12. Hold down the Command/Ctrl key and click the mask to convert it back into a selection.
13. Add a *Hue/Saturation* layer. Notice that the selection became its mask.
14. Drag the *Hue*, *Saturation*, and *Lightness* sliders to adjust the sky color to your taste.

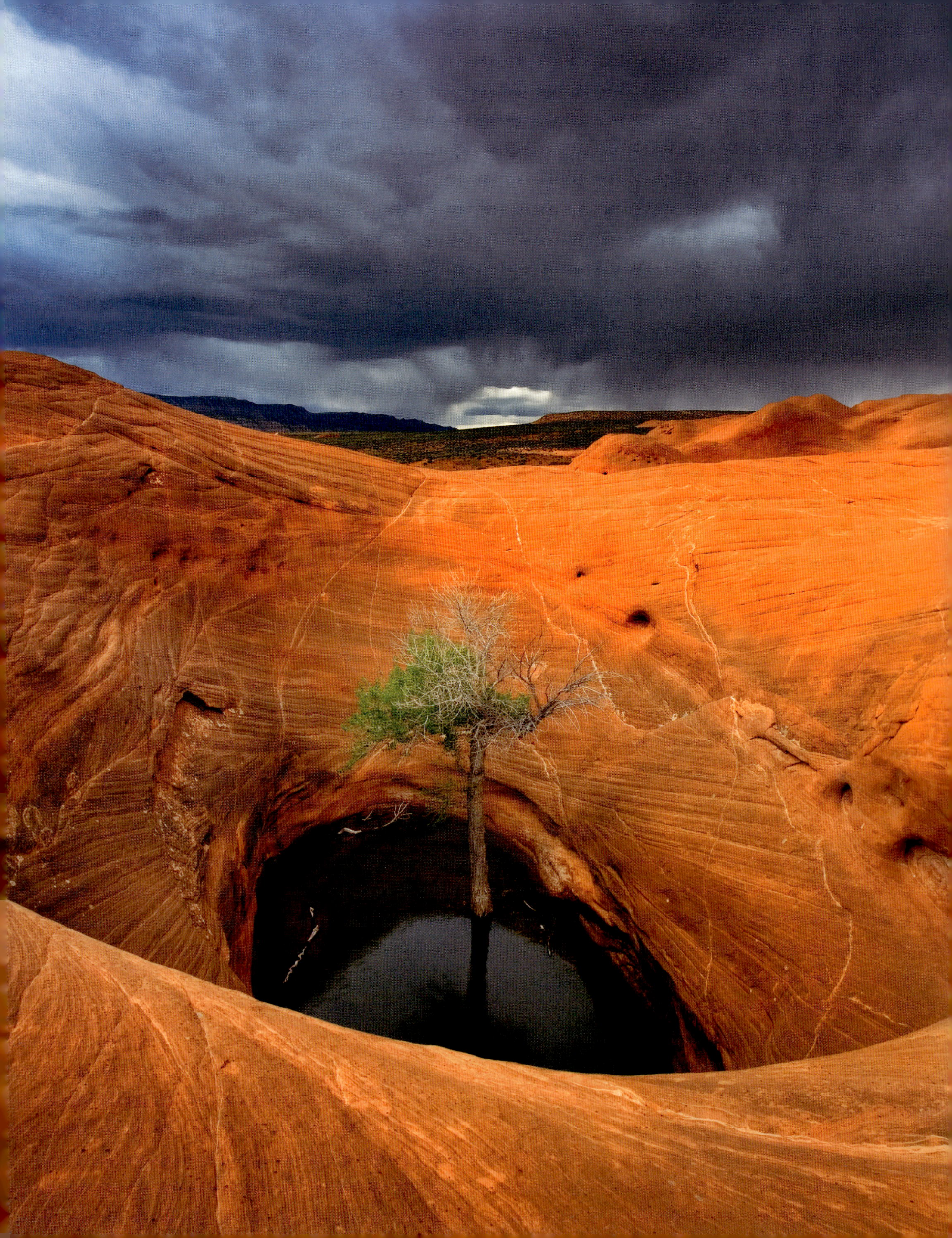

# Master Files

11

*The photographer's most important and likewise most difficult task is not learning to manage his camera, or to develop, or to print. It is learning to see photographically—that is, learning to see his subject matter in terms of the capacities of his tools and processes, so that he can instantaneously translate the elements and values in a scene before him into the photograph he wants to make.*

—EDWARD WESTON

Master files contain all the original image data (details and colors), as captured by the camera and converted from RAW (this is the layer shown as Background in Photoshop), and the subsequent edits that were made in the form of layers. Master files represent the best data that we have for the image, and are not explicitly optimized for any particular form of output (such as a web image or a print of a given size). Instead, the master file is a starting point from which we later derive other versions that are targeted to specific uses. Making output-specific adjustments to a master file is referred to as *targeting*.

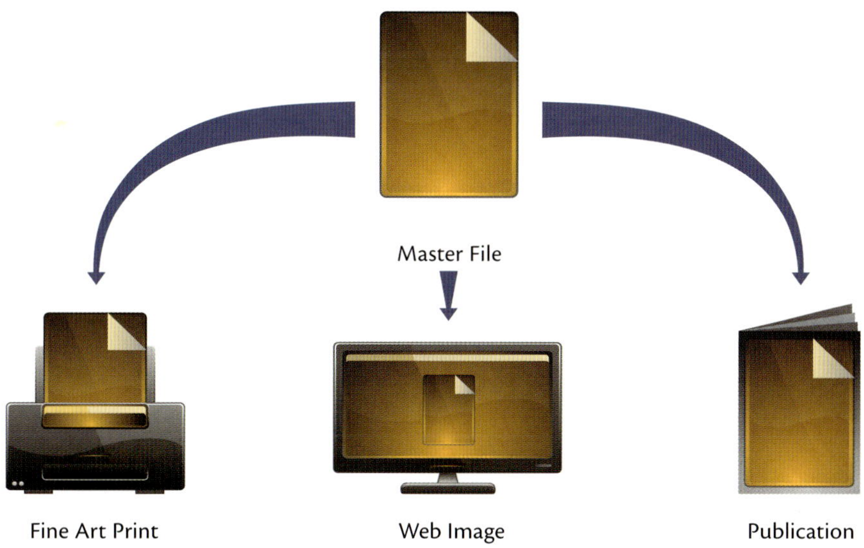


**FIGURE 11.1:** The master file is the repository of best data for an image. It serves as a starting point from which to derive device-specific versions.

## Targeting and Flexibility

Targeting always degrades the master file in some way. For example, to target a file for a large print, requiring more pixels than we have in the original capture, new pixels need to be artificially manufactured. Also, the file's color space should be converted to the limited gamut of colors supported by a given printer and paper (which is always smaller than the gamut of a computer screen). The same master file can also be targeted to create a web image by reducing its size (throwing away pixel data) and converting its color space to the small sRGB color space.

Master files should offer the utmost flexibility possible, allowing them to be targeted to any type of output. They must, therefore, contain as much detail and color information as possible.

Master files are also the files we'll want to archive and keyword in our image catalog, and back up to ensure we don't lose them in the event of a drive failure, data corruption, or a loss due to other reasons.

To make sure that our master files offer the utmost flexibility to be targeted to various output devices, the following requirements should be met:

- **Native pixel size:** Master files should retain the same pixel size as captured by the camera. In other words, pixels should not be added or eliminated (with the obvious exceptions of removing distracting elements such as dust spots, if needed, or cropping to a given aspect ratio, if dictated by a desired composition).

  Resizing an image, also known as *interpolation*, is a destructive adjustment, meaning it will discard or alter original image data so the resulting file fits within the required output dimensions. Keeping the master file at its native pixel size ensures that all original details recorded by the camera (as opposed to details manufactured by software) are preserved.

  Resizing should be applied only when the master file is targeted to meet the requirements of a specific output form, such as a print or a web image.

- **Large color space:** To retain the full range of colors captured by the camera and any that may have been added in processing, I recommend using a large color space such as Adobe RGB (1998) or ProPhoto RGB. Using smaller color spaces may result in loss of color data if out-of-gamut colors are changed to fit within a narrower gamut.

  Once an image is converted to a small color space, converting it back to a larger one cannot bring back any colors lost in the initial conversion.

- **High-bit format:** As I explain in chapter 4: "Speaking Digital," there is a significant difference in the number of discrete color gradations that can be represented in 8-bit versus 16-bit formats. In many cases, using an 8-bit format such as JPEG will discard potentially valuable image data.

  16-bit formats generally retain all color gradation that current sensors can resolve, and allow for smoother color transitions.

- **Nondestructive editing:** To the extent possible, methods such as layers and masks should be used instead of changing the original image pixels.

  Don't assume that you are done processing after the first pass. As your vision and skills evolve, and as better technology becomes available, you may want to revisit your image for additional processing. By using nondestructive editing methods, you can continually refine your image and even reverse prior processing without having to start from scratch each time.

  Also, if better RAW conversion software comes along, you may want to re-convert the original image and swap out the *Background* layer with the new version, and then retain or adjust your existing adjustment layers.

- **Lossless compression or no compression:** Lossy compression methods, such as the method used for standard JPEG files, discard and/or alter the original image data to reduce file size. Although this loss may not always be easily perceptible, it becomes more and more visible as the file needs to be enlarged or edited further (since data is changed each time the file is resaved).

  Lossless compression algorithms, such as ZIP or LZW, can be used in conjunction with TIFF and other file formats to reduce file size, if needed, without compromising the integrity of image data. Since drive space is relatively inexpensive, you may also want to consider saving your files uncompressed for improved performance (compressing and decompressing files require intensive computation).

- **Non-proprietary file format:** By default, Photoshop will save a file in its original format. For example, if you started with a JPEG file and tried to save it, Photoshop by default will keep the file in JPEG format. Files converted from RAW using ACR or Lightroom will by default be saved in Photoshop's own format, PSD (or PSB for very large files). PSD and PSB are proprietary formats, meaning that Adobe may decide, at its sole discretion, to cease support for them. I recommend instead to use an open file format such as TIFF, which is not subject to the whim of any one company, and has the advantage of being supported by a wide variety of software.

Photoshop knows how to embed its proprietary layers and masks in a TIFF file, which means that if opened in Photoshop, these features remain intact. However, other software that may not recognize Adobe's layer and mask data may still use the file but without utilizing these features. This is still a better scenario than not having access to your files at all, should you decide to use products other than Photoshop in the future.

## Saving Your Master File

To save your master file, open the *File* menu and select *Save As*. From the dropdown at the bottom of the window, select the file format (TIFF recommended), and be sure to check the *Layers* and *Embed Color Profile* checkboxes (figure 11.2).

The *Layers* checkbox ensures that layer and mask data will be preserved (even if only usable by Photoshop). The *Embed Color Profile* checkbox, as the name suggests, embeds the image's ICC profile in the file. This makes for a slightly larger file but also ensures that if you ever wish to open your master file in a color-managed application on a workstation that does not happen

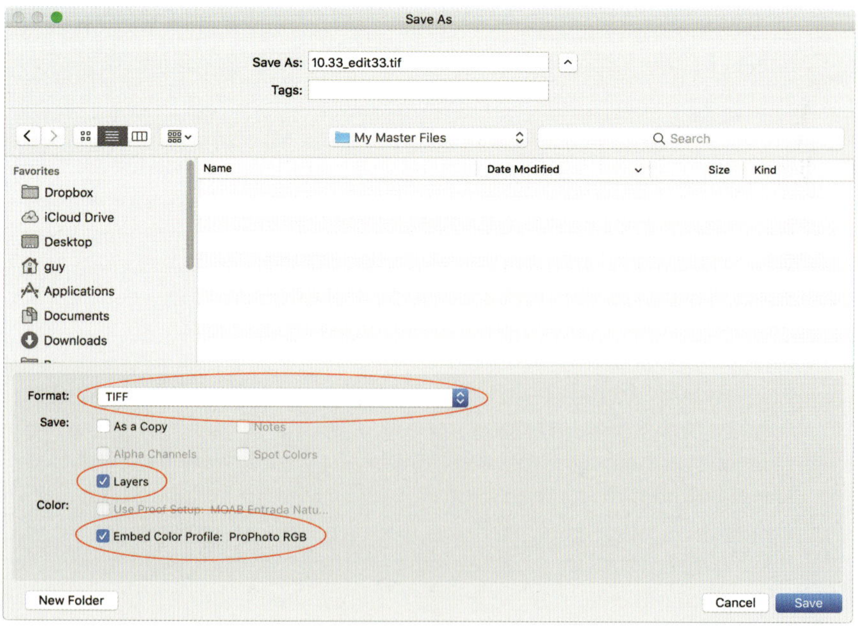


FIGURE 11.2: Note the options circled in red, which I recommend when saving master files.

to have the ICC profile needed (ProPhoto RGB, in the case of the example in figure 11.2), the application can extract it from the master file. If the profile was not embedded, the application may still know what color space the image was saved in, but will not be able to render it correctly on screen or to convert it to other profiles.

With the settings shown in figure 11.2, click the *Save* button. This will present you with additional options relevant to the TIFF format (figure 11.3).

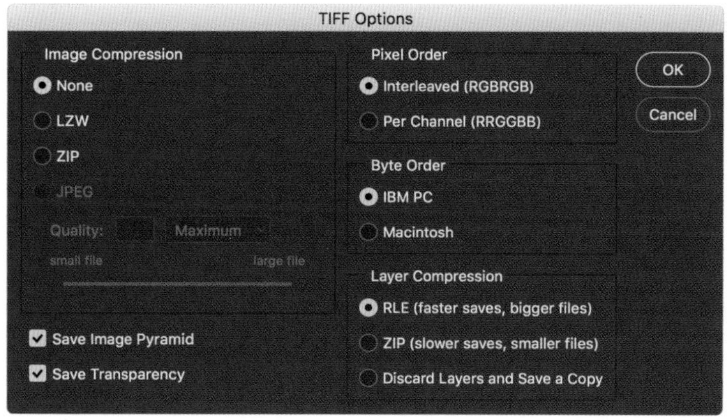


FIGURE 11.3: TIFF file options.

In the current version of Photoshop, only lossless compression options are available (lossy JPEG compression, which is greyed out here, used to be a valid option in older versions). ZIP compression generally produces very effective compression, but requires more processing power to compress/decompress the file, which somewhat degrades performance. LZW compression usually reduces the file size, but not always (in fact, in some cases it may even produce files that are larger than uncompressed versions). I choose to save my files uncompressed, making them usable by any application that supports the TIFF format.

Be sure to select one of the *Layer Compression* options for layers (anything other than *Discard Layers and Save a Copy*).

You may safely ignore the *Pixel Order, Byte Order,* and *Save Image Pyramid* settings. Some were important in the days when PC and Macintosh used different processors, which is no longer the case; or when some TIFF engines required pixels to be in a certain order, which is also no longer the case. The *Save Image Pyramid* option is not supported in Photoshop but is provided to preserve multi-resolution variations that may have been created by other applications.

If active, I recommend checking the *Save Transparency* option in case you wish to open the file in applications other than Photoshop (Photoshop will always preserve transparency, even if the box is not checked). If this is not important to you, you may ignore this option, too.

## Back Up!

Although I mentioned backups several times already, it is a point worth repeating and belaboring. I know several photographers who lost important work for lack of a backup copy. I strongly recommend backing up your master files as soon as they are created, and each time they are changed.

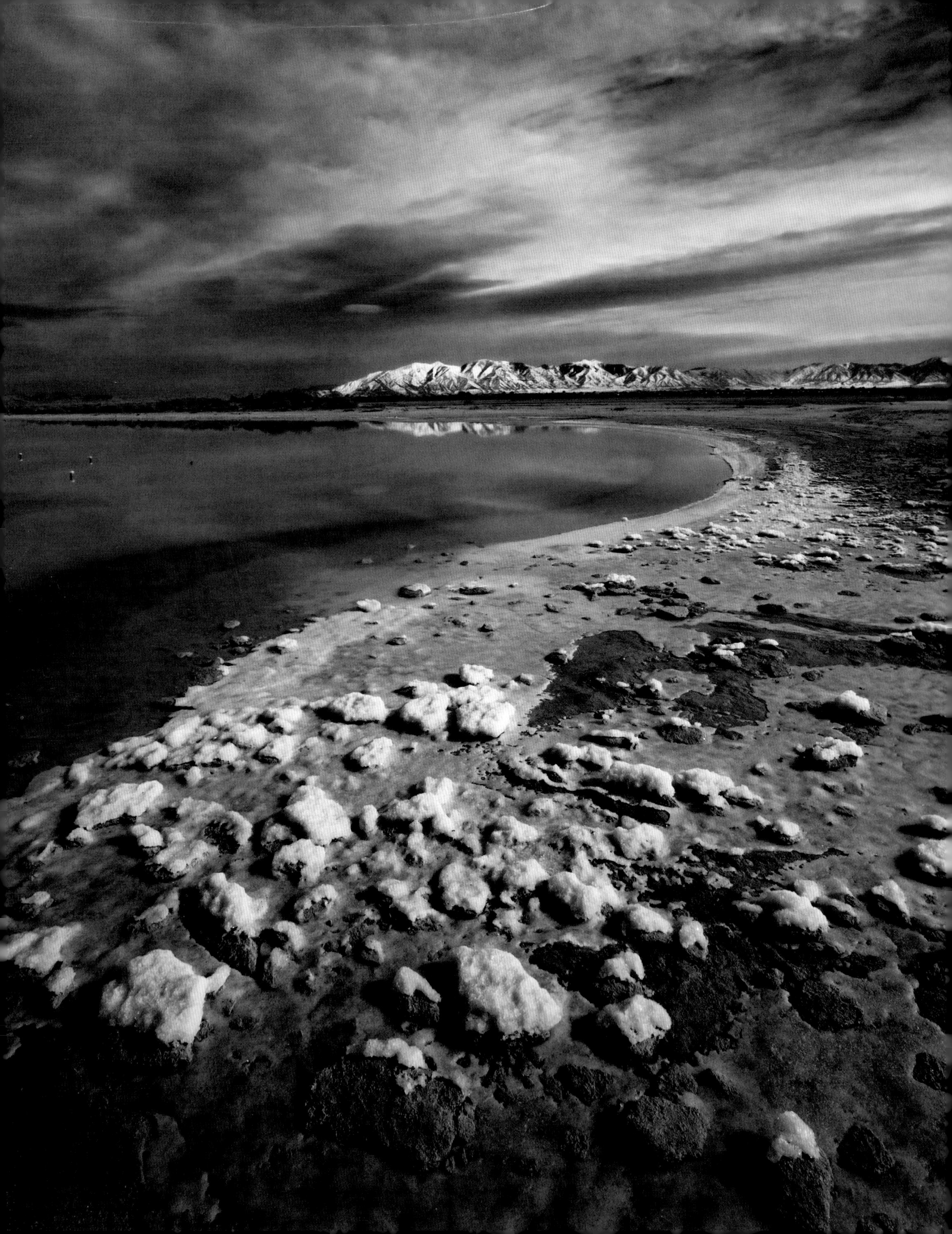

# 12

# Black-and-White

*The real voyage of discovery consists not in seeking new landscapes but in having new eyes.*

—MARCEL PROUST

Black-and-white images, for most people, are hidden in plain view. While all visual perception is a combination of physiological and cognitive processes, the ability to see (or, more accurately, to visualize) in black-and-white is almost entirely reliant on the cognitive part of our visual system. To determine what it is we are looking at and how we should respond to it, our brains are conditioned to interpret light in terms of color and intensity. However, visualizing images in black-and-white is not about recognizing what objects or scenes literally are, but as photographer Minor White put it, "...what else they are"—what they could be.

## From Color to Tone

While it may seem intuitive to think about making a black-and-white image of a colorful scene as simply eliminating color information from the captured data, and preserving only the degrees of lightness (tones), such characterization is inaccurate. Rather than eliminate color, we will convert (map) colors into tones. Note that this implies deliberate and subjective decisions regarding how each color will be rendered as a discrete shade along the continuum from pure white to pure black.

In the simplest black-and-white conversion, we can use the brightness of a given object (the amount of light it reflects or emits) to determine its tone. However, the results of such an approach (called desaturation) are rarely satisfactory. One common problem is that objects having different colors but that reflect the same amount of light will be rendered in black-and-white as the same tone, making them indistinguishable. In addition, such direct mapping bypasses a wide array of creative possibilities.

The first thing to keep in mind about black-and-white photography is that there isn't one "correct" way to convert a color image into one made of tones. An object under given lighting conditions can be made to appear very dark, very light, or anywhere in between without it seeming "wrong." The second thing to keep in mind is that color is an essential ingredient in the making of a black-and-white image, and makes possible the decision on how to map colors into tones. This ability to map different colors into different tones, independent of how bright they are, is known as separation.

Though I use the term *black-and-white*, other designations such as *monochrome* or *grayscale* are commonly used. Taken literally, none of these terms is very accurate. The tones in the final image do not necessarily need to be neutral (gray/colorless), and there are certainly more tones than just black and white.

In chapter 6, I discuss the HSL representation of color where colors are distinguished by their hue (e.g., red, green, purple); saturation (which represents the color's intensity); and lightness (which indicates how bright a color is perceived to be). Hue and saturation can be grouped into one quality called chromaticity, describing the characteristics of a given color that are independent of how bright it appears.

To better understand chromaticity, consider a painting hanging in a room with a dimmable light switch. As we increase the amount of light, the painting will appear progressively brighter, but its colors will not change (assuming a neutral white light source). In other words, the switch controls only lightness. All other qualities of the colors in the painting—their chromaticity—remain constant.

While it is quite intuitive to understand the role of lightness in how a given color will appear in black-and-white, in this chapter I discuss the less obvious role of chromaticity.

## How Color is Mapped into Tone

In chapter 4, I explain how various colors are represented in the RGB model. Considering our goal of rendering an image in black-and-white, however, most of these colors will not be of use to us and we need a method of mapping them into just one value representing a degree of lightness.

In the RGB model, neutral tones (white, gray, and black) are represented by all three channels having the same value. The higher the value, the brighter the tone. So, for example, the brightest white possible is represented as 255, 255, 255; middle gray is 128, 128, 128; and pure black is 0, 0, 0. Another way to think about it is this: rather than having three independent color channels that can be combined to produce a very large number of possibilities, in black-and-white we have only one (gray) channel and the number of possible variations is the cube root ($\sqrt[3]{\ }$) of what is possible using three channels.

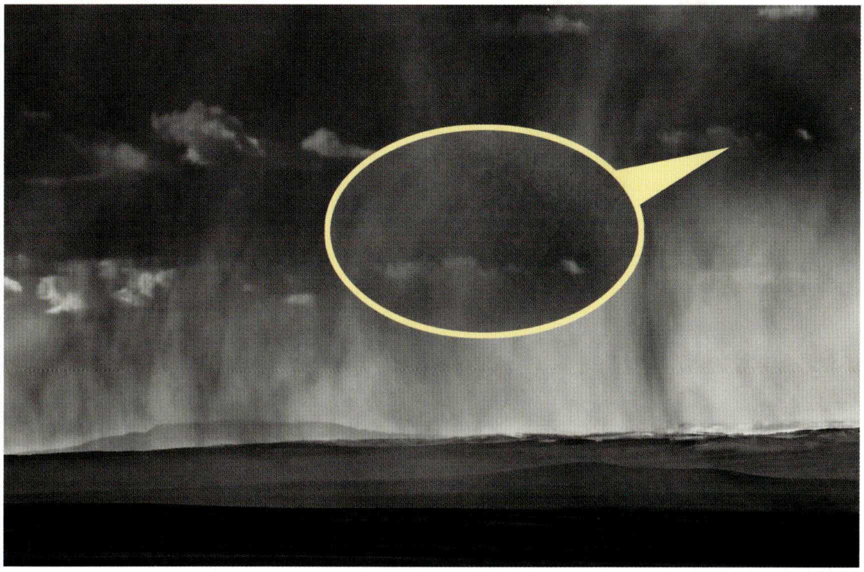

FIGURE 12.1: Section in the bubble shows artifacts resulting from insufficient gradation in an 8-bit file.

Although not obvious, an important implication of having just one gray channel is that an 8-bit file can only contain 256 tones. While possibly sufficient for some types of images, this number falls far short of ideal, especially when the image contains areas of smooth gradation, such as skies or reflections in water (figure 12.1). In these cases, an 8-bit file may not allow for sufficiently smooth gradation and may result in unsightly artifacts such as banding and posterization. Therefore, it is even more important when working in black-and-white to keep your image files in a 16-bit format.

### Calculating Lightness Based on RGB Values

It may seem plausible to guess that a conversion from an RGB color to a corresponding gray tone is as simple as averaging the red, green, and blue values. This, however, is incorrect. Our perception of how bright an object appears varies by its color. For example, a patch of yellow reflecting a given amount of light will appear much brighter to us than a patch of blue reflecting the exact same amount of light.

There are several variations of formulas to compute the lightness of a color based on its RGB values. One of the more commonly used is shown below, where L is lightness, R is the amount of red, G is the amount of green and B is the amount of blue:

$$L = \sqrt{R^2 \times 0.241 + G^2 \times 0.691 + B^2 \times 0.068}$$

Note the blue value is given much lower weight than green or red. This represents the difference in human perception of brightness and its dependence on color. There is no need to memorize the formula, of course, but readers who are mathematically inclined may find it useful in understanding how applications such as Photoshop (which has its own variation of this formula) handle the conversion.

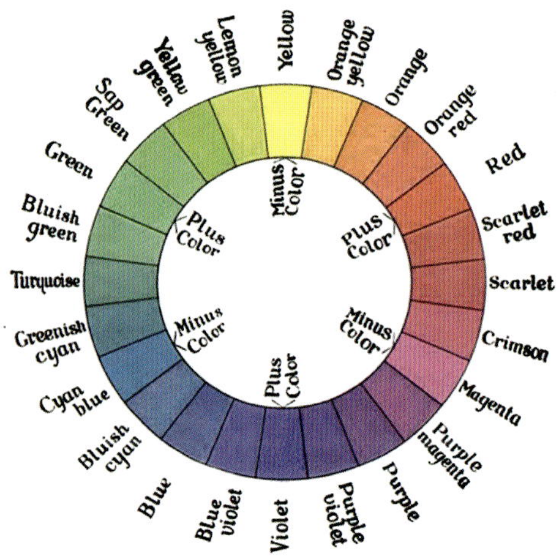


FIGURE 12.2: A color wheel created in 1908 by J. Arthur H. Hatt for his book, *The Colorist*.

## Color Filters

Black-and-white film photographers use a variety of color-tinted filters to achieve separation in tone based on color. Such separation is accomplished by physically blocking light of certain colors.

A filter allows light of its own color to pass through and blocks all other colors to varying degrees. For example, a red filter allows red light to pass through but blocks green and blue light to varying degrees. Thus, if used with an image containing red flowers, the flowers will appear much brighter than their green stems. Similarly, using a green filter will make the red flower darker than the green stem, and using a blue filter will make both the flower and stem appear dark.

Filters block to the highest degree those colors that are opposite them in a standard color wheel (figure 12.2).

The separation achievable using color filters can be quite striking, as seen in the example in figure 12.3.

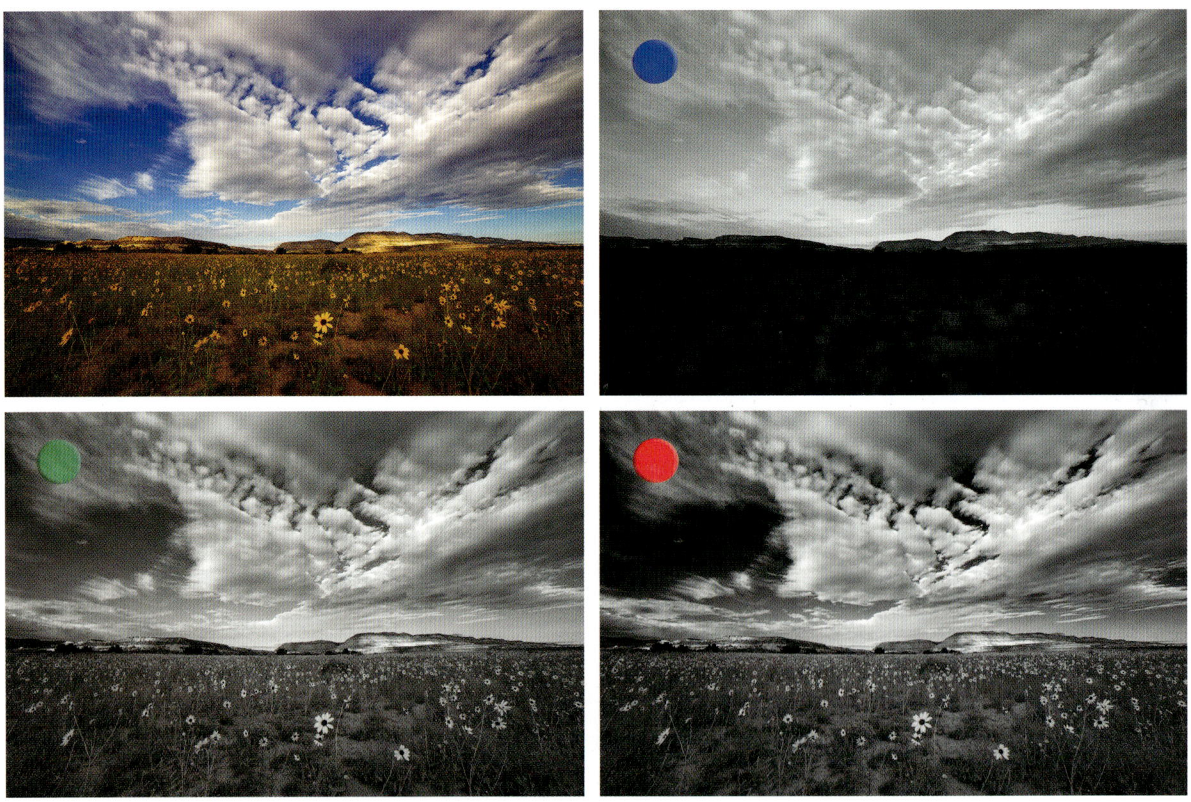

FIGURE 12.3: The color image (*top left*), converted to black-and-white using a blue filter (*top right*), a green filter (bottom left) and a red filter (bottom right). Note how each filter makes its own colors lighter and other colors darker to achieve separation of tones based on colors.

## The Digital Advantage

While very effective, the use of physical filters (made of glass, gel, or resin) imposes several limitations:

1. We are limited to the selection of filters we happen to have with us.
2. Filters are costly and prone to breakage, scratching, and other damage.
3. Physical filters have a physical size. Particular lenses may require a particular filter diameter. This may result in the need to purchase and carry multiple sizes of each filter to fit various lenses, or the use of step-up or step-down rings.
4. Since filters block light, exposure times need to be longer when using them. This may result in unwanted subject movement during exposure and it increases the potential for noise in digital capture.
5. Filter effects cannot be combined. For example, we cannot simultaneously use a red filter to brighten a red flower while using a green filter to brighten the stem and leaves.
6. Once used, the effect of a color filter cannot be easily (or at all) undone in later processing.
7. The placement of physical filters in front of the lens increases the risk of flare and, if the filter is dirty or of low quality, it may degrade the image.

The good news for digital photographers is that physical color filters are no longer required to achieve the desired separation effects. In fact, not even one of the limitations listed in this section applies to digital capture. The effect of these filters can be simulated with perfect accuracy, their strength can be applied in myriad discrete gradations rather than a limited selection, and there is no need to consider loss of light or other filter-related issues when capturing an image in the field. And, using common processing techniques such as layers and masks, the effects of multiple filters can be combined and applied to different areas in the image. For example, we can use a red filter to darken a blue sky and a green filter to lighten foliage all in the same image.

When converting a color image to black-and-white in Photoshop, we'll simulate the effect(s) of color filters to achieve tone separation. This is the most critical step in the conversion. After that, we'll be able to use Photoshop's *Curves* adjustment and other techniques to control contrast and other parameters, same as in a color image.

**Color Filters in Photoshop**

Photoshop's black-and-white conversion tool (the *Black & White* adjustment layer) gives us the equivalent of well over fifteen thousand trillion variations of color filters. Most of these variations do not exist as physical filters, and even if just a fraction of them do, that is a lot of filters to carry if you wanted to achieve a similar degree of precision using non-digital methods.

### EXERCISE 13

1. A photographer is contemplating making an image of a lush green forest scene and is attempting to visualize the effects of either a green filter or a red filter. Which filter will yield a darker image? Which will result in the greatest variation of tones?
2. A photographer is working on an image that includes interesting white clouds in a bright blue sky and wants to achieve high separation by darkening the blue to the greatest extent possible. What color filter will be best suited for the job?
3. Black-and-white film photographers sometimes use a green filter when photographing portraits of fair-skinned people. Can you think of a reason for doing so?

*See Appendix for answer key.*

## RAW Conversion

For the most part, the same RAW conversion considerations apply to images visualized in black-and-white as to images visualized in color. However, there are some considerations that are unique to black-and-white that will help produce a better outcome.

During RAW conversion, we should consider which color filter we will later use in Photoshop to convert the image to black-and-white. For example, we can decide that we want a red filter effect to achieve a very dark sky, or a blue filter effect to achieve a very light sky; or whether we want to use a yellow or red filter so that yellow flowers appear white, or a green or blue filter so the same flowers will appear as some darker shade of gray.

By varying such parameters as *White Balance* (*Temperature* and *Tint*), we can produce a version of the image that, once converted to black-and-white, will be more conducive to our visualization. For example, if we want the sky to appear dark, we might choose to later apply a red filter effect (which will make red and yellow hues lighter, and blue hues darker). However, if the image has an overall blue color cast, the use of a red filter may darken everything. By varying the *White Balance* controls, we can ensure that blues only exist in the sky.

We may also choose to deliberately add a color cast (figure 12.4) so when the image is later converted to black-and-white, it will appear darker or lighter overall.

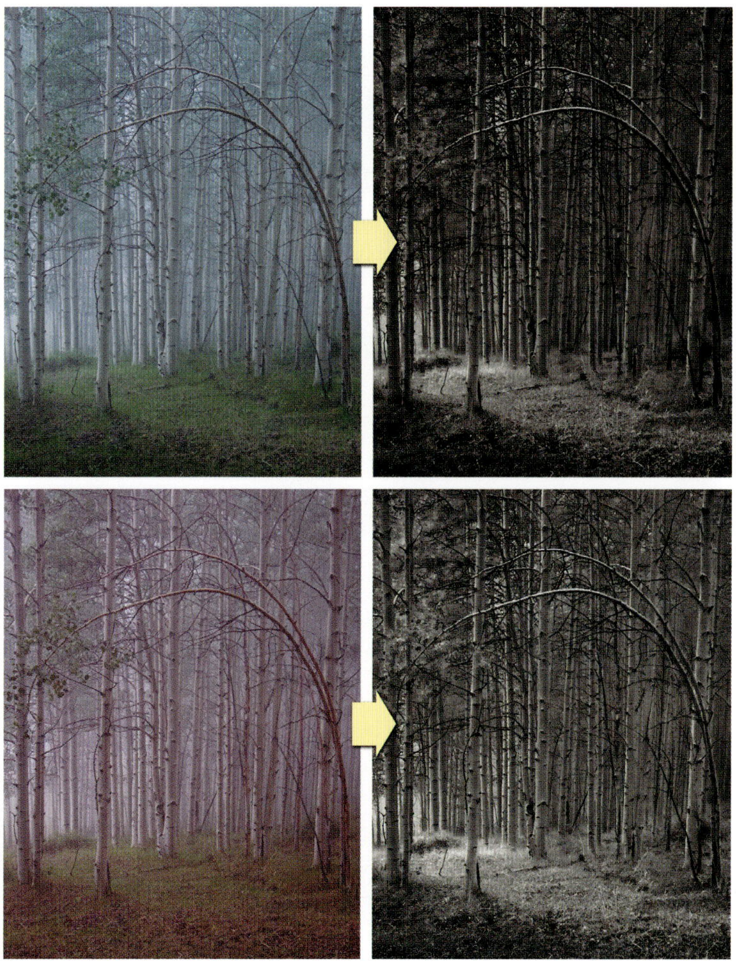

**FIGURE 12.4:** Two variations of the same images converted from RAW (*left*), then converted to black-and-white using a red filter effect (*right*). The image on the upper left is how I would convert from RAW if I intended to proceed in color (I liked the ethereal hint of blue in the woods). However, knowing that I intend to convert to black-and-white using a red filter, I opted to shift the Tint slider in ACR toward magenta, and the Temperature slider toward yellow (*lower left*). This resulted in mapping more data from the green and blue channels into the red channel, which helped add detail and subtle variations in tone to the red channel, and to make the shades of gray a bit lighter when converted to black-and-white with a red filter (*lower right*).

### Why Use White Balance?

While it might seem there are better ways to add a color cast than adjusting *White Balance* in RAW conversion, the reason I prefer this method is that it calculates pixel values using the RAW (Bayer) data. Once converted into pixels, using tools in Photoshop to add a color cast remaps the values of existing pixels, which is a step removed from the original RAW data, and some gradation in tone may have already been sacrificed.

## Converting to Black-and-White in Photoshop

Photoshop's tool for converting color images into black-and-white and for applying a filter effect to map colors to specific tones is the *Black & White* adjustment layer, which can be added using any of the methods discussed earlier in the book for adding new adjustment layers. Figure 12.5 shows one way to do it, using the *Create new fill or adjustment layer* button.

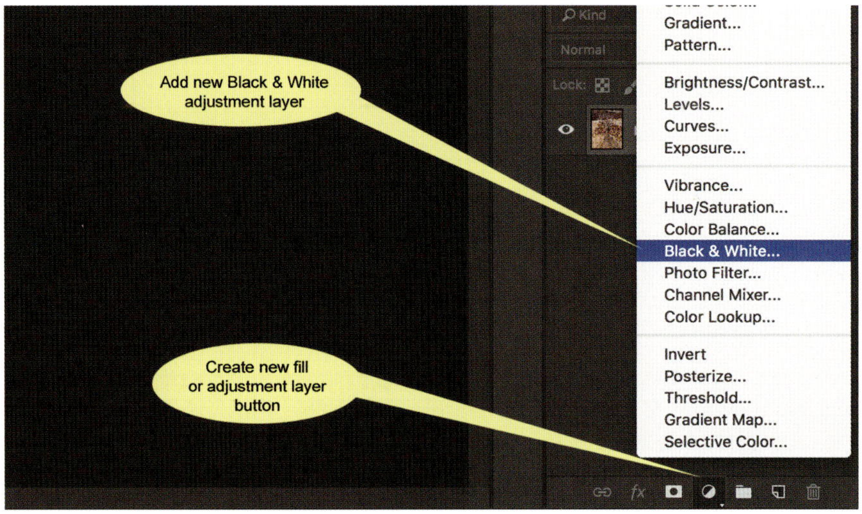


FIGURE 12.5: Adding a new *Black & White* adjustment layer using the *Create new fill or adjustment layer* button.

Once added, the *Properties* panel (figure 12.6) offers a *Preset* dropdown menu containing some preconfigured filter effects. There are six color sliders to either create a new filter effect or to fine-tune the effect chosen from the *Preset* menu. These sliders, in fact, allow us to decide the color of the conversion filter with extreme precision. With six sliders and about 500 possible values for each slider (ranging from –200 to +300, for some odd reason), we can simulate the effect of well over fifteen thousand trillion (or $500^6$) variations of color filters.

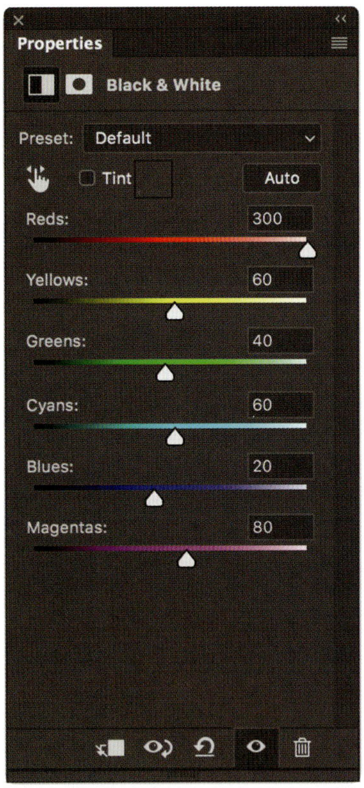


FIGURE 12.6: The *Black & White* adjustment *Properties* panel.

The way I prefer to work with the *Black & White* adjustment is to first select one of the preconfigured filter effects from the *Preset* menu (figure 12.7) as it contains the varieties normally used by traditional film photographers. I then fine-tune the effect using the sliders. For example, pulling the *Blues* and/or *Cyans* sliders to the left will make blue areas appear as darker tones, pulling the *Reds* slider to the right will make red and yellow areas appear as lighter tones, and so on.

The goal when working with the *Black & White* adjustment layer is not to create the final black-and-white image, but rather to establish the desired tonal relationships (what areas or objects need to be darker/lighter than what other areas or objects) using the effect of the color-separating filter. Remember that we still have at our disposal all the other tools and adjustments Photoshop offers—*Curves*, dodging and burning, etc.—to make fine adjustments to contrast, to lighten or darken areas that cannot be separated by color, or to make local adjustments to portions of the image.

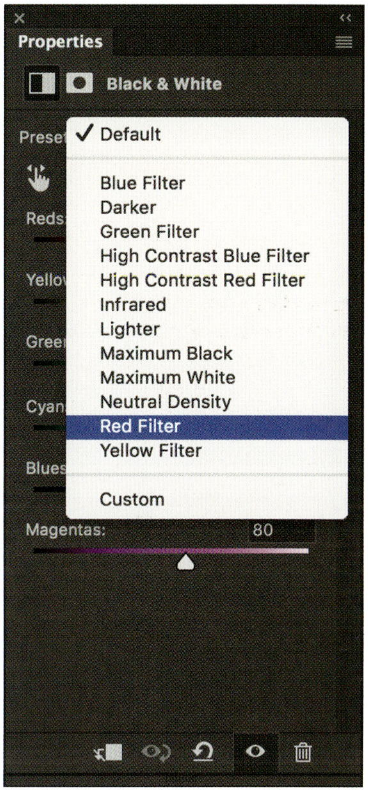


FIGURE 12.7: Selecting a red filter effect from the *Preset* menu.

## Toning

Since photography's early days, various techniques were used to add a hint of color to monochromatic images, long before color photography was even possible. The reason for doing so is this: human beings associate specific emotions and perceptions with some colors. A hint of blue, for example, may communicate chill, calmness, detachment, or sadness. To wit, many expressions in the English language refer to blue in such contexts: "feeling blue," "got the blues," etc. Alternatively, a hint of sepia or other yellow tint may communicate warmth, nostalgia, romance, or comfort.

Toning, also sometimes referred to as tinting, is the biasing of the otherwise-neutral grays that make up a black-and-white image toward a given color, often in subtle ways, but not always. Throughout the history of photography, we find a variety of toning methods that were accomplished using chemistry—from the use of exotic pigments such as sepia, precious metals such as platinum or gold, and a variety of other materials, such as selenium, or various dyes.

Toning was often applied not only for visual effect but also to create prints that are longer lasting and resistant to fading.

As with color filters, Photoshop offers a plethora of toning options—far more than what is possible using traditional methods in a chemical darkroom—and various ways to apply them.

The first thing to note is that our image, despite being converted to black-and-white, is still represented as an array of RGB pixels. That is, each pixel is still defined by separate values for red, green, and blue. It just so happens that immediately after conversion, all three channels have the same value, resulting in shades of neutral gray. Still, having the three channels available to us means that anything we do to nudge one or more color channels(s) relative to the others will result in some kind of color tint.

Photoshop offers many tools that can operate individually on each of the color channels—*Levels, Curves, Hue/Saturation,* and *Color Balance* adjustments can all be used for this purpose.

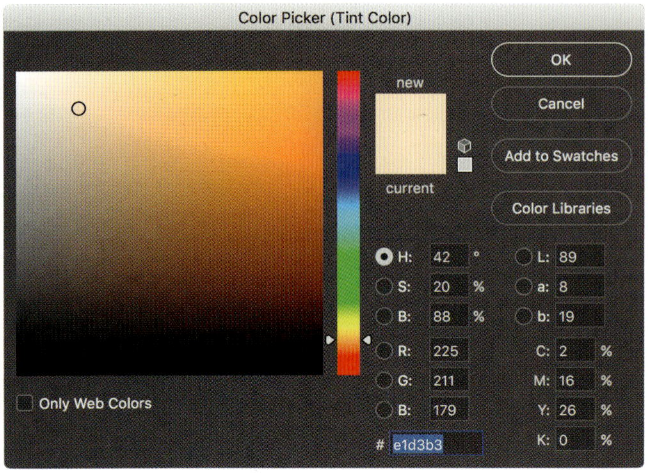


FIGURE 12.8: Photoshop's Color Picker can be used to select and fine-tune a color for tinting a black-and-white image.

## The *Color Picker* Method

Let's start with the one method explicitly designed for black-and-white image toning: the *Tint* checkbox in the *Black & White* adjustment layer properties. Checking the *Tint* box will bring up a color swatch next to it, indicating the color used to tone the image. Clicking on the swatch brings up Photoshop's *Color Picker* (figure 12.8), which offers myriad ways of selecting color. Selecting a color instantly shows its effect on the image, allowing for fine-tuning.

A useful feature accessible via the *Color Picker* is Photoshop's color swatches, which can be saved for later use. Once a desired tint color is found, click the *Add to Swatches* button, name your swatch for easy identification (say, "warm tone" or "cyanotype") and you will be able to access it later to repeat the effect consistently on other images.

One disadvantage of using this method is that it does not offer much flexibility (only one color can be selected to use evenly). Also, operations following the black-and-white conversion may skew the tint color, which is why I prefer to apply tinting as the last step, whereas black-and-white conversion generally is the first step before additional steps, such as dodging and burning, or contrast adjustment.

## The *Curves* Adjustment Layer Method

My preferred toning method is to use a *Curves* adjustment layer and to adjust one or more of the individual color channels to achieve the effect I want. I can then save curves for different toning effects so I can reuse them consistently with multiple images.

Following are the steps I use to create a toning preset using a *Curves* adjustment layer:

1. Convert an image to black-and-white using the *Black & White* adjustment layer, and perform all global and local adjustments to achieve the visualized result, except for toning.
2. Add a *Curves* adjustment layer. This should be the last (top) layer in your file, to avoid other adjustments that may affect color.
3. From the dropdown menu that by default says RGB, select one of the color channels and adjust to achieve the tint you are after. Repeat

with other color channels as needed. You may wish to refer to the reciprocal colors table on page 177. Remember that reducing the amount of any color channel increases the appearance of its reciprocal (reducing blue increases yellow, reducing green increases magenta, and reducing red increases cyan).

4. Once the desired effect has been accomplished, open the *Properties* menu (figure 12.9) and select *Save Curves Preset*; select a location to save your preset, and name it to something descriptive like "Sepia tone," "Warm tone," etc.

5. When the time comes to tone another image, once all other adjustments are complete, add a *Curves* adjustment layer, open the *Properties* menu and select *Load Curves Preset*. Now select the file you saved previously, and the same toning will be applied.

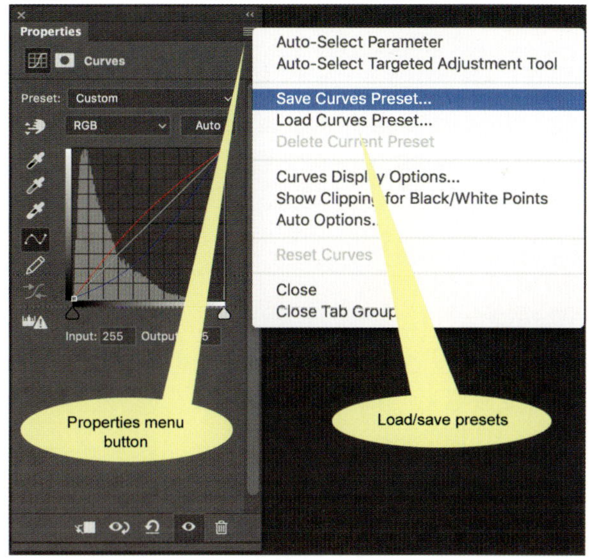


**Figure 12.9:** Saving a *Curves* preset. Note that I reduced the blue channel significantly (which has the effect of making the image more yellow) and increased the amount of red a bit. The combined effect is a rich sepia tone, so I will save this curve as "Sepia tone" so I can apply the same effect to other images later.

**Why use Curves and Not Color Balance?**

It seems that *Curves* may be an awkward way of creating the toning effect, and that a *Color Balance* adjustment layer may be easier to work with, which is true. Regrettably, at the time of this writing, Photoshop does not offer a mechanism for saving and loading presets for *Color Balance*, like it does for *Curves*. Also, such effects as split toning (described below) are not possible with the *Color Balance* adjustment.

## Split Toning

Split toning refers to a darkroom technique that allows toning the highlights and shadows in two different colors. When applied in a traditional darkroom, one's options are very limited, as the process requires finding chemicals of different colors that will bind to different parts of the image depending on its density (i.e., exposure). Using digital tools, on the other hand, split toning can be accomplished easily, and any combination of colors may be used.

A common split-toned look assigns blue hues to the dark areas of the image and a yellowish hue to the highlights. This can be accomplished easily using a *Curves* adjustment by selecting the blue channel, then pulling the curve above the 45° line on the left side of the scale (dark tones), and below the 45° line on the right side of the scale (which removes blue, and increases yellow in the light tones). The curve in figure 12.10 shows a blue/yellow split toning curve, and its effect can be seen in the lower-right variation in figure 12.11.

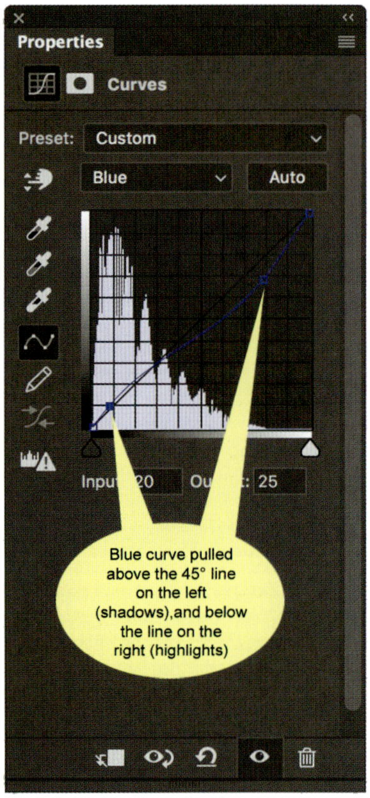


FIGURE 12.10: A curve designed to create a blue/yellow split toning effect.

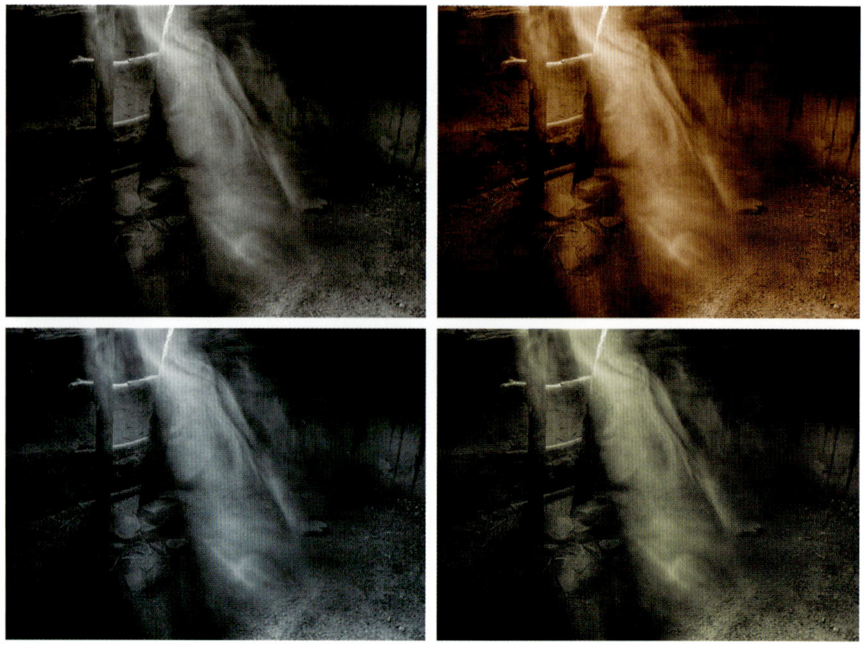

FIGURE 12.11: Toning variations applied to a black-and-white image using *Curves*. Clockwise from top left: neutral gray, sepia, blue/yellow split tone, cyanotype.

## Conversion Using Multiple Filters

Another advantage of converting to black-and-white digitally is the ability to convert various portions of an image using different filter effects, which is not possible with physical filters mounted over the lens. Physical filters accomplish tonal separation by blocking or reducing the amount of light in specific frequencies (which we perceive as colors) reaching the capture surface (film or digital sensor). For this reason, such filters cannot be combined. For example, I can't stack a red filter to darken the sky over a green filter to lighten foliage, since light passing through the red filter will have much of its green components stripped away before reaching the green filter. In Photoshop, such limitations do not exist since simulating the filter effect does not actually eliminate the underlying color information, which remains available to us should we need it.

Although it may seem counterintuitive at first, Photoshop's *Black & White* adjustment layer behaves like other adjustment layers in the sense that we are not limited to just one layer, and we can use a layer mask to limit a given layer's effect to just a portion of the image.

For example, the image in figure 12.12 contains both a blue sky and blue water. To illustrate the problem, let's say that my visualized result has a dark

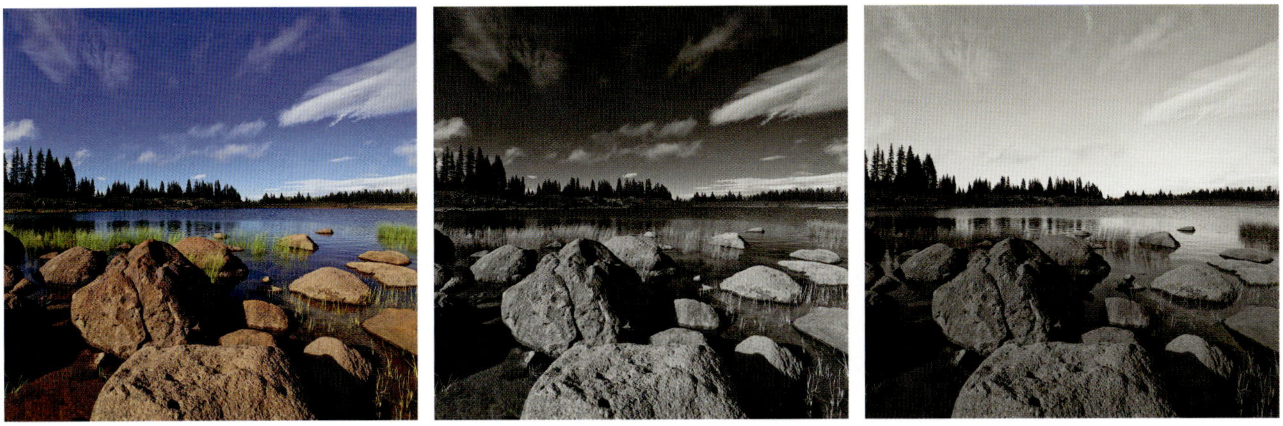

**Figure 12.12:** The original color image (*left*), converted with a red filter effect (*middle*) and with a blue filter effect (*right*).

sky (accomplished with a red filter effect), but lighter water (accomplished with a blue filter effect). However, if I use a red filter to darken the sky, the water will become dark, as well; and if I use a blue filter to lighten the water, the sky will become lighter, too.

Clearly, no one filter by itself can accomplish the tonal relationship I am after. To solve the problem, I used two *Black & White* adjustment layers: one for the sky (using a red filter) and the other for the foreground (using a blue filter), and I used a mask to target one layer to the sky and the other to the foreground. Figure 12.13 shows the result, as well as the layers and masks used.

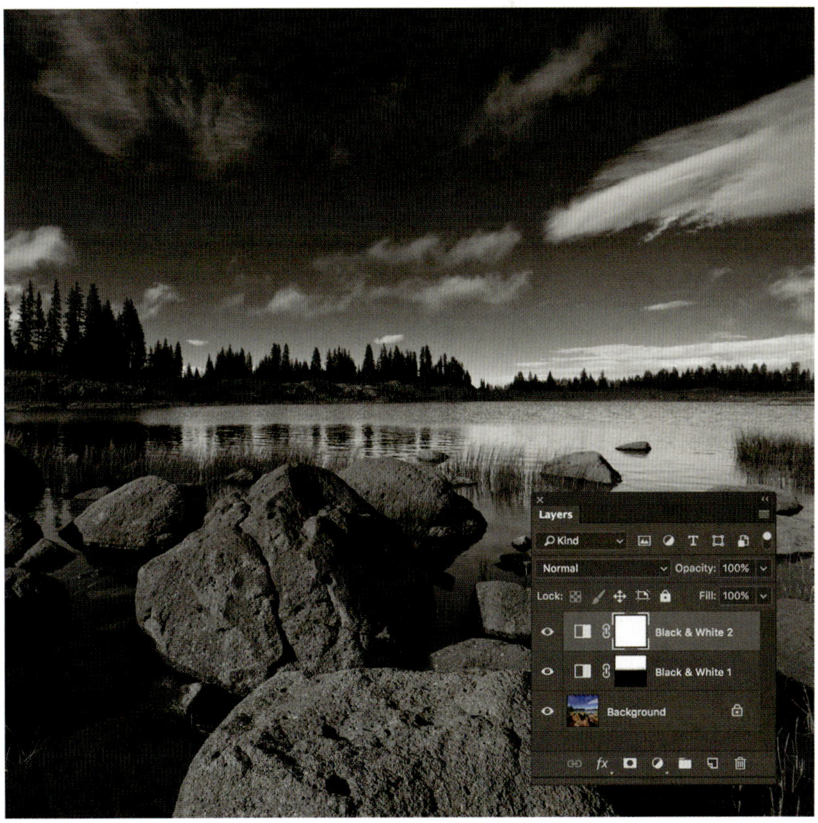


**Figure 12.13:** The image in figure 12.12 converted using two *Black & White* adjustment layers. The bottom layer applies a red filter effect, which is masked to block its effect in the foreground (so it only affects the sky). The top layer applies a blue filter effect. Note that it does not need a mask since it only converts colors into tones, but the sky has no color (already converted to gray by the previous layer), so it remains as is.

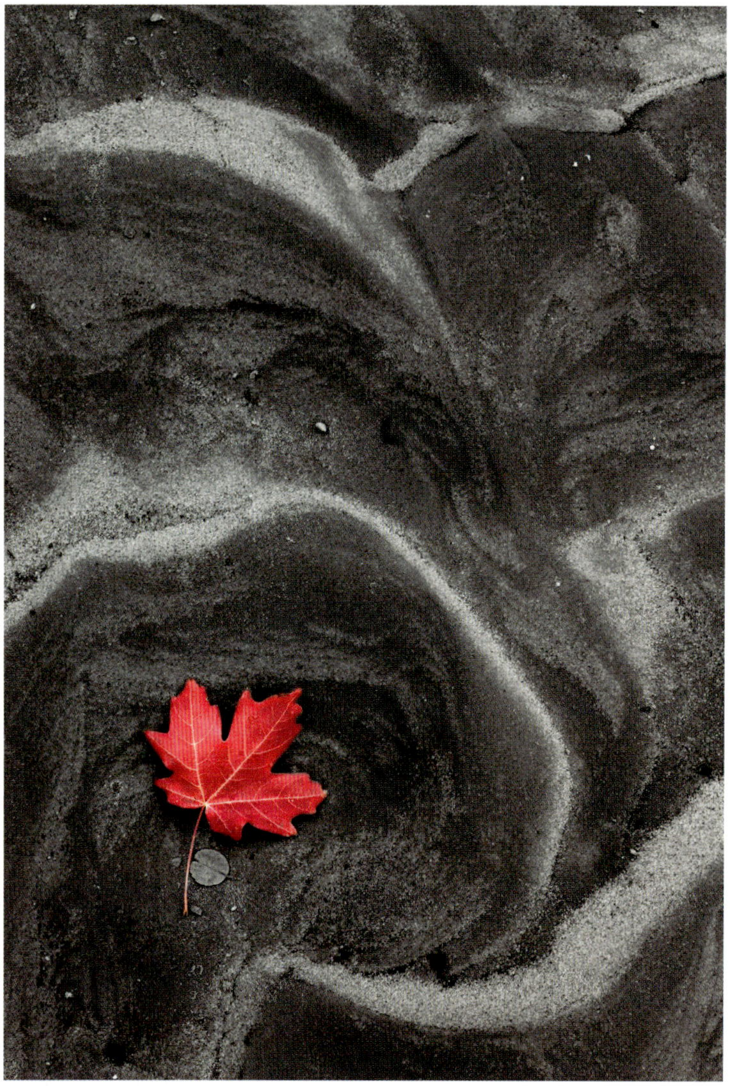

**Figure 12.14:** A hybrid color/black-and-white image.

## Hybrid Color/Black-and-White Images

Hybrid images are ones that combine black-and-white and color elements. Using the same masking technique described in the previous section, we can exclude elements in the image from being converted by the *Black & White* adjustment.

To create the image in figure 12.14, I used Photoshop's *Quick Selection* tool to select the maple leaf. I then inverted the selection by selecting the *Inverse* option from the *Select* menu. I then added a *Black & White* adjustment layer. Remember that when there's an active selection, adding an adjustment layer automatically converts the selection into a mask for that layer.

Since my selection covered everything except the leaf, the leaf was excluded from the effect of the black-and-white conversion.

The creative possibilities of such techniques are endless, but so is their gimmick potential. Use with caution.

## Hand-Tinted Images

Those possessing a love of both photography and painting may find hand-tinting black-and-white images a wonderful way to combine the two in creative and unique ways. Here, the black-and-white photographic image is used as a base to be colorized by hand.

To accomplish the tinting effect, I prefer to use the same type of *Soft Light* blended layer described in chapter 10 for dodging and burning. I then can use the *Brush* tool with various colors to subtly blend those colors onto the image.

Following is a description of the hand-tinting workflow:

1. Start with a neutral black-and-white image.

2. From the *Layer* menu, select *New* and then *Layer*. Change the layer's mode to *Soft Light* and check the box next to *Fill with Soft-Light-neutral color (50% gray)*.

3. Select a desired color from Photoshop's *Swatches* panel (if it is not visible, select it from the *Window* menu).

4. Using a soft *Brush* (I recommend an *Opacity* setting in the 5% to 10% range, depending on how vibrant you want the color to appear), paint the color where desired.

5. Repeat with other colors as needed.

Errors can be corrected by painting over them in 50% gray, which can be accomplished by setting the brush *Opacity* to 100% and selecting the *50% Gray* swatch from the *Swatches* panel (hovering over a swatch for a second will make its description pop up).

As with hybrid images, it's easy to get carried away, as I was in figure 12.15, in the name of illustrating the possibilities. Exercise good taste.

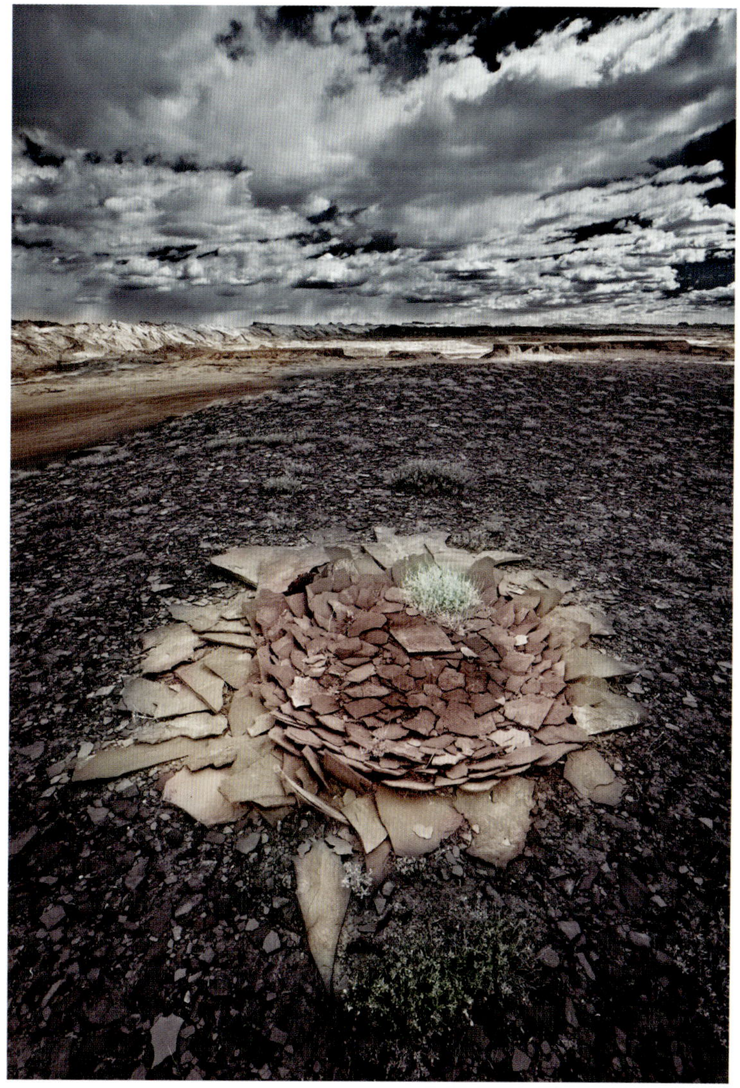

FIGURE 12.15: An illustration of a hand-tinted image, and of the reason I am not a painter.

## Applying Zone System Terminology

Although beyond the scope of this book, the Zone System has been a useful tool for traditional black-and-white photographers for several decades. Photographers familiar with the Zone System may use its terminology to assist in visualizing black-and-white images, as well as to document gaps and to apply processing decisions. Photographers not familiar with the Zone System may skip this section.

Ansel Adams and Fred Archer developed the Zone System around 1940. The Zone System created a standard vocabulary and methodology founded in the characteristics of black-and-white film and photographic paper. It allowed photographers to make predictably accurate exposure and development decisions in the days before cameras provided instant visual feedback and exposure tools such as the histogram.

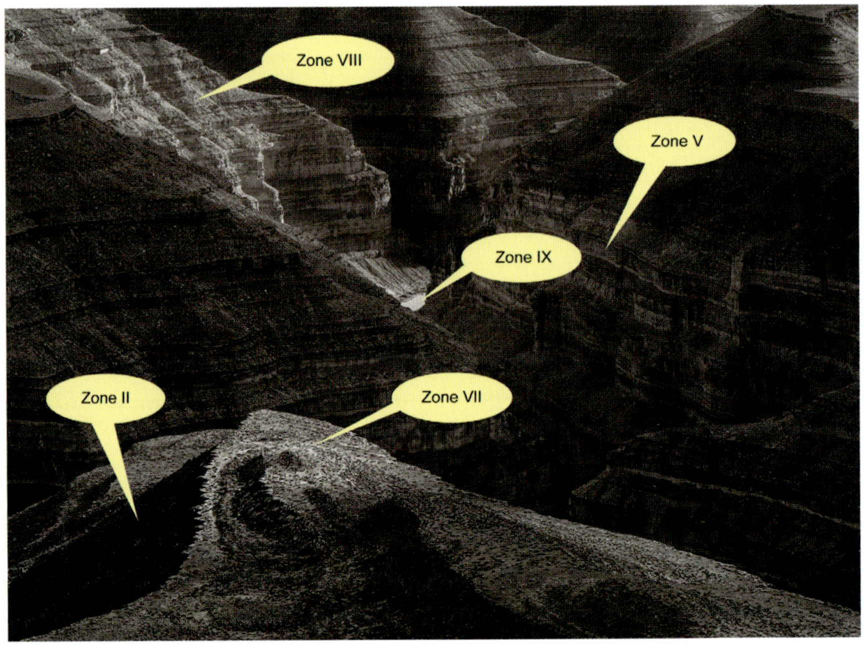


**Figure 12.16:** An image visualized using the Zone System.

Of the more useful Zone System concepts is placement. The idea of placement is to target a given tone to a given zone. For example, placing the shadows in Zone III would keep shadows fairly dark, but allow for a discernible degree of fine details; or, placing the sky in Zone VIII would make it appear bright, with clouds clearly visible.

Figure 12.16 demonstrates an image visualized using the Zone System, meaning that I consciously placed elements in the scene into known zones in order to later translate those decisions into processing adjustments.

One useful means of accomplishing Zone System placement is to use a *Curves* adjustment layer. Remember that it is possible to place a 10×10 grid behind the curve to provide 11 intersection points, which corresponds to the Zone System's 11 zones (figure 12.17, left). These points can be dragged toward lighter or darker values, essentially simulating the Zone System concept of placement (figure 12.17, right).

Following is the workflow to create a zone placement curve:

1. Add a *Curves* adjustment layer. I recommend this be the layer immediately following the *Black & White* adjustment layer used to convert the image.

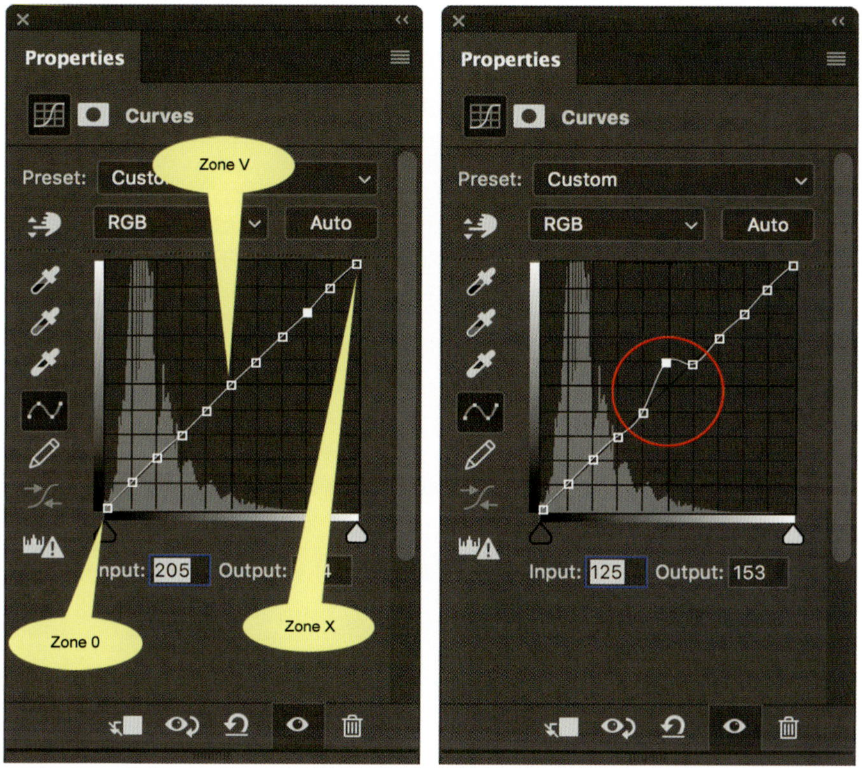


**Figure 12.17:** The intersection points on the grid correspond to 11 zones (*left*), and a curve showing placement of tones in Zone V into Zone VI (making them lighter by approximately one stop) (*right*).

2. If the 10×10 grid is not shown, hold down the *Option/Alt* key and click anywhere in the curve area in the *Properties* panel. Repeated clicking will toggle between a 4×4 grid and a 10×10 grid.
3. Carefully place an anchor point at each intersection point along the 45° line. There's no need to be perfectly accurate.
4. Once all anchors are set, you will have 11 anchors in total: the image's black point and white point (already shown as anchors on both extremes of the line) corresponding to *Zone 0* and *Zone X*, respectively; and 9 additional points at equal distances along the 45° line.
5. Pull the desired anchor points for each zone you wish to change and place it in another zone, as needed.

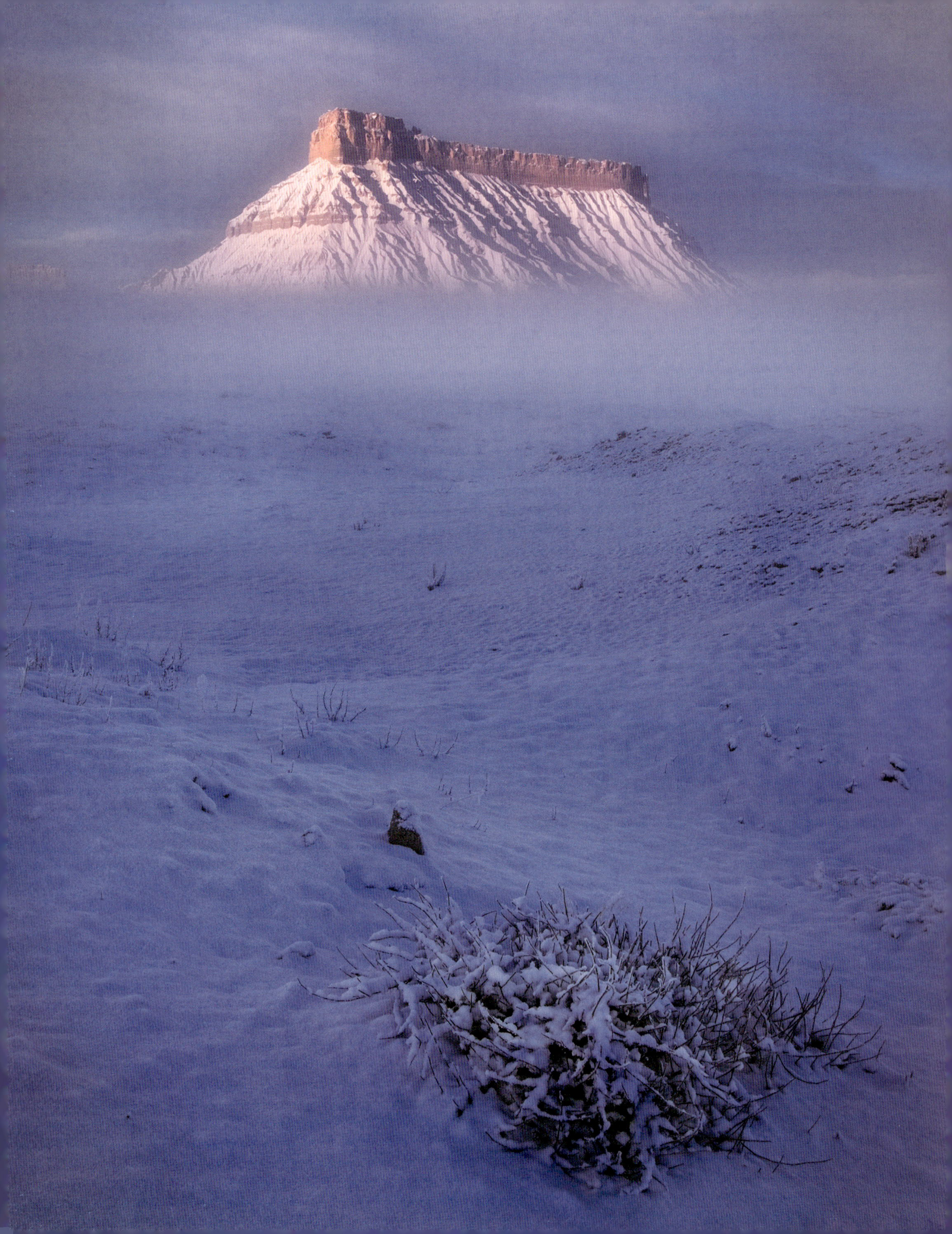

# Blending Images

13

*Living in a time of crucial struggle, the mechanization of men, photography for me became nothing but another example of this paradoxical problem: how to overcome, how to humanize the machine on which we are so very dependent—the camera.*

—ERNST HAAS

Blending multiple images (or variations of the same image) to produce a single composite image is useful in many ways. The ability to blend multiple bracketed exposures allows overcoming some technical constraints imposed by the camera, such as limitations of dynamic range (the range of tones in which the sensor can resolve a usable degree of detail) or limitation of the depth of field possible in a single exposure. We may also choose to blend multiple variations of the same image file, perhaps converted from RAW in multiple ways, each optimized for different qualities. Or, we may even want to blend portions of one image (say, an interesting foreground) with portions of a different image (say, an interesting sky).

The ability to blend multiple images offers a wide range of creative possibilities. While it may be tempting to push these possibilities to their extremes (and I recommend that you do, in the process of learning and practicing the technique), recall that our goal is to shape the resulting image into a visualized, expressive, outcome, and that such capabilities are best placed in the service of this outcome rather than to showcase the capabilities of Photoshop. Indeed, our process framework explicitly calls for dynamic visualization—revisiting our visualized image frequently—both to see if better possibilities exist, and to remind ourselves of our expressive intent so we don't become too bogged down in technical minutiae. The risk of losing sight of our expressive goals is that we may be tempted to focus on visual impact and technical gimmickry, rather than more complex and meaningful expressions.

**Bracketed Exposures**

The term "bracketed exposures" refers to taking multiple exposures of the same subject in quick succession while varying one or more parameters for each exposure, such as changing shutter speed or focus distance. These exposures are later combined, or "blended," during processing to create a single image file that contains data that cannot be obtained in a single exposure, such as extended dynamic range or depth of field.

**Automated Blending Tools**

While Photoshop offers automated functions for blending images, I have not been very impressed with their performance or accuracy. I found that I can produce more natural-looking results when blending images manually. The method I describe here usually requires only two exposures in most cases to accomplish a more natural-looking blend than can be achieved using automated tools.

The only scenarios in which I recommend using automated blending tools, rather than working manually, are those that require many bracketed exposures, like focus stacking in macro photography or when accurate selection of the areas to be masked is very difficult, such as detailed tree branches and leaves. If such cases make up a significant proportion of your work, I suggest investing in specialized third-party blending tools, at least until Photoshop's automated blending functions are improved.

## Blending Images Using Masks

In the previous chapter I described adjustment layers and image layers. I also introduced the use of layer masks to target adjustment layers to just portions of the image (for making local, rather than global, adjustments). Like adjustment layers, image layers can also take advantage of Photoshop's blending and masking features, giving us the ability to blend—to composite —portions of multiple image layers to make the final image.

## Blending Images for High Dynamic Range

High dynamic range (HDR) techniques are useful for tackling scenes having both deep shadows and bright highlights. In such situations, the camera's sensor may or may not have sufficient dynamic range to hold details in both the extreme highlights and the extreme shadows. And even if it did, shadow areas may still appear noisy since they don't reflect much light and therefore are more prone to sampling errors than well-lit areas.

With the ability to blend multiple exposures into a single image, we can capture one or more frame(s) where shadows are well-exposed (even if at the cost of clipping the highlights), and one or more frame(s) where the highlights are well exposed (even if at the cost of clipping the shadows). We can then blend the best-exposed portions from each frame into a single image.

When blending manually, it is rare that we'll need more than just two exposures: one for the shadows and one for the highlights. Digital sensors today have an exposure latitude of 7–14 stops (depending on camera model, as well as sensor size and quality) and there is no natural scene I know of that requires more than 14–15 stops to cover both extremely bright highlights and extremely dark shadows. This means even a sensor with only 7–8 stops of dynamic range can cover the range of brightness in any naturally lit composition with just two exposures, and with sufficient overlap between the two to make for a natural-looking blend.

Some automated HDR solutions benefit from bracketing more exposures in small increments to better calculate tonal relationships for a natural-looking outcome. However, since we are about to blend our exposures manually, we can decide, while looking at the result in real time, the proper blending ratios (what, and how much, to use from which exposure) based on our own taste.

I'll demonstrate the technique with an example. Figure 13.1 shows two exposures of the same scene; one optimized for the highlights and one for the shadows. I also included a snippet showing the histogram for each so you can see that the shadows are clipped in the exposure optimized for the highlights; and the highlights are clipped in the exposure optimized for the shadows.

Our first task is to stack the two exposures as separate layers in the same file. This can be accomplished in a variety of ways. For example:

- If you use Lightroom to manage your image catalog or to convert your images from RAW, you can select both images (hold down the Command/Ctrl key and click to highlight both) and then open the *Photo* menu, find the *Edit in* sub-menu, and select *Open as Layers in Photoshop*.
- If you do not use Lightroom, open both images as separate files, then copy and paste one over the other as follows:

**Figure 13.1:** The exposure on the left was optimized to capture detail in the highlights (note clipped shadows) and the exposure on the right was optimized to capture detail in the shadows (note clipped highlights).

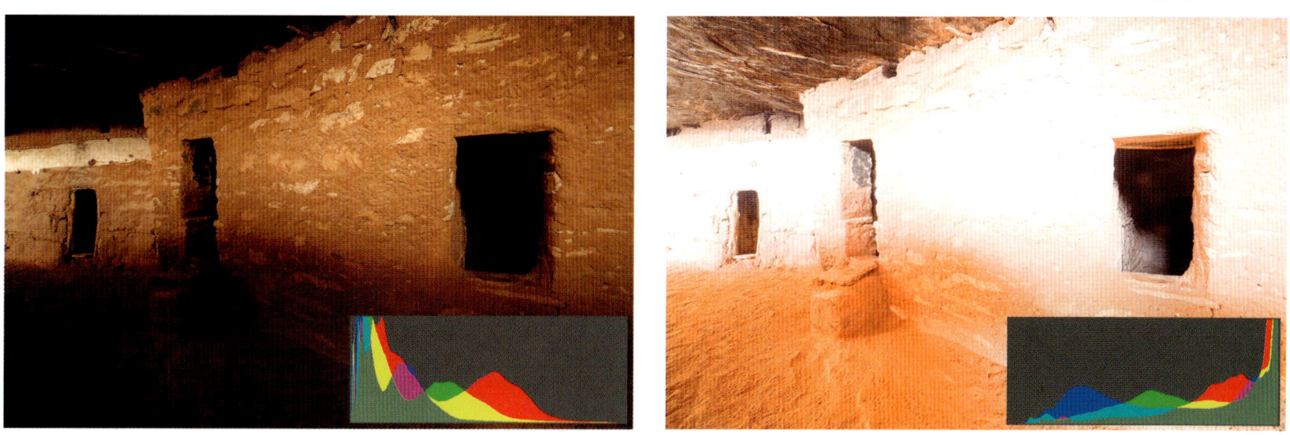

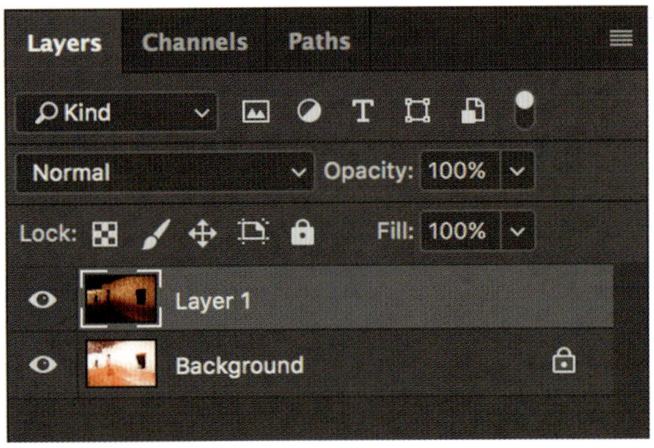


FIGURE 13.2: The *Layers* panel showing the two images as stacked layers.

1. With one of the images displayed, click Command/Ctrl+A (select all).
2. Click Command/Ctrl+C (copy).
3. Switch to the other image and click Command/Ctrl+V (paste).

Your *Layers* panel should now show both images as separate layers (figure 13.2).

In general, it doesn't matter which image is on top; the order just determines what portions of the top image will need to be masked (hidden) to show the image below it. However, since we'll need to create a mask to hide portions of the top image, it makes sense to place the image that will be easiest to mask on top. For example, if the blocked shadows are in a well-defined area that is easy to paint over (which we'll need to do to create the mask) but the highlights are scattered all over the frame and may require a lot more work to paint over accurately, I would favor placing the image with the blocked shadows (the one that was exposed for the highlights) on top.

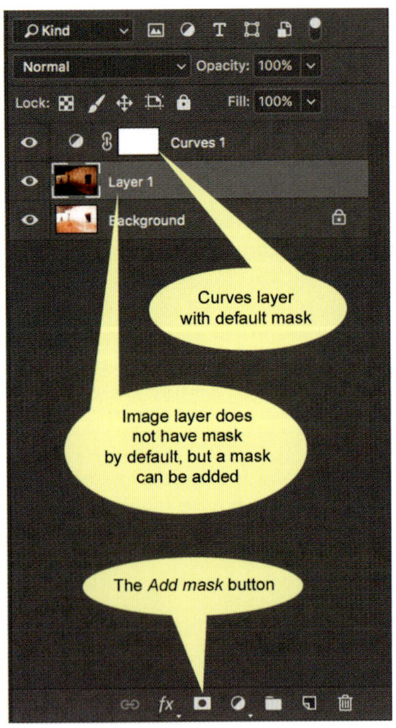


FIGURE 13.3: I added a *Curves* layer to the stacked image layers to show its default mask, as opposed to the image layer, titled Layer 1, which does not have a mask by default. Highlighting (by clicking on) Layer 1 and then clicking the *Add mask* button will add a mask to it.

We are now ready to blend the two layers; however, notice that we have a little problem. Earlier, when we added adjustment layers (such as *Levels* or *Curves*), each had a white mask already attached. Image layers, when added, do not have masks associated with them. This is just Photoshop's default behavior. We can add a mask to an image layer by highlighting it and then clicking the *Add mask* button (figure 13.3).

Once a mask is added to the top layer, we are ready to begin painting over it to hide portions of this layer to show the one below it. Recall that where the mask is black, the current layer is blocked, allowing the base (the sum of layers below it) to show. I recommend starting with a 20% brush *Opacity*, rather than with a higher value since we may not always want to completely block out the top layer. If using higher *Opacity* values, the transition may appear abrupt and unsightly. Brushing repeatedly with a 20% brush has a cumulative effect and we can visually judge how much is enough.

I like to start by brushing over the "transition zones"—the areas where portions of the two exposures transition into each other, at low opacity (sometimes as low as 10%) to avoid what is known as the "HDR look," which may appear unsightly and artificial.

Here's the workflow I followed to produce the blended final image seen in figure 13.4:

1. I stacked both images as layers with the darker exposure on top.
2. Using the *Add mask* button, I added a mask to the top layer.

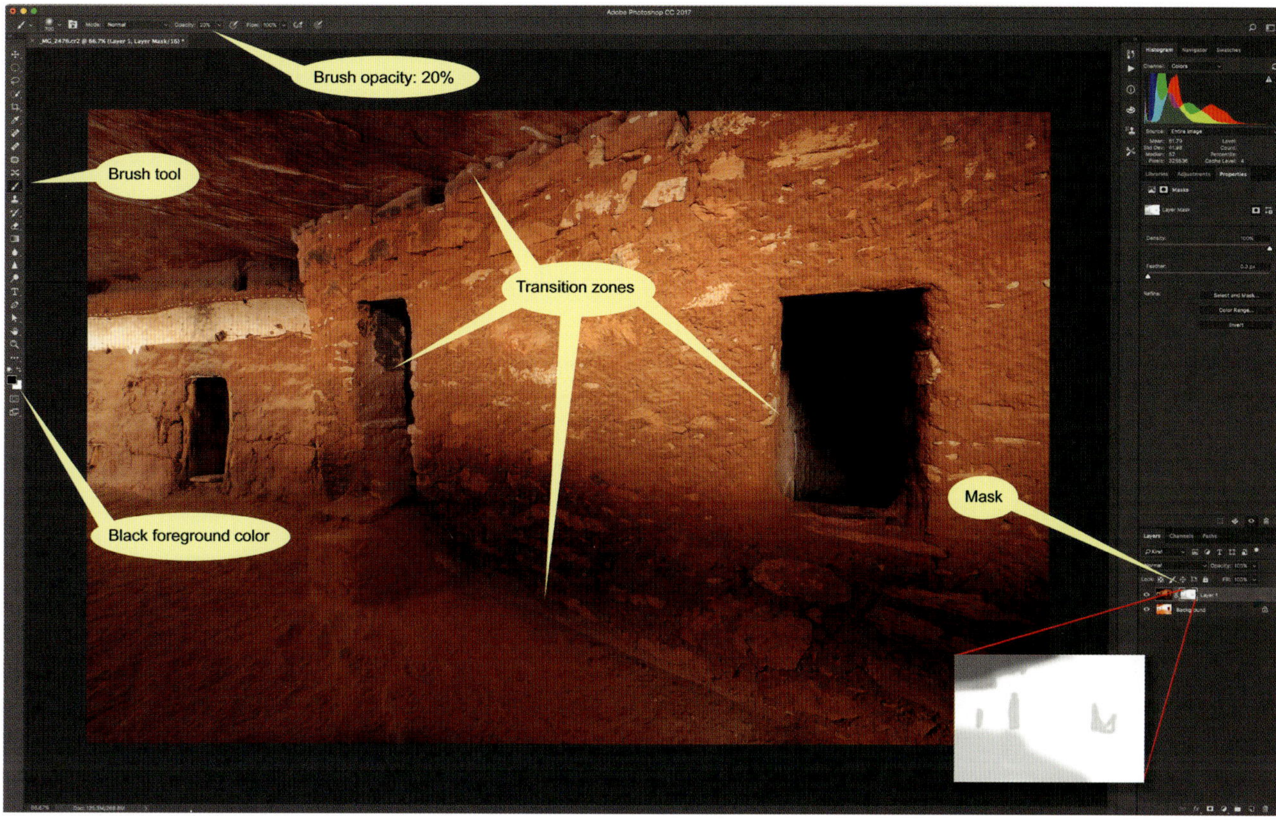


FIGURE 13.4: The tools, settings, and mask I used to blend the two images.

3. I selected the *Brush* tool, made sure my foreground color was black and set brush *Opacity* to 20%.
4. Using the square brace keys, I set the brush *Size* to about half the width of the leftmost doorway, which was the narrowest area I wished to paint over (i.e., mask).
5. I painted over all transition zones: along the edge of the upper-left dark area, within the doorways, and along the edge of the foreground floor.
6. Once the transition zones were to my liking, I increased the brush size and, staying a bit off the transition areas, painted the rest of the shadow areas to reveal the lighter details in the layer below. The upper-left corner required brushing over a couple of times to bring out a little more detail than other areas (as evidenced by the mask being darker in that area).

Note that I decided to leave the very deep shadows inside the doorways pure black (see shadow clipping in the histogram in figure 13.4). There is no law that says we must retrieve all possible details in every situation. Bringing out visible detail inside the doorways would have looked decidedly unnatural and would eliminate some of the sense of mystery of the image. Remember that our primary goal in processing images is to stay true to our expressive (visualized) intent, not necessarily to create a technically "perfect" file just because we can.

## Blending Images for Focus Stacking

Many landscape images may benefit from sharp foreground-to-background focus. Achieving this by using traditional means may require the use of tilt/shift lenses or hyperfocal focusing along with very small aperture settings. However, these mechanical and optical solutions also come with various limitations, which can be overcome by digitally blending multiple exposures focused at different distances (figure 13.5).

FIGURE 13.5: These two images were captured at different focus settings: the image on the left has sharp details in the foreground (flowers) while the image on the right has sharp details in the background (monolith). The insets show snippets of each file at 100% magnification.

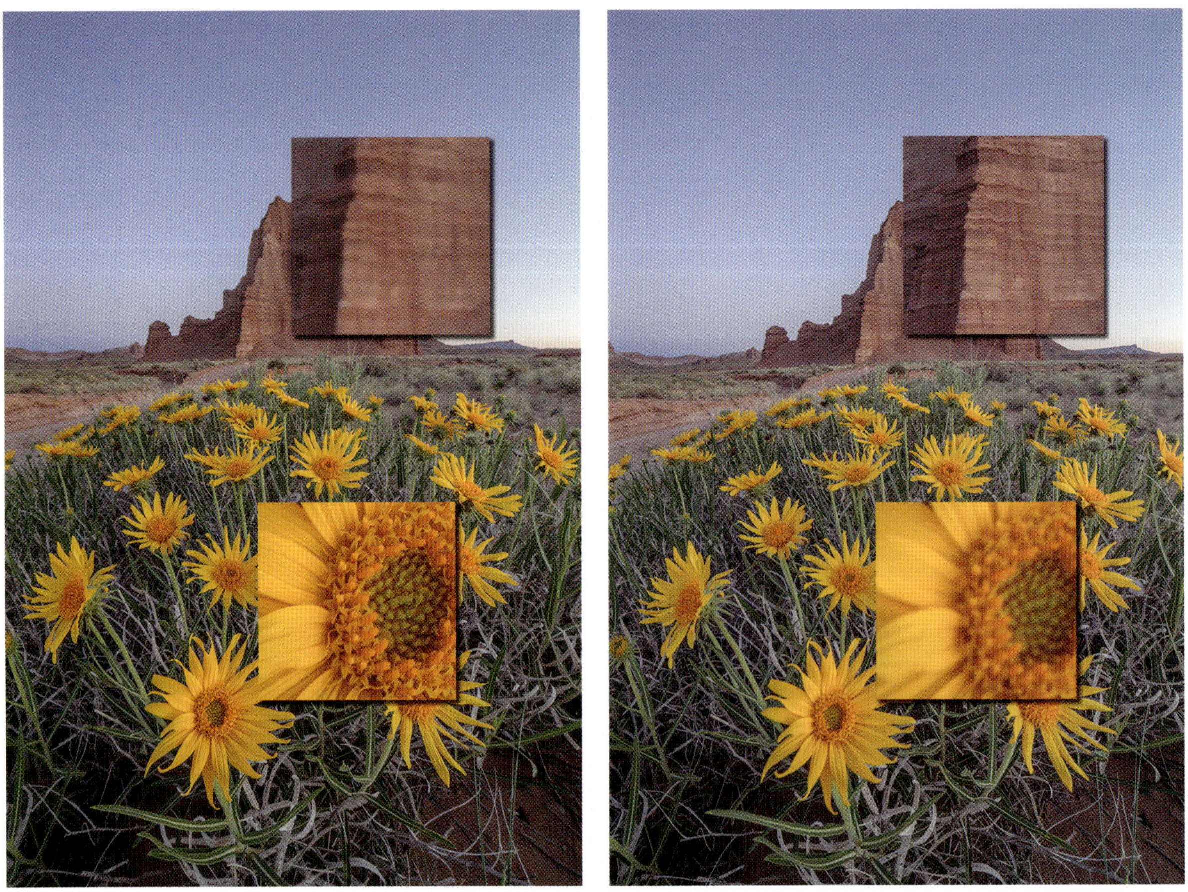

Tilt/shift lenses do not provide greater depth of field, as some believe; rather, they allow tilting the plane of focus, which would otherwise be parallel to the sensor. This may be sufficient to capture sharp detail throughout the composition at optimal aperture settings, but not always. These lenses also are available in only a limited selection of focal lengths and only from a handful of manufacturers. If your optimal composition requires a focal length of, say 180mm, and you wish for sharp foreground-to-background detail, a tilt/shift lens is not an option. Also, if using hyperfocal focusing, the use of very small apertures may cause loss of detail due to diffraction (light bending around the edges of the small aperture, resulting in loss of resolution, especially at the edges of the frame).

With exposure blending, we can overcome such limitations by making separate exposures, each focused at different distances and using optimal aperture settings (for most lenses, around f/11), and then blending the sharp portions from each exposure into a single composite image. This is called focus stacking.

The technique for focus stacking is similar to the blending technique I describe above for HDR, but with one small caveat, which is this: changing the focus setting on the lens also slightly changes its magnification, which means that the alignment (also referred to as registration) of images captured at different focus settings will not be perfect. For this purpose, Photoshop offers the ability to align separate image layers prior to blending them.

To align exposures, first stack them as layers and then follow these steps:

1. Hold down the Command/Ctrl key and click on the name (not the icon) of each of the image layers in the *Layers* panel.
2. Once the layers are highlighted, open the *Edit* menu and select *Auto-Align Layers*.
3. I recommend keeping the default (*Auto*) option before clicking OK.

Figure 13.6 shows the two highlighted layers and the *Auto-Align Layers* dialog.

The *Auto-Align Layers* function will slightly warp the layers so they align perfectly. Note this may leave some blank areas around the edges where one layer had detail and the other did not. These blank edges may be very thin and require inspecting the image at 100% or greater magnification to see. Use the *Crop* tool to remove these edges if they occur.

Once the layers are aligned we may blend the layers using the same technique demonstrated above for HDR: add a mask to the top layer and use a brush to mask out the un-sharp portions and reveal the sharp details in the layer below. In this case, there is no harm in using a brush opacity of 100%

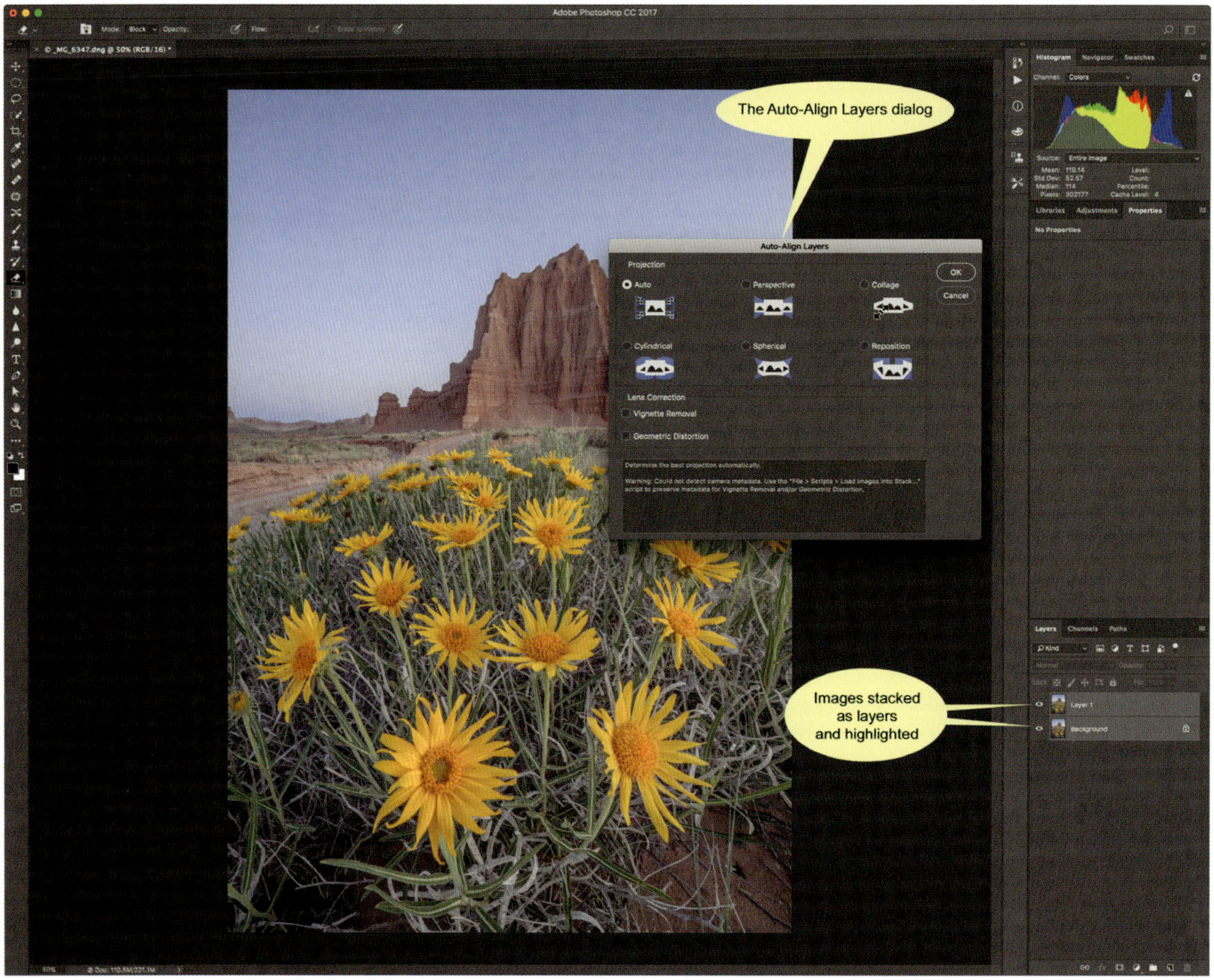


**FIGURE 13.6:** The two images that are shown in figure 13.5 stacked as layers and highlighted.

since the sharp/un-sharp portions are well-delineated around the center of the frame and there is some overlap of sharpness between the two.

## Blending Multiple RAW Conversions

There are times when we may want to use certain RAW conversion parameters to enhance only some portions of an image. For example, we may want to render our foreground with one combination of white balance settings (*Temperature* and *Tint*) to simulate the blue light found in open shade, and the

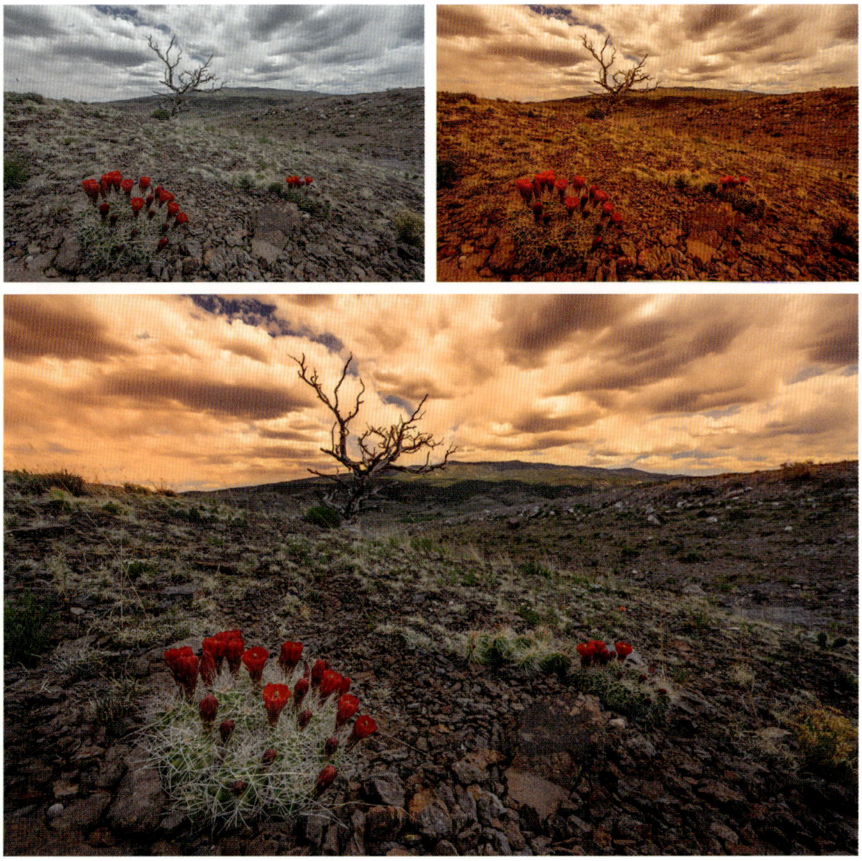

**Figure 13.7:** The two images at the top were converted from RAW with different *Temperature* settings: 5,050°K (*left*) and 10,600°K (*right*). They were then blended together to produce the composite image on the bottom. I deliberately exaggerated the effect for this example. I would not push it to this extreme in my own work.

background with different white balance settings to simulate the warm light in the golden hours (figure 13.7).

## Blending Images to Mitigate Noise

Digital noise is a difficult artifact to remove. To properly address noise, we need to detect where it exists (and effectively distinguish it from actual image detail), and then smooth out the affected area(s). Although Photoshop—as well as ACR and Lightroom—offers very good tools for the latter (smoothing out noisy areas), it doesn't do a very good job of the former (distinguishing noise from image details). Thankfully, our brains are far more adept than computers for this type of task, and noise is easy to detect by eye when studying the image at 100% or greater magnification.

It is rarely a good idea to apply noise reduction as a global adjustment. Doing so will almost always degrade useful image detail, and in almost every case some areas of an image need more noise reduction than others. For example, even if the noise is spread across the image evenly, it will be less visible in detailed areas and more visible in smooth areas, such as skies or bodies of water.

Noise removal is also an area where Photoshop offers an ability that ACR and Lightroom do not: removing noise only in one or two color channels, but not all three. This is a particularly useful function since you will often find the blue channel (and to a lesser degree the red channel) more prone to noise than the green channel. (Remember that digital camera sensors have twice as many green photosites as blue or red.)

None of the noise reduction tools available in Photoshop, ACR, or Lightroom offer a means of applying noise reduction as a local adjustment. To apply noise reduction locally in Photoshop, two methods can be used:

- **Destructive method:** Highlight the *Background* layer (where the original image pixels are stored) then use one of Photoshop's selection tools to isolate an area and apply noise reduction to it. This method has the disadvantage of being destructive (altering the image in a way that cannot be undone).
- **Nondestructive method:** Copy the *Background* layer, then apply noise reduction to the copy and selectively blend it into the original *Background* layer using a mask, as explained in the previous sections in this chapter. This effectively doubles the file size, but I believe it is a better way to approach noise reduction as it is not destructive, and it allows targeting noise reduction locally and in varying amounts as needed.

In order to make a copy of the *Background* layer, drag it to the *Create a new layer* button at the bottom of the *Layers* panel. This will create a new layer titled *Background copy*. I recommend double-clicking the layer's name and titling it "Noise Reduction" so its function is clear. Next, add a mask to this layer by clicking the *Add layer* mask button (figure 13.8).

Now that we have the *Noise Reduction* layer in place, we'll apply whatever noise reduction tools are needed to it, then use the mask to apply the effect only where, and to the extent, it is needed.

Before proceeding to apply noise reduction to this layer, make sure the layer itself is selected, and not the mask. Remember that when a mask is selected its corners are highlighted. Click the layer's icon to select the layer so that noise reduction is applied to the image pixels (figure 13.9).

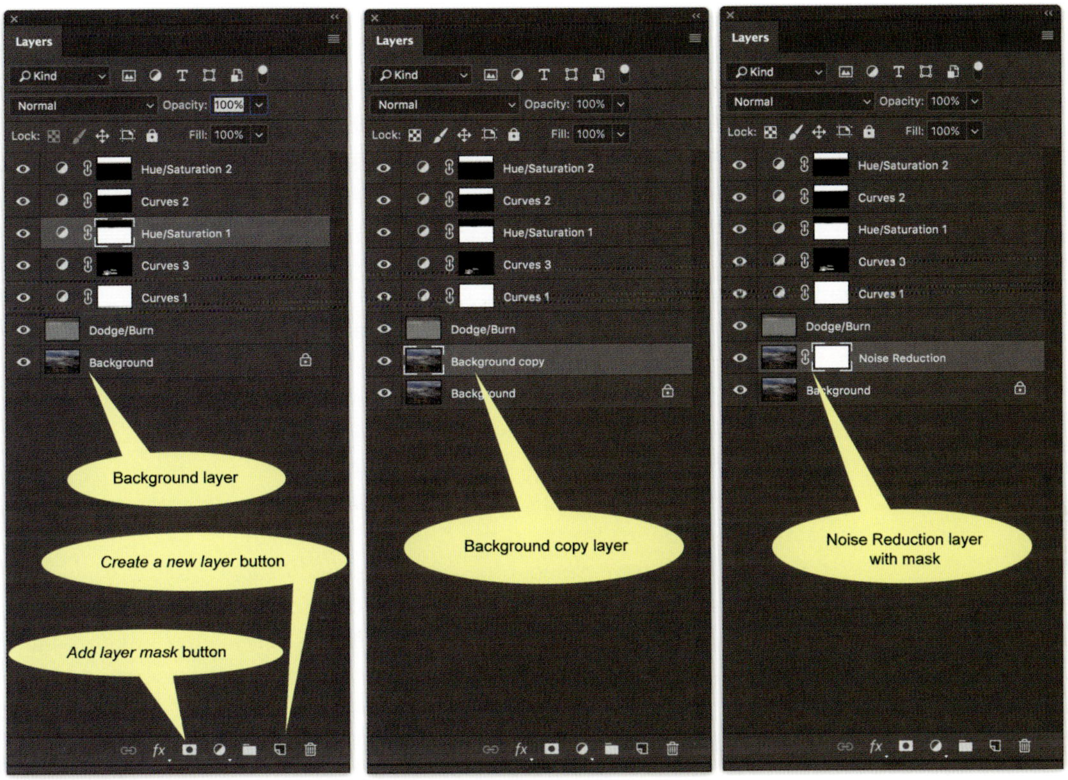


FIGURE 13.8: The *Layers* panel showing the Background layer (*left*). Dragging the Background layer to the *Create a new layer* button creates a new layer titled "Background copy" (*middle*). Double clicking the layer name allows us to rename it, and clicking the *Add layer mask* button adds a mask to it (*right*).

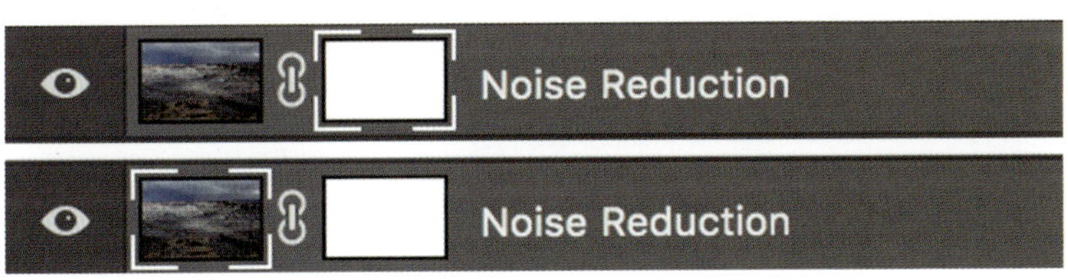


FIGURE 13.9: Mask selected (*top*) vs. layer selected (*bottom*). Make sure the layer is selected before applying noise reduction.

## Noise Analysis

Before proceeding to remove noise, we should first know where it resides and to what degree. We should also apply some common sense in deciding where not to remove noise, even if it is present.

As a first step, zoom to 100% magnification and slowly scroll around all areas of the image to see where noise is visible. Note those areas and particularly where the worst noise is to be found.

Next, we should identify areas of smooth tone, such as skies, as well as areas of important fine detail. In smooth areas, we should not be concerned about the appearance of sharp details and therefore can apply a high degree of noise reduction to them, if needed. On the other hand, in areas where fine details are important we should only apply little—or preferably no—noise reduction.

Especially prone to noise are areas of deep shadows. This is because these areas do not reflect much light for the sensor to measure, and sampling errors become more likely. These areas, unless prominent, are also less likely to draw much attention from the viewer, who will focus on the lighter areas in the frame, making these dark areas safe to apply a moderate amount of noise reduction, if needed.

Figure 13.10 shows a sample image that contains both sky and foreground elements, as well as areas of deep shadows. I noted those areas most prone to noise and where noise reduction can be applied without concern for detail, as well as areas where little or no noise reduction is desirable, even if noise exists.

Next, let's see if any of the color channels have significantly more noise than others. To do so, bring up the *Channels* panel (figure 13.11). If it is not within your workspace, select *Channels* from the *Window* menu.

The *Channels* panel shows the individual red, green, and blue channels, as well as any active layer masks. I mention earlier that in Photoshop, selections and masks are interchangeable. In fact, selections, masks, and

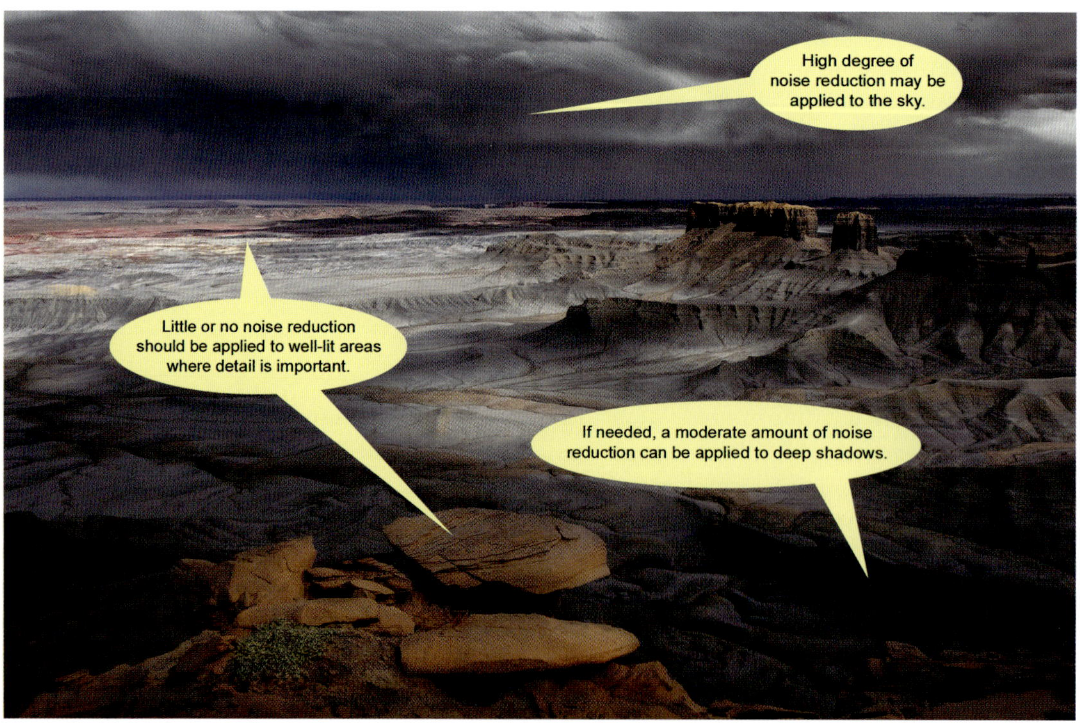


**FIGURE 13.10:** A common-sense analysis of where noise reduction may be needed and where it is not desirable.

channels are all interchangeable and we may create channels from selections (or masks), masks from channels (or selections), and so on.

Clicking on the name or icon of a channel turns "off" other channels and gives us a black-and-white representation of the data in that channel. Clicking sequentially on the red, green, and bluc channels at high magnification (100% or more), allows us to see which of them are noisy. Figure 13.12 shows a portion of an image, and sections of the red, green, and blue channels magnified to 200%, showing that the red channel is particularly noisy. If we could clean up the noise only (or mostly) from the red channel, we can still retain the details in the other channels. This is a good scenario since it allows excellent noise reduction with hardly any impact to image detail. If, however, all channels are equally noisy, there is no reason to focus on just one or two.

Now that we know where noise exists, and how much noise reduction to apply to different parts of the image (or to specific channels), we should determine whether we are dealing with luminance noise or color (chroma) noise. If you are unsure, refer to the "Noise" section in chapter 6.

Before proceeding be sure to select RGB in the *Channels* panel to make sure the image appears as it should. You may now close or hide the *Channels* panel as we will not have further use for it.

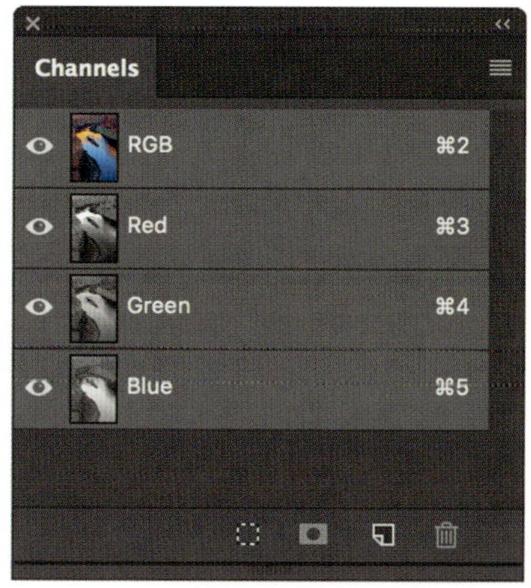


FIGURE 13.11: The *Channels* panel.

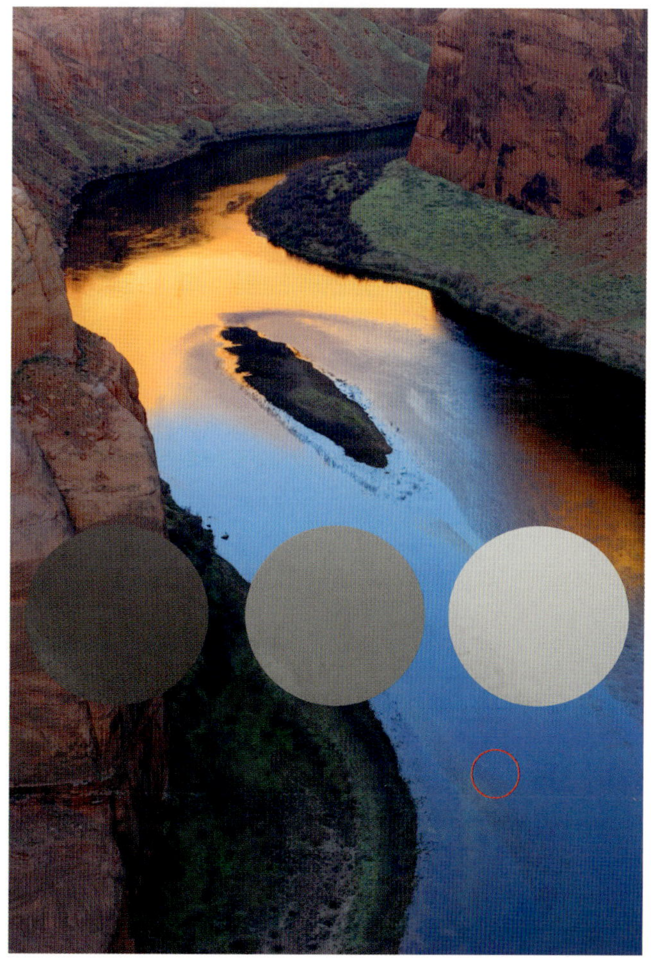

FIGURE 13.12: Each of the gray circles is a portion of the red (*left*), green (*middle*), and blue (*right*) channels corresponding to the area circled in red.

## Reducing Noise

Before applying noise reduction, be sure that the *Noise Reduction* layer we created

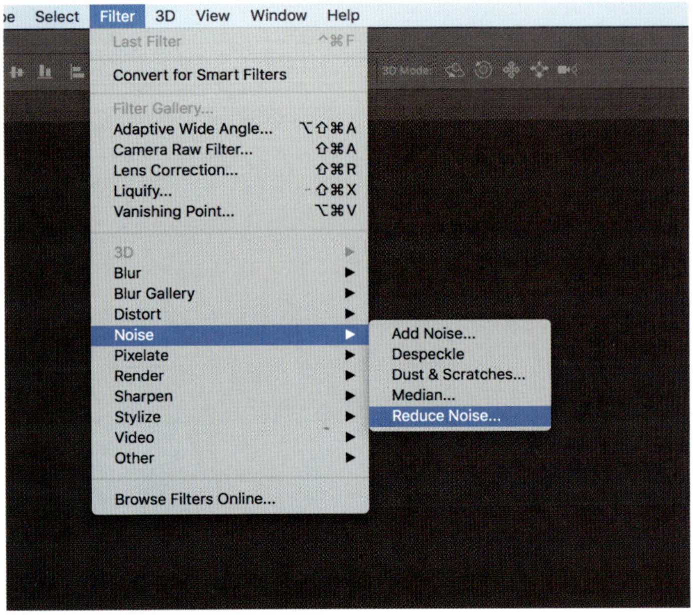


**Figure 13.13:** Activating Photoshop's *Reduce Noise* filter.

above is selected and that there are no active selections (otherwise the noise reduction will only be applied to the selected area). If a selection exists, click Command/Ctrl+D to de-select all.

Photoshop's noise reduction tool is found under the *Filter* menu. Open this menu, select *Noise*, then *Reduce Noise* (figure 13.13).

Our goal at this point is to apply noise reduction globally to meet the needs of the area(s) where the most unsightly noise is. Later, we will paint over the mask to remove this effect partially or completely where it is not desirable.

Figure 13.14 shows the *Reduce Noise* filter interface. Before starting, be sure to check the *Preview* box. This may slow things down a bit (some delay may occur between when you adjust a setting and when you see its effect, due to the complex calculations required), but it gives us the advantage of seeing the effect as we tune the various parameters. Also, be sure to select the *Advanced* mode, which gives us the option to reduce noise either overall or per channel.

Note that the *Reduce Noise* filter has a small preview window. Make sure it shows the noisiest part of the image, identified in the previous section. To do so, hover over the image (note the cursor will change into a square) and click on the desired area.

If noise exists in all channels and/or if we need to correct color noise, we should use the *Overall* tab. This tab provides the following sliders:

- *Strength* and *Preserve Details* control the amount of luminance noise reduction applied. I suggest starting with the *Strength* slider at its middle setting (5), and then setting the *Preserve Details* slider to ensure that important details are preserved. If the effect is too pronounced, or insufficient, return to the *Strength* slider and adjust as needed.
- *Reduce Color Noise* controls the amount of color (chroma) noise reduction.
- *Sharpen Details* applies a degree of sharpening to the details remaining after noise reduction, to make them more visible. I suggest setting it to about 25% as you adjust the other sliders, so that details are more visible, then set it back to 0 before applying the filter. There are better

tools to control sharpening, so I prefer to leave it to a later time, when targeting the image to a given output.

- Once the desired noise reduction effect is achieved, click the *OK* button.

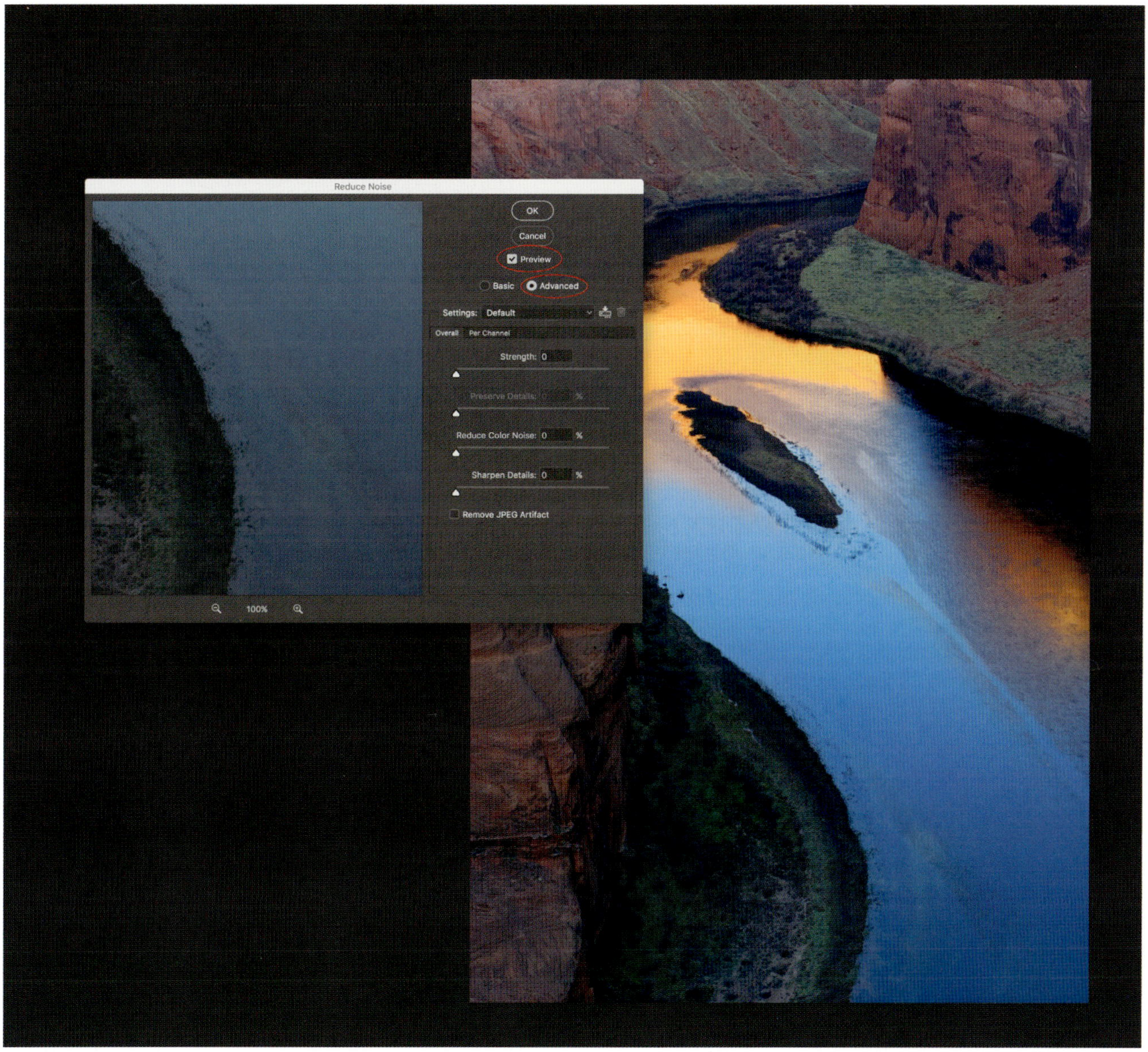


**FIGURE 13.14:** The *Reduce Noise* filter set to *Advanced* mode and to show a preview of noise reduction in real time.

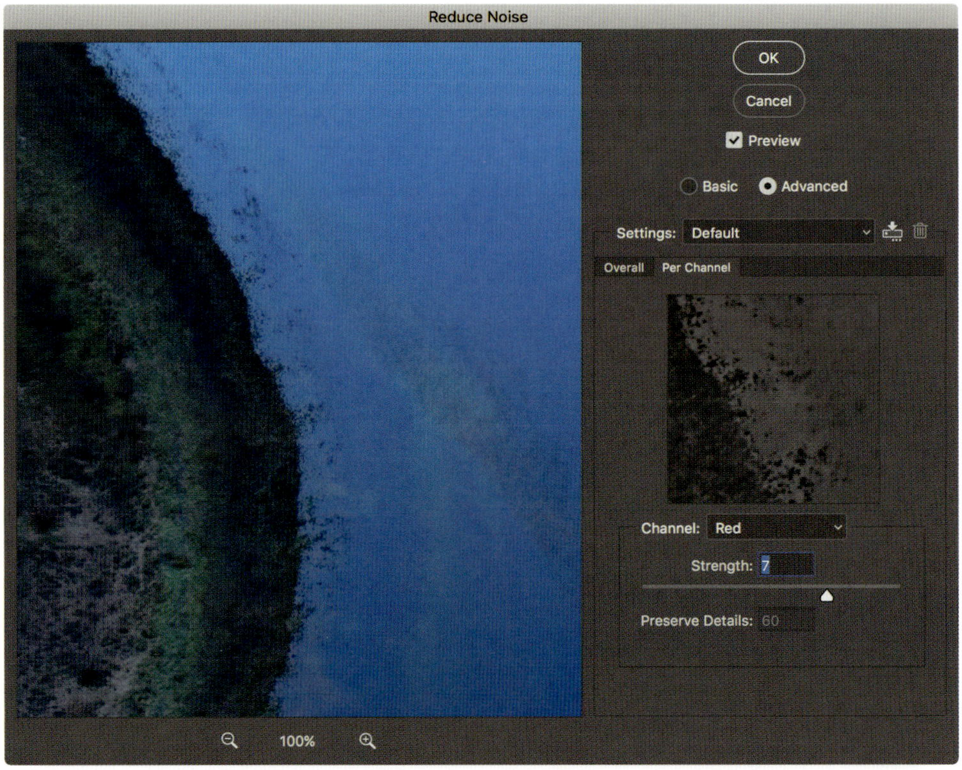


**FIGURE 13.15:** *Per Channel* noise reduction (here, showing the red channel).

If only one or two of the color channels are noisy, use the *Per Channel* tab (figure 13.15). This tab allows reducing noise to varying amounts for each color channel.

### Applying the *Reduce Noise* Filter More Than Once

In some cases, when noise is extremely heavy or when both luminance and color noise need to be corrected, you may need to apply the *Reduce Noise* filter multiple times. Click *OK* after each correction and then reselect the *Reduce Noise* filter from the *Filter* menu to reapply it.

Finally, when the desired noise reduction has been applied globally to the *Noise Reduction* layer we created, select the *Brush* tool and set the foreground color to black, make sure to select the mask (by clicking on it), and paint over the areas where noise reduction is not desired.

I suggest using a brush *Opacity* of 100% for areas where no noise reduction is needed, and then setting a lower *Opacity* value (20% or so) and brushing over areas where only some noise reduction is desired. Brushing over the same area multiple times will gradually reduce more and more noise.

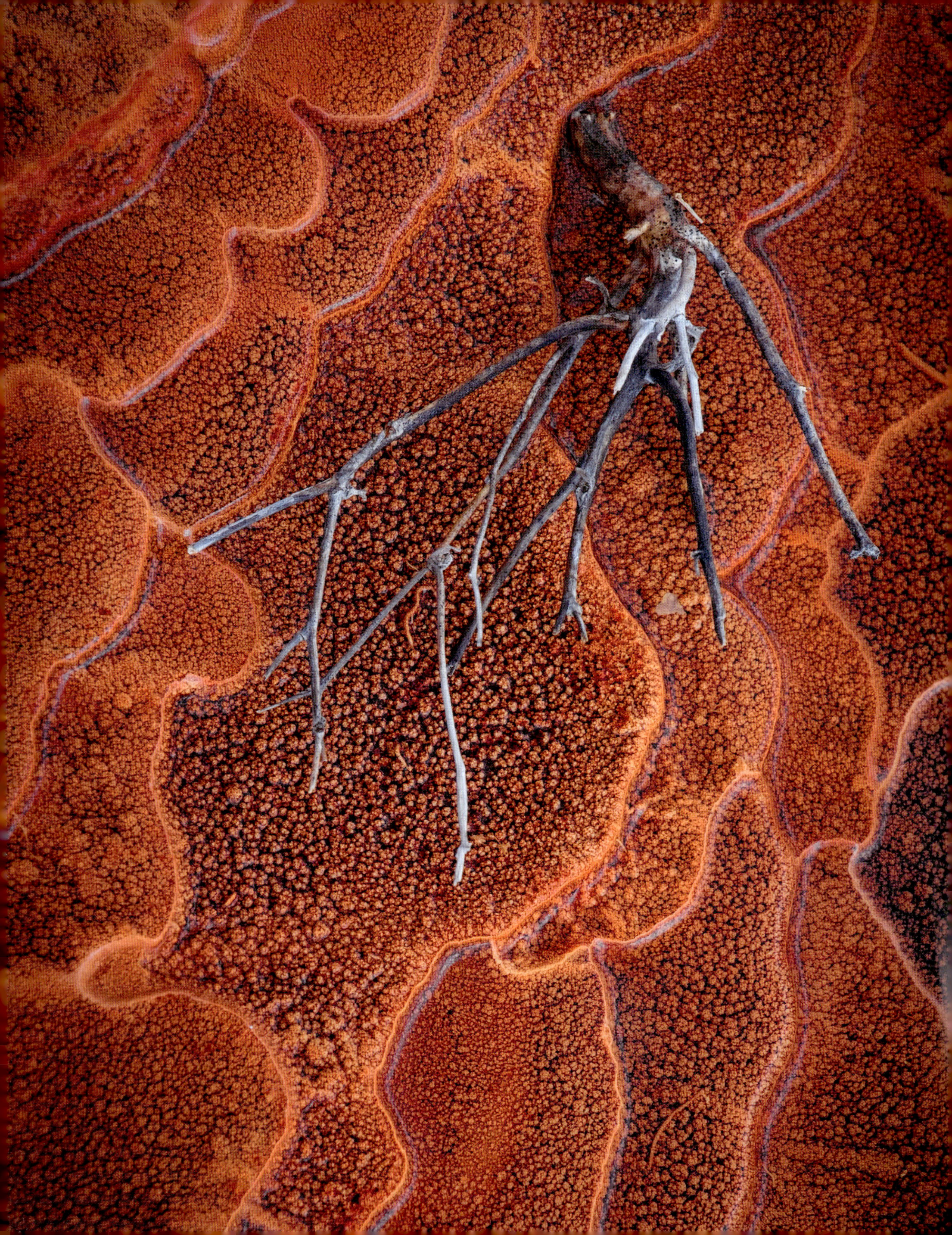

# 14 Using Images

*We are confronted today with a dichotomy; as our equipment and materials constantly grow in scope and quality the creative and technical standards appear to be diminishing; there is a near-cult of photographers who seem to intentionally avoid the beautiful and precise image, concentrating only on subject and obvious function. My personal reaction to this attitude is a determination to go as far in the opposite direction as possible. I believe in the most beautiful and appropriate prints, and the most clarifying and revealing approach of mind, heart, and craft. I believe that firm objectives in this direction can fulfill the promise of photography as one of the great visual arts.*

—ANSEL ADAMS

The workflow I described up to this point has one goal, which is to guide a captured RAW image to a point where it looks on screen as we visualized it—to give tangible form to a creation that previously existed only in the mind. This is the image we save as a master file.

We have not yet considered using our images—whether printing them at a given size, posting them to Internet sites, emailing them, using them in a projected slideshow, or using them for any other form of output.

Adapting a master file to any form of output requires degrading the data to account for the capabilities and limitations of an output device. For example, to display an image on an Internet site, its pixel size needs to be reduced considerably; and to make a print, pixels need to either be eliminated or added to accomplish a desired physical size.

In this chapter, I discuss the steps needed to optimize a master file for output, accounting for the capabilities of the output device, and with minimal loss of color and detail information.

## Targeting

The process of creating an output-specific version from the master file is called *targeting*. Following are the three factors we must consider when targeting:

- **Sizing:** It is unlikely that the original image size, whether in pixels (for digital output) or in physical units (for hard copies) is precisely what we need for any form of output. The master file, therefore, almost always needs to be resized to fit the desired output dimensions.

- **Color management:** Remember that we saved our master files in a large color space, such as ProPhoto RGB or AdobeRGB (1998). While some high-end screens can reproduce all the colors in Adobe RGB (1998), at the time of this writing no device exists that can reproduce ProPhoto RGB. Therefore, we will need to make sure the colors in our output file fit within the destination color space and that out-of-gamut colors are effectively mapped to the most desirable alternatives.
- **Sharpening:** Resizing a digital file often makes it look less sharp, or, even if it does appear sharp, chances are that the appearance of sharpness can be further optimized. Therefore, we need to sharpen our images for best results after resizing.

Before proceeding to the next sections, I recommend brushing up on the "Pixels and Dots" and the "Color" sections of chapter 4.

## Flattening an Image

Before targeting a master file to a given output, I suggest flattening the image—consolidating all layers into one. Following are several reasons to flatten an image:

- **Processing is complete:** At this point, the image already looks as we visualized it and no further edits or adjustments are needed (if that is not the case, the image is not ready for output, yet).
- **Reducing file size:** Flattening an image makes the amount of data Photoshop must manipulate and keep track of much smaller, making targeting tasks (sizing, color management, sharpening) faster and more efficient.
- **Avoiding errors:** Flattening the image helps avoid some common pitfalls, such as attempting to sharpen a mask or an adjustment layer, rather than the image.
- **Sending files:** If sending the image to a third party (print lab, or even just email to a friend), there is no point in sending all our adjustment and blending layers along. The recipient has no use for them, and the flattened file is much smaller.

To flatten an image, either select *Flatten Image* from the *Layer* menu, or from the menu in the upper-right corner of the *Layers* panel (figure 14.1).

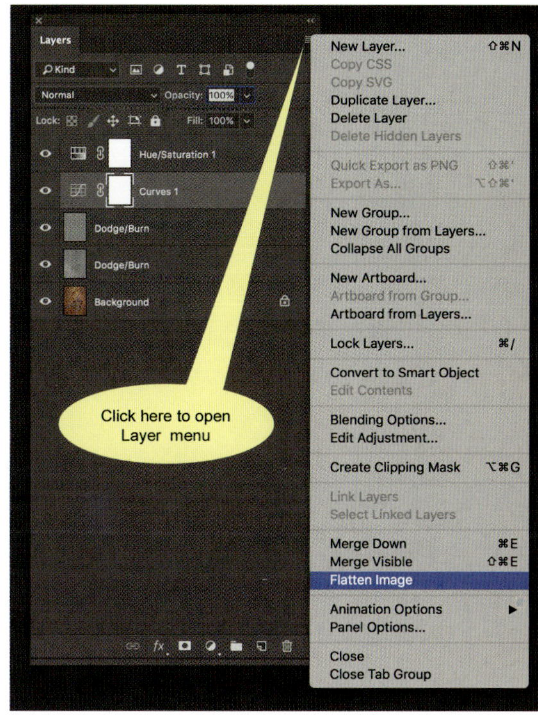


FIGURE 14.1: The *Flatten Image* option in the *Layer* menu found in the upper right corner of the *Layers* panel.

## Sizing and Interpolation

When using analog media, such as film, enlarging or reducing the size of an image to specific physical dimensions can be accomplished by optical means. Readers experienced with printing images in a chemical darkroom should be familiar with enlargers, which project light through a piece of film onto photographic paper, and allow changing the projected image size by using various enlarging lenses and by varying the distance between the film and the paper.

Digital images have a fixed pixel size, which is determined by the camera's sensor and any subsequent cropping we chose to apply. To change the size of a digital image we need to use computational algorithms to either throw away the least important pixel data (in the case of reducing image size) or to manufacture new data that looks as close as possible to the original pixels (in the case of enlarging image size).

The term *interpolation* refers to mathematical methods of estimating values for new data based on known reference points—in our case, the pixels in our image, originating from the camera's sensor and adjusted in Photoshop to match our visualization.

Following is a review of the various controls found in Photoshop's *Image Size* dialog (figure 14.2), which can be accessed by selecting *Image Size* from the *Image* menu.

### Image Size in Megabytes

The image size in megabytes (MB) is a useful indication for whether we are enlarging the image from its original size (and need to manufacture new pixels) or reducing the image from its original size (and need to throw away some pixels).

Once we enter a new number into either the *Width* or *Height* field, at the top of the *Image Size* window, we will see the new image size in megabytes compared with the original size (shown in parentheses, prefixed with "was").

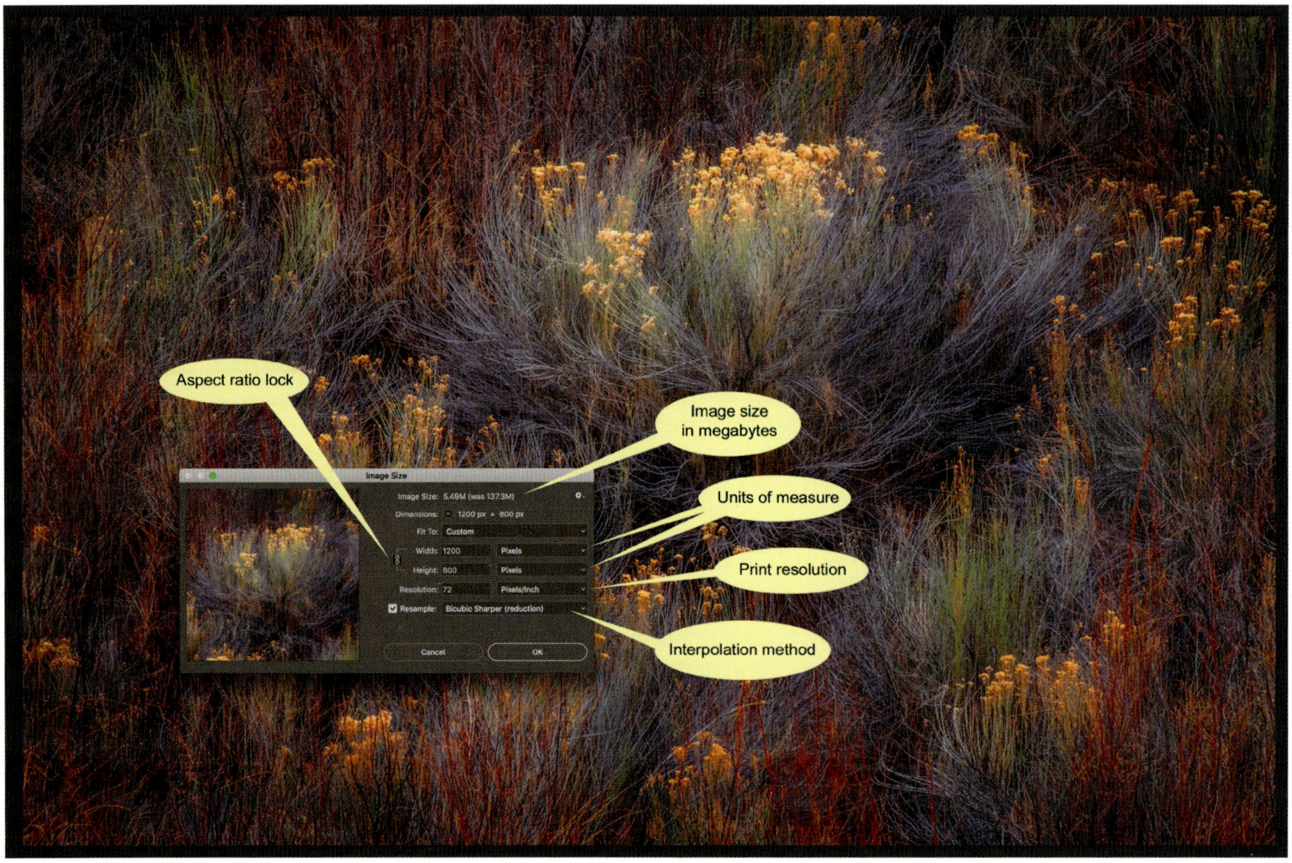


FIGURE 14.2: Photoshop's *Image Size* dialog.

The actual number is of less importance than whether the new number is greater or lower than the original, and by how much (giving us a sense of the ratio of pixels that need to be added or discarded).

Image size in megabytes is calculated as follows (8,388,608 is the number of bits in a megabyte):

The image in figure 14.2 was originally captured using a 24-megapixel camera and measures 6,000 × 4,000 pixels. The master file uses 16 bits per color channel, giving us:

$$(6{,}000 \times 4{,}000 \times 3 \text{ x } 16)/8{,}388{,}608 = 137.3\text{MB}$$

The *Image Size* field shows that reducing the image to a width of 1,200 pixels, as shown in figure 14.2, will result in a file that is only 5.49MB, meaning that about 96% of the original image pixels need to be discarded to make the smaller version, calculated as follows:

$$(1 - (5.49 / 137.3)) \times 100 = 96$$

The resulting image, measuring 1,200 × 800 pixels, is less than one megapixel in size and will work very well for Internet sharing (say, on a website or via email). This tells you that for any practical purpose, multi-megapixel files are mostly needed to make prints. For digital presentation, most of the data captured by multi-megapixel cameras is superfluous.

## Dimensions and Units of Measure

The *Width* and *Height* fields allow entering values using a variety of units, both virtual (pixels) and physical (inches, centimeters). To the left of these fields is an *Aspect Ratio Lock* button (see figure 14.2), which is locked by default, meaning that entering a value in one of the fields automatically calculates the value for the other field to maintain the same aspect ratio as the original image. Clicking the lock toggles its position and, when unlocked, allows entering *Width* and *Height* values independently, although doing so may warp the image.

## Print Resolution

The *Resolution* field may be a bit confusing since it is only applicable in uses that require converting from virtual units (pixels) to physical ones (inches, centimeters), which is only the case when printing. This number has no effect on files presented digitally, with one exception, which is text.

Photoshop, by default, uses PostScript resolution (72 pixels/inch) when rendering text. This means that if you set your print resolution to 72 PPI, text at a given point size will look as you might expect from working with word processors and other applications. If the print resolution is set to a value other than 72 PPI, text may appear larger or smaller than you expect.

While 72 may be a useful setting for Internet images where we may want to include text (perhaps a copyright notice), it is generally *not* a proper setting for printing images. I explain how to determine the best value for this field in the "Printing" section of this chapter.

## Interpolation Methods

When the *Resample* box is checked (which it should be when resizing an image to a size different from its original pixels), Photoshop offers a vari-

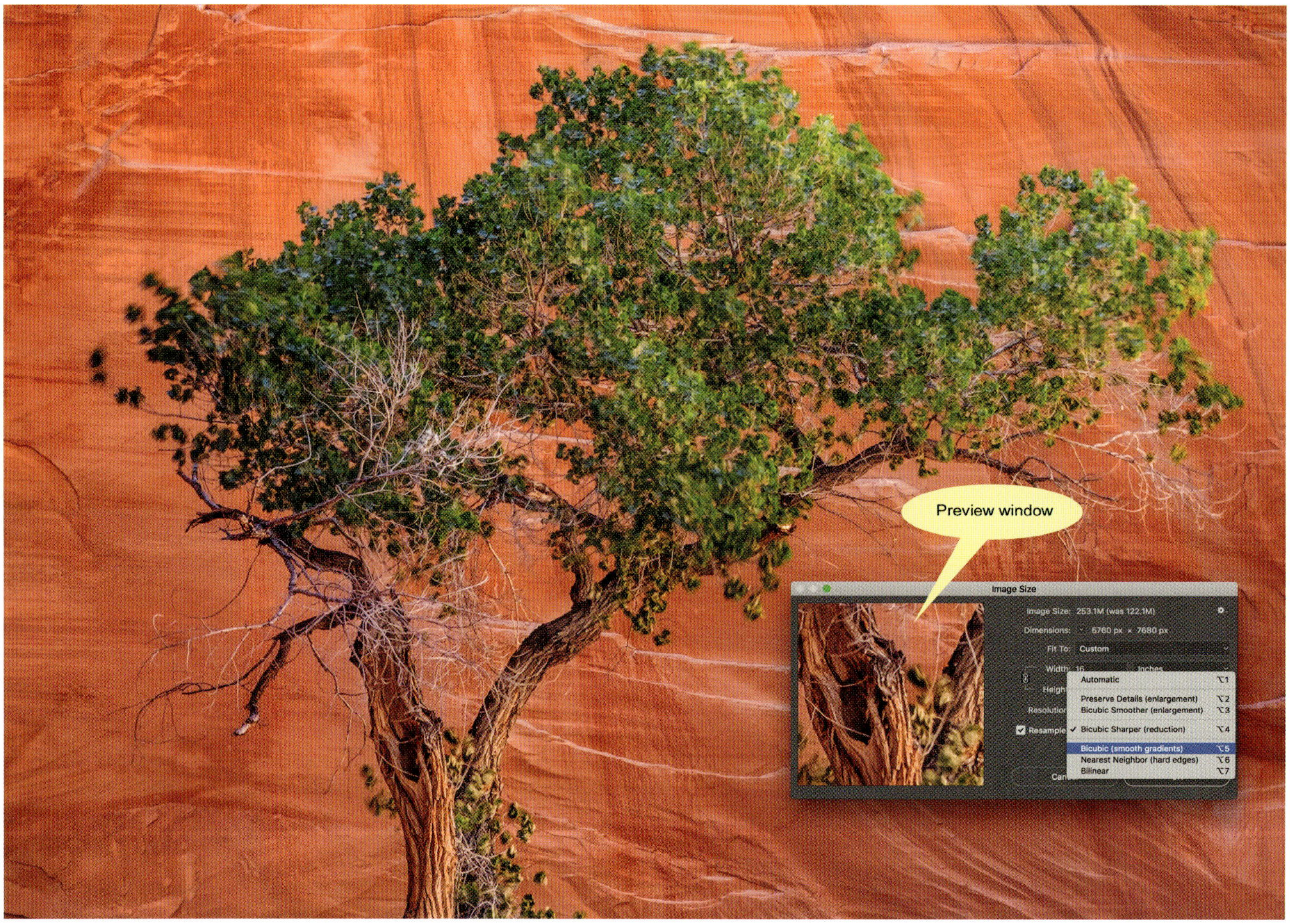


**Figure 14.3:** The interpolation methods offered in Photoshop.

ety of interpolation algorithms to calculate new pixel data or to determine which data to eliminate, as needed. Some of these algorithms are optimized for enlarging and some for reducing image size. Photoshop provides hints (in parentheses) next to each option, suggesting whether the option is optimized for enlargement or reduction (figure 14.3), however these should be taken with a grain of salt, as I explain below. At the time of this writing, these are the interpolation options available, in the order they appear in the menu:

- **Automatic:** When this option is chosen, Photoshop will attempt to decide which interpolation method is best, based on whether the image is being enlarged or reduced. If you are a control freak like me, avoid this option.

- **Preserve Details:** This is Adobe's latest addition to the list of interpolation methods. In my opinion this method produces the best enlargements for images that are very detailed and have well-defined lines. When selected, Photoshop also offers a *Reduce Noise* slider. I recommend avoiding it (leaving it at 0) and instead using the localized noise reduction method I describe in chapter 13.
- **Bicubic Smoother:** This is a variation of Photoshop's older Bicubic algorithm (described below) that is optimized for enlargement, producing smooth tonal transitions, which helps avoid artifacts such as posterization. This method also avoids exacerbating the appearance of noise, if present. Bicubic Smoother sometimes produces better results than Preserve Details when enlarging images that do not rely on very fine or sharp details (for example, water abstracts).
- **Bicubic Sharper:** This is another variation of the Bicubic algorithm, except that it is optimized for reduction of size, applying a degree of sharpening to the image and making it appear crisper. This is an excellent reduction algorithm with one caveat, which is this: sharpening may, in some cases, produce unsightly halos around high-contrast lines.

  If using this method, be sure to check the image at high magnification to see if the interpolation produced such halos (the preview window can be helpful in this). If so, undo the operation and resize using a different method. I generally prefer to avoid this option since I find that sharpening is almost always best applied as a local adjustment (since not all areas of the image need the same amount of sharpening). I explain my method of sharpening below.
- **Bicubic:** This was Photoshop's best resizing algorithm before the addition of newer variations, such as Bicubic Smoother, Bicubic Sharper, and Preserve Details. It produces excellent results for both enlargement and reduction.

  In my work I generally use Bicubic for reduction, and Preserve Details as my first choice for enlargement, with Bicubic as my second choice, comparing the two to see which produces the most desirable result for a given image.
- **Nearest Neighbor:** This method is *not* intended for resizing photographs. It stretches horizontal and vertical pixel edges which, when enlarging, makes an image appear very(!) pixelated. This method is useful when rendering such things as screen captures of application buttons or other small graphical icons, in print. Since the

original screen capture generally is too small for print publications, this method allows enlargement while preserving the pixelated appearance.

- **Bilinear:** This is a simpler algorithm than Bicubic, making it suitable for underpowered computers in the days when computers were much slower. While producing very good results in general, Bicubic interpolation tends to produce sharper-looking edges than Bilinear. Considering the quality of results produced by the other options available, there is little reason to use Bilinear.

## Color Management

The goal of color management is to maintain consistency in color reproduction among various devices. Color management ensures that our images as they appear in print, or displayed on other people's screens, look as close as possible to the way they appear on our screen.

Note that I used the words "consistency" and "as close as possible," rather than stronger terms, like "matching" or "identical." This is because some variation is to be expected. It may seem intuitive that we want foliage to have the same shade of green in our prints as it does on our screen; that the sky will be the same shade of blue; and red flowers will appear to viewers using a web browser as vibrant and as rich as they do when we view them in Photoshop. However, different devices render images in different ways, and a perfect match is usually not possible. Still, with proper color management, we can get very close.

At the heart of color management is the ability to represent, in a standard format, the color capabilities—also referred to as the gamut, or the color space—of a given device. Having this information, we can use it to identify what colors in the source image are, or are not, reproducible by the output device. We can then apply any number of techniques to address the outlying colors: colors that exist in the source image but that are outside the gamut of the output device. These are referred to as *out-of-gamut* colors.

The standard method of representing a color space is called an ICC profile (after the International Color Consortium—the body responsible for maintaining the standard). An ICC profile describes in mathematical terms the color capabilities of a given device, enabling computer algorithms to compare color spaces, identify gamut mismatches, and apply computation to map colors from one into another.

**Color Space vs. Gamut vs. ICC Profile**

As you noticed, I use the terms "color space," "gamut," and "ICC profile" interchangeably. They all refer to the color capabilities of a given device. For the sake of accuracy, "gamut" is a generic term that's applicable in areas other than just digital imaging; "color space" is a specific term referring to devices that reproduce colors; and "ICC profile" is a standard format for representing a device's color space, which is why the process of measuring the color capabilities of a device and encoding them in an ICC format is also referred to as "profiling."

No two devices have the exact same gamut. Even screens or printers of the same make and model will have slightly different gamuts based on their ages, environmental conditions (temperature, humidity, etc.), and manufacturing tolerances. To ensure the most accurate handling of color, a custom ICC profile can be created specifically for your screen (and, if printing, also for any paper you wish to use with your printer).

The screen we use when processing our images is the first link in a color-managed chain. If the screen is not calibrated, we cannot use our master file as a reliable reference point for color accuracy.

Some photographers create custom profiles for their cameras, making the camera the first link in the color-managed chain. This may be useful when precise reproduction of colors as captured is desirable. However, when practicing creative, expressive photography, precise fidelity to colors as captured by the camera is of little value. Indeed, in practically every case we will customize these colors with an aesthetic or expressive goal in mind when processing our work, making our workstation screen a more important reference point since that is where the appearance of colors in the image is decided (and not in the camera).

When working on a calibrated screen, we can use ICC profile-aware applications (such as Photoshop) to convert our images so they fit within the capabilities of other calibrated devices, and even to improve the chance of our images looking consistent on uncalibrated devices (as is the case with Internet images, discussed below). If you are serious about digital image processing, a calibration device for your screen is every bit as important to the quality of your work as any other piece of photographic gear.

## Converting Between Color Spaces

Our master files are saved in a large color space, such as ProPhoto RGB or Adobe RGB (1998). Therefore, these files may contain colors that are not reproducible on some, or any, device—not even on our screen. The reason

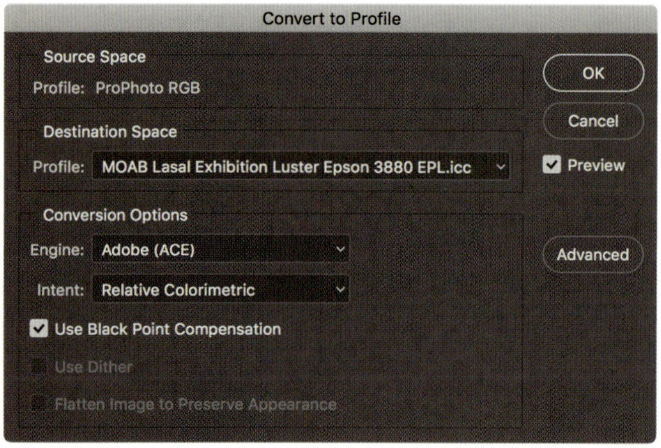


**FIGURE 14.4:** Photoshop's profile conversion tool, shown here converting from my master file, which is in the ProPhoto RGB color space, to a profile for Moab Lasal Exhibition Luster paper used with my Epson 3880 printer. I selected *Relative Colorimetric* as my rendering intent, for reasons I explain below.

images in a large color space appear properly on our screen is that the operating system (Windows or OS X) implicitly converts their colors behind the scenes. When we calibrate our screen, the operating system will use the custom ICC profile created by the calibration software to make the conversion, otherwise it will use a generic screen ICC profile.

When explicitly targeting an image to a device other than our screen, we get to decide which ICC profile to use, and what conversion method—known as *rendering intent*—to use. A couple of useful rendering intents for photographs—Perceptual, and Relative Colorimetric—are described in chapter 4.

Photoshop's color space conversion functions can be accessed by selecting *Convert to Profile* from the *Edit* menu (figure 14.4).

Note that the profile conversion tool has an *Advanced* mode, which extends its capabilities to conversion between different color models. However, for our purposes we'll remain within the RGB model and the functions offered in the *Basic* mode are sufficient.

**Black Point Compensation**

The *Use Black Point Compensation* (BPC) checkbox (figure 14.4) tells Photoshop to compensate for differences between the black point (darkest black possible) of the source color space and that of the destination color space. Although a matter of some heated debate among color experts, I recommend checking this box. Regardless of reasons offered by naysayers, I find that compensating for black point produces more accurate prints. And, as they say, the proof is in the pudding.

## Soft-Proofing

Soft-proofing is a way of simulating the appearance of colors as they will be rendered by a given device, based on the device's color space. Soft-proofing is most useful for printing. If you are targeting your image for Internet use or projection, odds are you will end up converting the image to the sRGB color space (discussed below), rather than using a device-specific profile.

To set up a soft proof, we first need to have a profile for the output device. This can be a profile downloaded from the website of a paper manufacturer, a custom profile created for our own printer, or (if outsourcing) a profile pro-

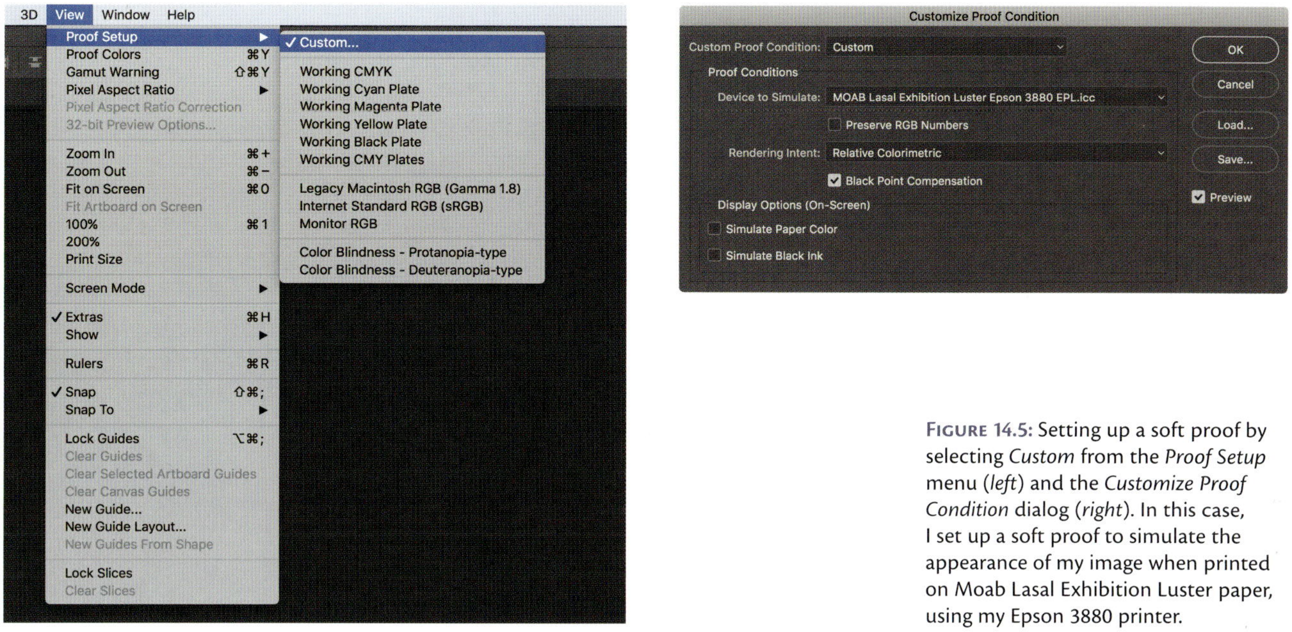


FIGURE 14.5: Setting up a soft proof by selecting *Custom* from the *Proof Setup* menu (*left*) and the *Customize Proof Condition* dialog (*right*). In this case, I set up a soft proof to simulate the appearance of my image when printed on Moab Lasal Exhibition Luster paper, using my Epson 3880 printer.

vided by a third party for their printer. The method for installing new profiles is explained in chapter 4.

Once the destination profile is installed on our system, we can set up the proof by selecting the *Proof Setup* option from the *View* menu, and then *Custom* from the sub-menu (figure 14.5, left). This will bring up the *Customize Proof Condition* dialog (figure 14.5, right).

When customizing the proofing parameters, first select the desired destination profile (this will usually be a paper profile for your printer). You can then try different rendering intents to see how they affect colors and contrast.

Once you set the proof parameters and click the *OK* button, you can toggle between the normal view and the simulated proof view using Command/Ctrl+Y. Note that the title of the image will indicate when the image is rendered to simulate a device (figure 14.6).

Perhaps more important than simulating colors—which should be treated as an approximation, rather than an exact match—is the ability to identify if and where out-of-gamut colors exist in the image so they can be managed. Once a proof is set up, you may select the *Gamut Warning* option from the *View* menu to see if, and where, out-of-gamut colors are found. When *Gamut Warning* is active, areas that are out of gamut will be rendered in gray (figure 14.7).

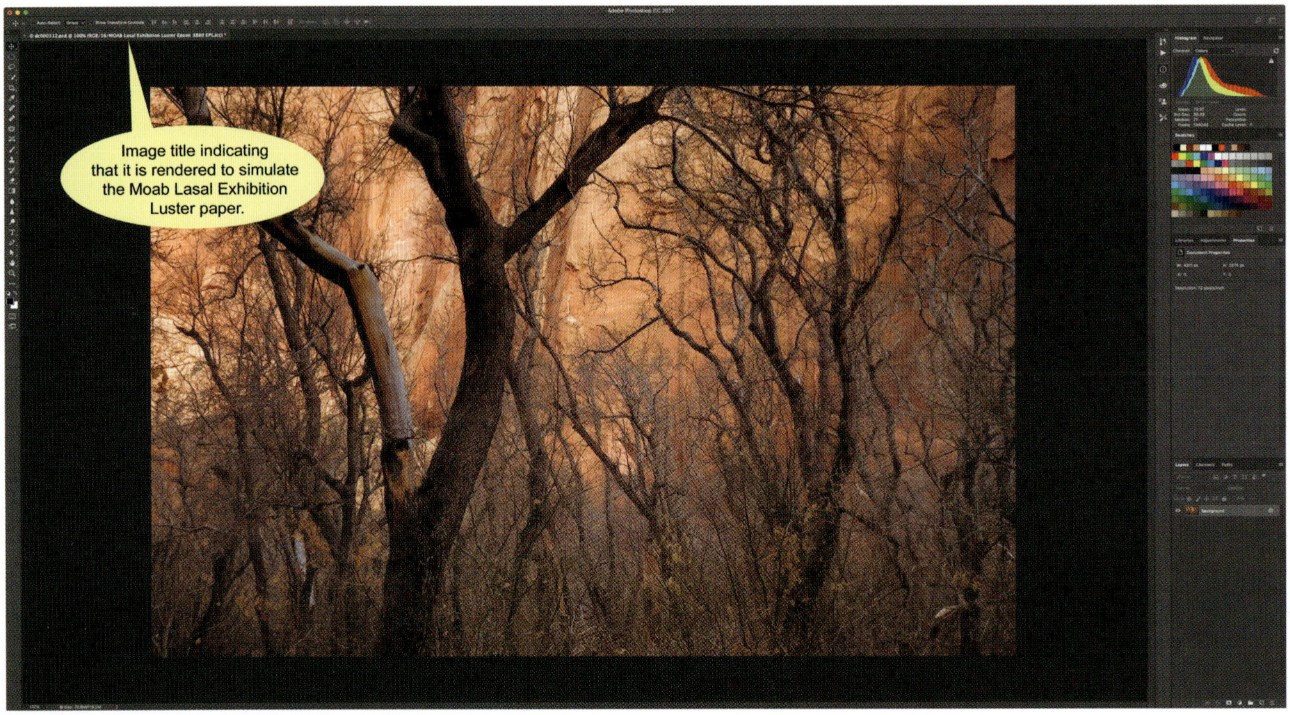


**Figure 14.6:** The image title indicating that the view is rendered to simulate the appearance of the image as if printed on Moab Lasal Exhibition Luster paper. Clicking Command/Ctrl+Y toggles between this view and the normal view.

**Figure 14.7:** As an example, I used Photoshop's soft-proofing feature to simulate the way the image on the left would appear on Epson's Enhanced Matte paper (chosen specifically since it has a relatively small color gamut). I then activated the *Gamut Warning* feature to show that many of the saturated oranges and reds in the image (now appearing as gray) are not available when printing on this paper. These areas will need to be managed for optimal reproduction.

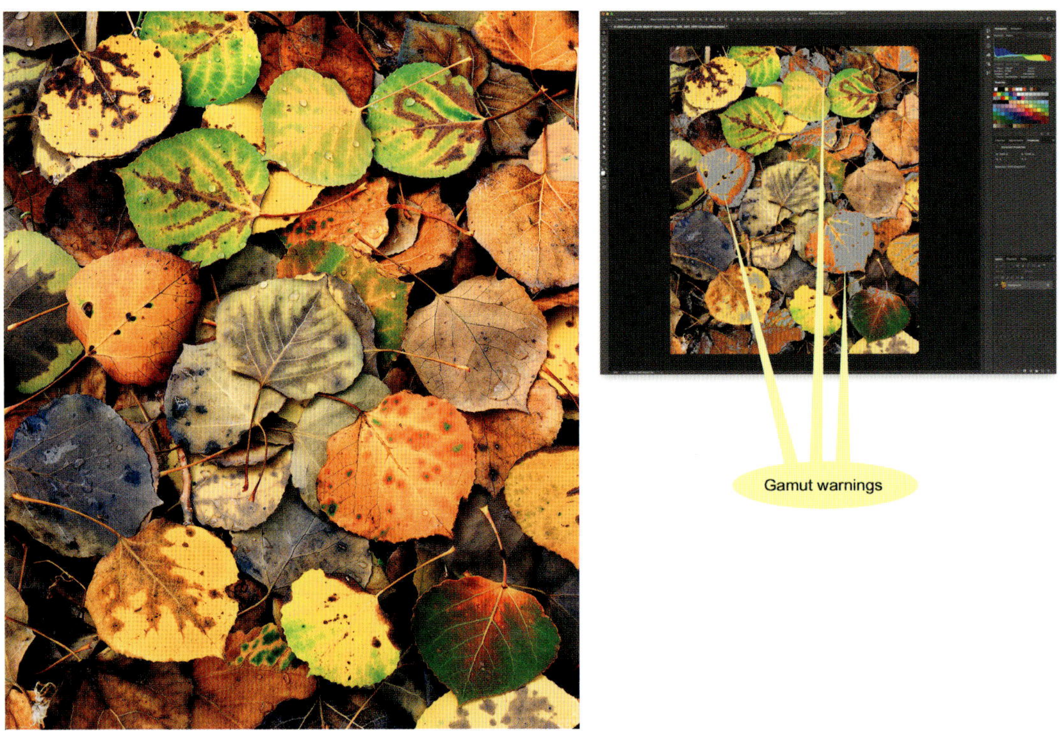

## Managing Out-Of-Gamut Colors

As with the previous section, managing out-of-gamut colors is most useful when printing, and not as useful when targeting an image for Internet use or projection.

I mention earlier that rendering intent tells the color conversion engine how to automatically map the colors in an image from one color space to another. However, for optimal results, this mapping can also be accomplished manually.

Figure 14.8 shows the color space of the Epson Enhanced Matte paper (in color) compared with the color space of the Moab Lasal Exhibition Luster paper (in gray). When reading this type of graph, consider that colors become progressively more saturated the farther they are from the intersection point of the axes, meaning that the larger the color space, the more saturated colors it includes.

Clearly, the matte paper has a much smaller gamut than the luster paper, which is to be expected as the coating on the luster paper, holding ink on its surface, can render more saturated colors than the matte paper, which absorbs ink. This, however, doesn't mean that the luster paper is unequivocally a "better" choice than the matte paper, just like an oil painting is not unequivocally "better" than a watercolor painting. Matte paper has its own

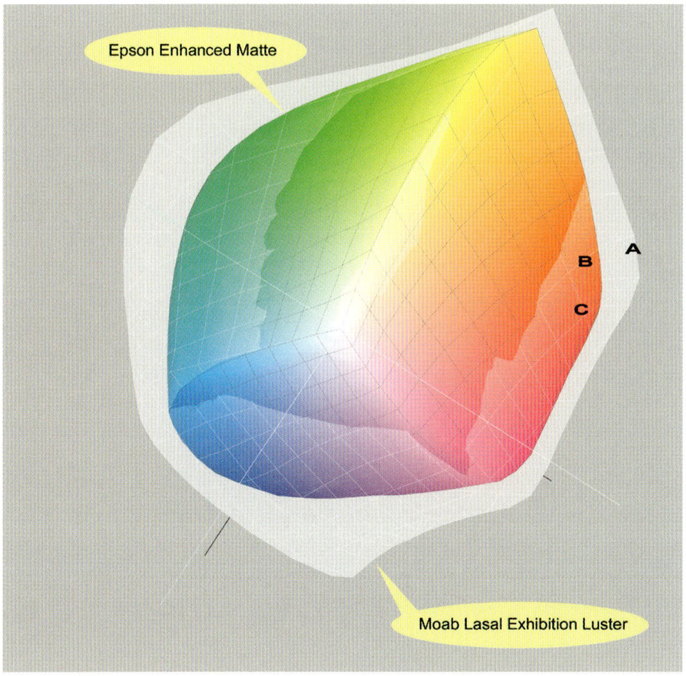


**FIGURE 14.8:** A graph comparing the color spaces of Moab Lasal Exhibition Luster paper (background, in gray) with the color space of Epson Enhanced Matte paper (foreground, in color).

aesthetic properties that are very different from luster. Subjective preference should be the primary factor in deciding the type of paper to use.

In figure 14.8, Point A marks a color I arbitrarily choose, which is in-gamut when using the luster paper, but out-of-gamut when using the matte paper. If I decide to use the matte paper, the color in Point A (assuming it exists in the image) will need to be mapped to a different shade that is within the matte paper's gamut. If I choose to use the Relative Colorimetric rendering intent (which leaves in-gamut colors as-is, and maps out-of-gamut colors to the closest available color), the color in Point A will be mapped to Point B, which is the closest shade that is within the paper's gamut. This may be perfectly acceptable. However, what if I prefer, instead, to map the color in Point A to Point C? This requires manual intervention.

To manually map out-of-gamut colors, use the following method:

1. Set up a soft proof using the desired paper profile, and Relative Colorimetric as the rendering intent. This will leave in-gamut colors as-is.
2. Activate *Gamut Warning*. If no warnings (gray areas) exist, all colors are in-gamut and you are ready to print. However, if warnings appear that indicate out-of-gamut colors, proceed as follows:
   - Add a *Hue/Saturation* adjustment layer.
   - Use the *Saturation* slider to reduce saturation (either overall, or individually for specific color ranges) until the warnings disappear.
   - If needed, also adjust the *Hue* and/or *Lightness* to fine-tune the mapping to your taste. If you venture outside the destination gamut, the gray warnings reappear.
   - Once no gray warnings exist, fill the layer mask with black, to eliminate the layer's effect (causing the gamut warnings to reappear). An easy way to do so is:
     — Make sure the mask is selected by clicking on it.
     — Select the entire mask by clicking Command/Ctrl+A.
     — Set black as your foreground color.
     — On PC, click Alt+Backspace; or, on Mac, click Option+Delete. This is a shortcut to fill a selection with the foreground color.
   - Select the *Brush* tool and adjust the brush size so you can easily paint over the gamut warnings. Set brush *Opacity* to 50%.
   - Set your foreground color to white.

- With the mask selected, paint over the gamut warnings. If a single stroke does not remove the warning completely from a given area, paint over it again until the warning disappears.

Using the *Hue/Saturation* layer, we can map out-of-gamut colors to our liking, rather than relying on the rendering intent algorithm. The mask allows us to apply the correction locally, only where needed.

Once gamut warnings are gone, all colors are in-gamut and the image is ready to print to the desired paper.

Be sure to flatten the image before proceeding.

## Sharpening

Sharpening digital images is, regrettably, an area where there is more lore and uninformed opinions than there are facts. This is because sharpness is not a quality that can be quantified or measured accurately. Sharpness is a perception, meaning that something either "looks sharp(er)" or it doesn't.

Two factors affect our perception of sharpness, which are these:

- **Detail:** Areas where our eyes can resolve finer/smaller details are perceived as sharper than areas where details are absent or blurry.
- **Acutance:** Also described as "edge contrast," acutance refers to how pronounced the lines (edges) are that separate visual elements.

When reducing an image size, we start with more data than we need and therefore (assuming a well-focused and well-exposed capture) more than enough fine details to fill the available space, allowing for very sharp-looking derivations to be made from our full-size master file. When enlarging, however, much as we would want to be able to add details to our images, that is not possible—the details are either there (captured by the camera) or they are not.

This leaves us with just acutance as a factor of sharpness that we can control post-capture.

To enhance acutance (edge contrast), a sharpening algorithm needs to do two things, which are these:

- Detect where edges are found in an image.
- Increase contrast along these edges by making one side of the edge more different (lighter or darker) than the other side.

Increasing contrast along the lines, once detected, would seem to be the easier of the tasks, but that is not necessarily the case. Consider that edges in the image don't all start off with the same degree of contrast: some are already well-defined and others may be subtler. This means that to optimize sharpness we need to apply different amounts of contrast increases to different edges. If we apply the same degree of sharpening to all lines in the image, odds are it will either be too little to bring out some of the subtle lines, or too much for lines that are already well-defined (resulting in artifacts that appear as halos along those lines).

Indeed, what makes some sharpening methods better than others is how good they are at finding edges, and then determining which edges need greater or lesser contrast increase than others.

Photoshop gives us a means of detecting the lines and increasing contrast along those lines. It does not, however, have a way of automatically determining which lines need a greater or lesser contrast boost than others. That is for us to decide.

Photoshop's sharpening algorithms are accessible from the *Filter* menu, under *Sharpen* (figure 14.9). Note that several sharpening methods are offered, although some are older and I do not recommend their use.

Of the newer methods, these are the most useful:

- **Shake Reduction:** This is the most recent addition to Photoshop's sharpening arsenal. *Shake Reduction* is especially formulated to reduce the appearance of camera shake. As it turns out, some things you *can* fix in Photoshop.

- **Smart Sharpen:** This is Photoshop's most sophisticated sharpening tool. It offers more functionality and options for optimizing sharpness than any other Photoshop sharpening tool. I cover it in more detail below.

- **Unsharp Mask:** This was Photoshop's most powerful sharpening method for many years until the introduction of *Smart Sharpen*. While still the method of choice for many photographers, *Unsharp Mask* offers a limited range of controls compared with *Smart Sharpen*. *Unsharp Mask* simulates a common traditional darkroom sharpening technique in which a second, unsharp (slightly out of focus), negative is created, then the two negatives are sandwiched together for printing. The slight blur of the second negative causes lines to appear thicker and more defined and the image to appear sharper overall.

FIGURE 14.9: Photoshop's sharpening filters are listed under *Sharpen* in the *Filter* menu.

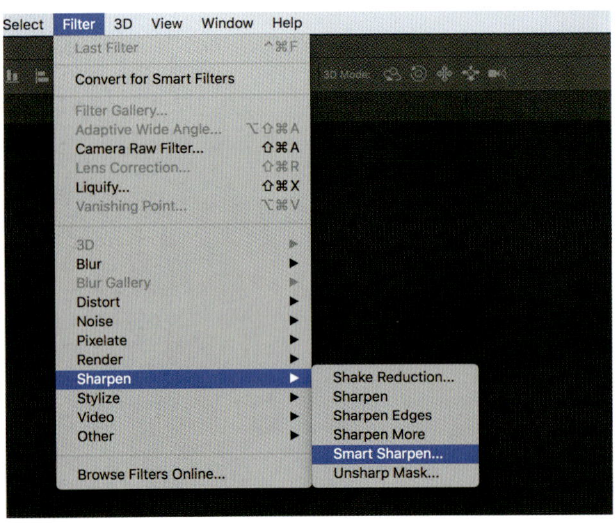

## Using the Smart Sharpen Filter

The *Smart Sharpen* filter (figure 14.10) has gone through a few permutations since its introduction. If you are using an older version of Photoshop, the interface may appear somewhat different but the functions described here should still be available.

Prior to using the *Smart Sharpen* filter, I suggest flattening the image, as I explain above, and making sure there is no active selection (as a general practice, I suggest clicking Command/Ctrl+D to deselect everything, just in case). I also recommend having your image displayed at 100% magnification so the sharpening effect can be easily previewed while tuning the various parameters.

When no active selections exist, the filter acts as a global adjustment. Since sharpening is destructive (alters pixel values), it is important to only apply it in the targeting process after resizing the image, and not earlier (our saved master files should *not* be sharpened).

There are some cases in which optimal sharpness can be accomplished using a single global adjustment. These are cases when all areas in the image need the same amount of sharpening, such as scenes with even lighting, low contrast, and where detail is distributed uniformly across the frame (figure 14.11, left). I will start by explaining the case of global sharpening, and

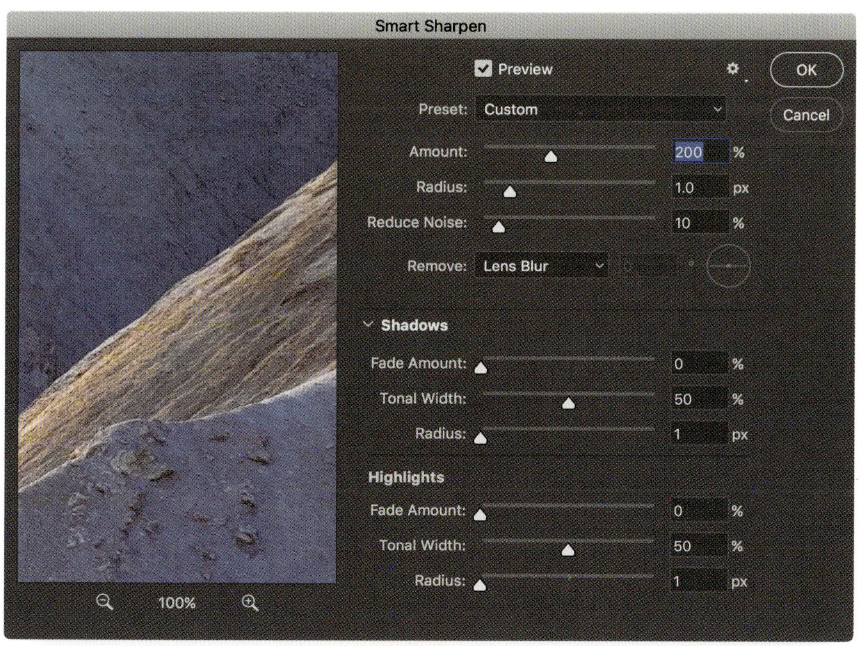


FIGURE 14.10: The *Smart Sharpen* filter shown here with the *Shadows/Highlights* section expanded.

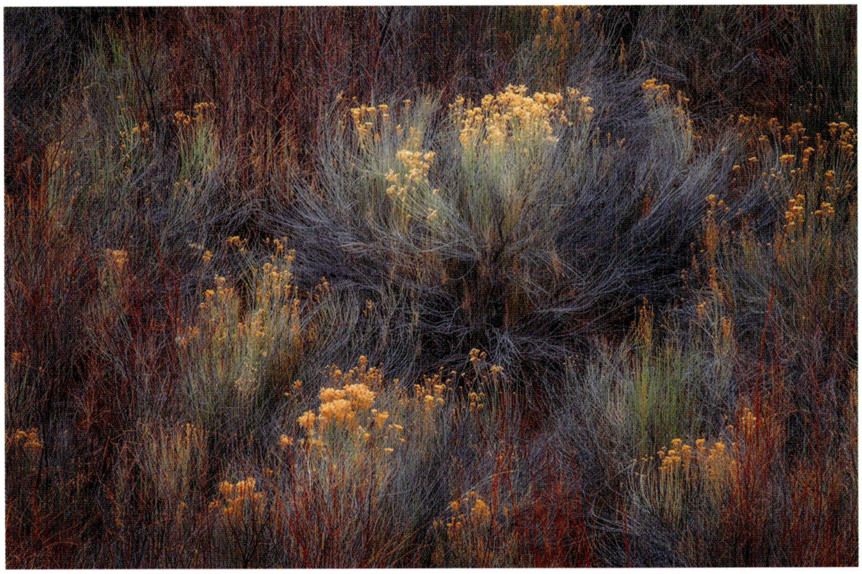

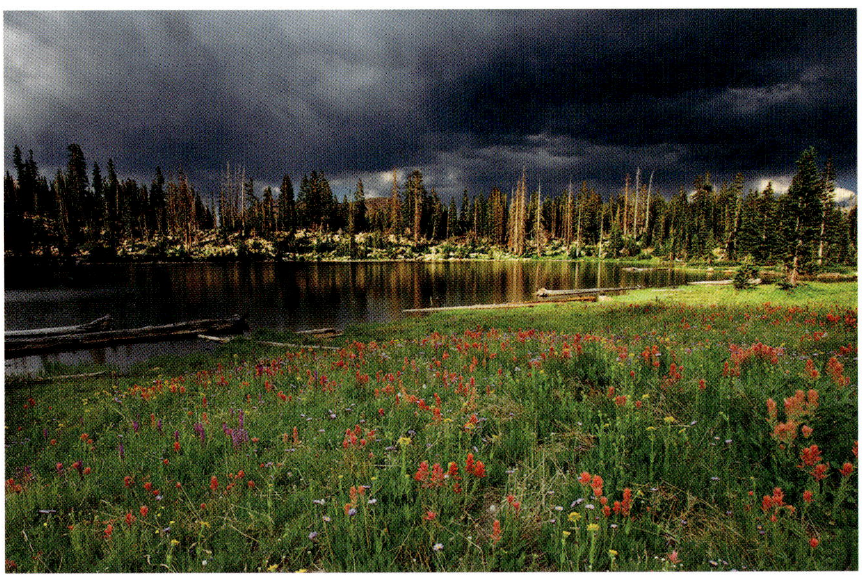

**Figure 14.11:** The image at the top has low contrast and detail is spread uniformly across the frame making it suitable for sharpening using a single global adjustment. The image on the bottom has distinctive areas of low contrast (*foreground*) and high contrast (*background*), as well as a sky where we may not want to apply any sharpening at all, making the image more suitable for selective sharpening using a local adjustment.

then I'll explain what to do when sharpening needs to be applied as a local adjustment—in different amounts to different parts of the image.

Once *Smart Sharpen* has been selected from the menu, make sure the *Preview* checkbox is checked. This will apply the sharpening effect to the portion of the image visible on the screen (rather than just to the small preview window). Having the image displayed at 100% magnification is very helpful in fine-tuning the various parameters and noticing over-sharpening artifacts (such as halos or pronounced noise). If the image area exceeds your screen, you may still scroll around while the sharpening dialog is active to see the sharpening effects in other parts of the image. To do so, hold down the *Space bar* key and, with the mouse button pressed, drag the image to view the area(s) you wish to inspect.

## Amount and Radius

The *Amount* and *Radius* settings control the sharpening algorithm's edge detection and contrast enhancement. *Radius* controls the detection of edges by scanning the image and comparing the lightness of pixels within a circular area of the specified radius. When an area is found where pixels on one side of the circle are significantly lighter or darker than those on the other side of the circle, Photoshop will examine adjacent areas to determine if the same difference between adjacent pixels continues to form a line. If the *Radius* value is too small, the algorithm may miss some thicker lines; and if set too high, some finer/thinner lines may not be detected. As a starting point, I find that *Radius* values in the 0.5 to 1.5 range work well, but each image is unique.

Once edges are detected, the *Amount* setting determines the amount of contrast increase (the difference in lightness between the light and dark sides of the edge line) to apply. The higher the number, the more defined the lines will become. In most cases, the ideal setting is in the 200% to 400% range.

Note that the higher the *Radius* is set, the thicker the detected lines are assumed to be, which may cause the appearance of halos as *Amount* is increased.

## Reduce Noise

The *Reduce Noise* slider offers a way of reducing noise as part of the sharpening process. The reason is that, as we increase sharpness, noise becomes more visible and it is convenient to have a means of correcting it as it appears. However, since noise reduction, like sharpening, is often best applied as a local, rather than global, adjustment, I suggest that if noise is present, you cancel the sharpening operation and correct the noise as I describe in chapter 13 before attempting to sharpen again.

To determine if noise is problematic, I suggest setting the *Reduce Noise* slider to 0% to make the noise more visible.

### Remove Blur

The word *Remove* is a bit misleading here. *Smart Sharpen* uses a method similar to *Unsharp Mask*, using a slightly blurry version of the image to enhance the appearance of edges. Since lines in the blurry version are a bit thicker and "fuzzier," they create a slight halo along sharp edges (and, if applying too much blur, the halo effect may become unsightly).

While the *Unsharp Mask* algorithm uses the *Gaussian* blurring algorithm exclusively, *Smart Sharpen* also offers the options of *Lens Blur* and *Motion Blur*. *Motion Blur*, obviously, is only useful when motion blur is present. When selecting this option, *Smart Sharpen* lets you set the direction of the motion. *Lens Blur* is a finer blurring than *Gaussian Blur*, making it a better choice for digitally captured images, which tend to be cleaner and smoother than high-resolution film scans, where film grain is visible. Therefore, I recommend using *Lens Blur* as your default option.

### Shadows/Highlights

The *Shadows/Highlights* section of the *Smart Sharpen* dialog is usually collapsed by default, and I recommend leaving it that way. *Smart Sharpen* allows fading (reducing) the sharpening effect by different amounts in either the highlights or the shadows. The ability to apply different amounts of sharpening to shadows and highlights may be useful in images with noisy shadows (which we do not want to sharpen, or at least not as much as much as we may want to sharpen well-lit detail). While seemingly a useful function, it is a very poor substitute to applying noise reduction and sharpening manually as local adjustments, allowing us to decide what amount of sharpening is appropriate to what part of the image, regardless of whether the areas where sharpening is needed happen to be in the shadows or the highlights.

## Sharpening as a Local Adjustment

To apply sharpening in different amounts to different areas, we can use a method like the one I describe for noise reduction in chapter 13. That is, make a copy of the image layer, sharpen the copy, then add a mask to the sharpened layer so its effect can be blocked to varying degrees (or completely) from different parts of the image (figure 14.12).

To use *Smart Sharpen* as a local adjustment, follow these steps:

1. After applying noise reduction as needed and flattening the image, make a second copy of the image layer (by dragging the *Background*

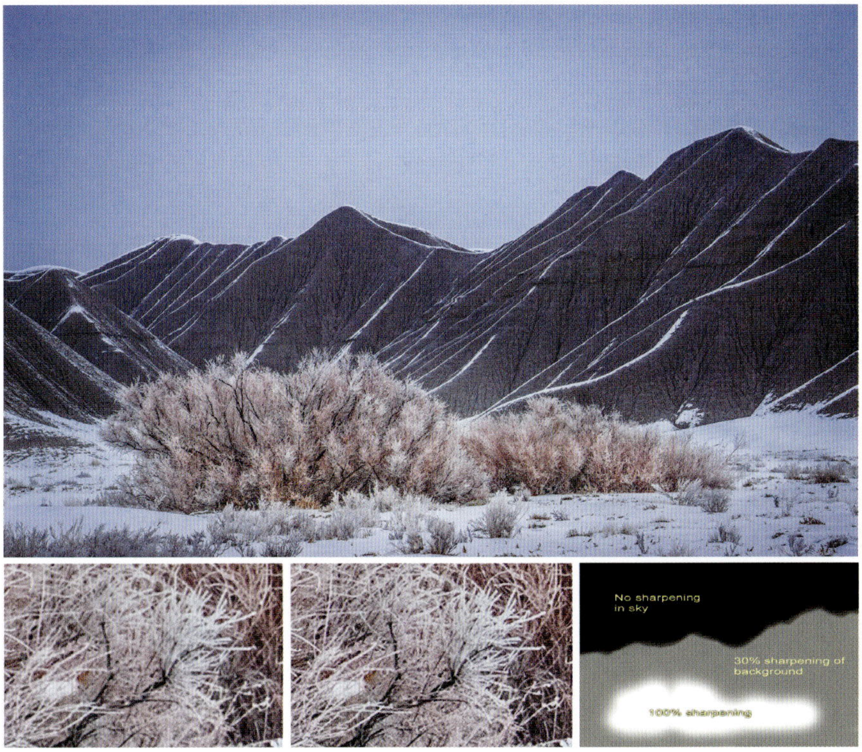


**Figure 14.12:** The image on top was resized for a large 60″x40″ print at 300 PPI. The original interpolated pixels (*bottom left*) show the blurring caused by stretching the image to this size. I made a copy of this layer and sharpened it with an *Amount* of 300% and a *Radius* of 1.2px (*bottom middle*). I then added a mask to the sharpened layer and painted it so no sharpening is applied to the sky, 30% of the sharpening effect is applied to the hills and snow (which had a bit of noise I did not want to exacerbate), and the full sharpening effect is applied to the tamarisk bush. I also created a 50% transition zone along the line separating the hills from the sky, to avoid the appearance of halos along the high-contrast edge between land and sky. The mask I ended up with is shown on the *bottom right*.

layer to the *Create a new layer* button, as shown in figure 13.8 in chapter 13).

2. Double-click the *Background copy* layer's name and give it a more descriptive title (e.g., "Sharpened copy").

3. Apply the *Smart Sharpen* filter as described above and tune the parameters to their optimal settings for the area(s) of the image that require the *most* sharpening. These will usually be areas of low contrast. Note that this may make areas of high contrast appear over-sharpened, but you may ignore that. Later, we will use a mask to remove the sharpening effect where it is not needed, or where a lower amount is needed.

   To optimize sharpening for where it is needed most, follow these steps:

   - Make sure the image is displayed at 100% magnification and that the layer titled *Sharpened copy* (or whatever you decided to name it) is selected.
   - Select *Smart Sharpen* from the *Filter* menu (under *Sharpen*) and make sure the *Preview* box is checked.

- Hold down the *Space bar* key and drag the image until the part of the image with the lowest contrast is visible.
- Tune the *Smart Sharpen* parameters as explained above until the desired area is properly sharpened. Ignore other areas that may appear overly sharpened.
- Click *OK*.

4. Add a layer mask to the sharpened layer and fill it with black, as explained in the *Managing Out-Of-Gamut Colors* section earlier in this chapter. This will hide the effect of this layer.
5. Change your foreground color to white, select the *Brush* tool and set the brush *Opacity* to 25%.
6. Paint over the mask in areas where you want to add sharpness. Repeated brushing has a cumulative effect so you may paint repeatedly to increase the sharpening effect where needed. Do not paint over areas where no sharpening is desired (such as sky or noisy shadows).

## To Save or Not to Save?

When explaining the targeting process in workshops, I'm often asked whether I save the targeted files in addition to the master files. The general answer is this: I do not. There are two exceptions to this rule: 1) Saving reduced versions for use on a website, in a slideshow, or to send over the Internet. 2) On the rare occasion that I prepare a file to be printed by a third party.

Other than these cases, I target the file in Photoshop, print it on my local printer, and when the print is ready and meets my expectations I close it without saving.

The reasons I don't bother saving my targeted files are as follows:

- Although the theory may take some time to learn, in practice targeting is not very time- or labor-intensive, and I can always recreate a targeted file from my master files quickly, rather than dedicate disk space to keep files I may rarely, if ever, need again.
- As my skills and sensibilities evolve over time, I almost always end up fine-tuning an image before printing it, rather than printing it the same way each time.

- As technology improves, new interpolation or sharpening methods may become available, which could produce better results than what was possible before.

## Preparing Internet Images

Preparing images for Internet use is among the simplest forms of output. Such images are optimized for sharing via the Internet, posting to a website, sending as an email attachment, or any other form that does not require making a hard copy and where we have no knowledge of, or control over, the screens used to view the image.

### Sizing Images for Internet Use

Since Internet images are displayed digitally, we generally have no control over their physical size. An image of a given pixel size may measure an inch or two when displayed on a mobile phone, or it may be several inches if displayed on a large desktop screen. When it comes to digital display, our concern is pixel size: how many pixels in height and how many pixels in width make up the image.

A typical high-end screen may support resolutions of 1,920×1,080 or 2,560×1,600, or thereabouts, meaning that the entire screen area can be filled with a 2- to 4-megapixel image. Some high definition monitors today, designated as 4K, 5K or even 8K (an approximation of the number of pixels on the long edge), can display full-resolution images from around 8 megapixels and upward of 30 megapixels; however, they employ various technologies to ensure consistency in size with screens of similar physical size and lower resolutions when browsing the Internet.

Considering the limitations of resolution and bandwidth, Internet images generally are sized from about 800 to 1,200 pixels on the long edge. This makes them appear sufficiently large on most current monitors, while keeping file size (and therefore download time) within reason.

Of the interpolation methods offered, *Bicubic Sharper* generally produces excellent reductions with crisp details, requiring little or no additional sharpening. I suggest trying it first. However, sharpening may also result in the appearance of unsightly halos along high-contrast edges. If this happens, I suggest using a different algorithm (such as *Bicubic* or even *Bicubic Smoother* in extreme cases), to reduce the appearance of halos, then selectively sharpening only those areas that require it.

## The sRGB Color Space

Other than being a standard color space supported by practically all screens, projectors, and scanners, sRGB is also the proposed standard color space for the Internet. This means that when a web browser or other Internet application does not (or cannot) detect a color profile associated with an image, it will assume the image is in the sRGB color space.

> **sRGB Profile Name**
>
> sRGB simply stands for *Standard Red, Green, Blue.* The International Electrotechnical Commission (IEC)—a standards organization based in Geneva, Switzerland—formalized the sRGB standard and gave it the designation "IEC 61966-2-1:1999," which is why it sometimes appears as: sRGB IEC61966-2.1.

sRGB is a unique color space in that it was created not to represent the capabilities of a specific device but rather to serve as a low common denominator for a variety of devices. This makes sRGB a handy color space to use when we know nothing about, or have no control over, the screens used to display our images, which is usually the case when we post an image to a website, and most often the case when we send images via email.

Converting an image to sRGB can be accomplished explicitly using the *Convert to Profile* option in the *Edit* menu, as described above, or, you may prefer to use Photoshop's *Export As* function in the *File* menu (figure 14.13) to both convert the image to sRGB and to save it in any of several formats.

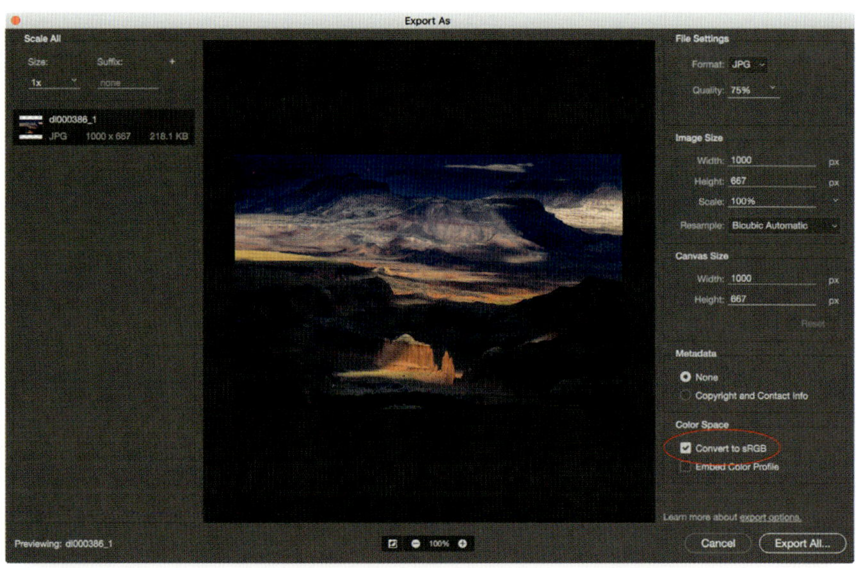


FIGURE 14.13: Photoshop's *Export As* dialog allows exporting images for a variety of uses and is useful when saving images for the Internet. I recommend not using it to resize images, as this is better accomplished as described earlier in the book. However, note the ability to convert to sRGB on the fly (circled in red), and to save the image with limited metadata in case you don't want viewers to be able to extract such information as keywords and GPS coordinates from the EXIF data.

For web images, I recommend using JPEG with a *Quality* setting of 75% to 80%, which is more than sufficient for most uses and produces a reasonably sized file.

## Printing

Printing generally requires much larger files than we need for Internet sharing. Also, the gamut of colors reproducible in ink on paper is different (usually much smaller) than what is possible on a device that generates its own light, such as a screen (figure 14.14).

A print's color space is determined by both the printer's capabilities (the range of colors it can produce using its ink set) and the characteristics of the paper used: colors that may be possible when printing on a coated glossy paper, for example, may not be available when printing on matte paper, canvas, or other materials.

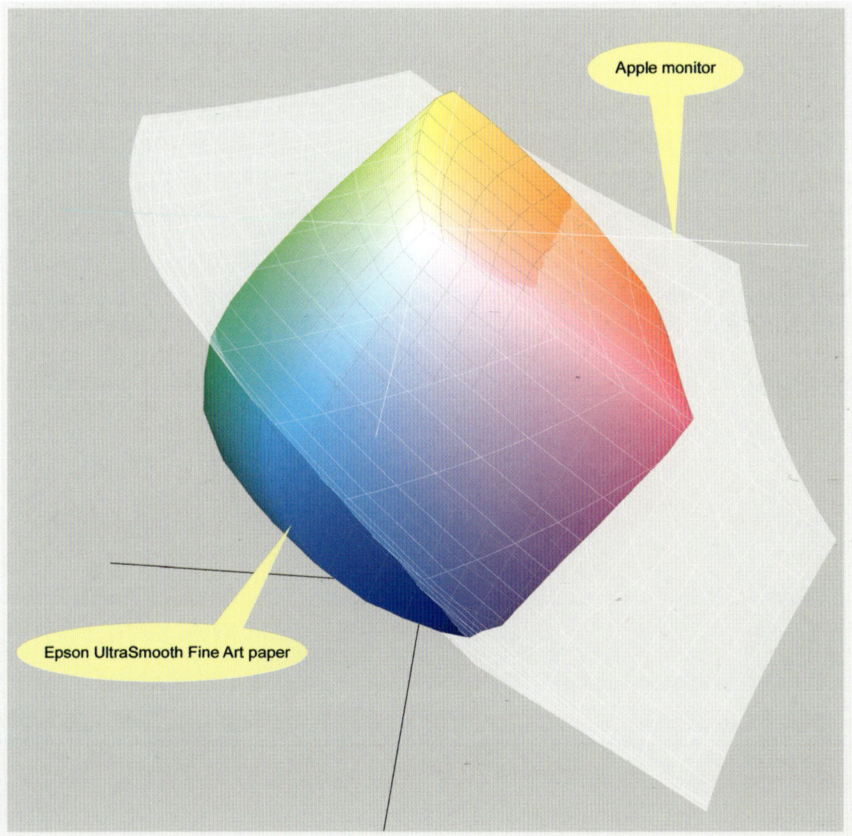


FIGURE 14.14: The color space for Epson UltraSmooth Fine Art paper (using an Epson 3880 printer), rendered in color against the color space of my Apple monitor (gray), shows that the monitor is capable of much more vibrant greens, reds, and magentas than the paper, but falls short of being able to reproduce the saturated yellows and blues possible using Epson's inks with this paper.

Printer and paper manufacturers provide ICC profiles for their products. These profiles are often quite accurate but not perfect. Given the low cost of purchasing custom printer profiles, it's hard to argue against having them produced for your own personal printer and favorite papers, rather than using generic profiles.

If you send your files to a lab for printing, ask for their custom profiles so you can soft-proof your files and, if desired, manage out-of-gamut colors to fit your taste before sending the files. Note that some labs may be reluctant to provide their profiles and will ask you to just send the file, in whatever color space it happens to be, so they can handle the conversion themselves. That usually works out well but, being very particular about my prints, I would not use a lab that will not provide me a soft-proofing profile.

Beware of labs that ask you to convert your images to generic small-gamut color spaces, such as sRGB. These labs target inexperienced photographers and cut costs by using a low common denominator, which will often not get the most out of the printer's capabilities, as illustrated in figure 14.15. My

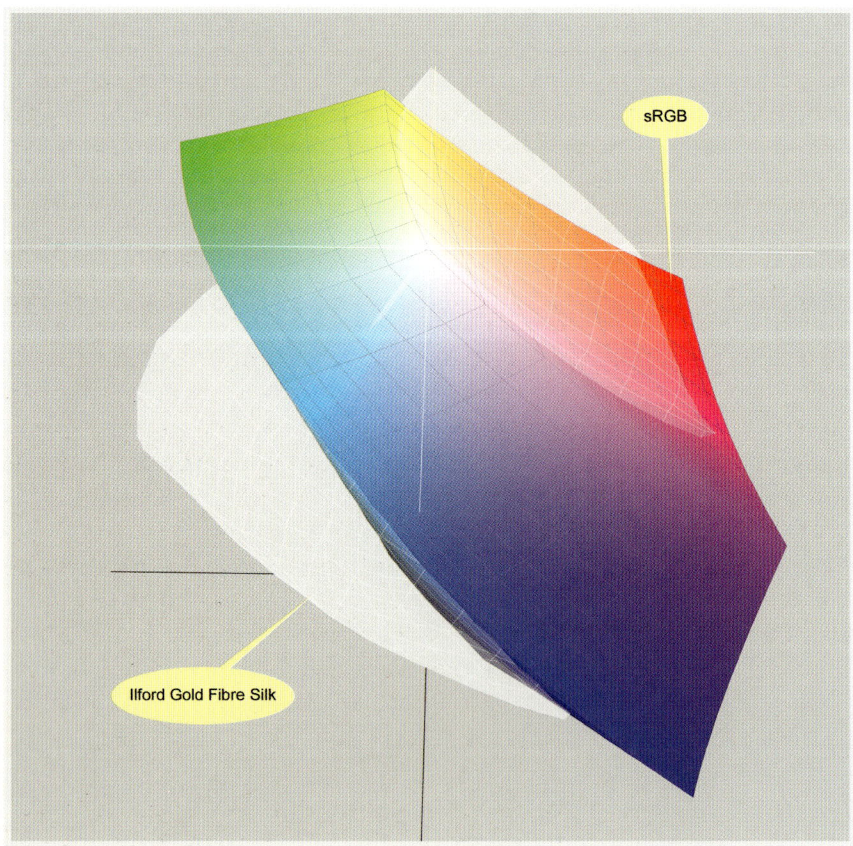


**Figure 14.15:** The sRGB color space shown in color against the color space of Ilford Gold Fibre Silk paper when used with an Epson 3880 printer (in gray). Note that if the image was converted to sRGB prior to printing, some colors (such as saturated oranges or cyans) that may have been present in the image and reproducible on the paper, may have been discarded, while some colors (saturated blues, reds, greens) in sRGB exceed the capabilities of the paper and will not reproduce as they appear on screen.

advice is this: if a print lab insists that you provide them with files in sRGB, find a different lab.

## What Makes a Fine Print?

Before jumping into the technical aspects of printing, it is important to establish a definition for *fine printing*, as distinguished from the common push-button automated printing functions available in most computer applications, such as word processors or others.

A fine print is primarily one that represents the photographer's subjective sensibilities and style. The immediate implication is that the photographer makes subjective choices, both aesthetic (color, tone, contrast) and technical (size, sharpness, choice of materials), regarding every aspect of the print. Such direct control also personalizes and elevates the value of the work as a product of the artist rather than one created by a technician or generated by a machine.

A fine print is not merely the transference of an image onto paper but is a unique rendition of that image. Just like a great photograph is more than just "a picture of" something, so is a print more than just "a paper copy of" something. Instead, the print possesses its own characteristics, aesthetics, and values ensuing out of the photographer's mind and skill, independent of the subjects portrayed or the technical details of its creation.

It is important to distinguish the role of the computer and printer in making the print from that of the photographer. In the digital studio, the computer and printer are no different in function from the chemicals, trays, drums, thermometer, and timer found in a traditional darkroom: they are means to an end. By themselves, the computer and printer don't make fine prints; rather, they act as extensions of the photographer's creative mind to be skillfully controlled, manipulated, and instructed to do his bidding.

Other than materials and techniques, perhaps the greatest difference between digital and traditional processes is the computer's ability to be programmed to perform complex operations and even to make informed decisions on the photographer's behalf. Still, it is the photographer's duty to decide which aspects of the print to control versus those that do not require creative decision-making and can be left to the computer. In the balance between automation and manual control, the most personal and meaningful creations are those where automation is kept to a minimum.

Considerations generally associated with fine printing include:

- **Permanence:** Sometimes described in terms of *archivability, durability,* or *lightfastness*, referring to the print's ability to maintain its appearance (color, tone, contrast) over time and to resist fading or discoloration. Present day pigment-based photographic printers, when used with archival paper, produce prints that may resist fading for upward of 100 years.

- **Impeccability:** Freedom from defects and undesired artifacts, such as banding, posterization, halos, and others; exhibiting proper sharpness, continuity of tone, and fidelity to the photographer's visualization.
- **Personalization:** The degree to which the print is directly associated with its creator. Personalization is manifested not only in the photographer's direct control over the printing process but also in such things as uniqueness, continued refinement, the artist's signature, and choice of presentation.

## Printer Types

Photographic printers come in various flavors, each with its own distinguishing characteristics. Printers can render images on paper in various ways. Among these ways are:

- Painting the image onto the paper's surface using microscopic drops of ink. This method is known as either *inkjet* or *giclée* (pronounced "zhee-clay") printing.
- Exposing light-sensitive (chromogenic) paper using very accurate light sources, such as laser beams or tiny light-emitting diodes (LEDs). The exposed paper is then chemically developed, the same as it would be in traditional darkroom processes.
- Using heat to transfer dyes onto paper or other materials. This process is known as *Dye Sublimation* (or dye-sub, for short).

## Inkjet Printers

Inkjet printers are the most popular and widely available photographic printers. They come in a variety of sizes, from small desktop models capable of making letter-size (8.5"×11") or A4 (210mm×297mm) prints, all the way to commercial wide-format printers, as much as 64 inches in width.

Other than their size, inkjet printers are also distinguishable by their ink sets (the type and number of inks they use). Ink sets generally come in two varieties:

- **Pigment:** Pigments are insoluble, meaning they don't dissolve in liquid but are suspended in it. Once the liquid evaporates, the pigment will remain on the paper and won't smear if accidentally moistened. This characteristic of pigments makes for very stable prints. Pigment-based inks also have excellent archival qualities.
- **Dye:** Dye-based inks are water-soluble, meaning that your print will be susceptible to damage from moisture and will smear if wet. Dye inks are considered to have a slightly wider color gamut than pigments, although their archival qualities fall short.

  Some specialized technologies exist to make dye-based prints more archival by sealing the dyes into specially coated "swellable" paper. These technologies (e.g., *HP's Vivera* dye inks) result in beautiful prints, but they severely limit available paper choices. On the other hand, pigment ink sets have now advanced to a point where any gamut differences between them and dyes are practically negligible.

As a general recommendation, archival pigment ink sets (such as *Epson's Ultrachrome K3, Canon's Lucia,* or *HP's Vivera* pigment inks) are your best choices for producing archival digital prints and for having the widest available selections of papers and other substrates to choose from.

Different manufacturers offer different numbers of individual inks in their photographic printers. Some may use as few as six or eight, while others may go as high as twelve. While it may seem logical to assume that more inks translate into better tonality (more discrete shades), this is not always the case.

There is, however, one reason to favor larger numbers of inks, which is this: the number of neutral (black or gray) inks within the set is usually an indicator of the printer's ability to produce smooth tonality in black-and-white prints. If you plan to make fine art black-and-white prints, you may want to favor printers offering three or more gradations of neutral inks over those that offer just one or two.

Another point worth considering is the printer's ability to switch between photo (glossy) and matte black inks. Pure black is an especially important ink, as the success of many prints relies on the depth and purity of their blacks. To render very dark blacks, glossy coated papers require a different type of black ink than matte papers. Many printers can switch between photo black and matte black inks automatically. However, some models require the user to make the switch manually, often involving significant waste as the black ink line needs to be flushed and replenished with new ink each time. For the greatest efficiency and economy, I recommend selecting a printer that can house both photo and matte blacks simultaneously and can handle the switching automatically.

Since inkjet printers form an image by placing microscopic drops of individual inks onto the paper, they are not capable of true continuous tone (seamless transition from one tone to the next). Inks cannot be mixed to form new colors. Instead, the printer uses a technique known as *dithering*—arranging tiny drops of different inks in patterns that are too fine to be resolved by eye—to achieve the *appearance* of smooth transitions.

Dithering used to be a point of concern in the early days of photographic inkjet printing because the technology was not yet capable of rendering small enough ink drops to make dithering patterns completely invisible. Current printer models, however, boast sufficiently high resolutions so that their dithering patterns appear completely seamless to the human eye. Indeed, you will need to view the print under a powerful magnifying glass or a microscope to see dithering.

Inkjet print permanence varies significantly based on the characteristics of the ink set and paper used. Pigment-based ink sets offer the greatest longevity, sometimes rating up to 200 years when properly finished and presented. Dye inks, on the other hand, generally rate up to 20–25 years.

### Chromogenic Printers

Printers exposing photo-sensitive paper are not suitable for home use, and generally are only offered by commercial printing services. Their size and operation require a significant amount of space, bulk-purchased chemistry, and well-trained engineers.

Chromogenic printers do have some advantages over inkjets, primarily because they offer true continuous tone and don't require the use of dithering.

Inside the printer, laser beams or very accurate LEDs are used with extreme precision to expose photographic paper. The exposed paper is then developed using traditional chemistry to fix the image.

Some common chromogenic printers are: Lightjet, made by Océ Display Graphics Systems (now owned by Canon); Chromira, made by ZBE (figure 14.16); and Durst Lambda, owned by Kodak.

A potential downside to these printers, other than the need to send your work to a lab rather than printing it yourself, is the relatively limited selection of papers available for them. On the other hand, some types of paper, such as Fuji Crystal Archive and Kodak Endura, can be used only in chromogenic printers and are not available to inkjet printers. If you are a fan of these specific papers, a chromogenic print is your only option.

Chromogenic prints are generally rated to last around 40 years when properly presented and finished.

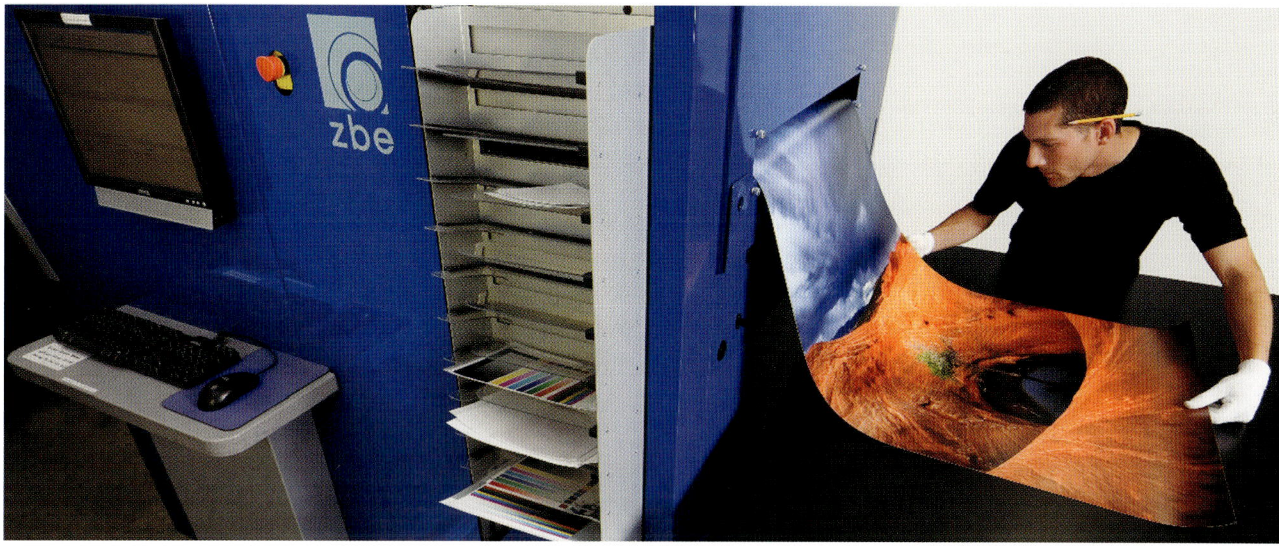


FIGURE 14.16: Bojh Parker inspecting a print of one of my images as it emerges from a ZBE Chromira chromogenic printer owned by Metal & Paper—an excellent professional lab in Oakhurst, California (metalandpaper.photo).

## Dye Sublimation Printers

Dye-sublimation, or dye-sub, printers used to be a mainstay of commercial photo labs. Today, most have converted to inkjet printers, which are less expensive and easier to operate.

Like their chromogenic brethren, dye-sub printers offer continuous tone printing and do not use dithering.

As the name suggests, dye-sub printers use dyes, which are water-soluble. To protect the print from moisture, most dye-sub printers apply a clear protective layer to the paper as part of the printing process. This layer offers a degree of water resistance. However, the coating tends to be brittle and does not provide very robust protection. Dye-sub prints should be handled with great care to avoid damaging their protective coating.

In terms of print permanence, dye-sub prints generally rank below both inkjet and chromogenic prints and are rated to last between 4–25 years when properly displayed.

## Under the Hood

Most applications offer simple and easy-to-use printing functionality. While suitable for text or the modest image printing needs of most users, these rudimentary functions are not sufficient to control all aspects of fine printing. To simplify life for most users, many of the controls needed to manage accurate color, print resolution, paper handling, and page layout are either automated or, at best, placed in a separate "advanced" section of the printer driver.

To get the most out of your printer and to preempt common problems, it is useful to understand how Photoshop "talks" to your printer and how your image (represented as an array of RGB values) gets translated into drops of ink, sublimated dyes, or the colors of laser beams exposing photographic paper.

Let's start on the printer end and work our way backward. The printer is a complex machine with many moving parts. For the sake of this discussion, let's assume we are making an inkjet print. Gears and rollers handle accurate feeding and advancement of paper; belts and pulleys transport the print head back and forth with extreme precision; and tiny pumps and nozzles feed a variety of inks to the print head, placing each drop on the paper at precisely the right spot. The printer has its own little computerized brain controlling every function to make sure they all operate in perfect unison. Each printer's computer, however, is a little different and "speaks" its own proprietary language. The computer built into a Canon printer, for example, will not be able to make sense of the data formats needed by, say, an Epson or an HP printer. For your computer to communicate with the printer, it needs a way of translating image data into the printer's native language.

In theory, application developers can write code to talk directly to the printer (and some do, creating specialized proprietary applications known as Raster Image Processors, or RIPs for short), but the need to support a myriad of different printer models makes this a daunting proposition. Having to communicate directly with the printer, using its proprietary data formats and communication protocol, also will likely result in some applications supporting some printers and not others, making it difficult for users to find software that supports the printer they happen to own.

Instead, applications wishing to send data to the printer "talk" to the computer's operating system, rather than directly to the printer. Operating systems control many low-level functions, among them communications with various peripheral devices, including printers. Application developers, therefore, only need to know how to send print data to one (or a handful of) operating system(s) to access any kind of printer compatible with that operating system.

Operating systems do not know how to control every function of every printer from every manufacturer. (Imagine if Apple or Microsoft had to update their operating systems every time a new printer model is introduced.) Instead, operating system manufacturers use a standard format for print data and provide this format's specifications to every printer manufacturer who wishes to have their products supported. The printer manufacturer then has the responsibility to translate the common format into its printers' native language. This translation occurs in a software component called a printer driver. Once a printer driver is installed on your system, any application can use it to access that printer.

Like any communication where intermediaries are involved, sometimes things get lost or changed in translation, which is perhaps the primary cause for printing-related issues.

Since the printer driver does most of the translation, it is also the prime suspect when things go awry. If troubleshooting is needed, always start by making sure you have the most recent version of the driver (usually available from your printer manufacturer's website) before pursuing other possible causes for printing problems.

The most common challenge for photographic printing is color management. Most imaging applications offer color management functionality, as do most operating systems and printer drivers. The primary reason for color mismatches in print is having too many components trying to decide how color values in the image should appear in print. There can only be one "color boss" managing color, and for our purposes we want to make sure this boss is Photoshop. This means we need to make sure color management is turned off in the printer driver and that the *Photoshop Manages Colors* option is selected in the *Color Handling* menu (more about this in the "Color Management for Printing" section below).

Printer drivers are proprietary components and the driver for one printer may appear very different from a driver for other printers. Be sure to find out how to turn color management off in the driver for your printer (figure 14.17).

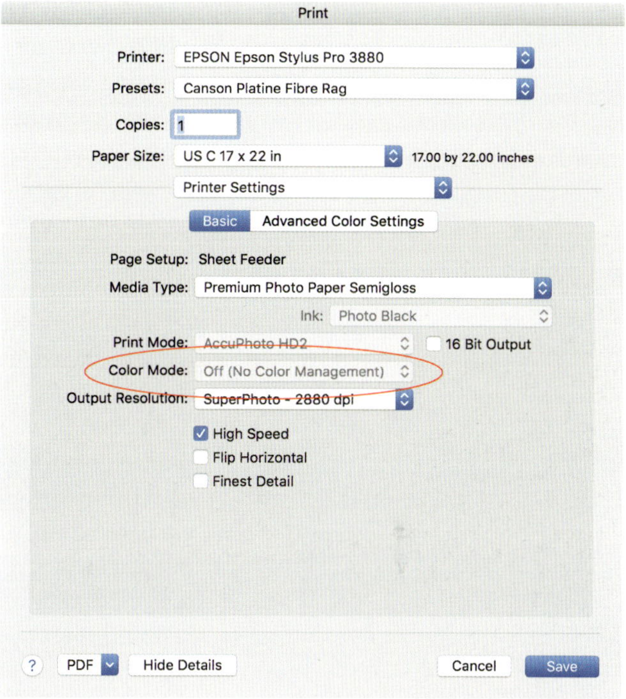


**Figure 14.17:** The *Color Mode* menu in the Epson 3880 printer driver for Apple OS X allows turning color management off. To avoid unexpected color management problems, make sure to find out how to turn color management off in the driver for your printer and operating system.

## Sizing for Printing

Digital images are measured in pixels. A pixel doesn't have consistent physical dimensions—its physical size is determined by the output device. Prints, on the other hand, are measured in physical units such as inches or centimeters. When setting out to make a print, we already know what its dimensions should be, but need to decide on the optimal print resolution: how many pixels to cram into a given unit of physical space.

The physical dimensions, the original pixel size, the type of printer used, and the way the print will be presented should all be accounted for when deciding what print resolution is best.

The inevitable question is this: "How many pixels per inch (PPI) are required to produce a sharp-looking print?" The answer is not as straightforward as you may think.

For purposes of estimation, consider that the human eye can resolve between 5 and 10 line pairs per millimeter (lp/mm) when looking at resolution charts consisting of alternating black and white lines ("pair" here refers to adjacent black and white lines). This translates to about 250–500 PPI. Indeed, the industry standard for commercial printing of photographs is 300 PPI, falling squarely within this range.

In theory, we want to make all our prints at 300 PPI or higher, making them appear sharp whether viewed up close or from a distance. However, given that we are limited by the number of pixels captured by the camera, this is not always possible. Indeed, to have the exact number of pixels needed for a given size print is unlikely. In almost every case we either have too many pixels or too few, requiring some amount of interpolation.

Interpolation is a necessary evil: it degrades the image to make it fit within desired dimensions. Therefore, we want to keep interpolation to a minimum, which dictates the following rules of thumb:

- When enlarging an image (adding pixels), we want to use the lowest print resolution possible that will still result in a sharp print. If we add pixels beyond that, we degrade the image further without any real advantage.
- When reducing an image, we want to use the highest resolution the printer is capable of, so we retain as many of the original pixels as possible (or, conversely, we discard as few of the original pixels as necessary).

For example, let's assume my camera captures images sized 3000×2000 pixels, and I want to make a 12"×18" print. And let's also assume that my printer is capable of printing at either 300 PPI or 200 PPI.

If I use 300 PPI, I need to enlarge the original file to 5400×3600 pixels, which is 3.24 times larger than the original capture (try to work out the math yourself to make sure you understand why).

However, if I use 200 PPI, the image will need to be enlarged to 3600×2400 pixels, which is only 1.44 times larger than the original capture.

Enlarging the file to 3.24 times its original size requires a lot more interpolation (i.e., manufacturing new pixels) than enlarging it to just 1.44 times its original size. Therefore, in this case, using 200 PPI rather than 300 PPI will result in a better print. The fact that this number falls slightly outside the optimal range for sharp prints does not matter, since manufacturing more new pixels will not make the image any more detailed. Also, generally speaking, the larger the print, the greater the viewing distance will be, which reduces the eye's ability to resolve fine details, so a print can still be made to appear sharp at lower resolutions.

If I want to make a 4"×6" print from the same file, using a resolution of 300 PPI requires reducing the image to 1800×1200 pixels, corresponding to a reduction of 64% from the original size. At 200 PPI, on the other hand, the output file will need to measure just 1200×800 pixels, representing a reduction of 84% from the original size.

Reducing a file by 64% requires less interpolation than reducing it by 84%; so, in the case of reduction in size, using the higher print resolution (300 PPI) will result in a better print.

I mentioned that the human visual system can resolve 5–10 lp/mm when using a resolution chart of black and white line pairs. This is true at normal reading distance. The resolution declines dramatically as viewing distance increases, and when colors and tones other than pure black and pure white are used. No human can resolve 5–10 lp/mm when looking at a photograph from a few feet away. Therefore, prints can still look sharp in many uses even at lower resolutions than 300 PPI.

When enlarging a file for a print that will be presented in a home or a gallery, where it will be viewed from a few feet away, it is safe to use a print resolution in the 150–250 PPI range. For large prints that will be viewed from a considerable distance (e.g., wall-sized murals hanging in a large hall), print resolutions of 50–100 PPI are often sufficient. And for prints that will be viewed from a very long distance (hundreds of feet or more), such as billboards or on the sides of buildings, even resolutions as low as 10–20 PPI still work well.

In addition to the above, some characteristics of the image should also be accounted for. All other factors being equal, very detailed images may not withstand as much enlargement as ones consisting of large smooth areas. And of course, well-focused and noise-free images will retain the appearance of sharpness at higher enlargement ratios better than images suffering from lack of focus (or other reasons for blurry detail) and/or pronounced noise or grain.

## Native Printer Resolutions

I mention above that the industry standard for image printing is 300 PPI. Indeed, most publications and commercial labs will ask you to size your output files to this print resolution prior to submitting them.

Interpolation is applied not only when preparing the file for printing, but also internally by the printer. This is especially true for inkjet printers that need to translate the PPI resolution to the appropriate number of ink droplets produced by the print head (measured in dots per inch, or DPI).

For example, at the time of this writing, most Epson printers use print heads capable of printing 1,440 or 2,880 DPI. (In other words, the print head can squeeze either 1,440 or 2,880 droplets of ink into a single inch.) For files printed at 300 PPI, the printer will, theoretically, need to use 9.6 droplets for each pixel (= 2,880/300). However, the printer cannot create a fraction of a drop and will need to interpolate the file internally so it can use whole numbers. In the case of Epson printers, supported native resolutions are 180 PPI, 240 PPI, and 360 PPI, which allow the use of whole numbers of droplets at either 1,440 DPI or 2,880 DPI. Therefore, files sized for printing on Epson printers should use one of the natively supported resolutions to avoid additional interpolation by the printer.

Most photographic printers from Canon and HP have print resolutions allowing for 200 PPI or 300 PPI to be used without interpolation.

Chromogenic printers, such as Lightjet, Lambda, and Chromira, also do well at 300 PPI or 200 PPI, although they still may apply some internal algorithms to enhance resolution. For example, Chromira printers use a proprietary algorithm to generate an output resolution of 425 PPI, while Lightjet printers use resolutions of 304.8 PPI or 406 PPI (corresponding to 6 lp/mm and 8 lp/mm, respectively). Since these printers are capable of continuous tone, they are not restricted by ink drop size. These internal conversions are applied to optimize output to the printer's proprietary technology and, while interesting to note, they are generally outside the control of the photographer.

## Sharpening for Enlargement

While the selective sharpening method I describe earlier in the chapter works well when sharpening for printing, and especially when the original image size needs to be reduced to accommodate a small print, there are some cases in which additional steps may be desirable.

When enlarging images, the interpolation algorithms are unable to magically add detail that is not in the original capture. Instead, these algorithms stretch the image to accommodate the new desired dimensions.

As I mention, sharpening is a perception based on detail, which we cannot add, and acutance (edge contrast), which we can enhance. Therefore, the better-defined the edges in the image appear before stretching them, the better defined they will be after stretching them, too, making the image appear sharper. Any "fuzziness" present in the image will also become exaggerated when interpolating an image to a larger size.

Sharpening an image prior to enlarging it goes by a few names. Some refer to it as *pre-sharpening*, or as *capture sharpening*.

Just like edges stretch out when enlarging an image, so does noise, potentially making it more visible. Therefore, I recommend performing a round of noise reduction, and very light sharpening before enlarging an image. Figure 14.18 illustrates the difference.

Some advocate applying sharpening when converting an image from the RAW capture, but I don't. Sharpening may make the master file appear snappier but it also degrades data that may be important when the image is later resized.

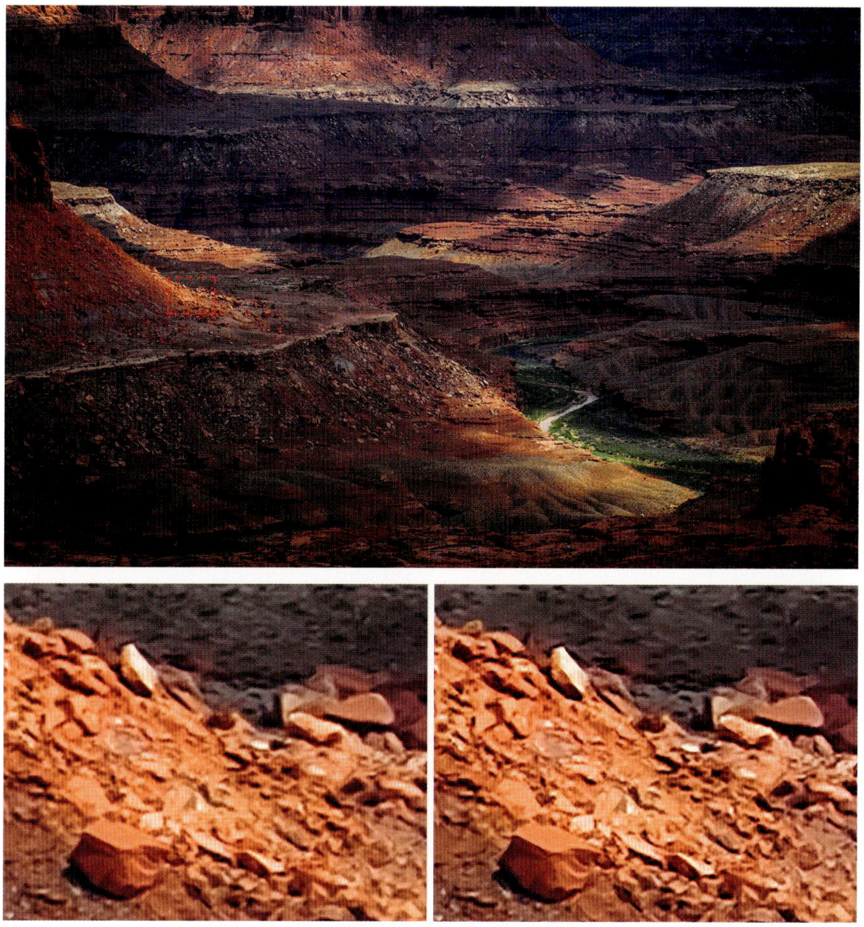

**FIGURE 14.18:** The image on top was made with a 16-megapixel camera and enlarged to make a 60"×40" print. Enlarging the image using the *Preserve Details* algorithm alone (*bottom left*) produced acceptable results. However, when I applied very slight noise reduction (*Strength:* 3, *Preserve Details:* 50%) and sharpening (*Smart Sharpen, Amount:* 50, *Radius:* 1) before enlarging, edge contrast post-enlargement is much more defined, with almost no loss of details (*bottom right*), resulting in a sharper-looking print.

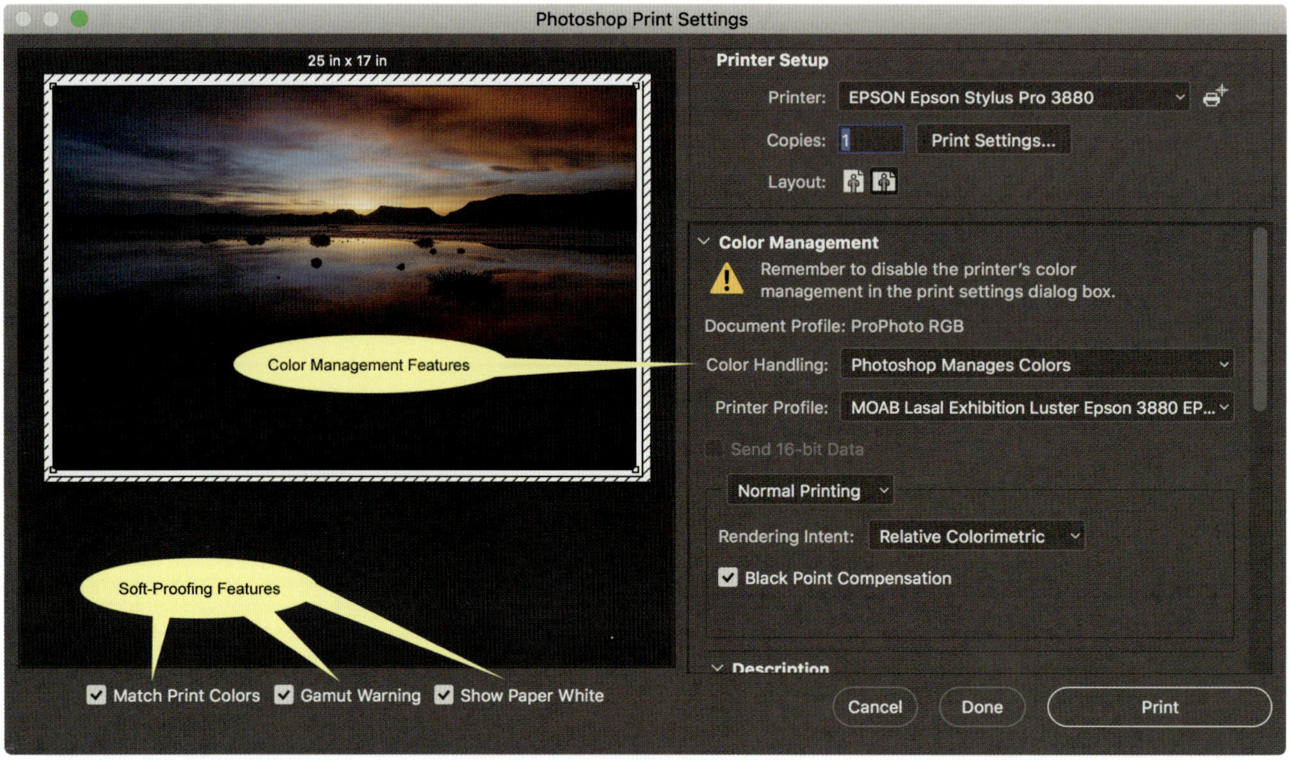


FIGURE 14.19: The *Print* dialog offers access to printer settings, color management, gamut warnings, and a host of other useful functions.

## Color Management for Printing

In addition to the color management measures already described, Photoshop offers useful and easily accessible color management features, including final soft-proofing, in its *Print* dialog (figure 14.19), accessible from the *File* menu.

Clicking the *Print Settings* button offers access to such parameters as paper size, as well as functions provided in the printer driver, such as color management, and printer-specific functions.

The *Print* dialog can also be used for scaling (resizing) and other operations, although I recommend using the methods described earlier in the book, rather than attempting to resize the image at this stage.

Be sure to select *Photoshop Manages Colors* from the *Color Handling* menu. This makes Photoshop the color boss, rather than allowing the printer driver or other components to attempt to manage color. Since we made all our color corrections and proofing in Photoshop, it makes sense to let Photoshop remain in charge.

When the three soft-proofing checkboxes are checked, pay attention to any gamut warnings (gray areas) that might appear in the preview window. If any warnings exist, cancel the printing and correct them as described earlier in this chapter.

If you followed my directions for manually managing out-of-gamut colors, be sure to select *Relative Colorimetric* as your rendering intent. Since all colors should be in-gamut at this point, this rendering intent will simply preserve colors as they appear, rather than attempt to remap them.

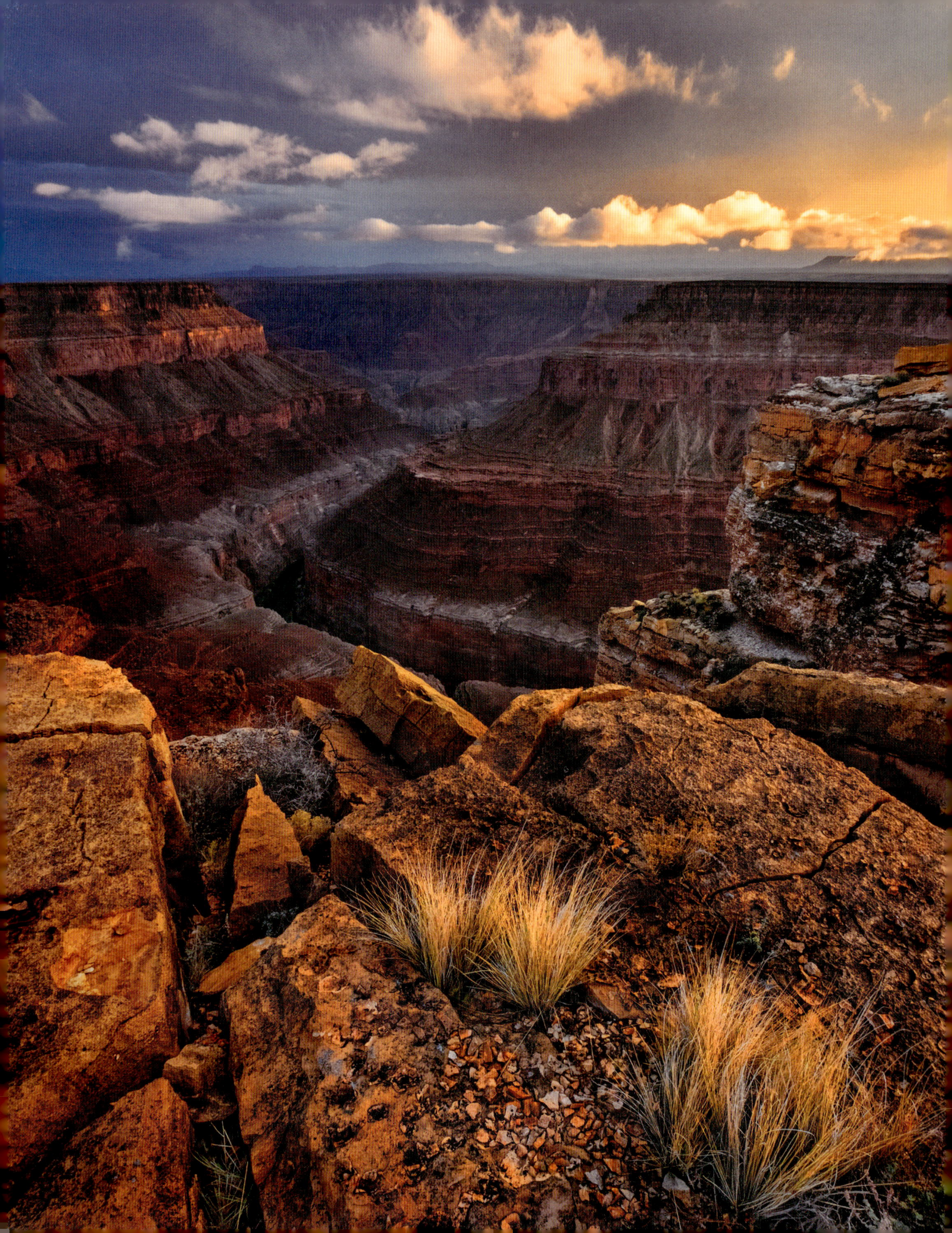

# 15

# Putting It All Together

> *But to put into expressive form the qualities of the natural world and its significance to humanity requires a very special technique, craft, and sensibility—also a great compassion.*
>
> —ANSEL ADAMS

Now that we covered both theory and practice in some detail, let's look at a real-world example.

When used as a medium for making creative, artistic images, it is important to approach the technical aspects of photography, as well as aesthetic characteristics of the subject or scene photographed, as means to an expressive end. Therefore, I place great emphasis on the inner experience I wish to express and to evoke in my viewers. Without having such an experience and making it the explicit goal for an image, we may end up with images that are aesthetically pleasing but that are devoid of meaning. Such images are often referred to as "eye candy," which is an excellent metaphor as such images, like candy, can be momentarily satisfying but do not nourish the viewer. In fact, when consumed in abundance, they may overwhelm the senses to a point of desensitization.

Therefore, in this example, pay attention not just to the techniques applied, but also (and especially) to the thought process and methods I employ to make the work emotionally and intellectually engaging. As I describe my approach, take from it what you find useful, but if your sensibilities call for other means of relating to, and finding purpose in, making an image, use what works for you. Among the many benefits of practicing expressive art are the things you learn, or acknowledge, about yourself in the process of creating.

In particular—and this may be a hard pill for some to swallow—make it your goal not to (just) portray appearances, but to also overlay appearances with a subjective message or story, or even an abstract emotion. In the words of painter Georges Braque, "The goal is not to be concerned with the reconstitution of an anecdotal fact, but with the constitution of a pictorial fact." You are not offering testimony to the existence of something, you are bringing something into existence—something that did not exist before, and that would not exist if it were not for you.

## Preparation

When setting out to process a meaningful image, and before delving into technical minutiae, I recommend taking a few moments to reconnect with the emotional state and the expressive intent you felt when you were moved to capture the image in the first place.

The greatest pleasures to be found when immersing ourselves in creative work are only possible when approaching the work with the right attitude and state of mind, with seriousness and with dignity. If you are short on time, unable to isolate yourself for a period, or are not feeling up to the task of investing your whole attention in processing your work, I suggest waiting for a more auspicious time.

Set up your environment so you are comfortable. If desired, play music or pour a drink. Breathe slowly and deeply to relax your mind and body. Now sit back and look at your image on the screen for a few moments, making it the focus of your attention.

Try to project yourself back in time. Think of the day you made the image—the events, thoughts, and feelings leading up to the moment you decided to reach for the camera. Recall the experience in all its dimensions: sounds, scents, temperature, light, who was with you (if anyone), and your feelings for the place and for any events unfolding in your life at the time.

Now recall your visualization of the finished image. Ask yourself if it is still worthy of expression, or, if otherwise inspired, revisualize the image in a new way. Whatever outcome you wish to pursue, make it as clear and vivid in your mind as possible. This visualized image will drive your decisions from this point on, until it becomes a reality on your screen.

## Visualization

The image in figure 15.1 was captured late in the morning on a cold December day. Winters in these parts are quiet, lonesome, and cold. I was struggling with an illness and not feeling well for some time, but I knew how rewarding it could be to commune with wild things, so I headed to a favorite canyon to spend a few solitary days among the red rocks and cottonwood trees, in search of inspiration and healing.

To better articulate the things I wish to express, I find that writing about an experience before I start processing an image helps me become conscious of bits and aspects of the experience that I would not have been able to recall otherwise. Following is a small blurb I wrote to help me revisualize the experience of capturing this image, how I intended it to appear, and the things I wished for it to express:

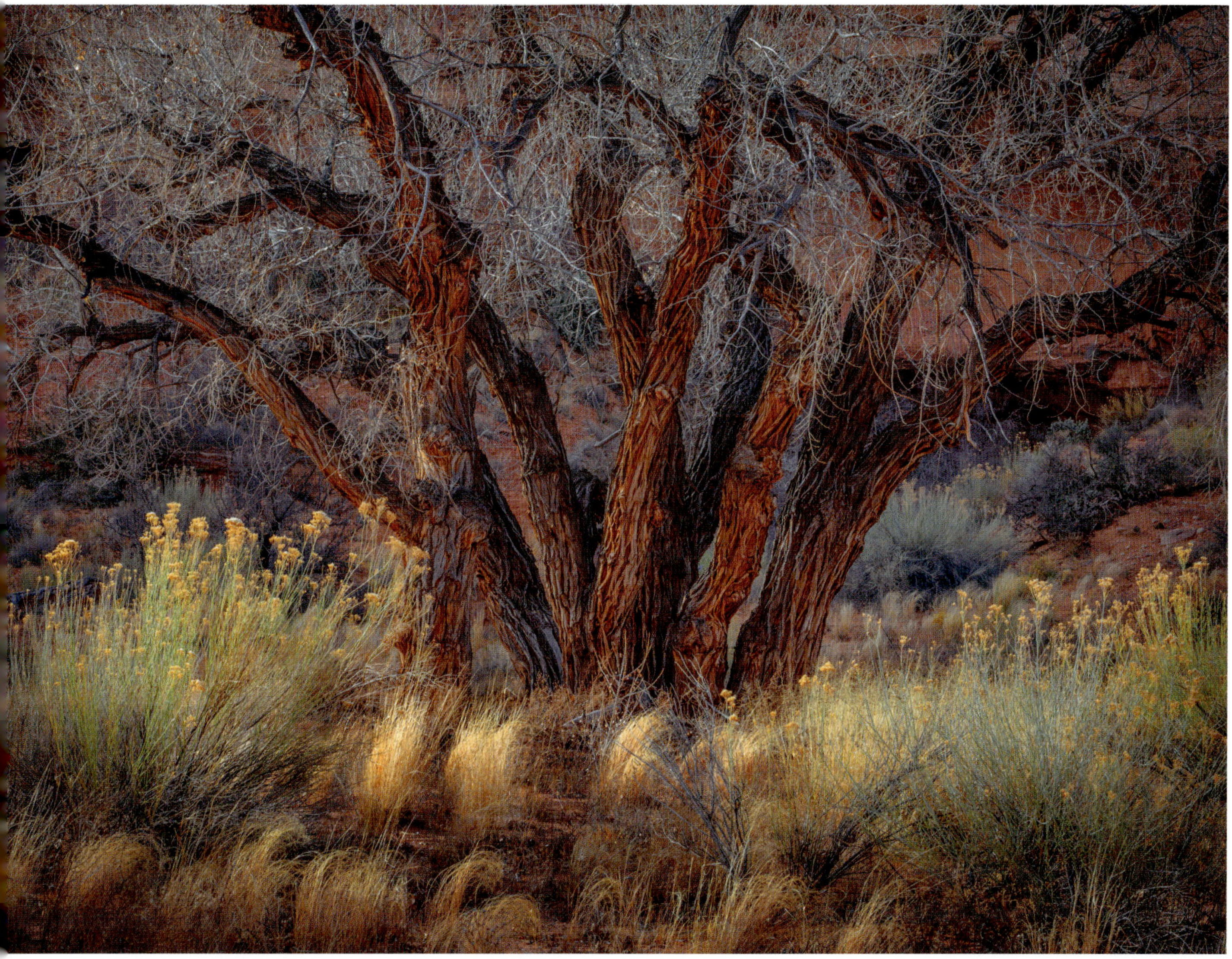

*The day was partly cloudy and very cold. Every so often, the sun—hanging low in the winter sky—peeked through the clouds for a short period, lighting the areas along the middle of the canyon, but never the canyon wall, which receives no direct sunlight at all this time of year. The glowing grasses, juxtaposed against the grooved trunk of a dormant old cottonwood tree, and flanked by a vermillion sandstone cliff in blue shade, stopped me in my tracks and sent my heart soaring. I stood there for a bit, appreciating the sunlight on my face, knowing the clouds would soon obscure it.*

FIGURE 15.1: The image as I visualized it, inspired by my wintry canyon experience, produced from my master file to fit the physical size of this book, and the color gamut of the paper this page is printed on. As I explain below, there were some nuances of the image that I visualized while processing it.

> *I decided to make an image. I wanted to convey the warm glow of the soft winter light while retaining some of the cold, icy, wintry mood. I also wanted to relay something of my mood, contemplating both the joy of the moment and the melancholy of my illness.*

As is evident from looking at the default rendition of the RAW file (figure 15.2), contrast was significantly higher than I would have liked, and a few errant branches added an unwanted distraction, but I knew I could address these in processing. If I waited for the light to soften, I would have lost the golden hues in the vegetation. My visualized image, therefore, was quite a bit different from the way the camera "saw" the scene.

With the visualized image clear in my mind, these are the notes I made while still at the scene:

- Although the scene possesses a great variety of colors, the two colors I wish to emphasize more than others are the warm gold in the glowing grasses and the cool blue in the shadows. Not only do these colors convey the mood I have in mind, but their combination, being

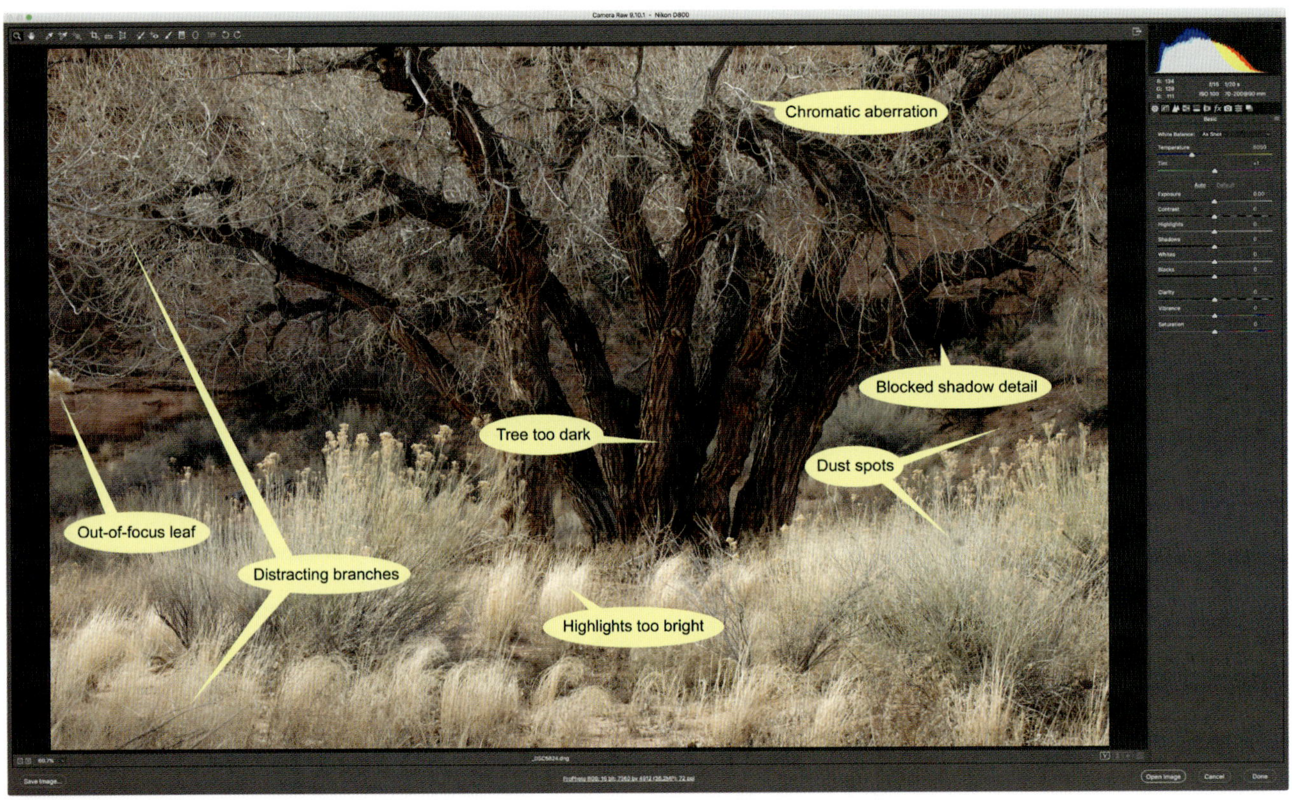


**Figure 15.2:** The image in figure 15.1 as rendered in ACR using the default conversion parameters.

complementary, has great visual appeal, making the image attractive to the eye.

- The camera's native aspect ratio of 3:2 is too wide and "skinny" for the sense of intimacy I wish for the viewer to feel. A crop to a more "squat" aspect ratio is needed.
- Contrast should to be reduced significantly for a softer, quieter, and more contemplative mood, and to avoid distracting areas of blotchy shadows or extreme highlights.

## RAW Conversion

When first opening the RAW file in ACR (figure 15.2), before adjusting any of the conversion settings, the image appears quite different from my visualized outcome. In this rendition, one may never know that the image was captured in below-freezing weather, or notice the myriad subtle hues throughout the scene. Left as-is, this would be an image of a tree, rather than an image about my subjective thoughts and mood. As I wish to create expressive art rather than a documentary illustration, my goal in processing is to transition from the former to the latter.

Before making any changes, I made sure the image would be mapped to the ProPhoto RGB color space and would open as a 16-bit file (note the line at the bottom of figure 15.2).

Examining the image closely and scrolling around it at 100% magnification, I identified several defects that required correction, as seen in figure 15.2.

Contrast was too high and the yellow color cast was too dominant to accurately assess such things as color balance or detail, therefore I started with the following adjustments:

- Increased *Saturation* so colors became more visible. My goal was not to achieve the desired final saturation, but to be better able to judge hues when I would adjust the *Temperature* and *Tint* settings.
- Set *Highlights* at –100, and *Shadows* at +100. This retrieved detail in the highlights and shadows that was either missing or difficult to discern. Although these would not necessarily be my final settings, they provided a good starting point.

With these settings, I began to move the *Temperature* and *Tint* sliders until arriving at my desired color balance. The settings ended up being 4,158 and +8, respectively. (Note that I decided to keep the *Highlights* and *Shadows* sliders at their maximum settings as the histogram looked good and the effect didn't seem too extreme. In other cases I might decide to move these to different settings once I had a chance to examine highlight and shadow detail.)

The increased color saturation also made it easier to see the chromatic aberration along high-contrast edges in the branches (figure 15.3). Switching to the *Lens Corrections* tab and checking the *Remove Chromatic Aberration* box eliminated the fringes.

I also used the *Spot Removal* tool to eliminate the two dust spots I identified earlier. I prefer to do spot removal in ACR (or Lightroom) as it is one of few functions that are implemented better in the RAW converter than in Photoshop, allowing me to select the area for the *Heal* algorithm to sample from, which at the time of this writing is not implemented in Photoshop.

After these adjustments, these were the remaining gaps I identified. I determined that all would be better handled using the tools offered in Photoshop, rather than in ACR.

| # | Description | Location | Possible Mitigation |
|---|---|---|---|
| 1 | Image too long and skinny | Global | Crop to more squat aspect ratio (4:3 or 5:4) |
| 2 | Contrast too high | Global | Adjust using *Curves* adjustment layer |
| 3 | Errant distracting branches | Lower left corner and just above middle of left edge | If still a distraction after crop, clone out |
| 4 | Out-of-focus leaf | Middle of left edge | If still a distraction after crop, clone out |
| 5 | Blocked shadow details | To the right of the tree | Dodge as needed |
| 6 | Foreground highlights too bright and distracting | Bottom of frame | Burn as needed, consider vignetting |
| 7 | Enhance gold and blue hues | Global | Adjust using *Hue/Saturation* adjustment layer |

Before opening the image in Photoshop, I set the *Saturation* slider back to 0 (preferring the more accurate color adjustment tools in Photoshop), and clicked on *Open Image*.

## First Iteration

The first thing I do when opening a new image in Photoshop is to add these layers, which I use with practically every image:

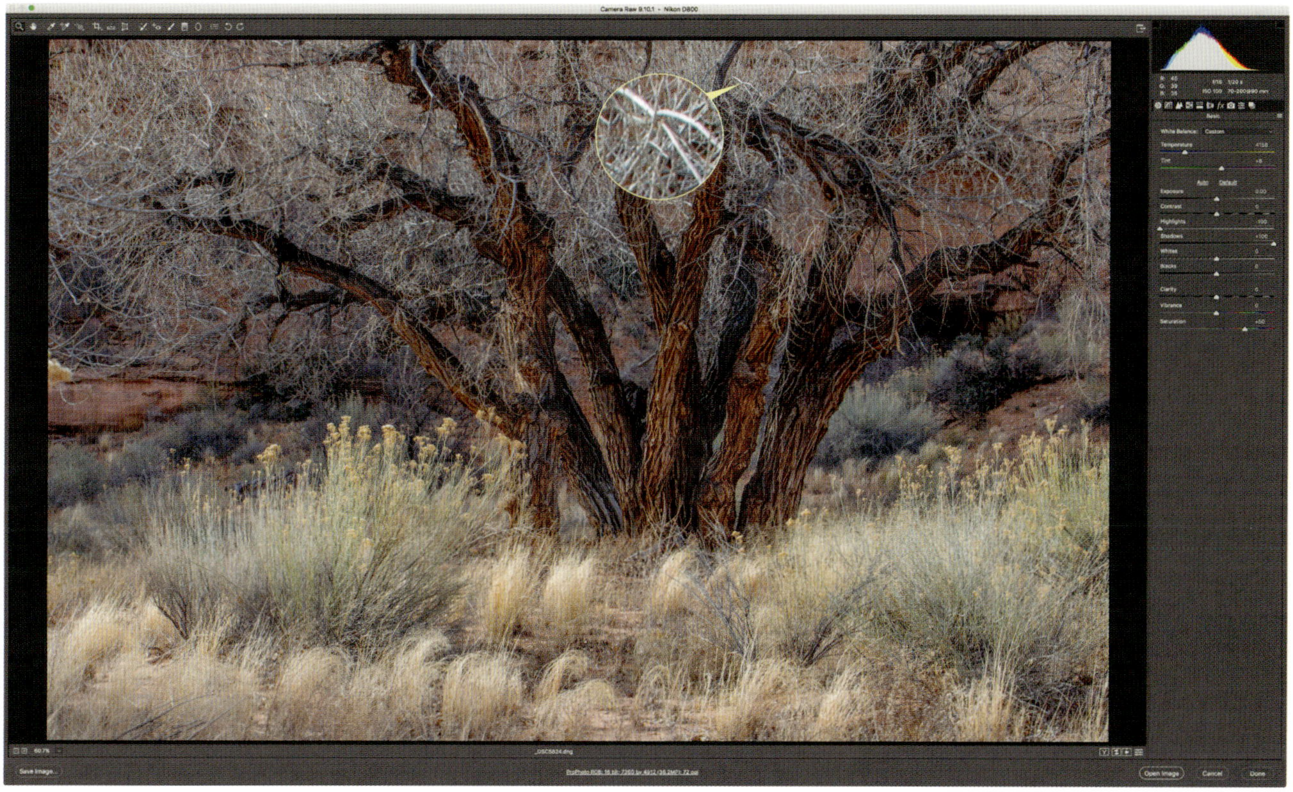

FIGURE 15.3: The image as seen in ACR, after increasing saturation and recovering highlight and shadow detail, making it easier to set the proper *Temperature* and *Tint*, as well as to see chromatic aberration.

- A Dodge/Burn layer
- A *Black & White* adjustment layer (if a black-and-white image)
- A *Curves* adjustment layer
- A *Hue/Saturation* adjustment layer (if a color image)

I then save the image to my master file folder. Although not yet finished, assigning the image a file name and saving it before applying adjustments allows me to then resave the file over and over with just a quick keystroke (Command/Ctrl+S) as I make incremental adjustments. Having worked with computers for more than three decades, I have learned (sometimes, the hard way) that Photoshop, like many other applications, may unexpectedly crash, and losing work in progress is never a pleasant experience.

The first processing iteration is best used for the most obvious and easiest-to-accomplish adjustments, such as black-and-white conversion (if a black-and-white image), cropping, and global contrast adjustment. These adjustments usually bring the image close to the visualized outcome, which is always a satisfying and motivating experience.

## Analysis

At this point I had a robust visualization in mind, as well as a list of the most obvious gaps to be mitigated. Analysis becomes more important in later iterations, as new ideas may present themselves after looking at and working on the image for some time.

## Adjustment

As this is a color image, I started with a similar technique to what I used in RAW conversion—I bumped the saturation a bit so colors became more visible and easier to adjust. I brought up the *Hue/Saturation* adjustment layer I created earlier and, with *Master* selected (to affect all colors), I set the *Saturation* slider to +35 (the value was determined by eye as I pulled the slider; other images may require a different setting). This had the effect of over-saturating all colors, but I later dialed it back down in the last iteration, when I made my final color adjustments.

Next, I adjusted the white point and black point using the *Curves* adjustment layer I added earlier, which also increased contrast a bit, exacerbating gap #2. But, at this early step, this was not reason for concern. I would mitigate this gap later in this iteration.

Examining the list of gaps and focusing on the easier and most obvious ones in this initial iteration, I chose to crop the image to a 4:3 aspect ratio and I removed a small section at the bottom using the *Crop* tool. This accomplished the greater sense of intimacy I was after (gap #1) and balanced the composition better, with the tree in the center and the midground green bushes on both its sides. It also eliminated most of the distracting branches on the lower-left corner and left edge, as well as the out-of-focus leaf (gap #4). I then cloned out what remained of the errant branches, mitigating gap #3.

Last for this iteration, I lowered contrast a bit by adding another *Curves* adjustment layer below the *Hue/Saturation* adjustment layer, and used a slight reverse S-curve to address gap #2. The reason I added this layer below the Hue/Saturation layer is that I did not want the curve effect to supersede the saturation increase I set earlier, and because I prefer to fine-tune colors

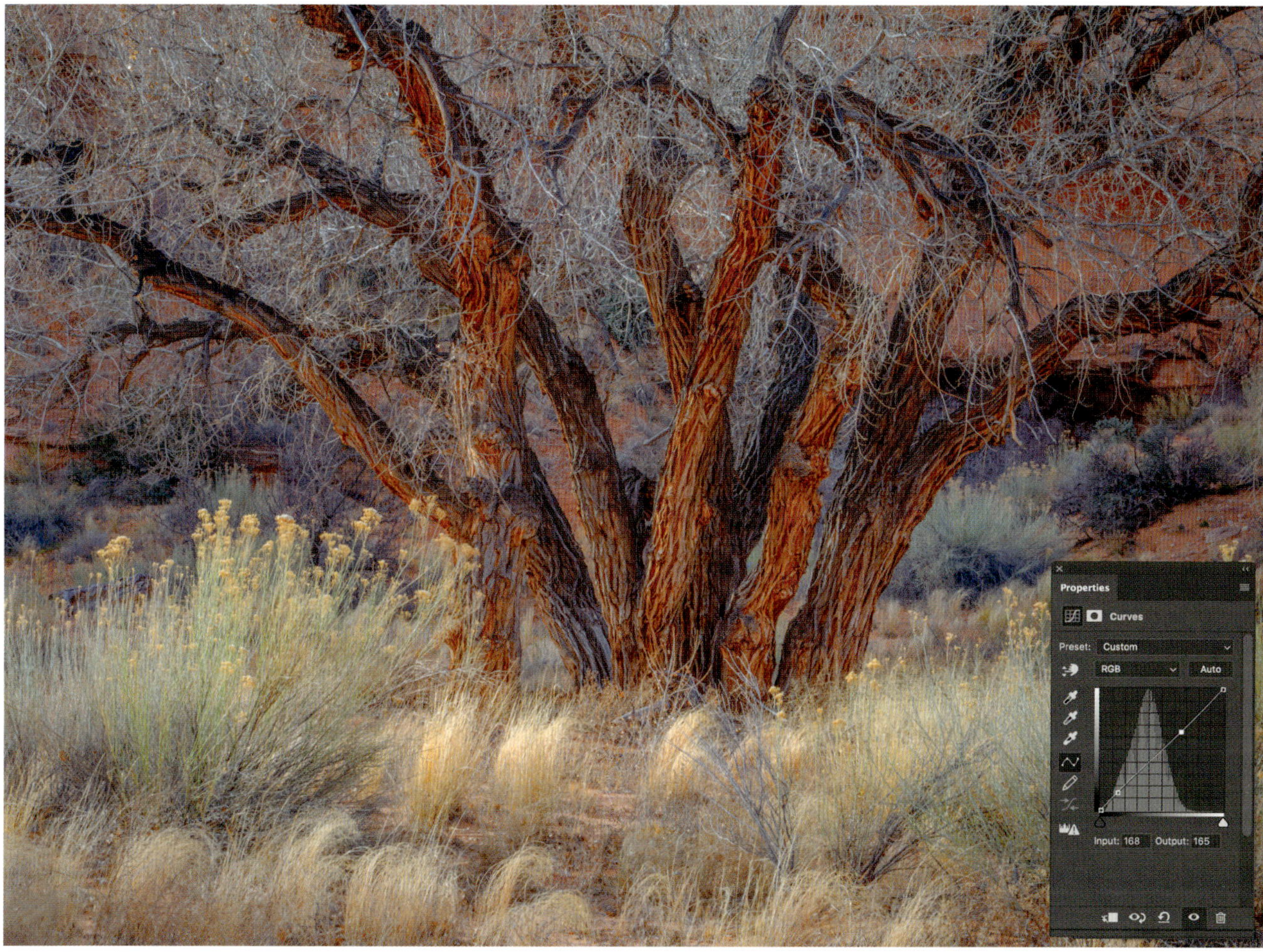


FIGURE 15.4: At the end of the first iteration, this is what my image looks like. I deliberately oversaturated colors so I could better judge the appearance of each hue, cropped to a 4:3 aspect ratio, and reduced contrast using the curve shown in the inset.

as the last step in creating my master file (to avoid having to redo it in case another adjustment alters colors).

Figure 15.4 shows the image at the end of this iteration.

## Dynamic Visualization

After spending some time with the image and getting to know its visual qualities better, I paused for a few moments to consider my original visualization and the impression I wished for it to have on the viewer. The adjustments I made in this iteration brought out some welcome aspects I did not originally consider, such as the red highlights in the tree bark (a result of light reflecting off the red cliff on the opposite side of the canyon). These were not quite visible when originally viewing the RAW file (figure 15.2) and, now that I became aware of these highlights, I liked their effect and decided to preserve and enhance them in the final image. Put another way, I "updated" my visualization to include this quality of the image I had not fully considered while at the scene.

Recall my admonition earlier in the book to not let your visualization become prescriptive. Creative ideas may arise at any time, and especially when focusing attention on an image while processing it. Don't lock yourself into just one possible outcome. Keep the door open to new epiphanies.

## Second Iteration

Although the image after the first iteration appeared somewhat less like the visualized result than it did after converting from RAW, it was in fact closer to my desired goal: the composition was better balanced and some of the most visible distractions had been removed.

### Analysis

After mitigating some of the original gaps, I updated my gap list to remove already-mitigated gaps, and to include my newfound revelation about the red highlights. As the composition is centered and I wish to keep the viewer focused, I also decided to add a slight vignetting effect—darkening the corners and edges.

Following is the new list (note, I retained the original numbers for easier reference):

| # | Description | Location | Possible Mitigation |
|---|---|---|---|
| 5 | Blocked shadow details | To the right of the tree | Dodge as needed |
| 6 | Foreground highlights too bright and distracting | Bottom of frame | Burn as needed, consider vignetting |
| 7 | Enhance gold and blue hues | Global | Adjust using *Hue/Saturation* adjustment layer |
| 8 | Red highlights in cottonwood bark need to be visible but not too saturated | Cottonwood tree | Adjust using *Hue/Saturation* adjustment layer |
| 9 | Add vignetting effect | Corners and edges | Slightly burn edges and corners |

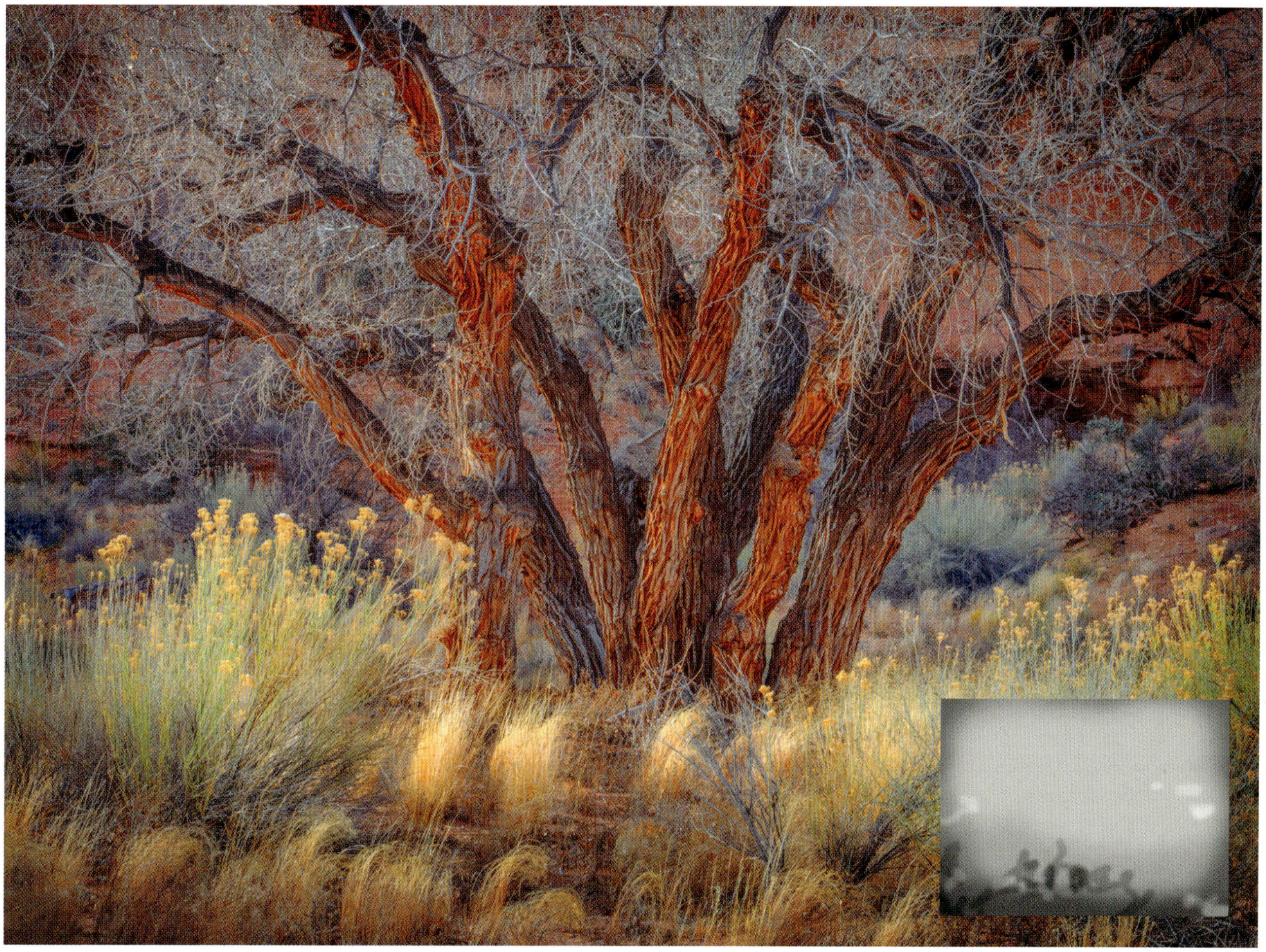

FIGURE 15.5: The image after painting the Dodge/Burn layer (shown in the inset).

## Adjustment

In this iteration, I decided to address the gaps requiring dodging or burning: #5, #6, and #9, leaving color adjustment to the final iteration.

Using the *Dodge/Burn* layer I added earlier, I painted in either black or white, using a soft brush set to 20% *Opacity*, to address the areas requiring lightening or darkening.

As I was working, I realized that some areas in the foreground could use varying amounts of dodging and burning, which I applied using different brush sizes.

Figure 15.5 shows the image after applying the desired amount of dodging and burning.

### Dynamic Visualization

At this point, I had been looking at the image for a fairly long time. Our brains, seeking to maintain consistency, sometimes get used to appearances that would otherwise call attention. Knowing this effect, something I like to do after a period is to either close my eyes for a couple of minutes, or even take a break and find something else to do before returning to the image and, again, asking myself whether I am still true to my expressive intent. Doing so in this case made me realize that the image appeared a bit lighter than I would have liked. A palette of darker hues would better convey the quiet and somewhat somber mood I was in. I added it to the list of gaps to be addressed in the next iteration.

## Third Iteration

The image is almost finished now, appearing close to the way I visualized (and revisualized) it, except for color adjustment. This was my indication that this would be my last iteration. Colors may be affected by other adjustments, which is why I defer fine-tuning them to the end.

### Analysis

With the realization that the image appeared a bit too light, I added gap #10 to the list below and removed the gaps already mitigated. Following is what remains to be done:

| # | Description | Location | Possible Mitigation |
|---|---|---|---|
| **7** | Enhance gold and blue hues | Global | Adjust using *Hue/Saturation* adjustment layer |
| **8** | Red highlights in cottonwood bark need to be visible but not too saturated | Cottonwood tree | Adjust using *Hue/Saturation* adjustment layer |
| **10** | Image too light overall | Global | Darken using *Curves* layer |

### Adjustment

Before adjusting colors, I brought up my *Hue/Saturation* adjustment layer properties and, with *Master* selected, set the *Saturation* slider—which I set at +35 earlier—back to 0. I recommend refraining from adjusting any of the

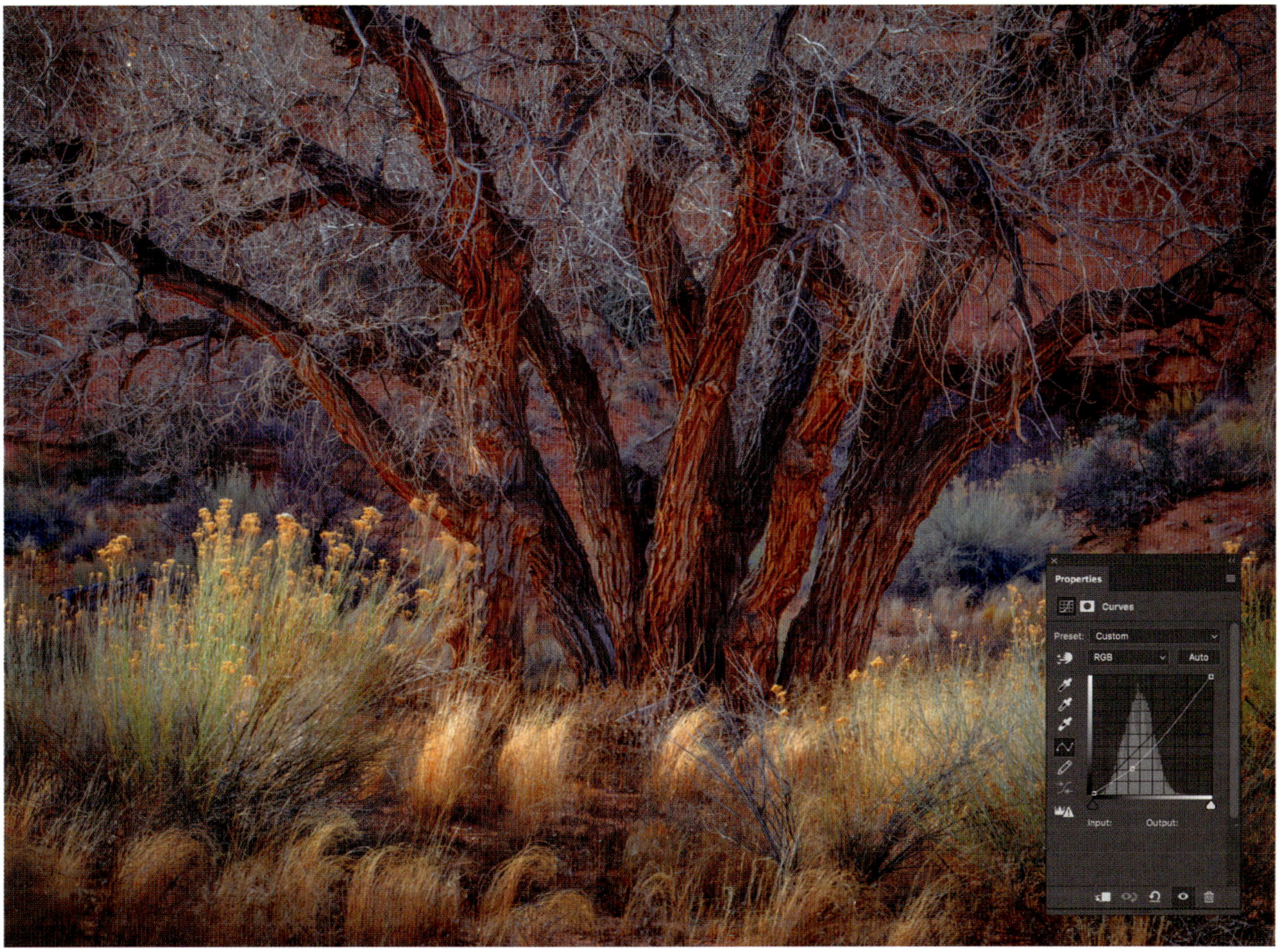


**FIGURE 15.6:** The image after all identified gaps have been mitigated. The curve used to darken the image is shown in the inset.

settings when *Master* is selected. Adjusting each color range independently is a better way of accomplishing the desired palette.

I started with *Yellows* as I determined earlier that yellow (along with blue) is of primary importance to the look I was after. I began by adjusting the *Saturation* slider, both to achieve the desired saturation and so the yellows became more visible, allowing for easier *Hue* adjustment. I ended up with a *Saturation* setting of +50, and a *Hue* setting of –3, which biased all yellows toward red, for the golden color I had in mind. I found no reason to adjust the *Lightness* slider here.

Next, I selected *Blues* as the second most important color in the way I visualized the image. I adjusted the *Saturation* slider until achieving the desired saturation at +35. I then continued to adjust the *Hue* slider to +2, which biased all the blues very slightly toward magenta. While I liked the result, it appeared a bit too punchy, so I lowered the *Lightness* setting to –20. This addressed gap #7.

Repeating the process for *Reds* resulted in a *Saturation* setting of +40, with no changes to *Hue* or *Lightness*, mitigating gap #8.

And last, I added another *Curves* adjustment layer and pulled the middle of it below the 45° line to darken the image (figure 15.6), eliminating gap #10.

### Dynamic Visualization

Before declaring the image finished, even when all identified gaps have been mitigated, I still like to lean back and study it for a few moments longer. Seeing an image with my eyes that previously only existed in my imagination is a satisfying experience that I like to savor. It is not so much the sense of accomplishment that I'm after, but the opportunity to relive an experience, to feel as I felt and to make sure I "said" all I had to say in the image.

If after a period, I am still satisfied with my work and have not identified other adjustments that need to be made, I save my finished (at least for now) master file one final time and immediately back it up for safety.

Done with processing for now, it is time for a little postprocessing, usually involving a beverage, a favorite jazz track, and sharing the image with a couple of close friends for initial feedback.

## Targeting for Publication

This section is offered to articulate some of the considerations that may be needed when submitting an image for commercial publication. In most cases, book publishers have well-trained staff to handle these tasks. However, when a publisher asks you to prepare the file to their specifications, you may need to target your image files before submitting them.

In preparing the images for publication in this book, I inquired with my friends at Rocky Nook for their printing requirements, and was provided with size information and an ICC profile for use when soft-proofing the image.

Before proceeding, I flattened the file as my adjustment layers will not be of use to the book printer.

### Size

The page width in this book is 8", which means that to fill the page from one end to the other—what publishers call "full bleed"—the image needs to be sized to 8". If a margin or gutter is required, it would need to be factored into the image's physical size. Generally, a book designer will make such choices and it is best to provide them with an image ready for full bleed, which they can always reduce. Also, when targeting images for commercial printing, be sure to inquire how much "bleed space" is required to accommodate trimming, to make sure that important elements in the image don't end up being cut off at the edges. For simplicity's sake, I sized the images to 8" wide and 300 PPI print resolution.

To accommodate the size requirements, the image size needed to be reduced from that of the master file, meaning I did not need to worry about having sufficient details.

*Bicubic Sharper* seems like it would be a good interpolation method to use in this example image, since the image does not have any high-contrast edges (which may result in halos if over-sharpened). However, knowing that the book designer may decide to resize the image again to fit a desired space, I did not want the image to be sharpened too much, as it might need to be sharpened again after resizing. I therefore chose *Bicubic* as the interpolation method.

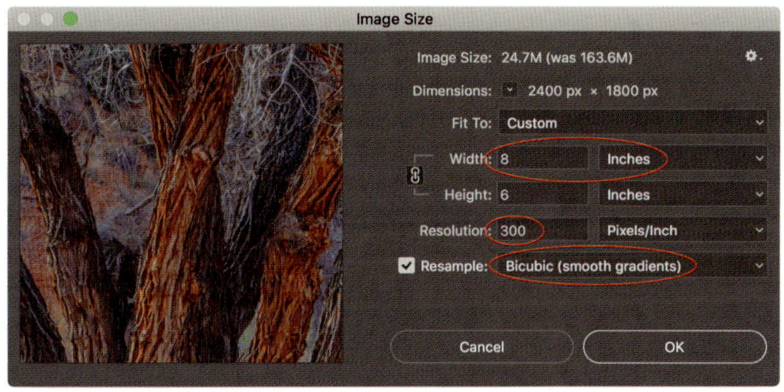


**FIGURE 15.7:** The *Image Size* dialog showing the parameters used for this book.

Figure 15.7 shows the sizing parameters I used.

## Color Management

Like most commercial print operations, Rocky Nook books are printed using a CMYK process, rather than RGB. In the past, CMYK printers tended to be limited in their color gamut, and photographs usually did not turn out as detailed and vibrant as you are seeing here. However, current printing technology allows for excellent results.

The ICC profile used for this process is a standard one, named *Coated GRACoL 2006*. After installing the profile on my system, I set up a custom soft proof using this profile, and selected *Relative Colorimetric* as the *Rendering Intent*, so I can identify and, if needed, manage the out-of-gamut colors (figure 15.8).

With the custom profile set, I activated the *Gamut Warning* feature by selecting it from the *View* menu. Figure 15.9 shows that the most saturated reds in the image are out of gamut and not within the capabilities of this printing method.

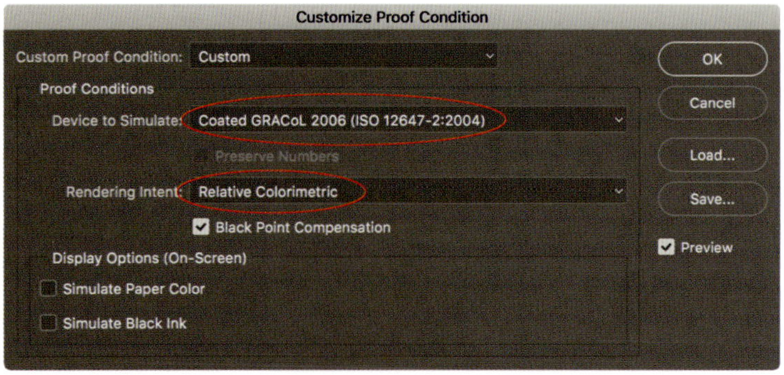


**Figure 15.8:** Setting up a soft-proof using the Coated GRACoL 2006 profile.

Normally, at this point I would add a *Hue/Saturation* adjustment layer to bring the out-of-gamut colors into gamut using the method described in chapter 14. However, this is an area where the expertise of a publisher and their experience working with their printing service can be invaluable in optimizing results, so I decided to wait for the proofs from the printing house to see if additional color work is needed.

## No Sharpening

When submitting an image to publication, knowing that it may be resized, it is best not to attempt to optimize sharpness as it may limit the designer in their sizing options.

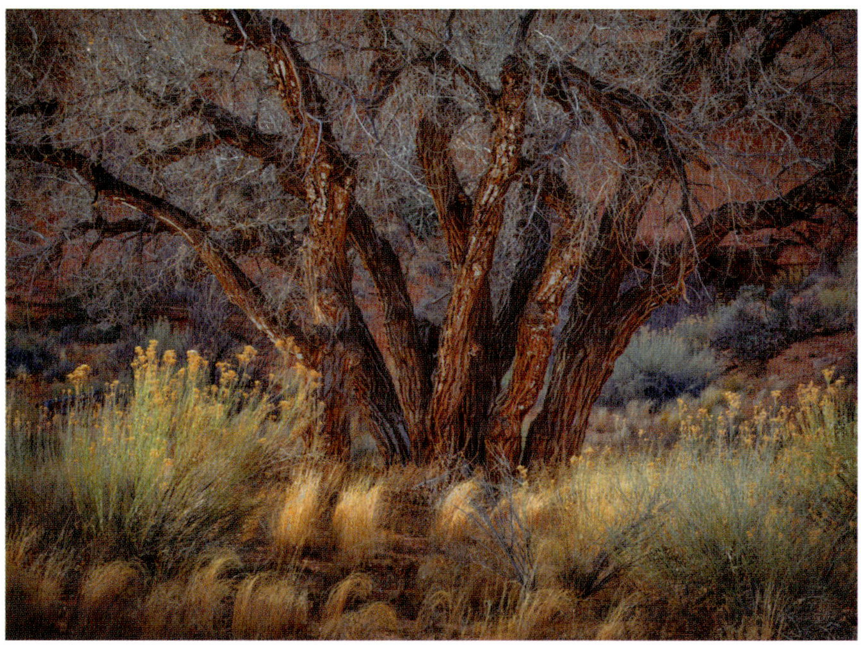

**Figure 15.9:** Photoshop's *Gamut Warning* feature renders in gray colors that are out of gamut.

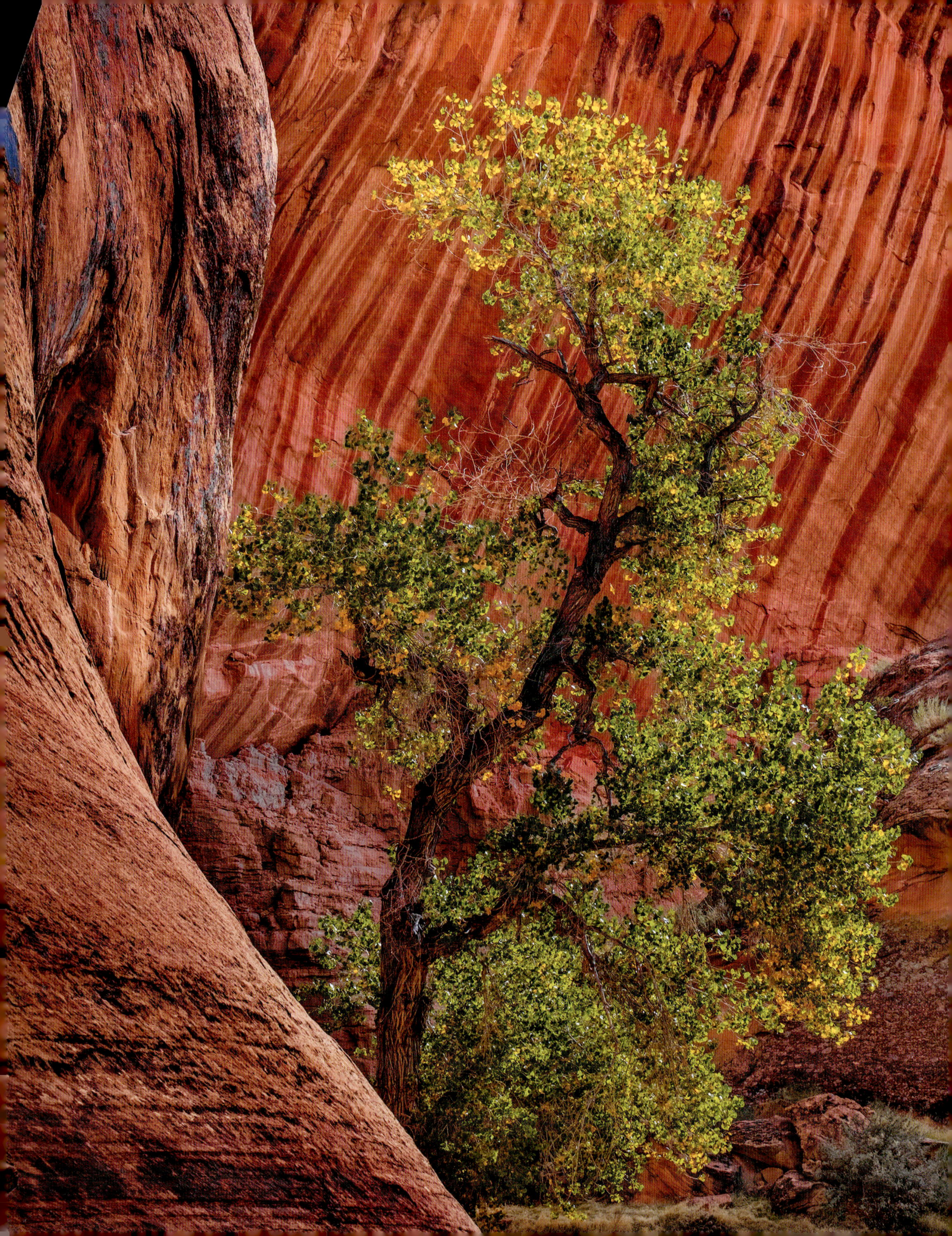

# Conclusion

*And in the end, the great artist under this climate is, above all, a great living being, it being understood that living in this case is just as much experiencing as reflecting.*

—ALBERT CAMUS

Having covered a fair amount of theoretical and technical knowledge, allow me just a few final words about the importance of placing such knowledge in the greater context of living artfully.

It has been my experience that the greatest rewards to be found in making art come from the making and not from the art—from engaging in creative thought and work as a way of life, rather than from whatever products such work culminates in.

It may seem plausible to think that if one considers himself an artist, his goal is to produce artistic artifacts (both words derived from the same origin: something created by human skill). In my opinion, however, works of art are but anecdotal pinnacles in the artist's life—milestones, and commemorations of significant events experienced at various times along his creative path.

While a beautiful image provides rewards in its own ways, such rewards are greatly amplified when an image also ensues out of a meaningful experience. The person who stumbles begrudgingly out of bed before dawn and heads out with the sole aim of recording a well-trodden sunrise view may be rewarded with a spectacular photograph, but his experience pales in comparison with that of the person who finds joy in exploring, visualizing, and contemplating his life, his surroundings, and his work, and rejoices in discovering new expressions or new views that stir in him deep emotions and epiphanies that he can express in a photograph. The viewer of the images may never know the difference, but to the artist—if he considers his reasons for practicing his work in the first place—there is a world of difference.

In this book, I discuss, for the most part, means of expression. But means are only of value if they are employed to accomplish worthy goals. I suggest you consider, often, your reasons for practicing landscape photography, if only to be reminded to remain true to yourself and your goals. Don't sacrifice your most noble motivations, or the profound inner rewards of pursuing them, for lesser ones. To live a creative, artful, deliberate life is a greater accomplishment than any photograph or number of photographs you will ever make.

—Guy Tal
November 2017

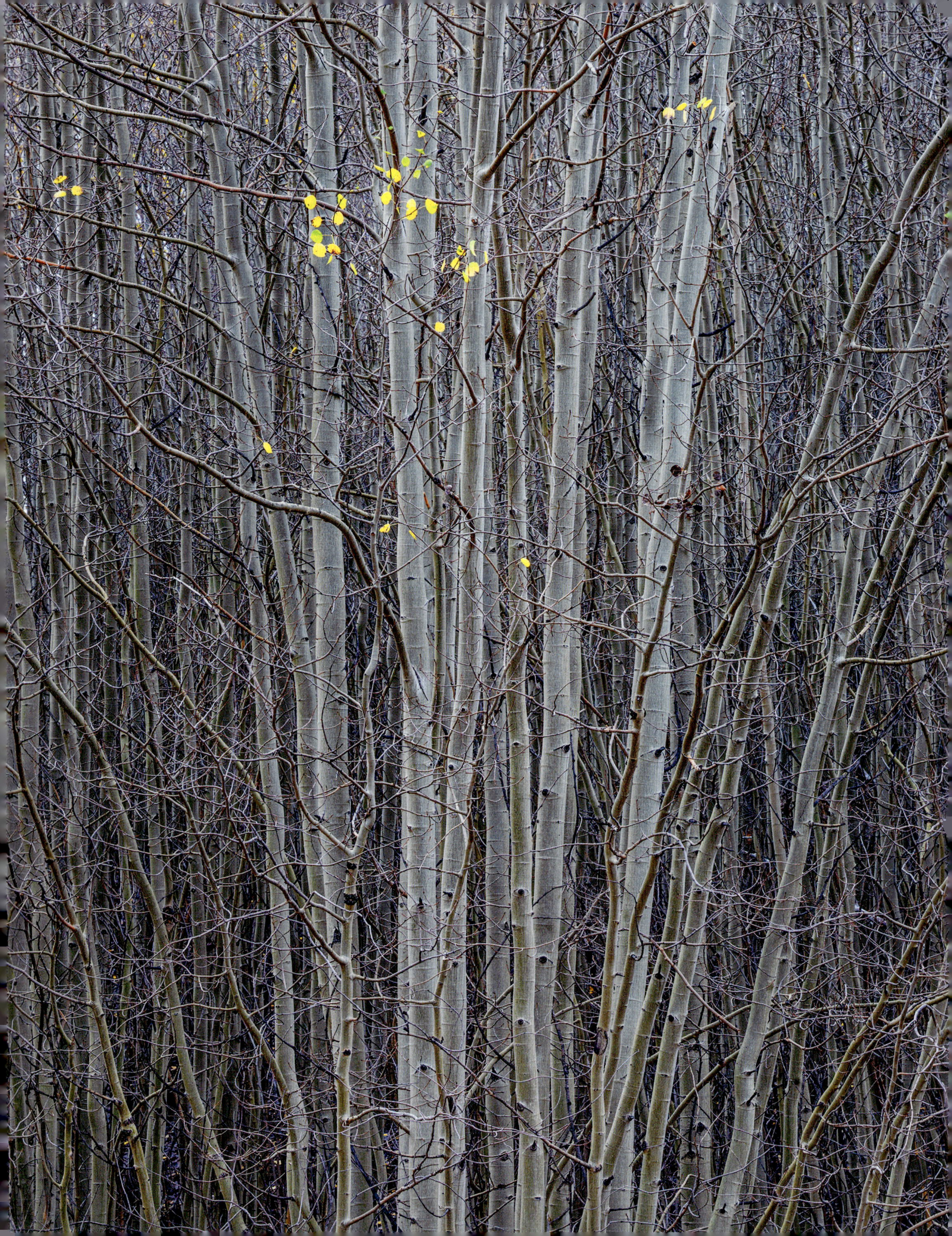

# Appendix

### Answer Key to Exercises

**Exercise 1**

1. Though many other possibilities exist, here are a few suggestions:
   - Things found in a natural landscape that can inspire a sense of drama: majestic mountain, stormy sky, long view, old tree, big river, ocean, sunbeams piercing through clouds, large-scale chiaroscuro (interplay of light and shadow), lone figure (human or animal) against a vast backdrop, reflected light in a canyon.
   - Things that can inspire a sense of intimacy: anthropomorphic features (natural elements resembling human qualities), abstract patterns, arrangements of leaves or rocks, warm colors, sinuous lines, flowers, delicate grasses or tree branches, figure (human or animal or other interesting formation) occupying most of the frame and juxtaposed against a natural background, muted/soft light, small-scale vignettes of rock walls or trees in a forest, ancient rock art or ruins, ripples in water.
2. Although the mood of an image derives out of its gestalt, or form—the totality of all elements in the composition and how they are arranged—some colors, if dominant, can make a profound difference. Yellows and oranges generally communicate a sense of joy and warmth while blues and magentas generally communicate a sense of quiet melancholy or peace. Reds inspire passion and desire. Greens feel quiet and harmonious.
3. Remember that the gestalt of the image is derived from the arrangement of elements in the composition. Nothing is benign; anything that doesn't contribute to the desired mood distracts from it. If your goal is to communicate a sense of peace, consider excluding elements having sharp angles; elements known to be associated with noise and turmoil, such as vehicles or industrial structures; elements that are visually dominant and that have characteristics incompatible with the sense of serenity, such as large featureless/colorless rocks, or bright red skies; elements that are disharmonious, such as large featureless dark patches, random lines intruding into the frame, etc.
4. The primary consideration in deciding whether an image "works" better in color or black-and-white is the concept (mood, idea, appearance, etc.) you wish to express in the image—what the image is about. If color does not directly contribute to accomplishing the concept, it most certainly will distract from it due to our innate tendency to associate meanings and moods with certain colors. If the concept is best conveyed through elements such as lines, shapes, textures, or patterns, make these more prominent by eliminating the distraction of color.
5. After studying the image and committing it to memory, I suggest reading each item, then closing your eyes for more effective visualization.
6. Same as 5.

**Exercise 2**

1. The histogram indicates that the image has a negligible amount of midtones. Most shades in the image are either very dark (blue shadows) or very light (yellow highlights).
2. Clipping on the left side of the histogram is not necessarily a bad thing. If all channels are clipped on the left side, it simply means the image contains areas that are pure black. If this accords with your visualization, there is nothing wrong with that. Clipping of all channels on the right side may be problematic when the image is printed, as an inkjet printer may not deposit any ink in those areas of pure white, causing an artifact known as a gloss differential (although

there are other reasons for a gloss differential, too). While some printers may still produce beautiful prints with pure whites (more accurately, the color of the paper), it is still something to watch for.

3. An RGB histogram aggregates all color channels, so clipping means that one or more of the channels are clipped, but there may still be information (details) in other channels. Think, for example of an image with a bright red and yellow sunset sky. In this scenario, there may be no blue at all in the highlights, therefore the RGB histogram will show clipping on the right side. But the red and/or green channels may still have details in the highlights. A luminosity histogram will show that detail exists in the highlights if at least one channel has such detail.
4. Yellow is produced by adding up red and green. If the Colors histogram shows yellow clipped on the left, it means the red and green channels have no shadow details, but blue does. This is usually OK, as shadows tend to be predominantly blue, but may still require noise reduction as the blue channel often tends to be noisy when underexposed.

**Exercise 3**

3. Blending multiple images may be desirable in these (and other) cases:
   - Insufficient dynamic range to render detail (or noise-free detail) in both highlights and shadows.
   - Insufficient depth of field to render sharp foreground-to-background detail (assuming it is desired).
   - When only some elements may introduce motion blur and should be photographed at a high ISO setting, but the rest of the composition can safely be photographed at a low ISO setting.
   - When, for creative reasons, you might wish to combine elements from one scene with elements from a different scene.
4. The most common form of chromatic aberration is best corrected in the RAW converter (ACR or Lightroom) rather than in Photoshop. This is because the correction can be applied more easily to RAW data, which is not available to Photoshop.
5. Orange is the hue, vibrant refers to saturation, and medium refers to lightness.
6. Vignetting makes the edges of the frame darker. Our attention is generally drawn to lighter elements in the frame, which means that darkening the edges will "pull" our attention toward the middle of the frame, rather than be distracted by elements along the edges.
7. Digital noise may be in the form of aberrations in lightness (also referred to as "luminosity" or "detail" in some noise reduction software), or aberrations in color (also referred to as "chroma" in some noise reduction software).

**Exercise 4**

1. Desired characteristics of a good starting point for processing (after RAW conversion) include:
   - Low contrast
   - Low color saturation
   - Large color space
   - 16-bit color depth
   - The adjustments best applied in RAW conversion, such as correcting chromatic aberration
2. Clipping of shadow details may be desirable when the image contains pure blacks. Clipping of individual color channels may be OK when the image includes areas that do not require all color channels (e.g., a vibrant red flower likely will not contain any blue).
3. The Saturation, Vibrance, and Contrast sliders offered in the RAW converter may be used to temporarily increase color saturation and/or contrast so adjustments to other parameters (such as the White Balance controls) are more visible and can be set more accurately before resetting Saturation, Vibrance, and Contrast back to their neutral position.
4. Reviewing the image at 100% magnification makes it easier to spot artifacts such as dust spots, chromatic aberration, and noise. It also helps in determining where fine adjustments are needed to such things as color or contrast.
5. RAW converters have access to RAW data (usually a Bayer pattern reading) and can use this

data to realign individual color channels before converting them into pixels. This ability allows the RAW converter to more accurately address such things as linear chromatic aberration.

**Exercise 8**

3. An S-Curve makes the light tones lighter (pulled above the 45° line) and the dark tones darker (pulled below the 45° line), increasing the difference in lightness between adjacent pixels, which is the definition of contrast.
7. The Luminosity blending mode prevents a layer from altering color, allowing it to only alter lightness (contrast), therefore any changes to color that may have resulted from this layer will be rolled back when changing the blending mode to Luminosity.
9. The eye icon next to a layer controls its visibility. When turned off, the layer has no effect at all. This feature is useful to assess the image before and after the layer's effect has been applied.

**Exercise 13**

1. Keeping in mind that a filter allows more light (greater exposure) of its own color and less light (less exposure) of other colors. A green filter will make green foliage appears very light while a red filter will darken green foliage considerably. In this case, the green filter will also result in greater variations of tone because the camera's sensor (and our eyes) are more sensitive to green light than to red light, and the green filter will allow more green light to pass through, whereas the red filter will block some of it.
2. Looking at the color wheel (page 212), it is evident that a red filter will block most of the blue light, rendering the blue sky very dark. The clouds generally are neutral in color (white or light gray) so will retain their appearance as they reflect all colors evenly.
3. Green filters block a portion of red/pink light and therefore will reduce the appearance of skin blemishes in people with light skin.

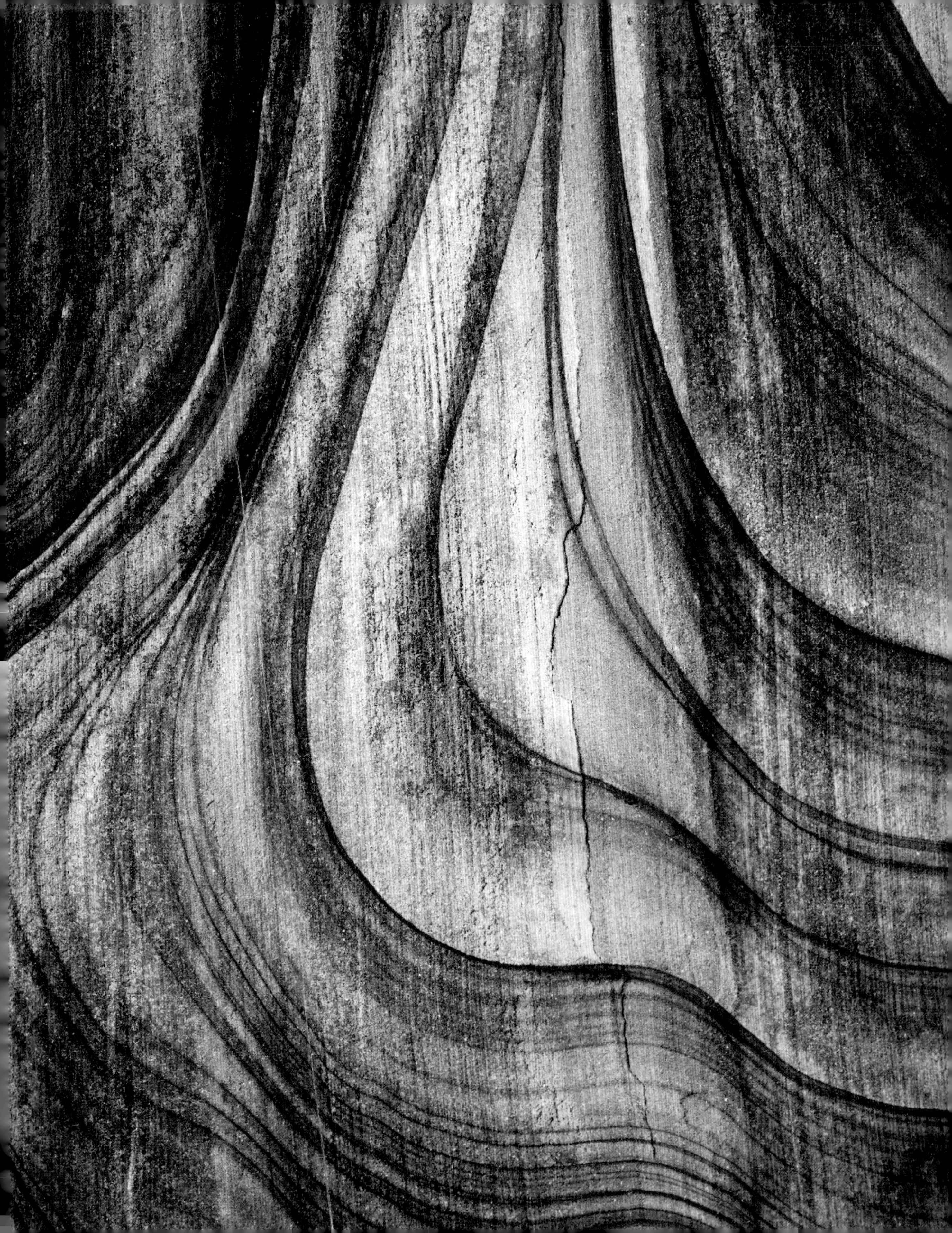

# Index

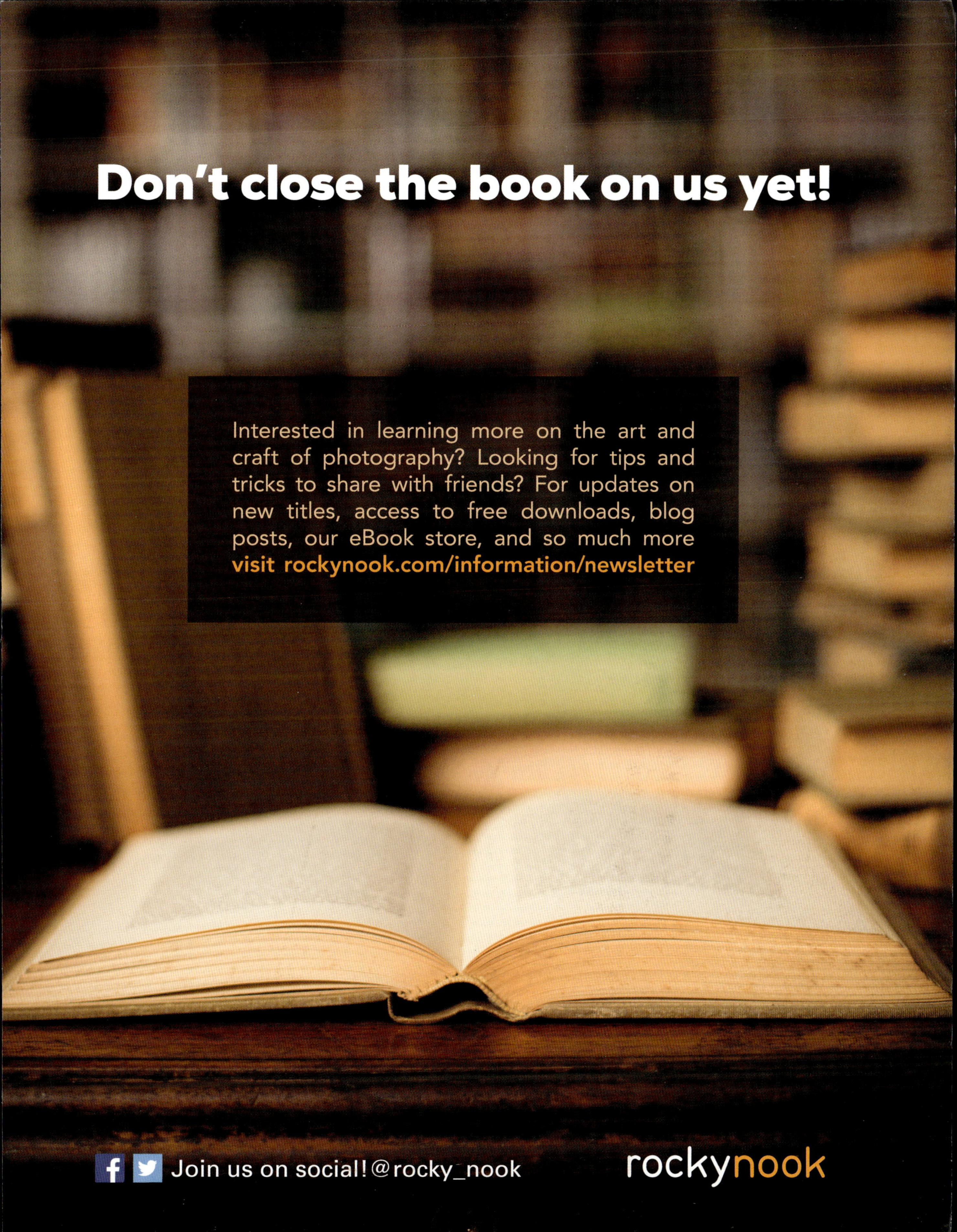
Don't close the book on us yet!
Interested in learning more on the art and craft of photography? Looking for tips and tricks to share with friends? For updates on new titles, access to free downloads, blog posts, our eBook store, and so much more visit rockynook.com/information/newsletter
Join us on social! @rocky_nook
rockynook